Wally Herbert
The Noose
of Laurels

Robert E. Peary and the
Race to the North Pole

ANCHOR BOOKS
DOUBLEDAY
NEW YORK LONDON TORONTO SYDNEY AUCKLAND

AN ANCHOR BOOK
PUBLISHED BY DOUBLEDAY
a division of Bantam Doubleday Dell Publishing Group, Inc.
666 Fifth Avenue, New York, New York 10103

ANCHOR BOOKS, DOUBLEDAY, and the portrayal of an anchor
are trademarks of Doubleday, a division of Bantam Doubleday
Dell Publishing Group, Inc.

First published in Great Britain by Hodder & Stoughton, Ltd.

The Noose of Laurels was originally published
in hardcover by Atheneum, a division of Macmillan Publishing Company,
in 1989. The Anchor Books edition is published
by arrangement with Atheneum.

Library of Congress Cataloging-in-Publication Data

Herbert, Wally.
    The noose of laurels: Robert E. Peary
and the race to the North Pole / by Wally Herbert.
—1st Anchor Books ed.
        p.   cm.
    Includes bibliographical references.
    1. Peary, Robert E. (Robert Edwin), 1856–1920.
2. Cook, Frederick Albert, 1865–1940.   3. North Pole.
4. Explorers—United States—Biography.
I. Title.
[G635.P4H4   1990]
919.804′092′2—dc20   90–31760
[B]   CIP

ISBN 0-385-41355-6

Contents

Maps and diagrams

Acknowledgments

The idea of writing this book was born on a winter's evening in 1980 in a cottage on bleak Bodmin Moor. My wife, who for some weeks had been working on a plot for a new novel, had suggested a brain-storming session in which she would record on tape the views of Allan Gill and myself concerning some of the more practical aspects of her story – a conflict between two ambitious explorers whose dreams of achieving lasting fame became focused on the same goal. Seeing her novel as a tragic tale, and one which in so many respects was similar to the bitter dispute which had raged in the early years of this century between Commander Robert E. Peary and his rival, Dr. Frederick A. Cook, over which of these two had discovered the North Pole, she had sought our opinion as polar travellers, not expecting for one moment the effect which that very lively discussion would have on the next eight years of our lives.

"You should be writing this story, not me," Marie had said with a hint of mixed feelings towards the end of our first tape that evening. And so my first expression of thanks goes to my wife for the idea, and to Allan Gill, my old sledging companion, for supporting her decision.

The research for *The Noose of Laurels*, however, took very much longer than I had expected. There were problems too in writing a novel so closely related to what, for me, was a deeply moving and intriguing true story – not least being the pressure of well-meaning friends to abandon the idea of a novel and write my own assessment of the claims of Peary and Cook.

Since this I was very reluctant to do, I must credit the charm, the Irish in him, and the persistence of Joe Judge. It was he, at the end of 1984, who persuaded me to accept the National Geographic Society's invitation to write an assessment of Peary's original 1909 diary and astronomical observations, and I would like to express my heartfelt thanks also to Bill Garrett, Dr. Barry Bishop, and the National Geographic Society's president, Gil Grosvenor, for the courageous initiative of that invitation and for the freedom I was given to write that assessment which ran to some 75,000 words. I would like to put it on record that I was given the very fullest cooperation of the Society throughout the nine months that I was working on that project, complete freedom of the Society's archive material on the North Pole controversy, and the most generous encouragement when, in September 1986, I started work on this book.

I am deeply indebted also to Alison Wilson at the National Archives, without whose patience and guidance through the masses of material in her care, I would almost certainly have lost my way – and many of the chance findings which, in this book, are presented for the first time. The staff at the Library of Congress were equally helpful as some of the pictures in this book will show, and for their help too I am grateful.

To Dr. Brad Washburn, the undisputed authority on Mount McKinley, I offer my thanks not only for his advice, but also for sending me some of his most treasured documents. Equally, others who have a very personal interest in some aspect of this intriguing story have offered me their opinions and findings. I thank Dr. Ray Thorsteinsson of the Geological Survey of Canada for sharing his thoughts with me on the location of "Bradley Land," and Jack Soper of the Department of Geology at the University of Sheffield with whom I have spent many hours discussing this same fascinating problem. I thank Professor James Helmer of the Department of Geography at the University of Calgary for his thoughts and his pictures of Dr. Cook's winter den on the north coast of Devon Island, and Caroline Phillips for her kindness in sending me information on the historic sites in northern Ellesmere Island.

I am particularly grateful to Rolf Gilberg of the National Museum of Denmark for the information he has supplied over many years, and to both him and the Greenland Society for permitting part of a paper, first published in the magazine *Grønland* in 1984, to be published in its first English translation as Appendix I to this book.

Over the thirty-three years that I have been involved in polar work I have discussed the claims of Peary and Cook with every one of my friends and colleagues, and particularly those with whom I have travelled. With Allan Gill and Roger Tufft I retraced Dr. Cook's route with dog teams in 1967, and with Allan, Dr. "Fritz" Koerner, and Major Ken Hedges I shared the long-drawn-out experience in 1968–9 of crossing the Arctic Ocean. I have made many journeys since then – some with Allan, some with Geoff Renner, some with Bryan Alexander, and many with the hunters from North-West Greenland, notably the late Peter Peary and Avatak Kaerngak, and more recently with Talilanguaq and Hissu. To these men, not only for their advice and companionship, but also their ability to suffer my love of history, I offer the rudest words of endearment that I can think of since any others in the printed form seem totally insincere.

Somewhat more formally I thank my academic friends – each distinguished in his field, and each of them, over the years, a fountain of kindly words of advice. Among these, my thanks go out especially to Sir

Acknowledgments

Vivian Fuchs, to Paul-Emile Victor, Dr. Gordon de Q. Robin, Dr. Terence Armstrong, Dr. Geoffrey Hattersley-Smith, Dr. Dick Laws, Dr. Charles Swithinbank, Dr. Peter Wadhams, Andrew Cowan, Robin Hanbury-Tenison and Dr. John Hemming. My thanks also to Commander Waldo Lyon and Fred McLaren, both of whom have spent as long under the pack ice of the Arctic Ocean as I have spent travelling on it, to Bob Lillestrand of the Control Data Corporation, to Professor Jean Malaurie, Directeur du Centre d'Etudes Arctiques, Susan Kaplan, Director of the Peary-MacMillan Museum, Brunswick, Maine, Cdr. George Michanowsky of the Explorers' Club, New York, Warren B. Cook, President of the Frederick A. Cook Society, Miss Janet Vetter and Sheldon Cook-Dorough.

Without help along the way in more practical terms I would not, however, have been able to get to the Arctic to check my reading against reality, and I am therefore especially grateful for the help and encouragement of Sven Adsersen of the Ministry for Greenland, my old friend Cdr. Martin Kilt, former Danish Liaison Officer at Thule Air Base, Rasmus Lau, Sven Petersen, Colonel James W. Knapp, USAF, Base Commander of Thule Air Base, the Commander of C.A.F. Alert, the Mayor of Qaanaaq and the Avanersuup Kommunia, George Hobson, Director of Polar Continental Shelf Project, and to Bradley Air Services.

But most of all I owe my thanks to the Peary family. Over the many years I have known Bob Peary, his son Bert, and Ed Stafford, the son of Marie Peary, I have, through the bonding of friendship and the closeness of shared experiences with Peary, come to regard them with the deepest affection. With the Eskimo branch of the Peary family I have also had a long and very close relationship and to them all I am indebted for the link they have offered me to the past and to one of the greatest polar travellers the world has ever seen.

Finally, to my wife, Marie, and my two daughters, Kari and Pascale, I owe the deepest debt of all. I promise to repay.

Sandridge
24th October, 1988

Prologue

The diary of Robert E. Peary for the months of March and April 1909, together with the astronomical observations and soundings made during that period, are the sole records upon which the explorer based his claim to have reached the North Pole on 6th April, 1909. And yet, amazing though it may seem, until as recently as April 1985, when I was invited to study and assess these historic documents, no one outside the Peary family and the staff of the Center for Polar Archives in Washington, D.C. has had access to them since the examination of these records by the seven-man Congressional subcommittee of the Committee on Naval Affairs (the so-called Peary Hearings) in 1911.

Not surprisingly, this silence had been interpreted by some of Peary's critics as a sure sign that something was being hidden, and by others as an indication of the possibility (some would even say certainty) that the documents no longer existed, that they had been deliberately destroyed in order to protect Peary's claim against the incriminating evidence of his original log of the journey. With their release we therefore have not only an unexpected and important contribution to the mass of material already available to students of the so-called North Pole Controversy, but also a fascinating and, until now, strictly private view of the recorded thoughts of one of the most determined explorers the world has ever seen.

It has, of course, been by no oversight that these documents have remained locked up and unavailable for study by polar historians for seventy-six years for, as Peary's critics correctly guessed, with documents as revealing as these, Peary and his family were naturally concerned for their safety. When requested by the Congressional subcommittee to leave his diary with them for examination, Peary had even been prepared to risk their suspicion by flatly refusing to comply. "I do not care to leave it with anyone," he had angrily replied. "I do not care to let it out of my possession; it never has been." His strong feeling on this issue had stunned his examiners into meekly accepting his ruling and, after a somewhat superficial examination of his original diary and observations, they were returned to their safe-deposit box in a bank vault where they remained until 1970.

To what extent the Peary family were influenced in their decision to keep these documents hidden after the death of the Admiral in 1920 it is difficult to say. There had certainly been no shortage of advice. It is known that close family friend, Isaiah Bowman, the distinguished geographer and Director of the American Geographical Society, had expressed the opinion that neither the diary nor the observations should be made available to the public. It was his view that this was the surest way to protect Peary's reputation from any possibility of defamation at the hands of critics who might misquote or otherwise distort the material to support their prejudice. It is, however, far more likely that it was by Peary's own request that the original diary and observations were hidden safely away.

Meanwhile the main body of the Peary Papers presented a very different problem. Whilst a good deal of the material might well be described as sensitive, the problem with the main mass of it was principally one of sheer bulk, since the boxes of documents took up two hundred cubic feet. Originally all of this material had been stored out at Peary's home on Eagle Island, in Casco Bay off the coast of Maine, and there it remained, a constant liability and worry to the family, until 1940 when it was decided, mainly for reasons of safety, to ship most of the material over to the mainland, and eventually on to the National Archives in Washington, D.C. where it was received into the care of the nation in 1967.

The original diary, however, together with the astronomical observations and some of Peary's personal memos, being in a different category of historical significance to the main body of the Peary Papers, and for security reasons separated from it, were not handed over to the National Archives for safe keeping until some three years later, and even then, because of the restrictions attached to these papers as a condition of the instrument of gift, they were examined only by the staff members of the Center for Polar Archives. And there they have remained ever since, in that great mausoleum on Pennyslvania Avenue, safe, but as inaccessible to the scholars, the iconoclasts, and the just plain curious as they have always been.

For how many more years they may have remained, safe but inaccessible, we shall never know. They had kept their silence throughout the most vicious debate that has ever focused its glaring attention on the stated claim of a renowned explorer, and these papers may well have kept their restriction right through to the end of the twentieth century had it not been for the television screening, early in 1984, of the CBS/ITT production *The Race to the Pole* – a dramatised documentary film which credited Dr. Frederick A. Cook with the discovery of the North Pole on 21st April, 1908. This film so angered and hurt those who supported Peary's position that, in February 1984, the Peary family were persuaded by the National Geographic Society that the time had finally come to release the Admiral's original diary, his observations, and his private memos for publication, the belief being that these documents would speak for themselves in defence of his claim and finally silence his critics.

The diary, however, was not written by Peary with publication in mind, as was the diary of Captain Scott. It was written as a private log of his journey, a log he had intended simply as a reminder of the events which he would later expand and polish for publication, and as a convenient notebook for ideas and memos, thoughts which it is truly astonishing that Peary should have taken the risk of committing to paper, let alone to his diary. One of these notes was a criticism of his old rival, the great Fridtjof Nansen, whose epic drift in the *Fram* across the Arctic Ocean, and his attempt to reach the North Pole by dog sledge from the drifting ship, is one of the most inspiring examples of courageous intelligence in the history of exploration:

Why did Nansen make no attempt to regain his ship when he found he could no longer advance? He had traveled about 130 miles, his earliest tracks were but three weeks old. He could certainly have followed his own trail back at least half the distance, and then he should at least have been able to hit within five miles of the ship and pick her up. She would drift very little in five or six weeks. Was he ashamed to go back after so short an absence, or had there been a row and the *Fram* made uncomfortable for him; or did he go off for Franz Joseph Land from sensational motives and business reasons?

There are notes which reek of delusions of grandeur, and others that show that, of all of his burdens, the hardest to bear was his craving for fame and his fear that he might not achieve it. They are committed as notes on the upper pages: memos, schemings, arguments in favour of his promotion to the rank of Rear-Admiral, notes on his final resting place: "Mark 1. monument for mausoleum? Faced with marble or granite, statue with flag on top, lighted room at base for two sarcophagi? Bronze figures Eskimo, Dog, Bear, Muskox, Walrus, etc or bronze tablets of flag on Pole and suitable inscription. Bust."

Even in the hands of someone who has made a sympathetic study of Peary's character and the complex issues of his claim, the deficiencies of the diary as a log of events would seem to weaken Peary's case. How much greater then would be the risk of publishing the full and unabridged text of that handwritten diary, knowing that in the hands of the less well informed or the more malicious of Peary's critics it would surely be seen as an open invitation to rush in and tear the material apart. Clearly the diary needed a preface, an informed comment by a scholar, or an assessment of Peary's claim by a polar explorer who knows the environment in which that historic journey was set, an appraisal not only of what was written, but what lies between the lines.

Read the hidden lines correctly and, at best, all one can say is that the searching light has caught another facet of the story, for the whole truth, by its nature, is impossible to see. But what if the reader should stumble upon a story that appears to be more human and therefore much more likely than the one the record shows? Should that reader challenge the accepted version, or accept that history always hides a good deal more than it reveals, and leave the hidden story undisturbed where it was buried by the need of men for heroes with whom they could relate?

This was the dilemma with which I was faced when, in November 1984, I accepted the invitation of the National Geographic Society to make an assessment of that diary and Peary's original observations – a confusing mixture of doubt and awe, for I found myself with an obligation not only to challenge and question Peary, but also to represent him. There was a conflict, too, at a deeper level, arising no doubt from the astonishing number of strange similarities between so many of the key events which Peary experienced during his lifetime and those occurring in mine.

During the first fourteen years of my polar career it had of course been the inspiring achievements of the great explorers that had been the focus of most of my interest, and Peary was no more real to me then than any of the other polar explorers through whose territories I was travelling with dogs, mapping what they had left unmapped in their more pressing need to be first at the Pole. And yet, even then, there had been at some level a contact with those whose routes I retraced – Shackleton, Scott and Amundsen in the Antarctic, and at the opposite end of the world through the far more hazardous and wilder territories of Peary, Sverdrup and Dr. Cook – and I had found my own experience being coloured by coincidences of date and place which made so much more personal for me an already intense sense of history.

With three companions and forty dogs I had set off from Point Barrow in Alaska on 21st February, 1968, on a journey of 3,800 miles across the longest axis of the Arctic Ocean, via the Pole of Relative Inaccessibility and the North Pole to the Arctic island of Spitsbergen. It was a journey which took sixteen months to make and completed not only the third and final achievement of the so-called trilogy of the first ascent of the earth's highest mountain and the first surface crossing of the southern and northern ice caps of the world, but one which also, in the historical sense, completed the last of the old-style geographical firsts on the face of the shrinking globe.

How strange that we should have sighted land at the end of that journey at precisely the moment the Apollo 10 astronauts took that first of many pictures of the "Earthrise" from the Moon. How strange that at the precise moment that our feet touched land, it was the sixteenth anniversary of the day, even to the hour, that Mount Everest was climbed. How strange, too, that after a journey of thirteen and a half months across drifting pack ice, we should reach the North Pole on 6th April, 1969 – the sixtieth anniversary of the date that Peary claimed to have reached that same desolate spot.

Since that memorable date, my interest in Peary's career has of course been very much more personal. I have retraced the track of his 1909 journey step by step and agonised over every detail in his diary and his published accounts with a critical understanding of Peary's claim which I dare say few others have equalled. Out of the total of thirteen years that I have spent in the Arctic and the Antarctic, during which I have travelled over twenty thousand miles with dog teams, I have, like Peary, spent nine winters in the polar regions and four winters in North-West Greenland among the children and grandchildren of the Eskimos with whom Peary lived and travelled between the years 1891–1909.

One of our neighbours during the years that my wife and I spent among the Polar Eskimos of North-West Greenland with our baby daughter was Peary's Eskimo son Kalipaluk; and one of my travelling companions, with whom I have travelled several thousands of miles, and a man whose life I have saved on at least three occasions, and who saved mine a great many more, was Peary's Eskimo grandson, Peter.

With what amazing foresight did Peter Peary's illustrious grandfather, at the age of twenty-nine, and before he had even embarked on his first Arctic expedition, write in his 1885 diary:

If colonization is to be a success in the polar regions let white men take with them native wives, then from this union may spring a race combining the hardiness of the mothers with the intelligence of the fathers. Such a race would surely reach the Pole if their fathers did not succeed in doing it.

In May 1971, Peter Peary reached the North Pole, together with Talilanguaq Peary (Peter's half-brother), Avatak Henson, the Eskimo grandson of Matthew Henson, Admiral Peary's black assistant, and ten other Eskimos in support of the Italian North Pole expedition of Count Guido Monzino. In 1978, Peter Peary did it again, this time as a guide for a Japanese expedition, and so became the first man, and the only man so far, to travel to the North Pole twice, both times with dog teams, and both times following the route taken by his grandfather's 1909 expedition.

I was passing through the weather station at Alert, on the north coast of Ellesmere Island when Peter Peary flew in from the North Pole after his second visit there in 1978, and vividly, and with great sadness, recall how he had begged me to teach him how to navigate so that he would no longer have to be the servant of the men from the south, but could lead his own party of Inuit to the Pole. He did not live to see that dream of his fulfilled. His tragic death a few months later on the eve of the anniversary of his grandfather's claimed discovery of the North Pole is still a mystery. Some say it was suicide, others not. Some say it was the Peary in him that needed recognition – that the simple cash bonuses he had received for taking his cargo of foreign adventurers across the drifting pack to their goal had undermined his self respect and finally destroyed his pride. But those who say this did not know the hunter with whom I travelled who now lies in a shallow grave in the cemetery at Qaanaq in North-West Greenland.

The craving for fame that had driven his grandfather Peter could never have understood, and this very difference between them was all the more poignant as a reminder that fame can be a tragedy disguised as a reward. For Peter, the North Pole was simply a point with which some of the crazier white men he knew (and one in particular about whom he had read) seemed to have had an obsession, a point far out on the Arctic Ocean to which, as far as he was concerned, there were hardly any good reasons to travel, and none of these included fame or offered the hope of a fortune.

He went because he enjoyed a diversion, and to collect a few stories to share with his friends through the long polar nights, stories invariably at the expense of the passengers he had carried to the Pole and whose flags he had wryly saluted. He went because he loved the feeling of being at the very limits of his range in those wild and trackless wastes of ice, his world where the human spirit breathes the purest air on earth and senses a real affinity with every living thing.

To have travelled with him, and learned the lore of the wilds from him has left me with some of the finest memories I have of the polar world. But his greatest gift was that same gift which had been given to Peter by the greatest hunters of the tribe: respect for the weather, for moving ice, and the readiness to laugh at one's inevitable misfortunes.

Peary must surely have had similar teachers and formed a similar bond between those hunters with whom he travelled. But these are only a few of the strands in this strangely repeating pattern of lives. What they mean I do not know. I offer them simply in part to account for the almost overwhelming excitement I felt on the morning of 26th April, 1985, as I signed in at the desk of the National Archives and was given directions to Room 11E of The Scientific, Economic, and Natural Resources Branch of the Civil Archives Division.

Welcomed warmly by Alison Wilson in the homely clutter of her polar den in that section which breathed more easily under the heading of the Center for Polar Archives, I was asked to be seated while she went out to fetch the diary. Even at that stage, I am bound to admit I could scarcely believe it existed. But there it was, protected by a clear plastic wallet, a much smaller book than I had imagined it might be at just under four inches wide and seven inches long, together with several less special documents in its grey National Archives storage box.

With more reverence than I can recall ever having handled an object before, I took the little notebook out of its box, carefully removed its protective wallet, and for a few moments held that diary in my hands. Here at last was that crowning journey of Peary's career out to the limit of human endurance, and miraculously back to reap the rewards of world-wide acclaim. The words which the Admiral had recorded for posterity shortly before he died in 1920, and which I had played and re-played so many times that they were deeply engraved upon my mind, were now ringing out as clearly as if he was standing right behind me:

> The discovery of the North Pole stands for the inevitable victory of courage, persistence, endurance, over all obstacles. In the discovery of the North Pole is written the final chapter of the last of the great geographical stories of the Western Hemisphere which began with the discovery of the New World by Columbus. Here is the cap and climax, the closing of the book on 400 years of history. The discovery of the North Pole on the 6th of April 1909, by the last expedition of the Peary Arctic Club, means that the splendid frozen jewel of the North, for which through centuries men of every nation have struggled, and suffered and died, is won at last, and is to be worn for ever, by the Stars and Stripes!

It was almost as though the very existence of the diary had become the proof of his attainment of the Pole – an astonishing admission, I confess. But the diary was certainly real enough to me, and the story, at the first reading, so very compelling that I could not bear the agony of the unreasonable doubts that were creeping into my mind. There could be no doubt, I kept telling myself, that the notebook was written by Peary's hand, and if, as he claimed, each entry was written on or within a day or so of the events he had recorded, then beyond a shadow of a doubt this record must be true. But there is that word doubt again. It creeps in even when the context of the phrase is trying so hard to deny it.

Slowly it now began to dawn on me that I had fallen into a trap which I had myself created. Through my admiration for the man as a polar traveller, and those coincidences which had somehow bridged two very different period settings and two very different temperaments, I had clearly become emotionally involved. From this standpoint, and from its other extreme – that of the reader who is unfamiliar with the complexities and the implications of Peary's controversial claim – it is impossible not to be impressed by the courage and the single-mindedness of this man and his companions. But the emotional involvement I was no longer permitted. My role demanded a dispassionate approach. So what were these unreasonable doubts, and where had they crept in?

Perhaps one might blame, among other things, those blank pages immediately following his arrival at the Pole. It had been to this part of the diary that I had turned first in search of Peary's entry for 6th April – the date which for both of us had been so fateful and so memorable – and I had by chance come upon those blank pages before finding the date I was looking for. The first one was headed "Thursday, April 8." I had then to turn back past six more blank pages before finding one that was headed "Wednesday, April 7" – his second day at the Pole. This page also was blank, and so too was the page before it on which I was expecting to find his entry for 6th April. Here, however, a loose-leaf page had been inserted – a note which, in Peary's book *The North Pole*, he claims to have written on the 6th:

> The first thing I did after awaking was to write these words in my diary: "The Pole at last. The prize of three centuries. My dream and goal for twenty years. Mine at last! I cannot bring myself to realize it. It all seems so simple and commonplace."

He does not quote accurately from the loose-leaf page. His diary had read:

> The Pole at last!!! The prize of 3 centuries, my dream & ambition for 23 years. *Mine* at last. I cannot bring myself to realize it. It all seems so simple and commonplace, as Bartlett said "just like every day". I wish Jo could be here with me to share my feelings. I have drunk her health & that of the kids from the Benedictine flask she sent me.

But more important than the differences: when was that note in Peary's hand written, and why is it not *in situ*? If, as Peary says in his book, this note was written "after awaking" some time during the afternoon of the 6th, then one would expect it to appear immediately after his diary entry for that date. But it does not. Nor is there any indication that the loose-leaf page had been torn from the diary at that point.

Having therefore set out to satisfy my curiosity concerning Peary's entry for 6th April and discovered that his diary offered no record of any of his activities during the thirty hours that he and his companions spent at the North Pole, I decided to read the diary right through from cover to cover, in the hope that by reading the entries in their correct sequence I would find some explanation for the gaps in the story. But I did not even get as far as the first entry before stumbling upon another mystery. On the title page of this log of his 1909 journey there is an inscription, in his own hand, which offers the surprisingly incomplete information: "No. 1, Roosevelt to —— and return, February 22 to April 27, R. E. Peary, United States Navy."

Why did he not insert the words North Pole? He states the date of his return to the ship; why then not complete the title page with those two words which together spelled out his very reason for living? Confronted by these two puzzles within only a few minutes, I determined to detach myself from all preconceptions and personal feelings and allow the diary to speak for itself.

And speak to me it did. It spoke to me of one of the most hazardous and amazing journeys ever made by man. It spoke to me of incredible courage and of a passionate, almost half-crazed need to succeed. It spoke also with a ring of truth, and yet, in spite of my respect, I had found the diary disturbing.

So what were those doubts: a few blank pages in an explorer's notebook and a title page which is incomplete? Sadly there were a great many others. At the first reading, however, it was far from easy to point to the places where those doubts had crept in.

Some of them were new-found doubts, which only a study of the original diary could possibly expose: the remarkable consistency, for example, of the handwriting throughout the diary, a consistency one surely could only expect of a diary that had been written in one sitting and in the comfort of the ship. But if that particular doubt was well founded, why had he not filled out the blank pages and left unrecorded those memos which might cause embarrassment to him if ever the diary was called upon to support his North Pole claim?

Others were doubts I had held for a long time: doubts which the handwritten entries of the diary now greatly seemed to amplify. Among these was the question, often raised by Peary's critics, concerning the sudden increase in speed immediately after the last of Peary's supporting parties (and the last of his reliable witnesses) had turned back to retrace the perilous journey across the drifting ice to the ship, circumstances that were remarkably similar to those of his previous attempt at the Pole in 1906. Another of these doubts, which a reading of the diary seemed only to increase, was Peary's astonishingly slack navigation.

There is no indication in his diary that he took a single observation for longitude on his outward journey to check the extent to which the winds and currents might be carrying him off his chosen course. He made, at most, only one casual check on his magnetic compass; but this compass check he mentions only in a loose-leaf memo which was written (along with several others) after his return to the ship, and his companions took only three latitude shots between Cape Columbia and the point at which the last of the supporting parties turned for home, some 133 nautical miles (in a straight line) from the Pole. And that final 133 miles – what of that?

In five marches over a period of four days and five hours, and without observations for latitude, longitude, or any checks on his compass variation, he claims to have made it to his goal in time for a sun shot on 6th April at local noon on the Cape Columbia meridian, a shot which placed that camp no more than three miles short of the Pole. Is such a feat of navigation credible? According to Peary, it certainly is, and his observations are proof of it. According to his detractors, however, it definitely is not, and the observations he claims to have made could easily have been faked.

Not surprisingly, I suffered a reaction to these doubts – an angry frustration that Peary had left us with only his word and a few pencil marks scratched on a pad. He could so easily have corrected his course and brought back a mass of acceptable proof that he and his five courageous companions had finally succeeded in reaching the Pole. But, incredibly, Peary had simply not bothered. He had merely offered as proof of his claim the sort of simple calculations which my companions and I, at local noon on a travelling day during our crossing of the Arctic Ocean, used to work out in a matter of seconds by scratching the numbers with the point of a ski stick on a smooth patch of wind-packed snow.

I thought of pulling out of the project and leaving someone else with the task of reading the conflict between the lines, but my respect for the man refused to release me. It appealed to me as a fellow explorer to support the driving spirit of Peary and side with him against his critics. But in trying to come to terms with the man I needed first to understand his pride and sense of purpose. I needed also to understand that self-destructive craving for fame which produced in Peary the tragic delusion that fame is the proof of true greatness. And what I found as I read on was a far more moving and tragic story than the one that I had been expecting – a conflict which exposed the truth as he himself perceived it.

CHAPTER I

Guests of Honour

It was the picture of the man that had first caught the eye, a studio portrait of a striking looking man; an erect, deep-chested, powerful man with a stern yet strongly handsome face, a rock-like jaw and a full moustache, a man perhaps of forty years, none of which had been easy.

The stunning effect of that studio portrait owed less, however, to the fierce intensity of his expression than it did to the unusual style of his dress, for although he seemed to be staring out from that picture in the *Sunday Herald* of 16th December, 1906, as though his eyes were fixed upon some goal which he alone could see, it was his elegant black fur hat and his truly magnificent sealskin cape which left no one in the slightest doubt that this was the famous polar explorer, Commander Robert E. Peary.

This, the headline had confirmed. "Peary awarded first gold medal" it announced in bold print above the picture, with several other smaller headlines leading the readers into the story of Peary's outstanding success.

Washington, D.C., December 15th, 1906. Commander Robert E. Peary was a highly honored dinner guest here tonight. His achievements in exploring "Farthest North" was the particular theme of the National Geographic Society, around whose annual banquet 400 prominent people gathered. The eulogies of men of science, of diplomacy and politics that Commander Peary heard during the entire evening found their climax in the presentation to him of the Society's first gold medal. President Roosevelt, who had been dining at the residence of Vice-President Fairbanks, entered the hall at the New Willard at 10.30, and from his hands, in the course of a simple but impressive ceremony, Commander Peary received the much prized trophy.

The medal, which was on exhibition as the guests assembled, excited much interest. Its intrinsic value is over $800. Circular in shape and three inches in diameter, it is of solid gold. Its face bears the great seal of the Society – a map of North and South America, with adjacent islands – and the legend "National Geographic Society, Incorporated 1888." The reverse bears at the top the words "The Hubbard Medal," as it was authorized by a bequest of the late Gardiner Green Hubbard. Just beneath that inscription is a little sapphire star, symbolic both of the navy, of which Peary is an officer, and of the "Farthest North." A further inscription on the reverse reads: "Awarded by the National Geographic Society to Robert E. Peary, for Arctic Explorations Farthest North, 87 degrees 6 minutes. December 15, 1906."

The dinner guests assembled in the reception rooms of the hotel at 7 o'clock and comprised a very interesting company.

They had indeed. There were no less than ten nations represented by titled members of the diplomatic corps, and some twenty states by Senators and Representatives. There were eminent churchmen, and men of science. There were millionaires who, through their patronage of various suitable cultural pursuits and their support of all things patriotic, had earned the privilege of being accepted as part of the distinguished gathering that moved along the receiving line in the parlours of the New Willard Hotel where one and all had been welcomed by the ebullient President of the Society and his wife, Mrs. Willis L. Moore. The guest of honour, Commander Peary, was also on the receiving line (illness preventing his wife from attending), along with the Hon. Charles J. Bonaparte who, as Secretary of the Navy, was there presumably to represent the official approval and the pride of the Navy in the man who was to be honoured with the great gold medal, which was on display. Its value as a work of art, as any discerning person could see, scarcely exceeded that of the metal from which it had been made, for although it bore the Tiffany stamp and the hallmark of its weight in gold, it also bore the sure sign of a job that had been done in a rush. And this, by checking back on the dates, it would appear it had.

Since 3rd October, when news of the successful first ascent of Mount McKinley in Alaska (the highest mountain in North America) had been reported in the *New York Times*, Dr. Frederick A. Cook had been the obvious choice to be the guest of honour that evening. Returning from Alaska with this prize, he had been invited to succeed Major General Adolphus W. Greely as the new President of the Explorers' Club (of which Cook had been one of the founder members in 1905) and without any question the record of Cook as a polar explorer, coupled with his most recent achievement, had earned him the honour intended. A month later, however, when news had come through that Commander Peary was on his way home claiming to have set a new Farthest North record, the organisers had found themselves faced with the problem of how to have two guests of honour without offending Commander Peary whose achievements were more widely known and respected. It had therefore been necessary to find some way of elevating Peary without belittling

Dr. Cook, and their solution, as one might expect, had been nothing short of brilliant. The Society would commission a special gold medal in honour of Peary's most recent achievement and invite the President of the United States to present it at their annual banquet.

But when had that decision been taken? Peary's first contact with the outside world on his voyage out from the Arctic had been two telegrams from Hopedale in Labrador on 2nd November: the first to his wife; the second to the President of the Peary Arctic Club, Morris K. Jesup. Both telegrams had stated his Farthest North as latitude 87°6′N, an advance of thirty-two nautical miles on the previous record set six years earlier by the expedition of the Italian, the Duke of the Abruzzi. He also sent the condensed story of his 1905–6 expedition to the *New York Herald* from Chateau Bay, Quebec, on 15th November, and this was published the following day.

Tiffany & Co. of New York had, at most, only forty days in which to design, make, and deliver the medal, if they had received the commission within two days of the arrival of Peary's first telegram, and only twenty-five days if the decision to strike a medal for Peary had been made in response to the newspaper story published on 16th November. It is therefore much more likely that the National Geographic Society had accepted the first telegram at its word, for even had Tiffany's given the medal their highest priority, the Dinner Committee of the National Geographic must surely have needed more than three weeks in which to incorporate their special arrangements into the banquet plan, not least of which the need to persuade the President to present a medal which made up in size for what it lacked in artistic value.

The *Sunday Herald* reporter tells us that the banquet hall was thrown open at 7.30 p.m., and the guests took their places at the "gridiron-shaped tables to inspiring strains from the Marine band." There were, in fact, twelve long tables laid out in that magnificent and yet surprisingly small banqueting hall, and "the decorations of roses, palms and hollies were superb." But, sadly, there is not a photograph, a seating plan, nor even a single souvenir menu which has survived to give us a picture of that historic event, and this seems odd considering that Peary was a collector of such mementos. There are boxes among the Peary collection at the National Archives in Washington, D.C. that are stuffed full of memorabilia of similar events. Why then not this one, the event which surely must have been the high point of Peary's career to that time? Could it be that something happened at that banquet which soured Peary's memory of the event?

We know that among the guests there were at least three who were friends of Cook and who harboured, for one reason or another, a deep dislike for Peary. We know also that there were several others who were highly suspicious of Cook. The two principal guests did not, however, at the start of that evening, appear to share their friends' distrust.

The doctor, who was nine years younger than Peary, had reason to be grateful to his old commander. As surgeon and ethnologist, Cook had accompanied Peary on his first wintering expedition to the Arctic in 1891–2, a highly successful and memorable expedition to North-West Greenland during which both men, each of them novices at that time in that cold and forbidding environment, had become enchanted by the native people of that world. Through hardships shared, the two had formed a bond of trust which had almost admitted to friendship. Even fifteen years later, with the affable doctor now a seasoned explorer in his own right and posing (according to some of Peary's friends) a serious threat to his own ambitions, Peary still had a genuine measure of gratitude for Cook which dated back to that day, right at the start of his 1891–2 expedition, when he had so narrowly averted being forced by his fare-paying passengers to abandon his expedition when his leg had been broken by an iron tiller. Not only had Cook supported his leader against the dissenting passengers, but he had so skilfully set the broken leg that within a matter of weeks Peary had returned to full mobility and to his usual vigorous optimism.

There was, in any case, another and perhaps more practical reason why Peary did not take the Cook threat seriously. He was, in the view of the older man, simply not in his class. Cook had made a couple of ill-fated summer expeditions to Greenland in 1893 and 1894, and had served as surgeon with the Belgian Antarctic expedition (the *Belgica* expedition) of 1897–9, which unintentionally had taken the honour of being the first expedition to winter south of the Antarctic Circle. This near disastrous expedition had, however, brought Cook's name to the admiring attention of a much wider audience, and stirred in him a need for fame which, although perhaps not at that time as obsessive or as specific as Peary's, was very nearly as deep. Peary's wife, Jo, had sensed this as long ago as March 1900. In a letter to her husband, who was then up in the Arctic, she had written: "The Belgian expedition is back from the Antarctic. Beyond puffing up Dr. Cook a little more I don't think it has accomplished anything." Cook was, nevertheless, a potential rival, and hardened as Peary was by his ambition, he regarded every man with suspicion whose own ambitions in any way might cross his path to success.

Nansen, Peary believed, had unfairly "forestalled" him in 1888 when he made the first crossing of the Greenland Ice Cap, and the fame-seeking Peary had been cut even deeper eight years later by Nansen's epic drift in the *Fram* across the Arctic Ocean, for it had established the Norwegian as, beyond any question, the greatest polar explorer of the age and this Peary could not bear. Captain Otto Sverdrup (who had been with Nansen on the Greenland crossing and as Captain of the *Fram*) was also unfairly accused by Peary of "appropriation" – a polite expression used by polar explorers who believed their domain invaded – and there was a whole string of others who had crossed Peary's tracks, some of them originally companions and friends, whom Peary later denounced. Eivind Astrup, Peary's sole companion on his hazardous 1,200-mile journey across the Greenland Ice Cap in 1892 was one. Dr. Cook, who with Peary and Astrup had almost perished on the depot-laying journey for that Greenland crossing, was another, and Peary's dislike for General Greely ran very much deeper than the normal so-called healthy hatred which most explorers secretly nurse for those who are their rivals.

Between Peary and Cook there had, however, been little cause for serious friction (with the possible exception of one event) since returning from the Arctic together in 1892. That one exception had occurred in the summer of 1901 when Cook had gone north on the *Erik* at the request of Herbert L. Bridgman, Secretary of the Peary Arctic Club. Representing the interests and the concern of Peary's financial backers, Bridgman had requested that Dr. Cook should examine Peary, and to this examination Peary had reluctantly submitted. Cook had later reported that he had found Peary "wrecked in ambition, wrecked in physique, and wrecked in hope" and had diagnosed him to be suffering the early symptoms of pernicious anaemia. He had evidently suggested to Peary that he should eat raw meat and liver, to which Peary is said to have replied: "I would rather die; besides, liver is poison."

With the evidence of Jo's remark made some seventeen months earlier, this reunion between Peary and Cook had been an uncomfortable one for Peary. Here was a man, nine years his junior, who was obviously eager to build upon his reputation as a polar explorer, advising his old leader: "You are through as a traveler." To this, we are told, Peary had not replied.

How many place-settings separated these two at the banquet we do not know, perhaps only one, two at the most, since they were both there as guests of honour. But with all of the glowing tributes that evening being paid to Peary, and with only the occasional mention of Cook, the proud explorer had relaxed. That evening was his, and rightly so in Peary's view – he had worked for it and earned it. Out of this pleasant reverie, however, the principal guest was suddenly shaken when the time came for the spotlight to shift and for the inventor, Alexander Graham Bell, to introduce the doctor.

I have been asked to say a few words about a man who must be known by name, at least, to all of us, Dr. Frederick A. Cook, President of the Explorers' Club, New York. We have had with us, and are glad to welcome, Commander Peary, of the Arctic regions, but in Dr. Cook we have one of the few Americans, if not the only American, who has explored both extremes of the world, the Arctic and the Antarctic regions. And now he has been to the top of the American continent, and therefore to the top of the world, and tonight I hope Dr. Frederick Cook will tell us something about Mount McKinley.

Here was a man, nine years Peary's junior, whose total travelled distance by dog sledge in the polar regions amounted to less than five hundred miles of relatively easy sledging; a man who had made no major geographical discoveries and led no major expeditions to the Arctic, being given credit for having reached "the top of the world."

Certainly it was clear that the remark in its context had referred to Mount McKinley. But to Peary's ears the misuse of the expression, merely for the sake of effect, was unforgivable before such a gathering and in the presence of a man who had already spent almost nine years in the Arctic and travelled 12,000 miles in pursuit of that goal. And Cook, had he noticed? Of course he had!

Smiling graciously at the applause, the doctor now rose to his modest five feet nine inches and politely began his address with words intended for Peary:

> Mr. Chairman, Ladies and Gentlemen: I would prefer to tell you tonight of the splendid achievement of Commander Peary and of the noble character of the man who has succeeded in pushing human endeavor to the utmost limit of endurance, all with the unselfish motive of carrying the honor and the flag of his country to the farthest north, but your chairman has put me to the task of getting to the top of our continent. In the conquest of Mount McKinley success was mostly due to our use of the working equipment of polar explorers, and among polar explorers Commander Peary has worked hardest to reduce the outfit to its utmost simplicity. Thus indirectly to Commander Peary should fall a part of the honor of scaling the arctic slopes of our greatest mountain.

Would he really have preferred to tell his audience about "the splendid achievement of Commander Peary and of the noble character of the man" than to tell that distinguished gathering about his own achievements? The answer is elusive. There may well have been a part of Cook's nature that had a genuine respect for Peary. It had, after all, been on Peary's expedition of 1891-2 that Cook had fallen under the spell of the Arctic – that "fascination which makes men risk their lives and endure inconceivable hardships for . . . no profitable personal purpose of any kind." Peary had also invited Cook to join him on his second expedition to North-West Greenland in 1893 but, although he had happily agreed, a disagreement with Peary had forced him to resign. Peary had refused to give Cook permission to publish an article in a medical journal, reminding Cook of the contract he had signed to refrain from writing or lecturing on the subject of the expedition. Cook had felt the ruling unfair; Peary had refused to shift on the issue, and so the two men had parted company. "Here was the only break I had with Peary," Cook was to write many years later in an unpublished autobiographical sketch. "I resigned then and there as volunteer, but did so in a friendly way. There really was no lingering malice between us."

Perhaps not. But by 1906 they were rivals, and Cook was as much in need of the admiration of the geographical establishment and its support-ing millionaires as Peary. This might explain the tone of those opening remarks in his speech, for although by then he had certainly seen for himself and heard from his friends enough evidence to convince him that Peary's motives for going north were almost entirely self-promoting, we find him saying only what was expected of him – what seemed generous, respectful, and socially polite. So how much more was he hiding?

We are safe enough in assuming that Cook had read the *New York Herald* report of Peary's last trip, for explorers always read the reports of those whom they regard as rivals. Even if Cook had not himself seen it, he would have heard opinions about it from friends who had his interests at heart, and there were at least three close friends of Cook's at that banquet who had less respect for Peary than they were publicly prepared to admit: Ralph Shainwald who had been with Cook on his reconnaissance of Mount McKinley in 1903 and was a neighbour of Cook's in Brooklyn; Anthony Fiala, another Brooklyn-based explorer, who had been the leader of the Ziegler Polar expedition of 1903–5 which had made an un-successful attempt to reach the North Pole from Franz Josef Land, and Rear-Admiral Winfield Scott Schley who had led the Greely relief ex-pedition in 1884.

To men such as these, Fiala and Cook especially, that despatch of Peary's giving the first details of his last trip and his report of having reached a new Farthest North of 87°6', was strangely unconvincing. No dates were given for any of the camps, except for the date of setting out from Point Moss, and the date he reached his highest latitude, 21st April, 1906, and he gave no longitudes. It must also to them have seemed "interesting" (which is the explorer's word for "suspicious") that having lost all communication with his supporting parties, he had made his dash with only six Eskimos, six teams of dogs, and Matthew Henson, his loyal black companion who had been with him on all of his polar expeditions, except his first summer trip to West Greenland. "Interesting," too, that at least one of these marches had covered a distance of thirty nautical miles which was unheard of at that time on moving pack ice, and that his new record was only thirty-two nautical miles beyond the latitude reached by the Italian expedition.

Without anyone with him on that dash to verify his observations, could it be that on this, his widely reported "final attempt" at the North Pole, he had exaggerated his distances in order to bring home the next best thing to the Pole – a new record Farthest North? Only an examination of his diary and observations would settle the question. But the question had not been asked, nor was it likely to be, for on the strength of his word alone the great gold medal had been struck, and already the Italians (who had themselves only beaten Nansen's record by 20.4 nautical miles) had conceded victory to Peary.

And now, in addition to this uncertain victory, Cook seemingly was offering his one-time friend some "part of the honor" of scaling Mount McKinley!

It is 20,300 feet high. Its summit pierces the frigid blue one thousand feet above any other mountain on the North American continent. It is, then, the top of our continent and the most arctic of the big mountains of the world. The country to the east was entirely unknown, and the country to the west but roughly outlined. A venture to ascend this mountain must therefore assume the responsibilities of an exploring enterprise and be prepared for all kinds of difficulties.

Three years ago, as Commander Peary was preparing for his assault upon the North Pole, I organized an expedition to ascend Mount McKinley from the west. In this we failed, but we carried a line of exploration through and around the range. Last spring I organized another expedition upon a similar general plan. My chief companions were Prof. H. C. Parker, Russell W. Porter, Belmore H. Browne, and Edward Barrille. We took twenty pack horses from Seattle for our difficult cross-country transportation, and for the river we built a powerful motor boat.

We reached Cook Inlet early in June. During June and July we forded and swam icy streams, pushed through thick underbrush, and over gloomy marshes, only to find that the part of the mountain which we finally reached was impossible for an ascent. A good deal of pioneering work was done at this time, but the opportunity to make an attempt to climb did not present itself until early in September, after all hope of mountaineering had been abandoned.

Here, strangely, were similarities with Peary's most recent attempt at the Pole: an apparent impasse is met; the party is split, and a final dash is made by the leader without reliable witnesses to a successful conclusion. Or as Belmore Browne, the artist on the expedition, later remarked:

With all thought of climbing Mount McKinley put aside for another year, our party broke up in mid-August, 1906, at Tyonek on Cook Inlet. Porter was left to finish up some topographical work, Professor Parker returned to New York, and Dr. Cook asked me to make a side trip . . . to secure some museum specimens. I told him that if he contemplated exploring the southern foothills of Mount McKinley I would prefer going with him. He answered that he would do no exploring outside of seeing whether or not the water route was practicable. Barrille (assistant horsepacker on the expedition just ended) and some prospectors picked up at Susitna station now accompanied the doctor.

Before leaving Tyonek I invited Dr. Cook aboard to take luncheon with me, and while he was on board or while the boat was at Seldovia he sent the following telegram to a well-known business man of New York City: "Am preparing for a last desperate attempt on Mount McKinley."

Some weeks later at the appointed time in early September, 1906, we met at Seldovia on the Kenai Peninsula. Printz and Miller were the first to join me. At this time we heard the rumor that Dr. Cook and Barrille had reached the top of Mount McKinley. We knew the character of country that guarded the southern face of the big mountain, we had traveled in that country, and we knew the time that Dr. Cook had been absent was too short to allow of his even reaching the mountain. We therefore denied the rumor. At last the Doctor and Barrille joined us and to my surprise Dr. Cook confirmed the rumor. After a word with Dr. Cook I called Barrille aside, and we walked up the Seldovia beach. Barrille and I had been through some hard times together. I liked Barrille and I know that he was fond of me for we were tied by the strong bond of having suffered together. As soon as we were alone I turned to him and asked him what he knew about Mount McKinley, and after a moment's hesitation he answered: "I can tell you all about the big peaks just south of the mountain, but if you want to know about Mount McKinley go and ask Cook." I had felt all along that Barrille would tell me the truth, and after his statement I kept the knowledge to myself.

I now found myself in an embarrassing position. I knew that Dr. Cook had not climbed Mount McKinley. Barrille had told me so and in addition I knew it in the same way that any New Yorker would know that no man could walk from the Brooklyn Bridge to Grant's tomb in ten minutes.

This knowledge, however, did not constitute proof, and I knew that before I could make the public believe the truth I should have to collect some facts. I wrote immediately on my return to Professor Parker telling him my opinions and knowledge concerning the climb, and I received a reply from him saying that he believed me implicitly and that the climb, under the existing conditions, was impossible.

I returned to New York as soon as possible and both Professor Parker and I stated our convictions to members of the American Geographical Society and the Explorers' Club.

The telegram Cook had sent out from Alaska on 27th September, 1906 – "We have reached the summit of Mount McKinley by a new route from the North" – had been sent to one of his financial backers, Herbert L. Bridgman, who was also a friend of Peary's, and Secretary of the Peary Arctic Club. Bridgman was one of the guests at that banquet who now listened with interest as Cook delivered his colourful report on his first ascent of Mount McKinley – the last fifteen thousand feet of which, according to the rumours, was pure imagination:

Hour after hour we dug our feet and hands into the snow in desperate effort to get from crevass to crevass, from grottos to cliffs, always gaining a little altitude and rising farther and farther into cloudland, with its awful cold and stormy agitation ... Here, on a cornice, we built a snow house and within we found rest and comfort, amid the cloud and storms.

Ever on and upward he guided his audience towards the summit of the mountain: "We were chilled to the marrow and our forces were about exhausted. Would we push on to the summit or return?" Here was the sort of question that audiences love, and Cook had them in the palm of his hand:

Starting early in the morning of the 16th of September, we began the last weary climb. It was hard to lift one foot above another; but the slope was easy, and with much forced effort we made a few hundred paces, leaned over our ice axes, puffed a few minutes, and then went farther. We dropped on a snow slope a few hundred feet below the summit and tried to rest, while we gasped for breath; but the piercing air chilled us; and so, with knees bent, and backs bent, and chests laboring like bellows, we digged one foot after another over the big blocks of granite at the top ...

An abrupt ending? Indeed it was, for although the report in the *National Geographic Magazine* does not say so, President Roosevelt entered the hall at 10.30 p.m. while Cook was speaking, and Cook's final few steps had to wait until the standing ovation for the President had died down and the President had waved him on to his climax:

> ... the summit at last – the top of the continent. Our North Pole had been reached. To an ice axe the flag was attached, and Barrille stood on the brink, as near heaven as he ever expects to get and live. We had been eight days in ascending, but we remained only twenty minutes. It would, however, take me several hours to tell you what we saw. This I will reserve for a future occasion.

With the words "Our North Pole had been reached" and the tremendous applause for Cook ringing in Peary's ears, Professor Moore rose to his feet to welcome the President and to invite him to present the medal to Peary "for distinguished service in exploration, and for having reached the Farthest North, 87 degrees and 6 minutes." And this of course the President did with all the enthusiasm for which he was renowned in a chest-bursting speech on the virtues of courage and hardihood, the "fighting virtues" as he called them, which wound itself up to the climax with the words:

> They can be shown in the work of the philanthropist, in the work of the scientist, and, most emphatically of all, in the work of the explorer, who faces and overcomes perils and hardships which the average soldier never in his life knows. In war, after all, it is only the man at the very head who is ever lonely. All the others, from the subordinate generals, down through the privates, are cheered and sustained by the sense of companionship and by the sense of divided responsibility.
>
> You, the man whom we join to honor tonight – you, who for months in and months out, year in and year out, had to face perils and overcome the greatest risks and difficulties, with resting on your shoulders the undivided responsibility which meant life or death to you and your followers – you had to show in addition what the modern commander with his great responsibility does not have to show – you had to show all the moral qualities in war, together with other qualities. You did a great deed, a deed that counted for all mankind, a deed which reacted credit upon you and upon your country, and on behalf of those present, and speaking also for the millions of your countrymen, I take pleasure in handing you this Hubbard Medal, and in welcoming you home from the great feat you have performed, Commander Peary.

The applause was thunderous, a sustained outpouring of patriotic pride. And according to the writer of the Special Despatch, the eyes of the

President "glistened." Now Peary was on his feet. His great moment had arrived:

President Roosevelt:
    On behalf of the Peary Arctic Club and its president, Morris K. Jesup, I beg to express our deep appreciation of the great honor confered by the National Geographic Society in this award of its gold medal, and the double honor of receiving this medal from the hand of President Roosevelt.
    Your continued interest, Mr. President, and permission to name the club's ship after you, has been most deeply valued by the club, and your name has proved a powerful talisman. Could I have foreseen this occasion it would have lightened many dark hours; but I will frankly say that it would not, for it could not, have increased my efforts.
    The true explorer does his work not for any hope of rewards or honor, but because the thing he has set himself to do is a part of his very being, and must be accomplished for the sake of accomplishment, and he counts lightly hardships, risks, obstacles, if only they do not bar him from his goal.
    To me the final and complete solution of the polar mystery which has engaged the best thought and interest of the best men of the most vigorous and enlightened nations of the world for more than three centuries, and today quickens the pulse of every man or woman whose veins hold red blood, is the thing which should be done for the honor and credit of this country, the thing which it is intended that I should do, and the thing that I must do.

There it was. He had chosen the perfect moment to let the world know that he was ready to try again and to remind all rivals (the one present at that banquet in particular) that the Pole was *his*, and through him it would be claimed to his country's credit. It was what the audience wanted to hear, and they beat their hands in sheer delight for here was a man – and a hero.

There could surely be no one now who stood between Peary and his goal. This must have been the impression of all who heard him winding his speech to its great conclusion, with but a single exception.

As regards the belief expressed by some, that the attainment of the North Pole possesses no value or interest, let me say that should an American first of all men place the Stars and Stripes at that coveted spot, there is not an American citizen at home or abroad, and there are millions of us, but what would feel a little better and a little prouder of being an American; and just that added increment of pride and patriotism to millions would of itself be ten times the value of all the cost of attaining the Pole.

President Roosevelt, for nearly four centuries the world dreamed of the union of the Atlantic and the Pacific. You have planted the Stars and Stripes at Panama and insured the realization of that dream. For over three centuries the world has dreamed of solving the mystery of the North. Tonight the Stars and Stripes stand nearest to that mystery, pointing and beckoning. God willing, I hope that your administration may yet see those Stars and Stripes planted at the Pole itself. For between these two great logical cosmic boundaries, Panama to the south and the North Pole to the north, lies the heritage and the future of that giant whose destinies you guide today, the United States of America.

To a standing ovation, swelled by the "bravos!" of the President himself, Peary proudly gestured his thanks. It was a triumph such as he had never before experienced. He had stirred in that audience their pride in their country. He had stirred in them their need of him. He had also skilfully forged a link with the President as a co-pioneer, and as a fellow boundary marker.

Here, then, was the fateful moment for Peary, the moment of commitment to one last attempt. But it was also a fateful moment for Cook. He, too, was desperately seeking some way in which to increase his fame, and through fame perhaps to find that fortune which it is always presumed goes with it. This much he was later prepared to admit: "I had no money. My work in exploration had netted me nothing, and all my professional income was soon spent. Unless you have felt the goading, devilish grind of poverty hindering you, dogging you, you cannot know the mental fury into which I was lashed."

Would such a man, at such a time, have missed the significance of that misused polar expression with which Alexander Graham Bell had introduced him, that slip of the tongue which in just four words had placed him ahead of Peary? Would Cook, sitting a few feet from the hero and watching him receive a medal and a standing ovation for what he was simply claiming to have done, have not felt the knife of envy and the need to fight – to win?

It is my belief that in one simple, swift, and stunning move, he had already, in his soaring dreams seen himself standing on top of the world, and even upon waking the following day to find that the odds were stacked heavily against him, Cook had found, to his surprise, that some parts of that dream remained and might yet, with some luck, be used to steal a march on Peary.

CHAPTER 2

The Sheltered Years

Peary had focused his craving for fame a good many years before he admitted it was his ambition to be the discoverer of the North Pole. But this, like so many of the statements and labels attached to his public image, is still very much a supposition and not, as so many historians imply, a clear and self-evident fact.

In the view of Commander Fitzhugh Green, Peary's first biographer, it was by the "purest accident" that Peary became interested in Arctic work, and the moment of inspiration, which had "consecrated" him to the task of "wrenching from the White Arctic the secret men had through centuries, died to learn," had come on the Greenland Ice Cap on 19th July, 1886, during his first short trip to Greenland.

John Edward Weems, a more recent biographer and the first to be given unrestricted access to Peary's papers, offers an earlier date for that moment of inspiration: a handwritten set of notes in his diary of 1885 in which Peary summarises what he had learned from his study of polar history:

> It is true that he did not seriously attempt to reach the North Pole until after severely testing his theories and equipment in the Arctic; but Peary's personal papers indicate that long before he first visited the Arctic he had dreamed of being the first man to reach the North Pole. Peary's early written references to the North Pole were no accident: in casting about for a way to fame, he had definitely imagined himself "the discoverer of the North Pole." His exhaustive preparations and planning and his steadfast work towards reaching his goal, which finally came twenty-three years after his first visit to Greenland, make one of the most amazing stories of dogged persistence ever recorded. If ever a man regulated his life – planned it, controlled it, was himself its master – Peary did.

If such an assumption is justifiable, it would add greater emphasis to the conviction which Peary, in the latter part of his polar career, was more openly prepared to express – the conviction that he had the *right* to be the first man to reach the North Pole. So what were Peary's own recollections of the evolution of his dream?

It is impossible to point to any day or month and to say, "Then the idea first came to me." The North Pole dream was a gradual and almost involuntary evolution from earlier work in which it had no part. My interest in Arctic work dates back to 1885, when as a young man my imagination was stirred by reading accounts of explorations by Nordenskjold in the interior of Greenland. These studies took full possession of my mind and led to my undertaking, entirely alone, a summer trip to Greenland in the following year. Somewhere in my subconscious self, even so long ago as that, there may have been gradually dawning a hope that I might some day reach the Pole itself. Certain it is, the lure of the North, the "Arctic fever," as it has been called, entered my veins then, and I came to have a feeling of fatality, a feeling that the reason and intent of my existence, was the solution of the mystery of the frozen fastness of the Arctic. But the actual naming of the Pole as the object of an expedition did not materialize until 1898, when the first expedition of the Peary Arctic Club went north with the avowed intention of reaching ninety north – if it were possible.

Here, then, we have a cautionary example of the pitfalls of trying to read a man's mind on the evidence of what he has written, for although there are several reasons why Peary's version is the more likely development of his dream, he was not consistent in his writings on this theme. We should be cautious also of the trap of assuming that by reading the life of Peary in reverse, we can pin-point the first stage of every development in the complex character of the man, and even more cautious of the trap of the "blood line" into which Green fell hook, line, and sinker:

One of the tonic themes of science is that of human heritage. Diet reddens our blood, but the quality of that blood's corpuscles is handed down from the generations who have gone before. So when one of the human swarm on this crowded globe stands head and shoulders above the multitude it is very interesting to contemplate whence came this rich blood's virtues.

With Peary the strain is clear that led to his unique life. On his father's side, some three generations back, we find in the south of France old Stephen Pierre, from which evolved the name Peary. Pierre was a man of the sea. No doubt his ancestry had run down the Spanish Main and rounded the Horn to the storied islands of the South Pacific ... Then came France's agony. Pierre's son could see no light ahead.

So he emigrated to the New World and helped lay the foundations of our nation.

On the mother's side the lead is clearly Anglo-Saxon: a long line of early pioneers straight from the solid blundering Empire of Britain. These pioneers were land owners and builders of great raftered barns. They were among the nameless patient army of early Americans who gathered a myriad rocky fragments left by prehistoric glaciers and piled them in tidy walls throughout New England ... Both the half-French Pearys and the wholly British Wileys (the mother's side) were of strong and virile stock ...

And so it goes on. A fascinating ascent from the wall builders of New England, through a score of "great eaters but moderate drinkers ... with a sterling set of human handles," including Eben Nutter (the brother of Peary's grandmother) who was successful in the "shook" trade of manufacturing barrel heads and staves, and on whose inspiration most of the family, including his nephew Charles Peary, had moved their business to the small town of Cresson in the Pennsylvania Appalachians.

Contemplate for a moment the atmosphere in which they lived ... an ethical entity, a microcosm, perched up there amid the clean summits of the mountains upon which shone nightly the glinting stars until a fresh sun strode over the curving horizon and bathed the green and virgin land in the glory of a new day. It is as though that group of good people were laid like an egg of Destiny in the womb of a clean nature for the single purpose of bringing forth a finer specimen of the race than the commonplace mechanics of gestation could achieve ...

It is more than family history, all this. It is an incredibly clear-cut series of events that points irrefutably toward a sentient scheming Ruler of the Universe. There was the Gallic heritage of fervor and inspired endeavour. There was the Anglo-Saxon strain of tenacity and fine undying courage. There was that group of splendid early American citizens led by an invisible hand to the mountain-tops. Whereupon, the stage all properly set, occured the birth of Robert Peary, destined to do a great thing.

It all fairly takes the breath away. Until, of course, one realises that within such a society, the union of every couple should have produced a child of the calibre of Peary, each with its manifest destiny of achieving world-wide fame – and since it clearly did not do so, the whole splendid build-up collapses.

The plain fact is, there was no star that kept its station directly above the lowly house of Charles and Mary Peary in Cresson, Pennsylvania, on 6th May, 1856, and the boy child who was born there on that date appeared to be blessed with about as much chance of becoming a famous polar explorer as the rest of his humble family and their equally humble friends. Indeed, he may arguably have even stood less of a chance, for within two years and eight months of his birth, his father, at the age of thirty, had died of pneumonia, and he was all that was left to his frail mother as an object upon which she could pour her love and, in later life, her self-pity.

What psychologist would not raise an eyebrow in instant recognition of what appears from the letters, the diaries and the family stories to have been a text-book example of a tight-hold mother's influence upon a son who during his early years was brought up almost as though he were a girl. In her biography of her father, Marie Peary Stafford explains:

> Gentle, pious Mary Peary had no previous experience with small children, especially small boys. Instead of recognizing her son's pranks as natural high spirits, she thought they were signs of a deep-rooted depravity which she was unable to stamp out. Being deprived of the help and advice of a husband, she tried her best to make her small son over into the gentle little girl whom she would have known so well how to handle. She tried to implant in him the idea that he was not strong, that he was too delicate to play with other boys ... On the rare occasions when he was allowed out to play, his mother, with unconscious cruelty, made him wear a sunbonnet to protect his fair, sensitive skin from sunburn. The bonnet and a lisp, which all his life betrayed him in moments of excitement, resulted in his being considered a sissy by the other boys, and he had many fights to prove the contrary. His mother never understood why Bertie invariably returned from play bruised, scratched, and disheveled, but the fact that he did was an additional argument in favour of keeping him at home.

With the end results seemingly justifying the means, biographer Green sees the role of Peary's mother as being one of the main contributing factors in his final success.

> ... living alone with his mother probably did more to make him a great explorer than any other single factor in his life. She it was who, recalling the lover of her other days, moulded the moral character of the son. Gently but firmly she led him into the right books and hobbies. She watched his food and his youthful friends with equal interest, and taught him of his family, holding them up as traditional examples of splendid men.

But his mother, who had returned home to Maine with her husband's body for burial, a three-year-old son, and the widow's share of her husband's business, which amounted to less than $12,000, was an inconsolable and melancholy woman, and the shadow which occasionally fell across her path, fell also across her son's. Small wonder the boy in seeking diversions had repeatedly broken the windows of the barn, with no explanation offered to account for his need to break the glass other than that he liked to hear the "jingle" as the glass shattered.

Had he not been sent away to school at the age of eight, that shadow surely would have deepened, and his mother's hold become a grip that may even have severed that vital force which gave the power to his ambition. But released from that hold, his school days were his chance to grow, to explore, and to experiment, to find his way, unaided and, for the most part, undirected by his over-protective mother.

This sense of release shines through his letters in spite of his devotion:

> I was very glad to hear from you and intended to write before but I have been putting it off for I have had such good times playing with the boys in the gymnasium and out on the baseball ground.

This he wrote to his mother from his boarding school at Topsham, Maine, on 30th April, 1865, six days before his ninth birthday. There is another letter among the Peary Papers, written seven weeks later, a few days after the birth of Frederick Albert Cook on 10th June, 1865, at Hortonville, in Sullivan County, New York, a hamlet not three hundred miles from that little school at Topsham from which Robert Peary wrote to his mother with evident pride:

> We had prizes for writing and I got the prize among the little boys for the most improvement it was a little pin in the shape of an anchor.

In another letter we see the fatherless boy trying to come to terms with his peers:

> The boys are playing tricks on me now, but I guess they won't after a while. They have made two holes in my chair seat to stick pins in, so when I sit down they will stick into me; and Wednesday night I found in my bed my brush, also Frank Patten's brush and knife, and my old jacket which they put there.

Meanwhile Frederick Cook, nine years his junior, was about to join him, through a similar tragedy, on the painful and uncertain road of life, for in the year that Peary entered High School, Cook's father, like Peary's, had died of pneumonia.

Born near Hanover, Germany, Dr. Theodore Cook had come to America, like so many other German liberals in the 1850s, in search of freedom, and about a year after setting up a practice in Jeffersonville, Sullivan County, New York, he had married Magdalena Long. She, like Dr. Koch (as he was known at that time) was German, her father a successful cigar manufacturer in New York City until the "plague" had struck that city and he had been forced to close his factory and flee into the wilderness of the lower Catskills for safety. The story goes that with all commercial transport in the city being at a standstill, he had made his escape on a home-made raft, which he, his family, and his friends had paddled up the Hudson River for sixty-two miles, before continuing their journey by covered wagon to Beechwood and the meeting between Dr. Koch and Magdalena which resulted in a family of four boys and a girl. By the time, however, that Frederick arrived, his father had changed his name to Cook, a name easier presumably for most of his patients to pronounce, for although his practice was extensive, it was a poor one in which his services were rewarded more often by the gift of dairy products than by the exchange of cash.

His death in 1870 therefore left his widow with a terrible burden, with no money, no work, and five children to raise. How they survived the first few years, none of the biographers seems to know, and the marks of those years appear to have been deeply engraved in Frederick Albert Cook:

In the early years of my childhood . . . I remembered a restless surge in my little bosom, a yearning for something that was vague and undefined. This was, I suppose, that nebulous desire which sometimes manifests itself in early youth and later is asserted in strivings toward some splendid, sometimes spectacular aim. My boyhood was not happy. As a tiny child I was discontented, and from the earliest days of consciousness I felt the burden of two things which accompanied me through later life – an innate and abnormal desire for exploration, then the manifestation of my yearning, and the constant struggle to make ends meet, that sting of poverty, which, while it tantalizes one with its horrid grind, sometimes drives men by reason of the strength developed in overcoming its concomitant obstacles to some extraordinary accomplishment.

Peary, by comparison, had an easier time, although easier only in the sense that he was slightly more protected than Cook from the cruel realities of poverty, and by a mother who, although frail, had only one child to support and encourage. She it was who when he was fourteen years of age and seriously ill with typhoid fever had nursed his fears and his frustrations, and bought him books on natural history to revive in him the will to live. She it was who had somehow found the strength to release him when he had finally come through the worst of his illness, and had sent him off for an extended period of convalescence with relatives in the southern states, a break from her which was a tonic that neither of them would ever admit. It was the sun that had revived his health. It was the ever changing scenes; the new-found friends; his growing love of natural history – never a thought of the possibility that it was his relationship with his mother and the lack of a masculine influence that had been weakening his spirit and confusing his emotions.

He returned from that convalescence in the South with the resolve in his diary "not to exaggerate," and a far more open and eager need to listen, learn and know:

The study of nature is a never-failing source of happiness to the earnest seeker after wisdom. Nature does not repel the student with monotony but shows a new side of her character every time we turn to her ... she has solace and amusement for every mood and phase of the human mind.

He returned to cram into just three months one whole year of normal schooling, and with a few kindred spirits still found time to explore his world, from the White Mountains over to Casco Bay and all the woods and rivers between, and through his trials and many errors he learned how to survive. He learned the art of taxidermy, and with his passion for natural history he became an authority on certain local animals and birds. Yet, that very singleness of purpose which so distinguished him from his peers seemed also to set him apart from them, for at heart he was a loner. He had admirers, even a girlfriend, but no one really understood him, not even his doting mother.

The closeness of his relationship with her had profoundly affected the character of the boy. He was self-reliant, yet reticent. He was sociable, and likeable, and yet beneath that outward show of confidence and self-assurance he was emotionally insecure, and his mother the very thread by which his life hung in the balance. With her he lived; with her he seemed to share his soul. At any moment she might die, and leave him all alone in the world, desolate and empty: "About nine o'clock as mother got up to go to bed she suddenly became very weak and cold on her left side so she could not walk. It scared me very much, but she laid on my bed and I chafed her hands and feet till she recovered and I then got the pistol in case of emergency."

This from a boy still sixteen who was studying desperately hard to win a scholarship to go to college. Would he, without her, have lost the incentive to achieve, his need to show through his success his gratitude and love for that woman who all alone had raised him? Fortunately his mother recovered, and the pistol was returned to the drawer. He won his scholarship, and at graduation was one of the speakers on the programme. His theme of "Nature's Mysteries" included the question that polar explorers had long been risking their lives to answer: what would man find at the Pole?

And so his four years at Portland High School "gloriously" had come to an end, and were followed by a further four years in that delightfully exclusive seat of learning, Bowdoin College, Maine. His mother, whose custom it had become to move house with every change of school, did so again, much to the dismay of Peary's relatives who felt, as evidently did most of his classmates, that it was too restricting for a college student, not to say decidedly odd, to be living off campus and still with his mother at the age of seventeen. But he had little choice. His mother was ill, and she needed his support as much as he needed hers during his first term at Bowdoin in the autumn of 1873 when he was feeling "lonesome, oh so lonesome," and so melancholy that even "the rustle of the leaves as they reach the earth seem as full of sorrow and lament . . . as a human sigh." It was a feeling that reached its lowest ebb during the first few days of January 1874, as he watched his mother sinking almost beyond his reach: "Mother is so weak she can hardly walk. If she gets through this she will probably be better but – it makes me dizzy to think of it – I don't believe she ever will."

But she did survive, and the reticent loner, the sensitive naturalist, the hardened out-doors-man who much preferred hiking to organised sports, now came under the influence of a young Professor of Civil Engineering, George Leonard Vose.

It may well have been Professor Vose who planted the idea in Peary's receptive subsconscious that the North Pole might some day be reached by the man who devised a system of supporting parties, for evidently Vose found this subject intriguing and often discussed it with his class as an exercise in problem solving related loosely to their subject through what he called "pioneering."

Peary never mentioned Vose's intellectual diversions into the polar field. But there can be little doubt that during his college days, through the encouragement of Vose and the respect of his fellow students, Peary was already beginning to set his own standards, and a course which diverged from that of his peers, for although just beneath the surface of the competitive and hard working student there was still the poetic and romantic dreamer who did not know where his life was leading, there was also, just beginning now to surface from his subconscious yearning for self expression, a growing need for fame.

We can see what may be taken as a hint of this in a passage from a letter he wrote a few days after his nineteenth birthday, one of many confiding letters he wrote during his college days to his girlfriend, Mary Kilby:

I have asked myself a thousand questions, which only time can answer. Where shall I be in ten years, in twenty years? Shall I be alive or dead, fortunate or unfortunate, shall I be trudging along in the narrow tracks many men make for themselves, or shall I be known outside the circle of my acquaintances? All these thoughts and many more present themselves to me whenever I have a chance to think. Shall I ever in the years to come think of my college days and the night I sat writing to you?

What ambitious nineteen-year-old does not indulge in these same formless thoughts. In Peary's case, however, such thoughts were evidently still troubling him on his twenty-first birthday:

How many have wished and wondered about the mysterious future as I do, and yet if the curtain were permitted to be drawn aside, would shrink ... for fear of gazing upon rugged rocks and yawning graves in place of the velvety paths they wish for.

Hardly the words of a young man who knows exactly what he wants to do with his life, and exactly how he will do it although, in fairness, this was written only a few weeks before graduation from Bowdoin with a degree in civil engineering. He had reached the finishing line in his "contest" with college in second place out of a class of fifty-two, and had been elected to the honorary fraternity of Phi Beta Kappa. A phase in his life which he had come to enjoy was ending, but the world beyond the college gates had a very dreary prospect for a young man who came very close to being the star student of his year.

One cannot follow the life story of Peary over the next few years without coming to junctions, rather more frequently than one might have expected, where he could so easily have taken the wrong road and ended up a nonentity. With his mother he had moved to the village of Fryeburg, Maine, a situation which, at first, seemed to drain from him almost every hope of one day being known outside the circle of his few friends and acquaintances.

It was a depression he was able to shake off only by walking in the hills alone; but these walks took him back to his passionate interest in natural history, which had been all consuming in him as a boy, and to his expression of that love of nature through the art of taxidermy. So with not enough professional commissions to earn him a respectable living, he set up in the business of mounting birds, and his skill, artistry, and knowledge in this field very soon won him a reputation and more orders than he was able to cope with. At the same time, he set himself a severe course in social self-improvement: "I am trying an experiment now. I am testing my ability to make myself agreeable ... I should like to gain that attractive personality that when I was with a person, they would always have to like me whether they wanted to or not."

But to what purpose? He still did not know. By the time he was twenty-three and had been out of college two full years, he had become engaged to Mary Kilby, his steady girlfriend from high school days, and had been appointed a Justice of the Peace – an office which he was proud and yet slightly embarrassed to admit indicated a social advancement to "the dizzy pinnacle of country squire" and gave him authority to "marry folks!"

It was during this period, and in his free moments between breaking horses and mounting birds, that he made a plan of the village of Fryeburg, his first real job since leaving college. During the course of his survey he established a line which pointed due north, and this was later marked by stones and even commemorated ten years after his death as the pointing finger of destiny. But his inclination at the time to follow that meridian line is neither hinted at in his diary, nor in any of his letters. Even allowing for his restless spirit, and his hope of one day being known outside the circle of his acquaintances, one would not expect, on the evidence of his career to this point, that Peary would have gone much further, and the break, when it came, as is often the case, was simply a step in the right direction, the one that had committed him to cutting the ties with home.

Indeed, the opportunity that presented itself, according to biographer Fitzhugh Green, was "so anemic in appearance that one is surprised that he even gave it a thought, unless one grants a 'guiding hand' in the young man's affairs," for Peary appears to have lowered his sights in responding to a notice he had seen in the village post office inviting applications from keen and qualified young men who were eager to compete for four vacant places as draughtsmen with the US Coast and Geodetic Survey in Washington, D.C.

With the notice posted in every post office and college across the United States, Peary had kept his application secret to avoid the almost certain embarrassment of failure. He had, however, with his application sent as a specimen of his work his "cherished plan" of Fryeburg, and it was his plan of that very place from which he was hoping to escape that had, with a suitable irony, won him the chance to begin his climb to his dream of world acclaim.

Chapter 3

The Uncertain Direction of Fame

It was an excited and yet perplexed young man who had set out from Fryeburg, Maine, on 4th July, 1879, to seek his fortune in the capital city. Twenty-three years of age at that time, he was still without the slightest idea of what he wanted to be in life, or for what he wished to be famous. But although at no other time in his life was his dream of fame so incomplete, at least it was not burdened by those heavy expectations that a definite goal in life creates.

After a few months in Washington, however, the realities started closing in, and the prospect of winning a permanent post with the US Coast and Geodetic Survey and advancing no further in life than a draughtsman began to fill him with dread. He found himself once again yearning for freedom and grasping at any passing thought that might relieve those hours of boredom in the Coast Survey Building on Capitol Hill, endless hours of practising lettering, until the day he actually read the notes that he was copying.

The subject was a proposed new shipping canal that would provide a linking waterway between the Atlantic and the Pacific, a "cut" through the isthmus of Nicaragua as brilliant as de Lesseps' Suez Canal, except this one would cut through jungles and swamps that had never before been penetrated, a far greater challenge, a far greater prize, his way to freedom and fame.

It had no doubt been this surge of hope as much as Peary's competitive spirit which carried him through that six months' trial to a permanent post with the Survey. During that time, however, he had also been preparing himself for the calling he was now certain would come by reading everything he could find on the subject of Nicaragua. It was his intention to become the authority, and thereby to win himself an appointment as one of the engineers on that project, should it ever go ahead. But between his dream and its fulfilment there also lay the deep devotion he felt for his ailing mother. He needed her approval of his plan, her emotional support, her blessing. And so, at the age of twenty-four, he wrote one of the most revealing letters he ever wrote in his life. It was a letter which poured out his heart, persuading, cajoling, pleading for his mother's permission to let him quit his post with the Survey and cut a new path towards fame.

My Dear Mother,

Among other things which I had counted on in the light September days which I cannot spend with you, were some good long talks. I had imagined myself with my head in your lap, telling you of things I have been thinking of the year that is past and had been gradually getting my thoughts into shape for that purpose, but perhaps it is better that I should write . . .

I feel myself overmastered by a resistless desire to do something. I do not wish to live and die without accomplishing anything or without being known beyond a narrow circle of friends. I wish to acquire a name which shall be an "open sesame" to circles of culture and refinement anywhere, a name which shall make my Mother proud and which shall make me feel that I am peer to anyone I may meet.

But I have got to the point where the years do not have leaden feet and I feel as if I must do something at once, before too many of them slip away. What good will fame or a name do me if it comes when I am an old man? I want to have some years to enjoy it in and then, my Mother, I want it to come soon enough for you to derive some pleasure from it.

Here I am, twenty-four years old, and what have I done, what am I doing, or what am I in the way of doing? Nothing. If I remain here till I am thirty and work hard and am fortunate, I may be drawing $2,000 per annum (never more than that) as a draughtsman, a machine, working so many hours a day, and known only on the payroll of the department . . .

Thinking of all these things and wondering what I could do that was fitted for me . . . it has seemed to me that there are more opportunities for lasting fame to be obtained on the little strip of land called 'The Isthmus' [of Nicaragua] in area about half as large as the state of Maine, than anywhere else on the globe.

Many men have made themselves world-famous by looking forward to something sure to be of importance in the future, making the subject thoroughly their own, and then when the right moment came stepping forward as the chief and only authority.

With enthusiasm, he now suggests that his mother should get out her atlas, and goes on to outline his plans for a reconnaissance journey which he was hoping to begin on 1st January, 1881. It is a bold idea. Too bold, perhaps, for his mother to approve: "This may seem a trifle wild to you at the first glance," he states, and then respectfully reprimands, "but remember I am a man now and many a seemingly wild thing has been accomplished by men who have struck out just as boldly, bent on accomplishing their object."

He goes on with delightfully simple logic to explain to his mother the pros and cons of giving up his job as a draughtsman in order to become an explorer:

> I am not of that phlegmatic temperament which permits one to become a machine ... There are men who are capable of becoming machines, and there are men who can do nothing except in their own way and at their own time, and the world has need of both.

He weighs the possibilities of catching some dreadful disease, or of losing his life in some "insalubrious" swamp, and concludes:

> But even supposing all the reports of danger and death are true ... would it not be just as well to meet the gray old mower in full harness, struggling for a grand object, as on a lingering bed of sickness? A nameless grave on the Isthmus is no worse than a marble surmounted one in the midst of homes and waving fields. Would it not sound just as well to say that he fell in that distant land working out a great idea as any way it could be put, and would not my Mother feel a touch of pride in the midst of her sorrow. But these are merely possibilities and I mention them simply to show that I have thought of them all. Let us turn now to the pros, and look at the magnificent possibilities of the step.
>
> First the grandest, and laden with glory which shall make the name of its discoverer the equal of any since history began, is the secret of the canal. This however we will set aside as too much to hope for. Next comes the fame which a thorough knowledge of the Isthmus is sure to bring, for when, as is certain to be the case some day, the Isthmus takes its place as a great center, he who knows it as he knows his native tongue can be no longer obscure. And finally if I was equal to nothing more, I could write for my Mother to read, and traveling never injures a man. And last but not least, I shall have half of the year to spend with you.

His final comment is perhaps the most revealing. He is offering his mother what amounts to a bribe: by allowing him to seek adventure and to risk his life in his quest for fame, he is promising that she will see more of him than if he remains at his office desk safely and securely a draughtsman.

He ends his letter by assuring his mother that this is not just a whim, nor an idea "fed on the glowing accounts of travelers." And then he seeks her blessing:

Think over all that I have written Mother and give me your consent, which is all that I lack, then I will come home and see you about New Year, just before starting, then after an absence of about five months, when the summer comes again with its birds and flowers, and light and happiness, I will come back to you, and together we will watch the happy days slip by. And perhaps another dream may come to pass, and there may be a little house on Eagle Island where we will laugh at the heat and in the strong health-giving sea air you will renew your youth and people more than ever, will think my little Mother is my wife.

Two weeks went by without a reply, and when eventually Peary received a letter from his mother, there was no mention of "the canal question." It was as though by ignoring it she was hoping it would go away. And so he had written a second letter begging her for an answer, and to this she had simply advised that he should "stay where he was; to be glad that he had a respectable job, and to try to be more contented." Incredibly, that night, 6th September, 1880, Peary wrote in his diary: "I bow to her wishes though it may change my entire life."

It is a response which seems at first almost to defy explanation. Here was a young man who, on the evidence of that letter to his mother, appears certain at last of his role in life, accepting with nothing more than a whimper the destruction of his dream. What was the nature of her hold on him that with a few well chosen words she could crush the confidence of a son who seemed in almost every respect to now be fully a man?

For years he had been preparing himself, testing himself, comparing and measuring himself against others:

I don't know whether it is my fortune or misfortune, or whether it is a sign of an ignoble spirit, but I cannot bear to associate with people who, age and advantage being equal, are my superiors. I must be the peer or superior of those about me to be comfortable, not that I care to show my superiority, simply to know it myself.

Such observations as one finds in his diaries, and occasionally in his letters to his mother, are self-assessments of what he saw as his steady progress and of his chances of success. The reading of them can leave no doubt that by 1880 he was ready physically for his first real challenge – for by his own admission he was: "Tall, erect, broad-shouldered, full-chested, tough, wiry-limbed, clear-eyed, full-mustached, clear-browed complexion, a dead shot, a powerful, tireless swimmer, a first-class rider [and] a skillful boxer and fencer."

He had even predicted with confidence that by the age of thirty, "or thirty-five at the latest," he would also have improved in other respects. He would then be "perfectly at home in any company, yet always bearing with me an indefinable atmosphere of the wildness and freedom of the woods and mountains, master of German, Spanish, and French, and as a speciality (all these things being mere accomplishments) a knowledge of the Isthmus equaled by no man living."

So what was lacking? The answer lies between the lines of his own assessment of himself, and at various places in that letter asking for his mother's blessing. But it is in the meekness with which he accepted his mother's wishes that Peary lays bare his greatest weakness: that he was at that time still bound to his mother, and at the age of twenty-four was emotionally immature.

Proof of this is the ease with which he had settled back into the city routine. A freer spirit would have rebelled, but with his increased salary as a member now of the permanent staff and little or nothing to do in the office, he joined a life class which met twice a week; enrolled for a course of dancing lessons, and developed a taste and a habit for the theatre, to which he would take the favoured from among his "ever increasing circle" of young and unattached lady friends. He became a member of an athletic club and set himself a tough training programme with a swim of at least a mile every day, or when he simply had not the time, a hundred feet under water. But at heart he was not a city man and, pleasant though all these diversions were, they could not heal his wounded pride or replace that need for the countryside which gave him a sense of freedom.

I never come under these glorious influences of Nature, the sound of a rushing stream, the dash of waves, the rustle of the wind in deep green boughs, or a glorious landscape losing itself in the distant sunshine, but my thoughts turn to those first few views which have burned themselves into the eyes of Columbus, Cortez, Balboa, de Soto, Livingstone, Mungo Park, and all the host of travelers and explorers. And sometimes I can feel something of the thrill and blended aroma of all such first views since the world was in its infancy. Do you know I have stood upon the summit of a mountain after a long day's climb through woods and over rocks and, looking toward the setting sun, have given my imagination full sway until I know I have felt something of that same thrill that Cortez felt when at the close of that beautiful spring day he gained the summit of the last range of mountains that lay between him and the city of the Aztecs and, looking westward, saw the valley nestling in the rays of the sun and the mysterious city glistening in the midst of its surrounding lakes.

And as for Balboa, one moment such as that when, bidding his followers halt, alone he climbed the last rock upon that "peak of Darien," and saw beyond the tree tops the flashing waves of that great mysterious ocean, was worth years of ordinary life.

Just think of the life of the travelers in an unknown country or on an unknown sea. Then think of the nights and their thoughts of the morrow – what will it bring? Some new strange sight, the realization of some wild dream – or will it bring disappointment, disaster and perhaps death?

Then there is the constant expectation of some new strange sight. You struggle on with feverish anxiety to see what is beyond this mountain or that turn in the river, or if you are sailing on some unknown sea you rack your imagination to fill the unknown region just beyond the misty horizon, and then when you least expect it, some glorious sunlit island, more beautiful than pen or brush can paint, some emerald shore, or wild rugged coast, bursts on your sight and then you go to work wondering what mysteries lie beyond the beautiful shores, what secrets the distant mountains are guarding and the distant valleys hiding in their unknown depths.

Tis a glorious life but, ah me! the poetry of the world in this respect is rapidly fading. I am glad that my lot is cast upon the world now rather than later when there will be no new places, when every spot will have felt the pressure of man's foot, and earth and air, and fire and water, the grand old primal elements and all that is in them, will be his abject slaves.

With fantasies such as these of course no woman (not even his mother) could compete, and sooner or later the power within them was bound to demand of Peary the dreamer that he should quit writing this sort of stuff and do something about them. In fairness to the man, being more realistic at twenty-five than he had been when a full year younger, that chasm between the life of a draughtsman and the sort of life he was wanting to lead had no doubt seemed an impossible leap. This is no mere speculation, for my own first "work experience," like Peary's, had been as a frustrated draughtsman. But in mid-July, 1881, the "guiding hand" (no doubt out of pity) had led him to a bridge.

His attention had been drawn, as before, to a notice, this one inviting civil engineers of the right age and of the right frame of mind to apply for a commission in the United States Navy and, as before, he did not confide his intentions to a single soul who might embarrass him with their pity should he fail to succeed. His drawings and notes on the canal project ensured him a high place in the qualifying examinations. Out of two hundred applicants, he emerged as one of the final four to be offered a commission. Though there were several questions he had not been able to answer, his examiners were of the opinion "that they were satisfied from his showing he was a man who if he did not know a thing, would keep at it until he did, and so was the kind of man the Navy needed."

It is interesting to speculate whether the Examining Board would have offered Peary a commission in the Navy had they known the true depth of his obsession, but with the security he had gained through that commission and the prospect also of increasing his prestige through his knowledge of Nicaragua, he now had a firm base upon which he could build his future. And his first assignment was as assistant to engineer A. G. Menocal, the undisputed authority on the proposed Nicaraguan canal.

Peary's delight and pride fairly rings through the note he wrote to his mother five days later:

It's different from the Coast Survey. I am "boss" instead of "bossed," have a room of my own, messenger, clerk, and draughtsman. Have over a hundred men under my control. But the thing which I have a good deal of to do for which I possess peculiar qualifications is signing my name. It is fun writing letters when you only have to write your name. The uniqueness of my signature has been remarked by the commodore commanding the yard.

Hastily, Bert

His work with Menocal was not to see any real action until the way was cleared politically by the treaty with Nicaragua in 1884, by which time Peary had served his first three years in the Navy, and earned himself not only a reputation as a first class and imaginative engineer by building a new pier at the US Naval Station at Key West, Florida; but had also earned the affections of Josephine Diebitsch, the stunning daughter of a professor at the Smithsonian Institution, whom he had first met at a dance in Washington in 1882. He had also, with money he had saved on the Key West project, bought Eagle Island in Casco Bay which, ever since his high school days, it had been his ambition to own and, with this as a tangible proof of success, he almost seemed content.

With the signing of the treaty with Nicaragua, the canal project was no longer a dream, and by the end of 1884, Peary was at last on his way. Whether he had risked asking his mother for her blessing a second time is not known, but as the Pacific Mail Steamer *Colon* ploughed her course south past San Salvador that Christmas, Peary wrote to his mother, musing on that island:

... which first gladdened the eyes of Columbus, purple against the yellow sunset as it was nearly four hundred years ago when it smiled a welcome to the man whose fame can be equalled only by him who shall one day stand with 360 degrees of longitude beneath his motionless foot, and for whom East and West shall have vanished; the discoverer of the North Pole.

It is too tempting to seize on this as a prophetic remark from a man already aware that he had been called to play a dramatic role in history. But if Peary had been aware of his destiny in 1885 it is unlikely he would have exerted so much energy in the jungles and swamps of Nicaragua when fame lay waiting for him at a point some 5,500 miles to the north.

Those three months in Nicaragua were spent hacking through dense undergrowth with "scarsely a place where fifty feet could be gained without cutting or clearing away a log or lifting the boats over one," and with all the men, Peary included, almost constantly in water to their knees, their waists, and even occasionally up to their necks "cutting, lifting, pushing, swimming." It was of course incomparable training in how to suffer cheerfully and to urge his men to follow his example by "singing with them, yelling at them, and at the last moment giving them a drink of gin all around, which brought them yelling into camp at 6:05 p.m., though everyone was thoroughly wet and tired, having been in the water over ten hours."

But he had not gone there for experience. He had gone in the hope of cutting out his name and he had not yet succeeded. Back in Washington and the Navy Yard again in the fall of 1885, Peary wandered one evening into one of his favourite haunts, an old book-store, where:

I came upon a fugitive paper on the Inland Ice of Greenland. A chord, which as a boy, had vibrated intensely in me at the reading of Kane's wonderful book, was touched again. I read all I could upon the subject, noted the conflicting experiences of Nordenskjold, Jensen, and the rest, and felt that I must see for myself what the truth was of this great mysterious interior.

And had Peary secretly set his sights on the North Pole at this time? If he had, it was certainly very wise of him to keep this glorious dream to himself, for as his reading must surely have warned him, he still had a long way to go.

CHAPTER 4

The Persistent Devil

One cannot read Peary's personal notes and memoranda of this period without sensing his excitement, and the North Pole does feature in these notes as an objective. Why then in his published writings did he make no mention of these earlier plans and always insist that his first expedition to set out with the "avowed intention" of reaching the North Pole was his expedition of 1898? The most probable explanation is Peary's reticence – a self-protecting secrecy which left him with the room to manoeuvre within the limits of his dream and thus reduce the risk of failure.

It is interesting too that Peary should choose to work out the fever of his private obsession within the protective embrace of his commission in the Navy. Aside from the attraction of the status this gave him and the security of a regular salary, the Navy fulfilled his need to belong, his need to be part of an established order which represented, justified, and to a great extent enhanced his sense of patriotic pride.

At the time he started planning his first expedition to the Arctic, however, he had been in the Navy a full four years, and in spite of his excellent service record, he still lacked the rank and political contacts needed if he was to advance and develop his dream of running two very separate careers with each supporting the other. A tactically important step in this plan was to get his six months' paid leave of absence revoked in favour of the more useful orders to special duty with the American Geographical Society – a ploy he had clearly considered worth trying since the Society had expressed some cautious interest in the summer reconnaissance trip to West Greenland that he was proposing, and Peary, in his innocence, had seen this as support. But the response he received from the Secretary of the Navy, "the service upon which you are about to engage can in no sense be considered naval duty," although a rejection he had half expected, was in the official tone of voice that seemed to shatter his dream of seeking fame outside the system, while yet remaining on full pay conveniently within it.

It was the first of many rebuffs he was to suffer during the early part of his naval career, for there was a flaw in the naval system of ranking which singled him out as a victim. No such flaw of course existed according to those of his fellow officers who were graduates of the Naval

Academy and clearly regarded themselves as superior to "civilians" such as Robert E. Peary whose commission was merely a relative rank. His official title, as the Academy officers had all too frequently reminded him during his years of learning the ropes, was not "Lieutenant," as his mother so proudly addressed her letters and as he himself preferred to be called, but "Civil Engineer, United States Navy." This denigration had hurt and angered Peary who on the issue of his naval rank was sensitive to say the least. But although his title was at the root of so many of Peary's problems in the Navy, his sensitivity was also the spur that goaded him into seeking a way of winning his laurels outside the Navy, beyond the reach of rank.

On the face of it this was the sort of challenge that suited Peary's temperament. His objective, however, was nothing like as clear cut or as certain as his diaries and letters appear to suggest, for Peary was an intensely secretive man, a man who was at pains to hide that other side of his driving force – that silent fear of failure.

What he needed was a remote arena, a setting somewhere in the Arctic that would be a place of his own choosing; a place where he would have the advantage that all the rules had been laid by him. Only in such a remote arena, where courage and determination would impress far more than social rank, could Peary hope to prove that he deserved a decent destiny and his right to lasting fame. But despite his outward self-assurance, he had no more "right" at that time to assume that he would be a success in that field than any of those who had gone before him and in his heart he knew it. And so he had read every book he could find on the subject of Arctic exploration.

At this time biographer John Edward Weems was convinced that Peary had committed his credo to paper – in his diary of 1885. And even allowing, as Peary implies, that his fascination with Arctic exploration was a long-standing one that dated back to his childhood reading of Elisha Kent Kane's "wonderful book" (a book which had also been read with enthusiasm by Ernest Shackleton as a boy), it is indeed surprising how close he came in his diary notes of 1885 to assessing correctly the practical problems of how to reach the North Pole:

The time has arrived now for an entire change in the expeditionary organization of Arctic research parties. The old method of large parties and several ships has been run into the ground and almost every American authority at least is beginning to see the necessity of a new departure. The English with true John Bull obstinacy still stick to the old plan. The new plan of a small party depending largely on native assistance, inaugurated by Schwatka, deserves to be recorded as the American plan, and another successful expedition will make it permanently such and put us far ahead in the race. Noting the opinion of various Arctic authorities it is interesting to observe that almost without exception those who are not biased by having failed themselves, and thus being as it were compelled in self-defense to assert that because their antiquated plan failed no other could succeed, are leaning more or less to the side of small parties.

One should be cautious, however, of crediting Peary with more original thinking than he deserves. Peary did not burden these notes with the claim that they were original thoughts. Nor did he ever publish them, for as well as being a reticent man, Peary was also a self-seeking man, and to have published them would have drawn public attention to the achievements of those who had gone before him and discovered *his* way to the Pole. Their value lies only in the record they offer of what he had learned from his reading, and his state of readiness now to compete with those whose books he had read and whose claims had clearly inspired him.

Foremost among these polar heroes, as Peary himself admitted, was the American explorer Elisha Kent Kane, and those who had followed this colourful doctor and had lived and travelled with the polar Eskimos in that area of Peary's greatest interest, the passage between Greenland and Ellesmere Island. Without, however, the slightest authority other than having read about it, Peary appears to have been convinced that this was the route that would lead to the Pole, and was already staking out his claim on the basis of the maps produced by those who had travelled the region before him – discoveries which, in certain cases, were every bit as dubious as Peary's right to claim them.

> Smith Sound is preeminently the American route. Almost the entire shores from Cape Sabine and Cairn Point north to both sides have been mapped by our expeditions and now we are farthest north on this road. Let the English, the Germans, the Austrians have the Spitzbergen and Franz Josef and all the other routes, but let us stick to Smith Sound.

This "American route," as Peary called it with the ringing patriotism of a peal of bells on the Fourth of July, was no more American than William Baffin who had discovered Smith Sound in 1616. Baffin had not only forced the *Discovery* to a new Farthest North in that part of the Arctic and discovered Sir Thomas Smith's Sound, but had also discovered Jones and Lancaster Sounds – all three key routes in this area which opened up the way for the eventual discovery of the North-West Passage and the North Pole.

Baffin had been following the tracks of the great Elizabethan navigators like John Davis, and Henry Hudson who was the first man to seek the North Pole. But it was the North-West Passage which was the prime concern of explorers seeking a northern trade route to the east, and the knowledge they brought back with them of travel on pack ice was invaluable background reading for Peary.

William Scoresby the younger on return from charting the east coast of Greenland in 1814 presented a paper on the "Polar Ice" which offered the original suggestion that the North Pole could be reached from Spitsbergen by travelling over the ice with "fleet quadrupeds, accustomed to harness." He also advocated an early start, "by the close of April." But on the still popular theory of an open polar sea he commented: "Were this really the case, the circumstance would certainly be an extraordinary one; but I consider it too improbable to render it necessary to hazard any opinion concerning it."

There had then begun what was for the most part a glorious, heroic, yet totally amateurish and ill-organised search for the North-West Passage by a whole string of Royal Navy expeditions, some of whose commanders had not even heard of the Scoresbys, knew little or nothing about the Arctic and, had they been told that a whaling skipper by the name of Scoresby was in the habit of amusing his sailors by lighting their pipes with "lenses" of ice, simply would not have believed it!

One of these expeditions under Commander John Ross (with Lieutenant Edward Parry as second in command) sailed west then north through the Davis Strait in 1818, and near Cape York discovered a small tribe of Eskimos who had evidently had no previous contact with ocean-going ships or the extraordinary creatures who sailed them. Ross tells us that despite the "imperious nature of [their] orders to proceed with all possible dispatch" towards their main objective – the North-West Passage – they were unwilling to leave "while any chance of a communication with a people, hitherto unknown, remained." And at about ten o'clock on the morning of 10th August, 1818, they "rejoiced to see eight sledges, driven by the natives, advancing by a circuitous route." Since they did not, however, venture any closer than the flag-staff which had been set up mid-way between the ship and the shore, and seemed unable to summon the courage to investigate it, an Eskimo interpreter had been dispatched "bearing a small white flag, with some presents, that he might endeavour, if possible, to bring them to a parley."

His efforts were met with extreme apprehension – a confusion of threats and frightened pleadings which rang out across a convenient fracture in the ice upon which the two parties stood. It was a fracture which seemed to separate two totally different worlds, and what finally brought them together was not some half-spoken word or some half-gestured sign of human goodwill, but the gift of a simple tool, a knife.

That was the moment at which they met and that meeting had struck a chord in Peary as surely as it had in me the first time I read about it. For the Eskimo, there was no turning back when, in their innocence, they had approached and "picked up the knife, then shouted and pulled their noses . . . Heigh yaw!"

Growing bolder, the Eskimos pointed to the ships and asked what great creatures they were: "Do they come from the sun or from the moon?" Meanwhile Ross and Parry had been observing this meeting through their telescopes and, hoping to create a friendly impression, dressed in their full naval finery and went out on to the ice tugging at their noses in return as though hauling themselves to their rendezvous, assuming this simple nose clearing to be an Eskimo salutation. This had of course delighted the Eskimos who immediately began to imitate the Englishmen, and even to this day the polar Eskimos relate how the very first men their ancestors ever met were almost continually pulling their noses, while the received histories of the western world quote this ritual as a witnessed example of the northernmost "savages" quaint salute.

Ross and Parry persuaded some of the Eskimos to go on board, where they delighted the crew with their reactions to everything they saw, and by their total ignorance of the outside world which was reflected in their response to every question they were asked. With the magnifying mirror "they looked first into it, and then behind it, in the hope of finding the monster which was exaggerating their hideous gestures." With a watch that was held to the ear of one of them, supposing it to be alive, he had asked if it was good to eat, and another, on being presented with a wine glass, "appeared very much astonished that it did not melt with the heat of his hand."

They were shown chairs, and appeared "to have no notion of any other seat than the ground." They were shown books and navigational instruments which produced the usual expression of surprise, and pictures to test their ability to comprehend "that they were representations of human beings." The sound of a flute seemed to excite attention, but one of the Eskimos, on discovering that he could not play it, "immediately threw it away." They were given biscuits to eat, but spat them out in evident disgust, and salt beef "produced the same effect." They seemed disconcerted by the tricks of a juggler; confused by the questioner's implication that they must know more numbers than ten; and on being told that there was "an omnipresent Being, who had created the sea and land, and all therein" and that this powerful God was everywhere, one of the Eskimos became "very impatient to be on deck" and would surely have fled had he not been distracted by the gift of a plank of wood.

Throughout this historic encounter Ross and his men had conducted themselves with courtesy and good-humoured kindness, and that meeting with the "Arctic Highlanders," as Ross called the natives, although a brief one, had at least diverted some of the malicious public attention away from his failure to find the North-West Passage.

That discovery of the northernmost tribe of Eskimos, however, had not distracted the attention of the Admiralty from his seemingly inexplicable retreat from the main object of his voyage. In the *Isabella* he had pushed into Lancaster Sound and made almost a hundred miles through fog (ahead of Parry in the *Alexander*) before becoming convinced that he saw a barrier of land up ahead. He even made a drawing of the feature, dutifully naming it the Croker Mountains after the First Secretary of the Navy, and a small bay to its south after the then Second Secretary, Barrow. Ross's mistake, however, was not in mistaking a mirage for land, but in turning about, for Parry was later to insist that he had seen open water ahead at the point where Ross had turned his ship, and that Ross had given up too soon. The fact that Parry in the *Alexander* had been five miles astern of the *Isabella* at the time that Ross had abandoned his quest was ignored by those who saw Ross as a convenient scapegoat for failure, and the implication of Parry's remarks not only damaged the career of Ross, but dramatically opened up the way for the spectacular advancement of Parry.

Peary could have taken a lesson from this to profit by much later in his career. Be wary of making any claim which others in the party might later be tempted to disclaim and publicly discredit. It would appear he learnt that lesson, and then, in part, forgot it.

Meanwhile Parry went on to attempt the North Pole by means of heavy "sledge boats over ice" and set a new Farthest North of 82°45′ which was not bettered for forty-eight years. He also set an example in courage. But as an example in travel technique, that final achievement of Parry's brilliant polar career pointed to the greatest weakness in the English attitude towards the Arctic: it was bold beyond question, but had still not come to terms with the fact that the Eskimos (and Scoresby) knew better, and that "light sledges drawn by dogs" were the only sensible means of Arctic travel.

In 1845 English Arctic exploration suffered a major blow with the disappearance of Sir John Franklin's elaborately equipped expedition with all hands. Now the search for Franklin became an objective of polar travel and one patron of this new quest was Henry Grinnell, first president of the newly founded American Geographical Society of New York, and the first of many devoted American patrons of polar exploration. It was through his influence in 1852 that Dr. Elisha Kent Kane was appointed to "conduct an expedition to the Arctic Seas in search of Sir John Franklin" – a covering objective for the real purpose of the expedition which was to reach the North Pole across what Kane believed would prove to be an open polar sea.

Kane was a larger than life figure who at first entirely lacked Ross's delicacy of touch with the natives of Smith Sound where he spent two terrible winters. When the Eskimo men stole from him, he made off with their womenfolk. But eventually he came to an arrangement whereby in return for knives and wood and sewing thread the Eskimos were to provide him with walrus and seal meat and promise not only to stop stealing, but to sell or lend him their dogs and teach his men how to hunt. Kane was the first polar explorer to live and travel with the Eskimos, and even by 1885 his was the only account of a people Peary would have to learn about himself at first hand if he was to carry out his grand design.

How very different to Dr. Kane, who died in 1857, was Dr. Isaac Israel Hayes, who was next on the scene. His objective, as he says in his book, *The Open Polar Sea*, was "to complete the survey of the north coast of Greenland and Grinnell Land, and to make such explorations as I might find practicable in the direction of the North Pole." His base, he proposed, would be on the coast of Grinnell Land which he falsely claims he himself had discovered and "traced beyond latitude 80 degrees," and from there he would transport a boat over the ice to the open sea, launch it and "push off northward."

It is quite astonishing that he was able to impress so many geographical, philosophical and scientific societies, and attract the support of so many distinguished and influential men (including Henry Grinnell), for the sum total of his Arctic "exploring" experience had been a twenty-five mile trip to the edge of the Inland Ice, and a ten-day journey to the west coast of Kane Basin in 1854 which was a total round-trip distance of only 180 nautical miles.

In this new expedition he was unable to penetrate Kane Basin and obliged to winter his ship at the mouth of Etah Fjord (south of Kane's winter quarters), and after the death of August Sonntag, his brilliant young astronomer and his second-in-command, the whole venture seemed to collapse, for with Sonntag's death there was no one left on the expedition capable of making maps. And yet Hayes produced them. He was even presented medals for his contribution to the exploration of that region and, as Peary must have noted, without any of the societies presenting those medals first asking to see his field notes or some proof that he really had reached a latitude 81°35', a new record Farthest North.

How far north Hayes went, no one now will ever know for his field diary went missing, and in Hayes' copy of his field data in the American Geographical Society's archives, the vital page has been neatly removed (the same expedient as used by Kane) and no doubt with the surgeon's scalpel.

Three more expeditions were to pass through Smith Sound during the course of the next twenty years, all of them aiming to reach the North Pole. But none of them added anything to the knowledge Peary had already gained through his study of Kane's observations on that tiny, isolated, and diminishing Eskimo population. Being more fortunate with the ice than the expeditions that had gone before, they had passed right through the hunting territory of the Smith Sound tribe. But those three expeditions, nevertheless, did offer Peary some clear examples in one dramatic form or another of what he certainly should not do, and implanted very firmly in his mind the conviction that every Arctic explorer returns more famous than the one that set out – or dies in the Arctic a hero.

The most unlikely explorer of the three and, potentially, the one with most vision, was undoubtedly the first in the field, the American, Charles Francis Hall. This moody, restless, irascible man has been described as "slightly mad" by polar historians who presumably mean that he was eccentric. Either way, he was unique, and however far removed from Peary he might have been in temperament, there was at least one conviction of Hall's that Peary deeply respected, the belief that the North Pole would only be reached by the Eskimo method of travelling.

He was to spend two years living among the Eskimos of Baffin Island "wearing Eskimo dress, eating raw seal-meat, living in their snow-houses, and travelling with dogs and sledge," and became convinced that the Arctic explorer of the future must learn "to Esquimeaux-ise himself." He had then spent five years without a break in the Canadian Arctic living and travelling alone with the Eskimos, and on his final expedition – the prime object of which was to reach the North Pole via the sea route through Smith Sound – he took the naval tug *Polaris* to a new record latitude in that part of the Arctic of 82°11', thus pioneering the final stage of that sea route to the very shores of the frozen Arctic Ocean. There he was to die on 8th November, 1871, at the age of fifty, poisoned, most probably, by one of his own men.

The British Arctic expedition of 1875–6 was lavish, impressive, determined, and incompetent. Goaded by Hall's new record northing on a route discovered by the English, and by the achievements of the Swede, Baron Nordenskjold, and the Austrians, Payer and Weyprect – all of whom had become rivals for the Royal Navy's hard-won place in the forefront of polar endeavour – the Admiralty had recalled from his command of HMS *Challenger* in the Antarctic their finest ice navigator, Captain George Nares, and sent him north to regain the record for Britain, and to counter the claims of the Americans to their assumed priority on the Smith Sound route.

It was an extraordinary expedition. The last in the line of the heroic Arctic endeavours in the Royal Naval tradition, accomplishing a great deal but, in the light of history, with an inexcusable waste of energy and courage. It is not possible to read the account of this expedition without being impressed by the sheer volume and quality of their scientific work and the achievements of their explorers. He had the best men and, in the *Alert* and the *Discovery*, the best ships for an assault on the Pole. He pushed them with brilliant seamanship through the ice-choked strait which on British maps now bears his name, correcting on his way the faulty charts made by Hayes and laying caches of supplies at key points along the coast as a safeguard against any possible misfortune. After finding suitable winter quarters for the *Discovery* in Lady Franklin Bay in the extreme north-eastern corner of Ellesmere Island, he had taken the *Alert* through the Robeson Channel and around the north coast to Cape Sheridan on the very shores of the Arctic Ocean.

But from that point on the men were committed to the worn out and hopeless ideas of the past, where only by incredible courage and through all the known shades of Arctic suffering could they carry the flag to a new Farthest North. And yet this, to their enormous credit, these scurvied sailors did – hauling their boats like the slaves they were to the mindless ways of the past. They set a new record on 12th May, 1876 at 83°20'. Had they hauled themselves only a few miles further it is probable that none of them would have returned, for on reaching the ship on 14th June, seventy-two days after setting out, only three men were left of the party of fifteen who were "capable of dragging the sledge."

In his sledging report to Nares on returning to the ship Lieutenant Albert Markham, the leader of that northern party, states the "utter impracticability of reaching the North Pole over the floe in this locality," and he goes on to say:

I am convinced that with the very lightest equipped sledges, carrying no boats, and with all the resources of the ship concentrated in the one direction, and also supposing that perfect health might be maintained, the latitude attained by the party I had the honour and pleasure of commanding, would not be exceeded by many miles, certainly not by a degree.

His hard-won Farthest North was, however, beaten six years later by four nautical miles, the new record being taken by Lieutenant James Lockwood and Sergeant Brainard of the American Lady Franklin Bay expedition. On the face of it, this expedition was the very antithesis of the Pole-seeking expeditions which had gone before. Conceived as a scientific project – part of The First International Polar Year 1882–3 – its main objectives appeared to be to collect meteorological and magnetic data in Grinnell Land. Its leader was Lieutenant Adolphus W. Greely, US Army.

But in spite of the mass of material collected, the expedition was a disaster. The failure of the relief expedition to get through had left Greely and his men with no choice but to make their way south as best they could and, with their numbers decreasing, they were reduced to eating their clothes, their shoes, and eventually each other. Only seven of the twenty-five men (Greely among them) were still alive when eventually they were rescued from Starvation Camp on Cape Sabine, on 22nd June, 1884 by Commander Winfield S. Schley, U.S.N. Of this tragedy, Greely was later to write:

> No pen could ever convey to the world an adequate idea of the abject misery at Cape Sabine ... yet we were never without courage, faith, and hope. The extraordinary spirit of loyalty, patience, charity, and self-denial – daily and almost universally exhibited by our famished and nearly maddened party – must be read between the lines in the account of our daily life penned under such desperate and untoward circumstances. Such words, written at such a time, I have not the heart to enlarge on.

And between the lines Peary did read, and not only when invited to by explorers such as Greely. He read every account of every explorer who had ever travelled in those regions before him, from some of them learning much more than from others. But it was from the sum of this reading that, one year after the return of Greely, he reached the starting point in his own polar career – the decision that he would take up the challenge, and succeed where others had failed.

The physical make-up of the party he would pattern on the physical structure of a tough, hardy man:

> There should be one head and but one, the body should be [small], compact, homogeneous, accustomed to cold and hardship, without an ounce of superfluous weight, and under absolute control of the head.
>
> Following this analogy, one intelligent white man would represent the head, two other white men selected solely for their courage, determination, physical strength, and devotion to the leader would represent the arms, and the driver and natives the body and legs. The presence of women an absolute necessity to render the men contented; farther than this they are in many respects as useful as men, and are nearly if not quite their equals in strength and endurance ... In all expeditions where women have taken part they have been of as much or more assistance than the men, notably in Hall's explorations, and I am not sure but what a party of which the larger proportion were women would be best.

Finally the head should be absolutely free and independent, free to risk his own life and his companions, in the dark of some supreme moment, which holds within its short grasp utter success or utter failure . . .

The whole history of attempts at colonization under circumstances of hardship and strange and untried dangers shows that though the results *may* be failure with women it is *sure* to be without them. It is asking too much of masculine human nature to expect it to remain in an Arctic climate enduring constant hardship, without one relieving feature. Feminine companionship not only causes greater contentment, but as a matter of both mental and physical health and the retention of the top notch of manhood it is a necessity.

. . . If colonization is to be a success in polar regions let white men take with them native wives, then from that union may spring a race combining the hardiness of the mothers with the intelligence and energy of the fathers. Such a race would surely reach the Pole if their fathers did not succeed in doing it.

All credit to Peary where credit is due. His ideas may not be original, but he has sorted out from all he has read a few of the basic priorities, and determined upon a simple plan in which he would first adopt, then adapt the native technique of travelling. Much of this he had learnt from Hall; but he had even learnt something from the Nares expedition – the laying of caches on the outward journey as a safeguard for his return.

He writes that he does not believe "in a perennial open polar sea," and indeed this is hardly surprising since the *Alert* was wintered on the shore of it and Markham and his men had sledged far enough north to put an end to that theory. But he clearly has studied his subject well, and knows now where his base should be – and that he must be patient:

The chances which an expedition of one season now and another a dozen or more years later have of striking a favorable season are small . . . The only way is to lie in wait at some favorable point and watch season after season ready to take advantage of a favorable one, and believe me, there will come that season when the fortunate man waiting on the verge of the unknown region can . . . when the moment arrives, shoot forward to the Pole like a ball from a cannon.

And how was he proposing to subsist and survive on the desolate shores of the Arctic Ocean without a lifeline to his world? He had evidently not thought this one through, but he clearly had the vision and courage:

Finally, to the patient waiter and the persistent devil all things come round in time, and I will be both. I will stake my life on the throw of that favorable season and with two companions, a Danish or half-breed driver and interpreter, and three natives and their wives will settle down and live there on the shore of the Northern ocean till the secret is wrested from the ice or I leave my life.

He knew then, as I knew myself at that same stage in my career, that all the reading and all the dreaming were merely the "other men" that were speaking. His test was not what he had heard, or what he had decided to do, but whether he could do it.

CHAPTER 5

Fame – One Way or Another

In April 1886, Peary read a paper before the National Academy of Sciences in Washington, D.C. outlining his plans for a crossing of the Greenland Ice Cap: "Not one single determined effort having for its goal the east coast of Greenland has ever been made, and there is nothing to show that an intelligent and determined effort and the devotion of an entire season to the work would not be crowned with success." He went on to outline two possible routes by which Greenland might be crossed: a four-hundred-mile crossing of the southern part of the ice cap, and a more ambitious and more "arduous" route which would cross the ice cap from Whale Sound in North-West Greenland, to the unknown region of North-East Greenland, a route which he believed to be "the key to the solution of the Greenland problem . . . the delineation and closing of its coast-line." This wording was sufficiently exciting to attract attention and respect, even though the object of his expedition was simply to make a reconnaissance and, as it turned out, that summer trip to West Greenland was all that a first-taste expedition to the Arctic should be: successful, exciting, and above all, inspiring.

It might have been otherwise had not Peary met up with Christian Maigaard, the Assistant Governor of Ritenbenk, and been persuaded by this eager young man that the journey should be made by two men as it was far too hazardous a trip to be made alone. Together they made an adventurous journey on to the ice cap, climbing to 7,525 feet above sea level at a point about a hundred miles from the coast, an "attainment," as Peary was later to claim, which was "of greater elevation than ever before reached on the Inland Ice" and a penetration of "a greater distance than any white man previously."

Among the other results of this first taste of Arctic adventure Peary mentions his "securing of an invaluable fund of definite practical knowledge and experience of actual ice-cap conditions and necessary equipment, as well as practical knowledge of arctic navigation." Some doubts, however, were later expressed about the reliability of Peary's navigation on this trip by Dr. Fridtjof Nansen, which make interesting reading in view of Peary's later claims:

Peary's longitude was only based, as it seems, on some observations of altitude taken with a theodolite about noon 19th July. The expression "circum-meridian sights," which both he and Maigaard use, is not quite clear in itself. These so-called "simple altitudes" are besides, notoriously uncertain for longitude reckonings ... The distance of a hundred miles from the margin of the ice cannot, therefore, be considered as established beyond all doubt.

Biographer Fitzhugh Green believed that Peary experienced some sort of spiritual revelation up on the Greenland Ice Cap – a sense of destiny which "consecrated" him to the task "of wrenching from the White Arctic the secret men had through four centuries, died to learn." But in Peary's letter to his mother of the 27th February, 1887, it would appear that his inspiration had a very different focus.

My last trip has brought my name before the world; my next will give me a standing in the world ... The trip means to me, my mother, first an enduring name and honor, second, certainty of being retained in the Navy even in case of adverse legislation in regard to the Civil Engineering Corps, third, social advancement, for with the prestige of my summer's work, and the assistance of friends whom I have made this winter, I will next winter be one of the foremost in the highest circles in the capital, and make powerful friends with whom I can shape my future instead of letting it come as it will ... Remember, mother, I *must* have fame, and I cannot reconcile myself to years of commonplace drudgery and a name late in life when I see an opportunity to gain it now and sip the delicious draughts while yet I have youth and strength and capacity to enjoy it to the utmost. And I am not entirely selfish, mother. I want my fame *now* while you too can enjoy it.

Back came the reply from a mother who, more than ever, was afraid of the fire that burned in her son, afraid that she might lose him to his possessive dream of fame:

If fame is dearer to you than anything else, what am I to say. I think if you should look at the matter calmly and dispassionately you would be less enthusiastic – such fame is dearly bought. I am only one year older than when you first talked of going to Greenland, but I feel as if I was ten. I do not care to repeat the last summer's experience. There, I am too dizzy to write more.

Peary's call to return to Nicaragua is seen by some writers as a diversion from his chosen course – and small wonder, since only eleven months earlier he had written in his diary while outward bound for Greenland: "I am too impatient to reach that northern region which holds my future name to enjoy anything and have paced the bridge all day."

And yet, it is clear from his letters that when the Maritime Canal Company was formed in April 1887, and Peary was chosen by Menocal, his former chief, to be second in command and with the impressive title of Sub-Chief Engineer, he was delighted by the order to change direction. Fame, after all, was fame by whatever course it was achieved, and fame was his objective. True enough, his first trip to Greenland had been successful and rewarding, and he was already preparing himself for his second assault; but here was a far greater opportunity for advancement. On this project he was to be responsible for the entire survey, and in command of some forty-five engineers and over a hundred labourers. The sheer size and importance of the project was of itself a guarantee that it would attract the attention of those with power and influence whose respect and friendship Peary needed, and he clearly found the whole challenging build-up to the project an exciting and heady experience.

Who is to say when a diversion from a chosen course is not the course of destiny? Was it merely by chance that Lieutenant Peary, in urgent need of a tropical helmet for his forthcoming trip to Nicaragua, should have gone to B. H. Steinmetz and Sons in Washington, D.C. and there met Matthew Henson? Second only to his meeting with Josephine Diebitsch, this proved to be the most fateful and fortuitous meeting in Peary's entire life. The two men were to become inseparable travelling companions: "I can't get along without him," Peary was to confide to Donald B. MacMillan shortly before the start of his final attempt at the Pole in 1909, although at the time of Peary's meeting with Henson twenty-two years earlier, all that Peary needed was a hat and a reliable young man he could employ as his personal valet.

But here, I suspect, we are straying once more into the intriguing mysteries of coincidence and pre-ordained destinies, when all there is for certain to offer (and all we should here be considering) are the well recorded facts.

Henson, a Negro who had some white blood in his veins – "just enough to lighten his skin the ochre color of a well-fingered copper coin" – was twenty-one at the time of this meeting, ten years younger than Peary. He was short in stature (a little under five feet seven), wiry, hard-working, extremely intelligent, and surprisingly well read. His mother had died when he was only two years old, and as an orphan at the age of eight he had come under the tyranny of a stepmother from whom he received his final and most vicious beating at the tender age of eleven. Convinced that the outside world could offer no worse terrors, he left home under cover of darkness and, in the dead of winter, walked all the way from

Washington in the hope of finding in Baltimore a ship that would take him to sea. It had been this courage and his innocent eagerness which had touched the heart of Captain Childs when Henson was only twelve, a vulnerability which the old sea captain had felt a duty to protect.

"Did you ever stop to think why I took you on my ship as a cabin boy?" Captain Childs asked him during their first voyage together. "I didn't have to, boy. You were under age, thin as a yardarm, and couldn't write your own name. I don't know a skipper on the entire seaboard who would have signed on a skinny flotsam like you; but I did. I took you aboard 'cause I wanted to give you a chance at life. How far do you think you'd gotten drifting around on land? You're colored, Matthew, that's a fact and God's wish, but you're a hell of a sight blacker on shore than you are on *my* ship."

And so Childs had taken Henson under his wing, and for five years had patiently nurtured him, taught him how to read and write, expanded his horizons at all the points of the mariner's compass, and prepared him for the world.

They made a strangely grotesque pair, the white-haired old giant and the small, eager-eyed, twelve-year-old Negro boy, the master and the pupil, holding class in the middle of the ocean. Hunched over the table with a child's primer opened before him, and his long white hair flowing down his broad back, Captain Childs had the look of an ancient priest listening with wise patience to the innocent confessions of an unworthy child. And across from him the eager Negro boy, his feet dangling above the floor, recited his lessons with the fervent enthusiasm of a blind child whose sight is gradually being restored to him, and for whom the world is unfolded for the first time.

In those five years of almost continuous sailing all over the world (which for Henson was to include, ten years in advance of Peary, his first experience of an Arctic winter when the *Katie Hines* was beset by ice in the Russian harbour of Murmansk) that gentle old sea captain not only moulded his cabin boy's character and gave him an education that would serve him for the rest of his life, but he also gave him the confidence and the courage to stand up against prejudice, and to look every man in the eye. "Your fight is with the ignorance in people's minds," the old man once told him, "and your best weapons are knowledge and intelligence. These books are the beginning. Make them your fists, Matthew."

Captain Childs was buried at sea on the final leg of the homeward voyage of 1883, and Henson, in his grief, felt part of his soul go with him. The boy was a man and a seaman now, and an all round master of his trade; but after one short voyage to Newfoundland, he knew he could no longer make the sea his life – that he had been prepared for something greater: to serve another man with the strength of character and the courage of his mentor, if such a man on the earth could be found. And it took him four years to find one.

"Matt," Sam Steinmetz called, "bring in a size seven and three-eighths sun helmet. They're on the shelf above the panamas." Henson felt the eyes of the Lieutenant on him as he entered the room, and sensed a powerful driving force behind the customer's terse introduction.

"My name is Peary," the man said as he adjusted the sun helmet on his head before the mirror. "I need a boy to go with me to Central America, as a valet. Keep my clothes and quarters clean. Must be honest with regular habits. Mr. Steinmetz recommends you."

Henson did not much care for the idea of being a valet; but the idea of going to Central America appealed to him, and so too did the confidence of the Lieutenant, whose response to Henson's eager acceptance was concise and straight to the point: Henson was to remain at Steinmetz and Sons until he received a letter confirming the agreement.

The idea of having a valet was a privilege that had been thrust upon Peary. The executives of the newly formed company, knowing of Peary's Arctic interests, were anxious to provide any status symbol which might appease the setback in the development of his still secret plans; but although flattered by this concern for his comfort, he had other problems on his mind, of which the company were unaware, that were the cause of far greater concern. One of these worries was the growing anxiety of his mother in whom he had felt compelled to confide his need to return to Nicaragua:

From my childhood I was not strong, less so since your birth. In my weakness and loneliness I have tried hard and earnestly to do what I thought was best for you. I do not tell you this to excite you but that you may judge me more leniently or justly. Now I cannot have your unhappiness laid at my door. Leave me entirely out of the question and do what you think will give you sunshine and happiness. The sudden though not unexpected announcement of your intentions wrung from me a cry of pain – It shall not happen again. All the clothes that you brought home I have put in as good order as my strength and ability would admit. You have only to say what else I can do to assist your preparations. If I have caused you the loss of a night's sleep you will forgive.

Mother

Peary's other worry was perhaps more in the nature of a dilemma: his attraction to Josephine Diebitsch was creating a conflict between his ambition and his love. By 18th September, 1887, however, the struggle was over. He would ask her to marry him, after, of course, confiding in his mother: "If she does not love me with her whole heart," he wrote, "then she is a most consummate and consistent actress. I shall take the risk and within the week shall ask her to wear my ring. I shall not think of marriage, however, until after my return from Nicaragua."

By the time the expedition sailed from New York on 30th November, 1887, Peary's concentration was more sharply focused on the demanding project which lay ahead than on anything he had attempted before. With his force of 145 engineers and labourers divided into six land parties, two boring parties and one hydrographic party, the entire route of the proposed canal was re-examined, relocated, mapped, levelled, and test-bored to bedrock, through jungles and swamps, cutting their way "through the tropical tangle" which separated one great ocean from another "until they knew the shape of every hill, the course of every stream." As Peary stated in the impressive report which he presented to a meeting of the American Association for the Advancement of Science in August 1888: "the expedition cut, ran with transit, or compass, and levelled, 500 miles of lines and 400 miles of soundings." And the results of his explorations and survey showed that in Nicaragua there were, and still are:

> ... two perfectly practicable locations of about equal cost, either of which is far superior to any other route across the Isthmus: and when the day comes, as it surely will, when one canal cannot accommodate the traffic seeking it, then the other can be built and give one canal for eastward, and one for westward bound vessels.

The estimated cost was $66,000,000 and the time needed to complete the canal system only five years, for by this route (via Lake Nicaragua) the actual cut canal would be less than thirty miles. In short, it was a masterly plan, for which of course Civil Engineer A. G. Menocal, U.S.N., quite rightly took the lion's share of the credit. But it was also a brilliantly organised survey on which Peary rose to the challenge and revelled in the complex problems of moving men and equipment around, particularly through those stretches of country that were wild and unexplored. From his letters to his mother it is equally clear that the enormous significance of his achievement had already excited his hopes of reward long before the work was completed, for the spotlight of public interest, as always looking for a hero, had fallen on him as the dynamic field leader through the despatches of a reporter from the *New York Herald*, and another from the *New York Times*.

Received by the president of Nicaragua on two occasions and warmly congratulated on his work, and entertained lavishly by the social élite in the capital, Managua, Peary had really begun to feel that he had arrived and was confident not only that the canal construction would go ahead, but also that he would be chosen as one of the key figures – the de Lesseps of Central America. "I am lifting myself," he said in a letter home, "I am writing my name before the world." And on his thirty-second birthday in a "progress report" to his mother:

> I shall be indispensable to the Canal Company after this trip and can make my own terms. At the same time am making myself known, as you see by the *Herald*. I am 32 today . . . and I hope you are satisfied with my progress. I am as far along as I dreamed eleven years ago when I left college, and I have prospects ahead of me beyond what I dreamed. I have now a firmer grip upon this canal matter than even Menocal himself, because in addition to his knowledge of the general scope of the work, I have a personal knowledge of every foot of the ground.

One cannot help but feel that his self-assurance, which at this stage in his career fell only one breath short of arrogance and two short of conceit, had been earned and was therefore justified. But as with every other determined effort that he made in his life from this point on, the full measure of his earned success was sadly, if not cruelly, denied him. The surveys made under his direction were assessed by a board of eminent consultant engineers and approved; the company was granted its charter, and work was started at Greytown. Even a special commission set up to examine the comparative merits of the Nicaraguan and Panama Canal projects reported in favour of Peary's plan. And yet, in the end, as we all know, Panama won the day.

It was, however, a while before all this came to a head, and Peary was still flushed with his success and confident about his future on 11th August, 1888 (a broiling hot day in Washington), when he finally married his Josephine, and he and his bride, with his mother in attendance, travelled in style to Seabright, New Jersey, where they were to spend their honeymoon.

For a while, Peary's yearning for fame died down and he devoted himself to his bride. "If he is as happy as I am," Jo wrote to his mother on 8th October, "then we must be the happiest people in the world." But that yearning could be rekindled at the merest mention of competition. His bride had seen the distress in his eyes only two weeks before, when the news had come through that Fridtjof Nansen had made the first crossing of the Greenland Ice Cap by a route which Peary had felt was his, and on which he had set his heart. The shortest route across the ice cap had been Peary's shortest route to fame.

Now he was left with no alternative but to set his sights on the longer and far more arduous journey from North-West Greenland to the unexplored area in the extreme north-east, a route he had originally proposed in the paper he had read before the National Academy of Science in April 1886, but with no intention at that time of taking on such a challenge. Now he was driven to attempt it by the bitterness behind the feeling that Nansen had forestalled him. And so began his determination to cut the name Peary so deeply into the frozen North that he would be regarded, for the rest of time, as the greatest polar explorer in the history of mankind.

The implication that Nansen had cheated him made by Peary in the introduction to his book *Northward Over the Great Ice* is, of course, unfair. Peary writes: "This forestalling of my work was a serious blow to me, but my duty to the Service left me helpless, and I could only fall back upon the other northern route." He even adds as a footnote a quote from Nansen's book which indicates that Nansen was aware that Peary's journey with Maigaard had been merely a reconnaissance, and that Nansen knew he had no time to lose if he did not want to be anticipated. But the fact is, Nansen had conceived his plan "of crossing Greenland on ski from coast to coast" in the autumn of 1883, some three years in advance of Peary's summer reconnaissance journey. It is interesting also to note that Nansen openly admits that Peary's journey spurred him on. Competition, after all, is one of the most effective instigators of progress in the western world, and Peary himself, in his early years, had been a master of the art of getting to the top; his technique being to prepare himself well, to study thoroughly the skills and techniques of those he considered as a serious threat, and to enter only those competitions in which he was certain of winning. By the time of Nansen's first crossing of Greenland, a change, however, had occurred in his thinking. Whilst still accepting the obvious need and the essential value of competition from a philosophical point of view, Peary had come to distrust it deeply in whatever shape or form it appeared to threaten him professionally, and was incensed by any competition that entered the territory which he shamelessly regarded as strictly and solely his own.

This presumption that he had first claim and the exclusive right to explore any region of the Arctic which suited him is, of course, ludicrous. No other polar explorer before him or since, with the possible exception of Captain Scott, had come anywhere near to matching Peary's sensitivity on this issue of territory, and this problem of Peary's, together with his fear of failing, was to grow stronger with each year, until the destructive forces of this paranoia began to undermine the very foundations of his confidence in himself, and his conviction that it was his destiny to be the first man at the Pole.

Without that obsession, there is not the slightest doubt in my mind that Peary would have failed to reach the shores of the Arctic Ocean, and he would, in August 1894, have abandoned all hope of reaching his goal. But that obsession became the counter-weight which kept him on his chosen course; which drove him beyond the limits of endurance, which faltered but never failed. If we are to understand Peary, we must first accept his obsession.

Scores of books have been written on the subject of Peary's claim to have reached the North Pole – as many concluding he attained his objective as there are those that discredit his story. It is, however, a general rule among historians to follow his polar career along the route he claims to have taken, with the result, of course, that they are confronted only by those physical problems which Peary himself was prepared to record, while those conflicts raging within the man go unnoticed or ignored.

Here we are looking at this polar career from a somewhat different point of view – an overview of Peary's journeys less concerned with detail than it is with the impression. Seen from this angle, the first thing that strikes one about the first period in this career – from the time of launching his first expedition to North-West Greenland in June 1891 to the bitter end of those eleven years of doubt and suffering in August 1902 – is the time lag between receiving the news of Nansen's successful first crossing of Greenland and Peary's response to the challenge. True, he had just got married. True also, he was still working on the reports of his Nicaraguan canal survey until October 1888, and had then little option but to put in some Navy duty to justify his salary. We should, however, remember that this is a man with a burning ambition, and that in May 1891 when he was given eighteen months' leave of absence from the Navy to prepare and conduct his first major polar expedition, he was already thirty-five years of age, the age at which most polar explorers are reaching the peak of their active careers. He had to weigh carefully the advantages of staying in the Navy, which gave him status and a regular salary, against the freedom to pursue his polar career whilst he was still young enough to be in with a chance of success. The former course might curtail his personal ambitions. The latter would be less wasteful in years, but financially far more precarious. It was a difficult choice, and he delayed his decision on it until he had the outcome of his application for eighteen months' leave of absence. He then opted for the safer course.

By this course he believed that, if he played his cards right, he could pursue his polar ambition in spite of the fact that his ambition lay outside the range of duties he was commissioned to perform, and that he succeeded, in the face of considerable resentment from some of his superior officers, is an indication of his tremendous power of persuasion, and his skill in the art of impressing those who had the authority to sweep aside all the departmental obstacles which lay in the way of his patriotic mission. To recognise the pressures under which he laboured it may suffice to quote from a memorandum from the Department of the Navy's Bureau of Navigation to the Secretary of the Navy dated 10th February, 1910:

> During his service in the Navy, Civil Engineer Peary has performed active duty for twelve years and nine days. He has been unemployed for sixteen years, one month and sixteen days. Of this unemployed duty approximately thirteen years and five months have been spent on leave while unattached, and the balance on waiting orders or leave on duty.

The statement of pay received by Peary from the date of his entry into the service on 26th October, 1881, to 31st December, 1909, which forms part of that same memorandum, is also interesting. It indicates that the total pay received by Peary while on duty was $33,703, and that the total he received while on leave or waiting duties was $38,148. For only six months during his entire service was he on leave without pay, and on 4th March, 1911, when the thanks of Congress were extended to Peary "for his Arctic explorations resulting in reaching the North Pole," those thanks carried with them an advance to the rank of Rear-Admiral, with retirement pay at that rank of $6,500 annually, effective from 6th April, 1909 – the date he claimed to have reached the North Pole.

It would appear that Peary made the right choice, and that those twelve years and nine days of active duty were a good deal in exchange for just over fifteen and a half years of paid leave, not to mention steadily climbing status: Lieutenant-Commander in 1901, rising to Commander in 1902 (on his forty-sixth birthday), on to Captain in 1910, and retiring with the rank of Rear-Admiral "and the highest retired pay of that grade under existing law." But what we should not overlook is that the outcome of this choice was by no means certain, and that Peary had to work hard to maintain the impetus of his rise in favour among those who believed in him and this, as we shall see, was a strain.

An assessment of Peary's explorations over the eleven-year period from 1891 to 1902 also uncovers a few surprises. During this period he made three major expeditions to what he called his "domain" (that north-western corner of Greenland and the east and north coast of Ellesmere Island); spent a total of seven years and four months in the field, and probably travelled somewhere in the region of nine thousand miles with dog teams, which by any criteria is an impressive performance. It is, however, all too easy to assume that these years were essentially a preparation, a period during which he built up a formidable background of experience that would stand him in good stead for his heroic 1906 attempt at the North Pole, and the great climax of his career in 1909. To some extent, of course, this is true. By the end of this period he was, unquestionably, the most experienced polar traveller of his day (allowing in this statement that the native peoples of the Arctic are entirely in a class of their own), and he was also one of the toughest.

Why then, if the man was such an exceptional polar traveller did he not reach the North Pole some ten years earlier? Look at the route maps in his first two books and you will find the country webbed with tracks; and yet his Farthest North in this period was only eighty-two miles out on to the pack ice from his starting point, Cape Hecla, and in spite of all that travelling – nine thousand miles, and some of the cruellest travelling conditions ever experienced by a polar explorer – he succeeded in mapping a total of only about 320 miles of previously unexplored coastline.

Such questions and facts need some explaining, particularly since one of the stated objectives of his 1893–5 expedition, and the "main purpose" of his 1898–1902 expedition, was the attainment of the North Pole. But where are we to go in search of answers? His published accounts covering these three expeditions offer some of the most fascinating reading in the history of exploration, but they are incomplete. His original diaries are more revealing, and some of the letters deeply moving. But his written words are guarded and we will not find the answers here, only the shape of the missing pieces and perhaps, from the uncompleted picture, an impression which may be true.

Of the three expeditions, only his first and shortest comes clear of any critical analysis with the verdict of successful. Perhaps it is therefore not surprising that this is the only one of the three in which the pieces are almost all there, for Peary was proud of this first expedition and had little to hide. It was a fresh, bold, even brilliant conception, on which the main objectives had been to determine the northern limit of Greenland and to seek a more practicable route to the Pole; both objectives being sought by an inland route across the ice cap. It was to be a small expedition with only seven members in the wintering party, three of whom were to play key roles in the on-going story of Peary's life. The first was Matthew Henson, whose "remarkable ingenuity," intelligence and loyalty so impressed Peary during the Nicaraguan survey that Peary promoted him from the role of man-servant to that of chain man with one of the survey crews. Henson was already regarded by Peary as an indispensable part of any plan he might conceive. The second was Dr. Frederick A. Cook, a Brooklyn physician, who joined the expedition as surgeon and ethnologist; and to the shocked amazement of the general public, Peary's wife, Jo, was the third.

CHAPTER 6

The Vision

It was five o'clock in the afternoon of 6th June, 1891, when Captain Richard Pike, master of the steam sealer *Kite*, gave the order to cast off from the pier at the foot of Baltic Street, Brooklyn. Ten years earlier, as commander of the *Proteus*, he had taken the Greely expedition to within only a few miles of the shores of the Arctic Ocean. Now it was Lieutenant Peary, in command of his first full scale expedition, who was standing at the rail with his wife beside him. They were bound for North Greenland and, as Peary records:

> Scores of whistles bade us good-bye and *bon voyage*. All the way up the East River dipping flags gave us hail and farewell. The fleet of big Sound steamers passed us one by one, whistles saluting and the decks crowded with passengers waving handkerchiefs. At Flushing, and other points, many yachts saluted with their guns; and it was not until night hid us that the inspiring God-speeds of our friends and well-wishers were heard no more.

With his wife beside him, Peary now believed himself invincible, a man with a God-given mission, as his letter to his mother reveals: "Now I feel that all is written in the irrevocable book that I have been selected for this work and shall be upheld or carried safely and successfully through."

And so he was, in spite of a setback even before the *Kite* reached her destination when Peary's leg was broken by the iron tiller. The wisdom of continuing the voyage with an injured leader was the subject of much debate among the nine fare-paying passengers on the ship (whose contributions represented a large part of the expedition's $10,000 budget), and Peary, suspicious as always of the intrigues of others, had a compass installed in his cabin in order to keep a check of the course until, on 27th July, 1891, the *Kite* reached her destination, McCormick Bay in North-West Greenland where Peary, suffering some indignity, was taken ashore "strapped to a plank."

It was an inauspicious start to an expedition on which he was hoping to make a crossing of the Greenland Ice Cap, an unnecessary test of his resolve. In his book *Northward Over the Great Ice* he gives credit to those who helped him through the ordeal: "Thanks to the professional skill of my surgeon, Dr. Cook, and the unwearying and thoughtful care of Mrs. Peary, my complete recovery was rapidly attained."

But as the relationship between Peary and Cook was to sour and eventually turn to hatred, so too did the relationship between Peary and several of his other polar companions over the years to come. A good organiser though he was, he was not a sensitive leader of men, and his craving for fame would not permit him to offer those who shared his triumphs anything more than a token measure of the credit for his success. What he needed in a companion was competence, courage, total loyalty and, above all, an emotional commitment to serve him without question or any thought of reward.

At the time of this first wintering expedition he was, however, still too inexperienced to recognise this need. Indeed, in terms of practical Arctic experience, he was almost as much a novice in this cold and forbidding environment as those he had taken with him. Through his reading Peary had seen the advantages of having a small party and, believing that "every man beyond the number absolutely essential is an element of danger and failure," he had selected from among the hundreds of applicants only five men to accompany him.

> They were all young, and in addition to possessing first-class physique and perfect health, were men of education and attainments. I believe this to be the type of men best fitted to endure with minimum unfavorable effect the ordeal of the arctic winter, and to effectively execute a two or three months' dash on sledges, where intelligent will-power, youthful elasticity, and enthusiasm rise superior to the stolid endurance of muscles hardened by years of work.

Their attainments, however, did not quite match up to Peary's listing of them. Dr. Frederick A. Cook, he describes as "the surgeon and ethnologist of the expedition," a twenty-six-year-old physician and surgeon, a native of New York State who "had been practicing his profession in New York City for several years." In fact Cook's practice in Manhattan had attracted only three patients in the first six months, and he had been greatly relieved when, only a year after graduating, and with little else to do but read books on exploration, his application to join Peary's expedition had been accepted.

Whether or not Peary knew this, it is evident that he was impressed by Cook's professional ability and by his relaxed and friendly attitude towards the native people. It is perhaps significant also that Cook heads the list of his five companions in the short introduction he offers his readers to each of the members of his expedition. Langdon Gibson was his "ornithologist and chief hunter"; Eivind Astrup, his Norwegian ski expert; John Verhoeff, his mineralogist and meteorologist who "contributed generously to the expenses of the expedition"; and the twenty-three-year-old Matthew Henson is described as his "body servant."

Bottom of the social status though Henson may have been on that expedition, Peary was bold enough (for that day and age) to leave his readers in no doubt as to the merits of his "hardy colored man" and of his own decision to take him: "His intelligence and faithfulness, combined with more than average pluck and endurance, as shown during several years that he has been with me through varying experiences, part of the time in Nicaraguan jungles, led me to regard him as a valuable member of the party."

But clearly the most vital member of that party from Peary's point of view was his wife Jo. She alone could Peary trust with any of his private thoughts. But this we only know years later through his letters to his wife, for what he told the readers of his books was very seldom more than he believed that they and history had the right to know:

> Possessed of health, youth, energy, and enthusiastic interest in the work, she saw no reason why she could not endure conditions and enivronment similar to those in which Danish wives in Greenland pass years of their life. I concurred in this opinion, and believed that in many ways her presence and assistance would contribute to the valuable results of the expedition, as they were invaluable to me in the preparation. Events proved the entire correctness of this belief.

Only once, in any of his published writings, did he venture to express the deep respect and love he had for this long-suffering, totally devoted, and remarkably brave woman. His comments appear in the preface he contributed to the book she wrote about their first expedition together, *My Arctic Journal*:

> She has been where no white woman has ever been, and where many a man has hesitated to go; and she has seen phases of the life of the most northerly tribe of human beings on the globe, and in many ways has been enabled to get a closer insight into their ways and customs than had been obtained before.
>
> I rarely, if ever take up the thread of our Arctic experiences without reverting to two pictures: one is the first night that we spent on the Greenland shore after the departure of the *Kite*, when, in a little tent on the rocks – a tent which the furious wind threatened every moment to carry away bodily – she watched by my side as I lay a helpless cripple with a broken leg, our small party the only human beings on

that shore, and the little *Kite*, from which we had landed, drifted far out among the ice by the storm, and invisible through the rain. Long afterwards she told me that every unwonted sound of the wind set her heart beating with the thoughts of some hungry bear roaming along the shore and attracted by the unusual sight of the tent; yet she never gave a sign at the time of her fears, lest it should disturb me.

The other picture is that of a scene perhaps a month or two later, when – myself still a cripple, but not entirely helpless – this same woman sat for an hour beside me in the stern of a boat, calmly reloading our empty firearms while a herd of infuriated walrus about us thrust their savage heads with gleaming tusks and bloodshot eyes out of the water close to the muzzles of our rifles, so that she could have touched them with her hand, in their efforts to get their tusks over the gunwale and capsize the boat. I may perhaps be pardoned for saying that I never think of these two experiences without a thrill of pride and admiration for her pluck.

Within sixty miles of where Kane and his little party endured such untold sufferings, within eighty miles of where Greely's men one by one starved to death, and within less than fifty miles of where Hayes and his party and one portion of the *Polaris* party underwent their Arctic trials and tribulations, this tenderly nurtured woman lived for a year in safety and comfort ... Perhaps no greater or more convincing proof than this could be desired of what great improvements have been made in Arctic methods.

His concluding remarks, although as much in praise of himself as they are of his courageous wife, are entirely justified. In his planning and equipment Peary had taken the best ideas of those explorers who had gone before, and invariably improved upon them. He had also, in choosing to spend the winter some sixty miles to the south of Etah and nearer to the Eskimo settlements on the shores of Whale and Murchison Sounds, shown how wisely he had read the signs which previous explorers had reported without fully understanding.

The actual site of his winter quarters on the south shore of McCormick Bay, although not the best site in the region, was nevertheless a suitable one, and with the building of Red Cliff House completed on 11th August, 1891, ten days after the *Kite* had sailed, the seven of them moved in.

The timber house, designed by Peary, was small, but well constructed. It consisted of an inner and an outer shell with a four-foot air-space in between, the inner shell being lined throughout with heavy Indian blankets. The outer wall, built to be impregnable to the winter storms, was constructed from specially designed wooden boxes in which their supplies had come north on the *Kite*, and with its roofing of canvas it served as

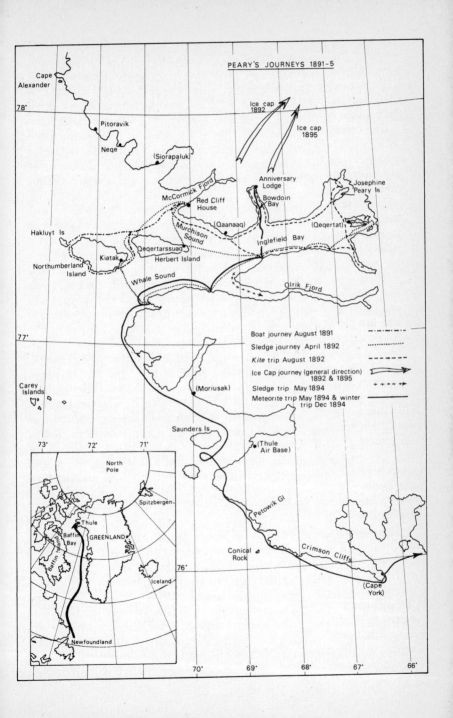

a protective corridor in which their supplies were "immediately and conveniently accessible." The interior offered a living space of only twenty-one feet by twelve, and was divided off to make a tiny bedroom for the Pearys while the main room served as a bunkhouse for the men, and with the stove set in a pit below the level of the floor, that hut was to prove a warm but somewhat cramped space for the seven who were to share it. Indeed, this was the only disadvantage of that hut. It was designed on the assumption that morale would be high and the seven would get along well together, a weakness some would blame on the plan, while others would blame the temperament of those who could not share that space without creating friction.

It was, however, a while before there were any signs of a downward turn in the general morale of Peary's men, for their adventure served as a bond between them, particularly their first and most important assignment, "to communicate with the natives." Crucial to the success of his plan, Peary needed the help of the Eskimos, although in writing his book he of course expressed this need differently. "I wished to become well acquainted with these most isolated and northerly of all peoples and, for the purposes of studying this interesting tribe, I hoped to induce not a few of them to spend the winter months at or near our camp."

This appears at first a paler plan than the one he had outlined six years earlier, but at least this idea was a comfortable compromise between the ship-based expedition of his one-time hero Dr. Kane and the very much closer-to-nature adventures of that other hero, Hall. And so Peary had sent Gibson, Dr. Cook, Verhoeff, and Astrup away on their mission in their well-equipped little whaleboat *Faith*, with provisions enough for fourteen days and directives which, if strictly obeyed, would steer them clear of trouble.

Their delightful adventure produced results, which the four were then required to present in the form of three handwritten reports, and from part of Cook's I quote:

Sir:

In pursuance of your instructions of August 12th, 1891, I submit to you the report on the duties you assigned me on the boat cruise around Hakluyt and Northumberland Islands, from August 12th to August 19th.

Hakluyt Island presented few signs of Eskimo habitation. We found fox-traps all along the south-west coast, but only one was set . . . The first indication of Eskimo habitation that we discovered on Northumberland Island was in a bay to the west of a large glacier. The deserted village was made up of two stone igloos, six dog-houses, and eight bird and blubber caches. All entrances of both the igloos and dog-house open directly on the south. The roofs of the igloos were either removed or fallen in. The general mode of construction was precisely the same as others that we examined, but large bones, such as whale, walrus, and narwhal, skulls, scapulae, and vertebrae, formed a large part of their walls.

The next Innuit houses we found in a large bay. When we first saw these igloos from a distance, we could see no life, but as we approached nearer and were about to land, we saw a man approaching down over some hummocks, at a short distance. His general appearance approached nearer that of a wild animal than a human being. He expressed no fear, but came right down and helped us with our boat, and smiled, and talked for minutes at a time. Soon a woman with two children also appeared at the scene. We had lunch, and offered them some of it. They seemed pleased at our generosity, ate what we gave them, but apparently did not enjoy any of our foods except the coffee and biscuits.

The next day . . . as we got around the cape, we saw a tupek [tent], and a man in a kayak came out to meet us. This kayaker seemed more than pleased to see us; his face was all aglow with smiles. He piloted us to the settlement, which had by this time all assembled, the men on the beach, the women and children in a row on the rocks in front of the first tupek. After lunch, I took a census of the village, the population of which numbered thirteen. Each man possessed a kayak, a harpoon, a lance, and a bird net; and two possessed bows and arrows, a number of rolls of line and narwhal sinew. The lack of fear in these men and their confidence in white men were clearly shewn the first night we camped there. At about ten o'clock, all the men suddenly started out in their kayaks after narwhal, leaving their women and children unprotected. At about five o'clock, they returned with a narwhal in tow.

. . . We tried to inform these people where our camp was, and that we had plenty of wood and knives, but [they] hesitated considerably. I again tried to persuade our former friend to come with us. He hesitated, but suddenly made up his mind, took his belongings and all he could borrow, put them in our boat, and came with us with his family. As we reached the place marked 5 on the map, we saw two stone igloos, but did not dare go ashore to examine these for fear of losing our prize, the Eskimo family. Ikwa told us before he came in our boat that his wife and children would get seasick, but when we crossed the Sound she and the children went asleep – and in this condition we brought them safely to Red Cliff.

Respectfully submitted,
F. A. Cook, MD,
Surgeon to North-Greenland Expedition

These Eskimos were "the queerest, dirtiest-looking individuals" that Jo had ever seen. Clad as they were entirely in furs, they reminded her "more of monkeys than of human beings," especially the man, Ikwah, whose "coarse black hair was allowed to straggle in tangles over his face, ears, and neck, to his shoulders, without any attempt at arrangement or order." But as the ice formed on the sea and the visitors to Red Cliff House were encouraged to set up camp nearby, she became more exposed to their strange ways, indeed, unable at times to avoid them:

> M'gipsu is sitting on the floor in my room (an unusual honor), and her husband, Annowkah, comes in as often as he can find an excuse for doing so. He frequently rubs his face against hers, and they sniffle at each other; this takes the place of kissing. I should think they could smell each other without doing this, but they are probably so accustomed to the (to me) terrible odor that they fail to notice it.
>
> I dislike very much to have the natives in my room, on account of their dirty condition, and especially as they are alive with parasites, of which I am in deadly fear, much to the amusement of our party. But it is impossible for the women to sew in the other room where the boys are at work on their sledges and ski, so I allow two at a time to come into my room, taking good care that they do not get near the bed.

Worse even than their habit of exchanging wives (since this habit did not directly affect her), was their custom of stripping off their clothes when they were in an igloo. To this she was not initiated until the following spring but, judging by her description, it was something of an ordeal:

> As the wind was blowing fiercely and the air was thick with drifting snow, Mr. Peary urged me to come into the igloo, which I did, rather to please him than to get out of the storm. Now as long as I have been in this country I have never entered an Eskimo hut; hearing about the filth and vermin was quite enough for me. But Mr. Peary said the snow-house was much cleaner, etc., etc., and seeing that it really made him uncomfortable to have me stay outside, I yielded. Can I ever describe it? First I crawled through a hole and along a passage, about six feet, on my hands and knees; this was level with the snow outside. Then I came to a hole at the end of the passage which seemed hardly large enough for me to get my head through, and through which I could see numberless legs.

Around the walls of the igloo she found a platform, the middle part of which was the bed, and this was "covered with two or three tooktoo [reindeer] skins which almost crawled away, they were so very much alive."

Mr. Peary had taken a seat on the edge of this bed, and the women immediately made room for me between them; but this was more than I could submit to, so excusing myself by saying that my clothing was wet from the drifting snow and that I could not think of getting their bedding wet, I sat down, not without a shiver, on the edge beside Mr. Peary, selfishly keeping him between the half-naked women and myself.

Besides the persons mentioned there were always as many visitors as could possibly pack in without standing on one another. These took turns with those unable to get in ... and this was kept up throughout the night. Of course the addition of our stove, together with the visitors, brought the temperature up rapidly, and to my dismay the Eskimo ladies belonging to the house took off all their clothing except their necklaces of sinishaw, just as unconcernedly as though no one were present.

The odor of the place was indescribable ... and leaning on my elbow, I sat from ten at night until ten in the morning, dressed just as I was on the sledge. But I made the best of the situation, and pretended to Mr. Peary that it was quite a lark.

Peary meanwhile, "as the result of a systematic series of interviews with the natives who came to Red Cliff," was soon in possession of "information as to the location and ownership of every dog in the tribe, and also the financial rating of their owners – just what each one's possessions were; what each one most desired, and what would be most effective in bartering for the dogs." He and Dr. Cook also made a study of the Eskimos themselves, measuring and photographing seventy-five somewhat puzzled natives during the course of the winter.

On one side of the stove, near the partition separating Mrs. Peary's apartment from the main room, I stationed myself to handle the camera. On the other side was Matt manipulating the flash-light. Dr. Cook would pose the subject at the other end of the room and near at hand was a table at which he recorded his anthropological measurements.

It was interesting to observe the modesty both of the women and the men. They could not understand at first why I desired to take their pictures in a nude condition, and I am not sure that they ever got a very clear idea of the matter. I told them that we wished to compare their bodies with those of other people in the world, and it was not long before some of them grasped the idea so far as to decide that our work was in the interests of a perfectly laudable and proper curiosity. At first, however, some of them asked Dr. Cook if I wanted the information he obtained for the purpose of making other people!! The flash-light work never failed to be a subject of lively gossip in the native community. All the fresh arrivals were told what was before them almost before they had unhitched their dogs, and as soon as a native was photographed, he would invariably tell of the experience to an admiring group, narrating every minute detail.

But in spite of these diversions, and all the feverish activity of preparing, testing, and modifying their equipment in readiness for the spring sledging journey across the Greenland Ice Cap, the four months of darkness, the cramped space of the hut, and Peary's forceful personality began to have an effect upon the morale of what was all too clearly an already divided party.

Worst of those affected by Peary's style of leadership had been Verhoeff. His resentment at having been reprimanded by Peary during the winter for having ventured beyond the five-hundred-yard limit (which Peary, perhaps in a tactless way, had imposed on them all for their safety) had alarmingly become a hatred of the leader and his wife, and Jo's dislike of Verhoeff was equally intense. Other members of his party were also giving Peary problems, his dilemma being who to take on his ice cap journey and who to leave behind with Jo.

Before setting out he also needed to make a practical test of his gear, and to test himself to see if his leg would take the strain of the longer journey that he was planning. And so he set out with Astrup and Cook on Sunday, 14th February, 1892, on a trial climb up to 2,000 feet to an igloo which, the day before, Gibson and Verhoeff had been unable (or unwilling) to complete. As it turned out, Peary's leg proved fine, but the igloo had been badly constructed, and instead of (more wisely) building a new one, they put a flat roof on the existing one, using their snowshoes and skis as supports for the heavy blocks of snow.

Had they spent more time that winter learning from the Eskimos the most basic of their techniques of survival, the next few hours would have probably produced nothing much more than a memorable experience of a night out on the ice cap. But after their supper they turned in, snugly nestling into their bags in nothing more than their underclothing, all of their furs having been removed and neatly stowed away.

At four o'clock Peary was awakened by the noise of the wind, and by drift which was pouring in a fine stream through a small hole in the igloo. But Cook having turned out and plugged the hole, they had all gone back to sleep. For how long they slept, he does not say. That they woke up only just in time there is, however, little doubt, judging by their predicament:

Looking over the foot of my bag, I could see, in the faint light of day, that the cutting drift had eaten off the angle of the igloo where the roof and end wall met, had completely filled that end, and was rapidly covering us.

Peary and Cook were able to haul themselves out of the drift, but Astrup lay buried and unable to move. The situation was desperate:

Telling Dr. Cook to keep a breathing hole open for Astrup, I rose up in my bag, forced the ski apart, rolled out over the wall, bag and all, and reached the shovel at the entrance, then rolled back to the end of the igloo, and crouched against the wall on the outside to get my breath. Then I crept around to the side where Astrup was, and crouching before the howling wind, tore through the side wall and freed his head and body, and with the Doctor's assistance, pulled him out.

For a full day and another night they crouched there in their sleeping bags with no shelter from the roaring wind. A search for their clothing had only succeeded in digging out Peary's dog-skin trousers. All of the rest lay deeply buried under the massive drift of snow, and with the blizzard then turning to freezing rain it had seemed as though they could never survive. But then the storm began to ease and, hanging by the thread of hope, the three men fell asleep.

When I next awoke, I found the opening of my hood closed with balls of ice, but the wind was much less violent, and the intervals between gusts were longer. Putting out a hand and tearing away the ice, I looked out, and to my delight found moonlight flooding the Inland Ice, the moon having just broken through a rift in the black clouds over Herbert Island. It had stopped snowing, but the wind was still whirling the fine snow along the surface.

I immediately conveyed the pleasing intelligence to the boys, and learning from the Doctor that he was cold, I got over to him as well as I could in my sleeping bag and curled myself around and against the head of his bag, to windward. This expedient did not succeed in making him more comfortable, and as the temperature was rapidly lowering I rolled back, got the shovel, and succeeded in digging a hole down into the snow. I then got the Doctor's bag loose, pulled the sleeves out of the frozen crust, adjusted his hood, and helped him to wriggle to the hole, down which he tumbled and curled himself up. I then placed my trousers over his head to keep the drift off, and curled myself round the windward edge of the hole above him. I was glad to find that the complete protection from the wind thus afforded him, together with the exercise of moving, restored his temperature and rendered him entirely comfortable.

In this way we lay for several hours, the wind gradually dying away, and the light of day increasing.

It was not until 11.45 a.m. on Tuesday, 16th that they finally came through their ordeal. By then they had succeeded in digging all of their clothing out of the drift, had warmed themselves with exercise, and the southern sky was aflame with colour:

> In an instant the snow waves of the Inland Ice about us danced, a sea of sparkling, molten gold. Neither gold, nor fame, nor aught can purchase from me the supreme memory of that moment when on the ice-cap, far above the earth, with the rustling of the Stars and Stripes in my ears, I laughed with the laughing waves of the great white sea, in greeting to the returning sun.

Returning to Red Cliff House, Peary's mind was now to focus on the main object of his first long sojourn in the North: the crossing of the ice cap to the extreme north-east corner of Greenland, and his preparation and training for this journey was to take him on several short trips. One of these he made on 5th April with Astrup and an Eskimo guide across to the deserted village at the east end of Herbert Island where there now stands a cluster of thirteen wooden huts, in one of which I lived for two years with my wife and baby daughter in 1971–3. Another he made with Jo, a delightful 250-mile sledge journey which took them on a tour of the Eskimo settlements and camps around Whale Sound and Inglefield Gulf in search of more dogs and additional furs and materials. On both of these trips he used a native dog driver, and his total sledging experience with dogs at the start of his great ice cap journey (largely as the result of his injury before even setting foot ashore) was surprisingly little, probably no more than about three hundred miles.

He knew even less about the ice cap and admits it:

> I was more or less in the dark ... as to the probable altitude to be reached, there was nothing to guide me. It might not be over 6,000 feet; it might be 15,000. I could only devise my equipment in such a way that it would meet, as far as possible, every contingency and every extreme.

Seen in this light, that journey he made from his winter quarters right over the ice cap and into the unknown region of North-East Greenland was certainly courageous. And yet that journey seems oddly out of step with the drummer of all of his earlier dreams.

His clothing and dogs were Eskimo, but not his method of driving dogs, and his fixation with the ice cap could hardly have been further from the native mind, for whilst to them the Inland Ice was a featureless and lifeless place, he seems to have somehow got the idea that it would be for him an "Imperial Highway" to the North Pole, a certain route to fame. Of the twenty dogs with which he set out from Red Cliff House on 3rd May, four died within a few days, one escaped, and two returned with the supporting party, leaving him only thirteen dogs with which to make the crossing and return safely. He was not carrying an ounce of food more than the minimum he would need and he planned on laying no depots. In short, he took an amazing risk, and with little or no chance of finding a single geographical feature which he could claim to discover, except at the very extreme of his range. And yet such a feature, indeed, a vista, he eventually found:

A few steps more, and the rocky plateau on which we stood dropped in a giant iron wall that would grace the Inferno, 3,800 feet to the level of the bay below us. We stood upon the north-east coast of Greenland and, looking far over the surface of a mighty glacier on our right and through the broad mouth of the bay, we saw stretching away to the horizon the great ice-fields of the Arctic Ocean.

From the edge of the towering cliff on which we stood, and in the clear light of the brilliant summer day, the view that spread away before us was magnificent beyond description. Silently Astrup and myself took off our packs and seated ourselves upon them to fix in memory every detail of the never-to-be-forgotten scene before us. All our fatigues of six weeks' struggle over the ice-cap were forgotten in the grandeur of that view.

. . . Looking to the west, we saw the opening of the fjord that had barred our northern advance . . . Now we knew that we had paralleled its course from Robeson Channel clear to the Arctic Ocean off the shores of north-east Greenland. For days we had kept constantly in view the mountain masses forming the southern boundary of this channel, and through rifts in the mountains we had from time to time seen this depression, and had now and then caught glimpses of the frozen channel occupying it; and we had seen beyond it mountains and fjords stretching between them. It was evident that this channel marked the northern boundary of the mainland of Greenland.

Peary had made that hazardous, 1,200-mile journey by cutting his margin of safety to the bone, and had he and his sole companion, Eivind Astrup, not found musk-oxen at the end of their outward journey, it is unlikely they would have returned to tell of their amazing trek and announce their discoveries.

Those discoveries in North-East Greenland, however, were not to survive the test of time, for Peary had fallen into the trap which lies waiting for every single explorer at the extreme limit of his range: the trap of guessing what lies beyond what he can clearly see. The outcome was a map that was virtually worthless and misled other explorers into taking risks they should not have taken, with loss of life and unnecessary suffering as the result. Eventually those errors in Peary's map of North-East Greenland (errors which showed the "Peary Channel") were acknowledged by the Hydrographic Office and, in response to a resolution introduced by Congressman Henry T. Helgesen in the House of Representatives in January 1916 (and later correspondence), the map was "officially cancelled and withdrawn."

Cook and Gibson, Peary's supporting party, returned to Red Cliff House on 3rd June to the enormous relief of Jo, for her relations with Verhoeff had deteriorated even further during the absence of Peary and, to ease the strain, the returning pair set out with Verhoeff on a boating trip, leaving Jo in the care of Matt Henson. But her nightmare was not yet over, for when the *Kite* returned on 24th July to take the expedition home, Peary and Astrup had still not arrived and there was pressure on Jo to abandon her husband to his fate. The Eskimos had also had their say: "Mr. Peary is dead!" But on 6th August, while Jo was on the *Kite* and half asleep, she was roused by the sounds of oars and men's voices; by someone jumping over the rail on to the deck above her head. She knew it was her husband, but found herself unable to move until he forced the door of her cabin open and proved to her he was there.

Now at last they could all go home – all, that is, except Verhoeff. From the boating party to the head of Bowdoin Bay he had set off to return to Red Cliff House by an overland route he had taken before, and was never seen again. Peary was to name the glacier on which presumably Verhoeff met his death after that young man who hated him, and in his book had these words to offer:

It is needless to say that this accident cast the deepest gloom upon every member of both parties; it was so sudden, so unexpected, like a flash of lightning from a clear sky, occurring as it did in the height of the summer, after all the possibilities of the winter and of the ice-cap work had been surmounted without the least accident. I could think of nothing else as the *Kite*, on the 24th, after six days of unremitting search, slowly swung out of Robertson Bay.

But perhaps Peary did have some other things on his mind as he sailed for home. The physical achievement of crossing the ice cap was clearly not enough to convince the scientific Establishment and his superiors in the Navy that the expedition had been worthwhile and whether his claims to have determined "the northern extension and the insularity of Greenland" and to have discovered "detached ice-free land-masses of less extent to the northward" was what he genuinely believed, or whether he was taking a chance on no other explorers visiting that area before he had revisited it and corrected his first impressions, it is difficult to be sure. Either way, it had been a rash claim.

What Peary was soon to discover, however, was its effect upon his standing as an explorer. Within weeks of returning he was lifted by all the approbation so far along the road to fame, that he was now committed to going on, if only to extend and consolidate his impressive discoveries in the far north of Greenland, and this must surely have been underlined by the letter of congratulations he received from his generous rival, Fridtjof Nansen, who signed himself "Your admirer":

I hope you will not think it impudent when I now send you my most heartfelt congratulations on your wonderful achievements and grand results. Certainly not many will better understand what a piece of work you have performed, and not many have awaited with more impatience to hear what you would find in the unknown North of the inland ice.

Peary now had to produce a plan even more eye-catching than the previous one in order to get another leave of absence, for there was now a strong undercurrent of envy and resentment flowing against him within the Navy. By this time, however, Peary not only had the strength of his own convictions and a "success" behind him, but he had found the formula for winning the support of those with power and influence – he offered himself discreetly, modestly, secretly as the man who would reach the North Pole.

CHAPTER 7

The Deepening Obsession

With the nagging doubt about his discoveries in North-East Greenland, it was of course prudent, at least when making his public statements and formally presenting his new objectives, that Peary should be slightly more cautious. He would, he stressed, continue the work of his previous expedition, but with a larger party would seek this time to define the limits "of the detached lands lying north of main Greenland," by which he was referring to Heilprin Land, the land mass to the north of the so-called Peary Channel, which in 1906 Mylius Erichsen was to discover to his cost did not exist. His second objective would be to fill in "the remaining gaps in the northern and north-eastern coast-line of Greenland," and his third, deceptively low in the list, would be to make "an attempt upon the Pole".

This plan, however, although impressive, needed some very powerful backing if Peary was to get his orders to report to the Navy Yard, Norfolk, replaced by three years' paid leave of absence. It needed an influential friend who could whisper into the official ear of the Secretary of the Navy. Such a man was the president of the Philadelphia Academy of Natural Sciences, General I. J. Wistar, and it was to him that Peary turned for help. The Academy had been one of Peary's sponsors on his last successful expedition, and Wistar, being a patriot, was determined that Peary should have his chance and carry the flag to the Pole. And so, after questioning Peary closely on almost all aspects of his plan except the overall cost of the expedition and from where or whom he proposed to get the money, he gave the anxious Lieutenant his blessing: "On the understanding that the Academy will not be called upon for any money, its endowment not being lawfully available for this purpose, and will not be responsible for the risks to yourself and your companions, I will use my best efforts to obtain your leave."

Hardly surprising that Peary's fellow officers were envious of his powerful friends, for without actually spending a single day on active duty after his triumphant return from his first expedition to North-West Greenland, and at the very moment when the full weight of his superiors' condemnation had been launched against any further official support of his aspirations, Peary had been granted, simply by the nod of a head, three years' paid leave of absence with the approval of the President of the United States to devote himself exclusively to planning, preparing and conducting his next Arctic expedition.

> I had six months in which to raise the funds, organise my party, and equip and fit my Expedition. It was too much work for the time, and though it was done, some of it was not carefully done. This applies specially to the selection of my party. Carried away by enthusiasm, and with no time in the rapid whirl of effort for a calm consideration of the matter, I made the fatal mistake of taking, contrary to my expressed theory, a large party. I found, when too late, that I had very little suitable timber for Arctic work in it.

He needed $80,000 to secure a ship and all his equipment, a formidable target, particularly since he was now determined to defray the entire expense himself and thereby avoid, on this occasion, the temptation of taking on board any man who might presume (as had John Verhoeff) that in return for a few thousand dollars he had some right of influence upon the leader's plans. There was no other way of raising the money than by throwing himself into a series of lectures. But Peary was no orator, nor did he ever waste his dreams in wishing he might be one. It is therefore very much to his credit that in spite of his loathing of public speaking he had, with Henson, tackled each lecture engagement head on – for their performances by all accounts were something of a sensation.

Dressed up in his Arctic furs Peary would shuffle on to the stage which was set to look like an Eskimo camp. Then on would come Henson, cracking his whip and driving a team of five Eskimo dogs, the latter having being trained by Henson to lie quietly at the feet of the master until his lecture had run its time, whereupon, or so it is said, the dogs would set up a plaintive howl and bring the show to a close.

For a full three months this two-man act with its five performing Eskimo dogs was almost continually on the move with their notoriety as entertainers always one town ahead of the show and an ever increasing number of incidents trailing away behind them. In ninety-six days on the lecture circuit they gave an astonishing 168 performances at a profit to Major Pond's lecture bureau of some $20,000, of which Peary is believed to have received $13,000. It was one of the most strenuous lecture tours that had ever been arranged by that great impresario. Indeed, he claimed it was "one of the greatest lecture tours America had ever seen." And yet throughout this exhausting tour, Peary was frantically organising an expedition that was set to leave within a few weeks of his return to New York.

In applications alone it is said he received very nearly two thousand letters from young men and women who wanted to join his next expedition, or had merely applied (as they still do today) to impress their less adventurous friends of their courage in having done so. Fortunately his task in selecting twelve intelligent and loyal young men for his second winter in North-West Greenland had been reduced by the almost immediate and eager response of three of the members of his previous trip: Eivind Astrup, in spite of the hard time he had on the ice cap; Matthew Henson, in spite of the fact that his social status would remain unchanged and he would still be at the bottom of the pack, and Dr. Cook, in spite (we can only suppose) of his better judgement.

Cook had been caught by the spell of the Arctic, but had a deep and nagging doubt about serving a second winter with Peary. There were no such doubts in the other direction. Peary needed Dr. Cook, as is evident from the tribute he paid him in the book in which he relates so vividly some of the hardships that they had shared:

> To Dr. Cook's care may be attributed the almost complete exemption of the party from even the mildest indispositions, and personally I owe much to his professional skill, and unruffled patience and coolness in an emergency. In addition to his work in his special ethnological field, in which he has obtained a large mass of most valuable material concerning a practically unstudied tribe, he was always helpful and an indefatigable worker.

His study of the Eskimos, as reported in some of the newspapers covering the achievements of Peary's expedition, had attracted the attention of a great many of his fellow physicians and, in response to many requests, Cook presented a lecture on certain anthropological aspects of the Smith Sound Eskimos at the King's County Medical Society in Brooklyn. The lecture had fascinated his audience, and many of those who had heard him that evening had urged him to publish his work in a medical journal, since only part of it had gone into the report Peary had made to the Philadelphia Academy of Natural Sciences, and this had been under Peary's name. He had of course given credit to Cook: "The report would be incomplete without an acknowledgement of my obligation to Dr. Cook, patient and skillful surgeon, indefatigable worker, earnest student of the peculiar people among whom we lived; he has obtained, I believe, a record of the tribe unapproachable in ethnological archives."

This acknowledgement, however, generous though it was, had merely underlined the point that the colleagues of Cook had been making: that the data now needed to be published in full and under the authorship of the researcher who had conducted the study. And so the doctor, who was on respectfully good terms with Peary and had already been appointed second-in-command, paid a courtesy call on Peary to ask permission to publish the article. But Peary flatly refused his request, reminding the astonished Cook of the contract he had signed, and pointing out that if, as a special favour to Cook, he was to release him from his agreement, that very same favour would be expected by all of the others in their party who might suddenly find the need or the urge to see themselves in print.

Cook felt the ruling unfair, since the article he was wanting to write would confine itself strictly to his medical and ethnological studies and could not conceivably have any effect on the sales of any book Peary would write. But Peary had refused to shift on the issue, and Cook "on a matter of principle" had politely resigned.

"Here was the only break I had with Peary," Cook was later to write in an autobiographic sketch. "I resigned then and there as a volunteer, but did so in a friendly way." But "friendly" though it may have been, that disagreement and its outcome had weakened Peary's team. He now had to find, and at very short notice, a suitable replacement for Dr. Cook, and although (according to the doctor) there was "no lingering malice" between them, Peary was shaken and even confused by Cook's inability, as Peary saw it, to understand the leader's need to protect his vested interests.

Cook's contract in fact had been no different to any of those which had been signed by the members of Peary's previous expedition, and the same form of contract he now was requiring each of the members of his new team to sign. It was a perfectly straightforward legal agreement which stated that Peary was the commander and that each signatory would be committed to "loyally aid and support the said Peary by all means in his power, to accomplish each and every object and purpose of the expedition aforesaid, in such manner as the said Peary shall deem best and require." It also committed each man who signed it to refrain from writing or lecturing on the subject of the expedition for one year after their return, and bound each member of the expedition to hand over all diaries, journals, scientific observations and notes to Peary. This is in fact the standard contract which even today all far-sighted leaders who are carrying the full financial responsibility insist on each member signing, especially if they are expecting to recoup some of the expenses through sales of an expedition book.

Sadly, in the case of Peary, it was not just a financial matter. He saw any aspirations in others as a direct and dangerous threat to his own. Even the mild-mannered Dr. Cook, who could have been such a useful companion, had to be discarded once he had shown the need to publish. This Peary went to some lengths to hide, telling reporters how much he regretted that Dr. Cook was unable to sail with them because of his "professional engagements." The excuse was specious. Only Astrup, Henson and Jo knew that the regret was genuine.

He was also to regret many of the other decisions he made under pressure during those last few hectic weeks before the departure of the *Falcon* from Philadelphia on that "raw and disagreeable" 23rd June, 1893. Besides his party, which was too large and which he had not taken enough care in selecting, he took eight burros from Santa Fe, New Mexico, which were to prove of no more use than as fresh meat for the ravenous dogs, and several homing pigeons, only one of which ever carried a message, the rest having either died of the cold or been caught by falcons.

Indeed the same sad thread seems to run right through almost every aspect of this disastrous expedition, for with the happy exception of his decision to take his wife Jo with him a second time, and the birth of his first child, Marie Ahnighito Peary, at Anniversary Lodge on 12th September, 1893, hardly a thing went right from the day the *Falcon* left the party at its winter quarters in Bowdoin Bay on 20th August, 1893, until two years later when the *Kite* came north to collect the very dispirited man who no longer had any illusions about the work that still lay before him.

How deeply consoling Marie's birth must have been in the midst of so much secret doubt and self-inflicted misery Peary himself makes clear:

This little blue-eyed snowflake, born at the close of the arctic summer day, deep in the heart of the White North, far beyond the farthest limits of civilized people or habitations, saw the cold, gray light of the arctic autumn once only before the great night settled upon us. Then she was bundled deep in soft, warm arctic furs, and wrapped in the Stars and Stripes.

Throughout the winter she was the source of the livest interest to the natives. Entire families journeyed from far-away Cape York to the south, and from Etah to the north, to satisfy themselves by actual touch that she was really a creature of warm flesh and blood, and not of snow, as they at first believed.

Within only a few days of this happy event, Astrup, who was away from base with orders "to establish a depot of supplies as far in on the Inland Ice as possible," was taken seriously ill with gastric fever; three sledges had been "blown away without leaving a vestige," and on the night of 31st October, while Peary was at the moraine waiting for an opportunity to get on to the ice cap:

. . . a big wave, caused by the breaking of a huge iceberg from Bowdoin Glacier, rushed into Falcon Harbour, burst up through the solid ice near the shore in a roaring cataract of water and foam; rolled the steam launch, which had been hauled up for the winter at the head of the harbour, over and over and stove her in; dashed the whale-boat *Faith*, which had been hauled up at the mouth of the brook, a hundred yards up the valley and ruined her; then receding, carried down with it into a vortex of grinding ice-cakes all [the] oil barrels, the dory, several bales of hay from the burro stable, and a number of puppies.

"The fates and all hell are against me," Peary is said to have cried out on hearing the bad news which young Hugh Lee rushed to bring him, "but I'll conquer yet!"

His plan had been to cross the ice cap with a party of eight men and, from somewhere in the region of Independence Bay, to split into three parties: two men staying in the musk-ox grounds to hunt and build up a large reserve of carcass meat, while one three-man party followed the coast south, and the other went north, even perhaps to the Pole itself. The elements, however, had other plans. Within eight days of setting out from Anniversary Lodge, Peary's party was reduced by sickness and frostbite, and then the storms hit them:

> For thirty-four hours the average wind velocity had been over forty-eight miles per hour, and the average temperature about minus 50 degrees Fahrenheit, with a minimum of over minus 60 . . . When these figures are considered in connection with our elevation of some 5,000 feet . . . the judgement will be that this storm beats the record as the most severe ever experienced by any Arctic party.

Two more men were forced to turn back, the dogs were failing, the sledges were breaking, and yet, with Peary's plan already shattered, he still pushed on way beyond the point of reason. Finally, on 10th April, with two of his companions frostbitten and the other suffering from severe cramps, and with an epidemic among his dogs that was threatening to halve his pack "or even exterminate it entirely," he "regretfully" called a halt, paid tribute to his companions who, as he says, "showed true grit and were willing to push on," then cached his supplies, and turned back. This cache, set up at an elevation of some 5,500 feet above sea level and about 128 miles from his winter quarters, was never seen again.

From this gruelling and heart-breaking journey, Peary and his companions returned on 18th April, and it was some two weeks before they recovered from the strain and their exposure to the storms. But for Peary the "inaction was unbearable," for he had been deeply hurt and angered on reaching the lodge to learn that Eivind Astrup, having recovered slightly from the illness which had prevented him from joining the ice cap party, had set off on 6th April with his "favorite native friend," Koolootingwah, on a journey south to Cape York in the hope of sledging eastward along the coast to get "a close view of the unexplored shores of Melville Bay". Peary makes no comment in his book on his reactions to this news. Nor does he comment on how he received Astrup on his return, thirty-seven days later, from that successful little expedition which he had made, unforgivably, without seeking Peary's permission. A clue to what Peary was feeling, however, can be seen in the excuses for having failed to cross the ice cap and his claim that their survival was in a sense success.

> The causes of failure of the trip are to be found primarily in the extremely antagonistic weather, and secondarily in my failure to properly appreciate the limits of endurance of the Eskimo dog. With regard to the weather, the number and duration of the storms, the incessancy and violence of the wind, and the uninterrupted low temperatures were exceptional even for this region; and the exemption of the members of the party from permanent injury, as a result of their continued exposure, shows conclusively the perfection and adequateness of their clothing.

But greater than Peary's self-delusion at this early stage in his career was Peary's need to dominate, and cast adrift without compunction any member of his party who would not accept his ruling or fell short of his demands. It would have been so easy had he been a natural leader to congratulate the younger man and openly and gratefully accept his contribution. But, sadly, Astrup's survey of the northern coast of Melville Bay had drawn attention to flaws within his own ambitious plans and this from Peary's point of view, half-blinded as he was by fear that he was losing all the ground that he had fought so hard to gain, he now saw as disloyalty.

Astrup, confused and hurt, and believing that Peary would not include the report of his journey to Melville Bay in his official account of the expedition, was persuaded to publish the results of his journey on his return to his homeland, Norway. This incensed Peary, who was now obliged to include Astrup's report and map in his book or to suffer the jibes of those who knew that he was suppressing what the Paris Geographical Society had described as "the principal result of the expedition." The sting is still there in Peary's footnote to that report:

> The contents of this chapter have already been published, Astrup having disposed of his paper immediately after his return home in 1894. Recognising, however, that his apparent discourtesy was only the natural result of youthful eagerness to see himself in print, I am only

too glad to give his work what I hope will be a more permanent form and wide-spread circulation than it would be likely to obtain in the form in which he himself published it.

Astrup did not live to read that footnote in Peary's book, *Northward Over the Great Ice*. He died at the age of twenty-four while skiing alone in the Doorefjeld Mountains of Norway in January 1896, two years before his own delightful book, *With Peary Near the Pole*, was published. The circumstances surrounding his death were, and are still, a mystery. Dr. Cook, however, writing in 1911 offers this contribution with surprisingly little concern for evidence to support his opinion:

Astrup was disabled by poisoning, due to Peary's carelessness in furnishing poisoned food. Recovering from this illness, he selected a trustworthy Eskimo companion, went south, and under almost inconceivable difficulties, explored and mapped the ice walls, with their glaciers and mountains, and the off-lying islands of Melville Bay. This proved a creditable piece of work of genuine discovery. Returning, he prepared his data and published it, thus bringing credit and honor on an expedition which was in other respects a failure.

Astrup's publication of this work aroused Peary's envy. Publicly Peary denounced Astrup. Astrup, being young and sensitive, brooded over this injustice and ingratitude until he had almost lost his reason. The abuse was of the same nature as that heaped on others ... For days and weeks, Astrup talked of nothing but the infamy of Peary's attack on himself and the contemptible charge of desertion which Peary made against Astrup's companions. Then he suddenly left my home, returned to Norway, and we next heard of his suicide. Here was one life directly chargeable to Peary's narrow and intolerant brutality. Directly this was not murder with a knife – but it was as heinous – for a young and noble life was cut short by the cowardly dictates of jealous egotism.

Cook in his venom against Peary was also quick to lay Verhoeff's death on the previous expedition to Peary's charge. Again, writing several years after the events, he recalls that Verhoeff "was treated with about the same consideration as that accorded the Eskimo dogs," although, in fairness, there is evidence also in the literature that both Peary and Jo on many occasions tried hard to appease and please Verhoeff. Cook, however, is adamant:

When I last saw him in camp, he was in tears, telling of Peary's injustice. Mrs. Peary – I advert to this with all possible reluctance –

had done much to make his life bitter, and over this he talked for days. Finally he said: "I will never go home in the same ship with that man and that woman." It was the last sentence he uttered in my hearing. He did not go home in that ship. Instead, he wandered off over the glacier, where he left his body in the blue depths of a crevass.

As for Peary, as soon as his dogs were in a condition to travel again after his abortive ice cap journey he set out with Jo on a five-day trip to explore and map Olriks Fjord. He tells us that he and Jo were "the first white persons ever to penetrate the innermost recesses of this striking fjord, which winds like a great river between giant cliffs and rolling deer pastures, to its source against the face of the Marie Glacier sweeping down from the 'Great Ice.'" But apart from that very local and insignificant discovery, and another short trip westward to complete his surveys and collect walrus meat, he did no serious travelling until after Astrup's return, when he was suddenly galvanised into action by the need to produce some results.

But what could he do? There was no time left in which to do any mapping, but he had to do something that would compete for attention with Astrup's embarrassingly successful journey down to Melville Bay. The idea then came to him. The Englishman, John Ross, who had discovered the local Eskimos in 1818, had seen knives and harpoon heads made from a "metal" which Peary believed might have come from a meteorite; so, with a reluctant Eskimo guide, he set off down the coast with a team of ten dogs in search of "the 'Iron Mountain' of Melville Bay," and eventually located three *saviksue*, as the native people called them. His only white companion on this journey was Lee, his youngest and most loyal assistant, and the only other member of his party (besides the ever faithful Matthew Henson) who volunteered to stay on with Peary for another year when the *Falcon* returned on 20th August, 1894, to take the party home. From Lee's touching letter to his mother the picture is so very clear:

Mr. Peary is having some quite hard luck. Sometimes it seems as if I could almost cry, but that would do no good of course. The boys have all gone back on him and I am about the only one who is faithful to him – poor little weak me. Oh, what can I do for him, what can I do for him! Almost nothing. If anything is the matter at home that you need me I shall be in a sad state for he needs me and I shall hate to leave him. It will be hard, hard indeed. You do not know how I feel towards that man. The more the boys talk against him, the more I like him ... All the boys are so down on him and if there is any fault on either side, and I believe there is, it is all on their side as nearly as I can make out ... All the boys know that I am true to my contract; that I am loyal to Mr. Peary.

Peary had, in effect, a mutiny on his hands, but in his book he would not admit it:

> Davidson and Carr were invalided, the former with a frosted heel, the latter with a weak back; the other members of my party had discovered that Arctic work was not entirely the picnic they had imagined, and wisely regarding discretion as the better part of valour, had decided to return home; Lee and Henson alone possessed the grit and loyalty to remain.

His men were disillusioned by the time the ship arrived, and bitter when later they read Peary's book, *Northward Over the Great Ice*. Commenting in 1910 on that very passage, Samuel J. Entrikin, the man who replaced Cook as his second-in-command, had written:

> No man of his rank should be found guilty of trying to belittle his men who had often risked their lives that he might eventually wear the coveted laurels (which are now fading). His men served him well, the best they could under the conditions. It was not long before some of the men lost confidence in Peary and saw they would get little credit for their labors. His own book shows he did not have sufficient outfit to keep the party another year. Several agreed to remain another year if Peary could show the outfit to remain on, which he could not do. We were living on short rations when the *Falcon* arrived without stores for another year. Some stores were secured for those who remained.

In a letter to Entrikin from Dr. Cook dated 25th September, 1895, there is an indication also of the growing rift between Cook and Peary: "Peary's failure is sad news, for it will throw another shadow on Polar work, but it is what you and all of us knew the bad shape of his equipment expected. He has fought hard and against tremendous odds to accomplish something. He deserves sympathy."

A letter also from Evelyn B. Baldwin – another member of that ill-fated 1893–4 expedition, supports Entrikin's view of things. Baldwin was to become a competitor of Peary's and was to feature in the Cook story, but here he is defending himself against that slur on his character in Peary's book, and coming up with a slightly different impression regarding Peary's original intention:

The members of the expedition were led to believe that we were to be absent two years. I believed Mr. Peary's statement to that effect implicitly ... Upon our arrival in Greenland that summer the report became current that the chartered expedition ship *Falcon* would come up for us a year later for the purpose of taking the entire party home. I doubted the reliability of the rumor until Captain Henry Bartlett, master of the ship, assured me that it was true.

I thereupon went to Lieutenant Peary regarding the matter, as I was desirous of sending word to friends for business as well as personal reasons. To my inquiry he replied: "Whoever told you any such thing may get fooled!" All of this was confirmed the next year when the *Falcon* arrived as empty as a drum so far as food was concerned.

In addition to what I have already stated, my reply includes the following facts which completely shatter Peary's charge of disloyalty: First, in the course of our return march from the sledge-journey in 1894, Mr. Peary had told Messrs. Entrikin, Clark and myself, who had remained in the field with him until he turned us back, that he would have supplies sufficient for the second year for three men only. On this occasion Peary asked the three of us if we would volunteer to remain the next year. I distinctly heard both Mr. Entrikin and Mr. Clark say they would. I replied that I preferred to reserve my answer till the arrival of the ship.

It was on 26th August, 1894, almost a year to the day after they had arrived in Bowdoin Bay, that the *Falcon* finally turned for home with all of the members of the expedition on board except for the desolate Lee. He had been left to look after the lodge while Peary and Henson, together with five Eskimo hunters, were to be taken some two hundred miles down the coast before leaving the ship near Petowik Glacier to make their own way back to the lodge in the whale-boat, *General Wistar*, doing some local surveys on the way.

On the morning of the 28th he parted from his wife and baby, fearing the worst and yet trying so very hard not to show it. In a letter to Jo which he wrote on 9th September he recalled:

As long as I could see I looked for the white handkerchief fluttering from your cabin port. My brave sweet wife. I wondered, dear, if you thought as you saw my little boat sail go tossing northwards into the coming Arctic night of these lines of Tennyson – "sad as the last beam glittering on a sail/That sinks with all we love below the verge."

And in his diary:

> So ends with the vanishing ship the ill-omened first half of my expedition and begins the second.

They arrived back at Anniversary Lodge on 6th September, having had to walk the last few miles because there was too much ice in the bay, and now there were only three of them left – one with an obsession that was cruelly misdirected, the other two still driven by their callow admiration to do whatever he would ask of them and risk their lives to please him. But in spite of the loyalty of his two companions, Peary's loneliness at first seemed crushing, for with it had come that first real taste of bitterness and failure. His letters to Jo and his diary tell it all:

> 9th Sept, 1894
>
> The night I returned to the lodge I stepped in your room for a few moments but I could not stay there and I slept on the bench in the dining room. I cannot sleep in the room yet. I know dear now just how I shall feel should you pass on before me to the great hereafter. But the sun is leaving and I am getting the blues. You will know wherever you are that I have been with you this evening.

> 30th December, 1894
>
> Ah! Darling, the room is cold and cheerless. Frost is on the walls and overhead. I throw myself across our bed; I stretch my dangling arms to you but I am too sad, too weary of myself and all the world for words.

> 6th January, 1895
>
> Cold and more cheerless yet seems the room tonight, and I stretch yearning across to you from a sad heart. Never have I felt more lonely than tonight, never if God grants me to take you in my arms again will I leave you for so long again. The past runs black, the future blacker. Matt is still sick, Lee is in a condition that I fear for his sanity, and I feel at times that I am going mad. I have lost my sanguine hope, my elan, I am an old man; I think at times perhaps I have lost you.

Only by brute force was he able to drag himself out of this depression to the hunting grounds to build up a supply of meat for the winter, and with this activity being more important than anything else, it was not until late in September that he was able to turn his thoughts once again to the ice cap and his need to check his caches, one of which was twenty-six miles from the lodge, the other, 128 miles. Never once did it appear to cross his mind that he might not be able to find them, and in sending out Henson, Lee and an Eskimo on 2nd October to re-erect any markers that might have blown down, he felt sure this would be the last activity before settling down to a comfortable winter. But to his dismay, they returned only four days later without having found the first cache and without going on to search for the second.

Compelled by the need to make another search, Peary set out on the 8th with Matt, an Eskimo and a team of ten dogs. By the end of the second day they were in the vicinity of the first cache but the weather was closing in. The Eskimo, seeing the storm coming, decided to leave and Peary made no effort to follow or stop him since "his absence would very materially economize our food supply, and enable us to stand a longer siege." It was to take that Eskimo four days to reach the lodge, by which time he was so weak with hunger and cold that he was barely able to crawl. Meanwhile, up on the ice cap, Peary and Matt were pinned down by the blizzard:

> After the first three days I could not sleep and could only lie and listen to the infernal driving of the snow against the tent, knowing that the demonic white downpour was destroying the last chance of finding my caches, destroying all the work of the previous year on which I had counted so largely to assist me the next spring, reducing my resources to the very minimum, and perhaps even destroying every chance of success next year. Plans for the future failed me. Interest in anything refused to be aroused; thoughts of wife and blue-eyed baby, or mother, pictures of boyhood, happy scenes and memories before this devil of Arctic exploration took possession of me, rose and ranged themselves opposite to the precious hours of my life being wasted, the sacrifices of me and mine, all perhaps to end in naught, till it seemed as if with this, and the unceasing hissing of the wind and snow, I should lose my reason.

All of his essential supplies for the following spring's sledging journey, which amounted to nearly a ton and a half and included every ounce of his alcohol and pemmican, lay buried and lost, "and yet," he later wrote, "the idea of abandoning the journey, even in the face of this apparently overwhelming disaster, never for a moment occurred to me, nor, I think, to either of my companions." He threw himself into the task of making-do with what he had got, of devising, planning, willing himself (and with him his men) across those vast and empty wastes to the game grounds of Independence Bay, knowing full well that his chances of even getting that far would depend entirely on luck.

Now came the nightmares – the recurring dream of failure: "I was back home again without having been able to make another attack upon the ice cap." And, finally:

Anniversary Lodge,
March 31, 1895

My Darling:

It is the eve of our departure for the great ice, and I sit down to write to you what I know I shall later hand you myself. I do not know why, but I cannot collect my thoughts to write as I wish. The winter has been a nightmare to me. I have been to the shrine regularly, but the cold, damp, frost-lined room has made me think of the tomb. The only bright moments have been when I was thinking of you and old times, my wife, my darling. I have kissed the place where your head rested, have kissed my blue-eyed baby's socks, and I carry with me next to my heart your last letter and your little guidon. These will go with me to the end, where and how it may be.

I start with provisions and equipment evolved almost from nothing. As you will see from my journal which is in the larger of the tin lock-boxes under the floor of our room, the enormous snowfall of last summer lost me everything on the icecap, biscuit, milk, pea soup, cranberry jam, pemmican, and worst of all, alcohol. I am obliged to use kerosene for fuel and this the Saint John's article of such poor quality that it becomes like condensed milk at temperatures not far below zero, and I have been obliged to devise a cooker in which I can keep a small flame going constantly during the upward trip. For meat I have venison, some cooked and some raw; and for dog food walrus meat. I can carry full rations only for the outward and return trips to Independence Bay ... beyond ... I must depend entirely upon the game of the country.

I have named my sledge made on the Greenland pattern the *Josephine* after the woman I love and a little trailer sledge *Chopsie* after my baby. I start with thirty-five dogs of my own and thirty hired ones. I have with me four natives who will form a supporting party and have promised to accompany us for ten days, which ought to carry us past our farthest of last spring. I have had a great deal of trouble in getting dogs, thanks to the loyalty of the Norwegian member of the expedition, who has told the natives that he was coming here in a year or two and if they kept dogs for him he would give a gun for every two. I owe Ingerapadoo and Akplisuahlio, members of the boat crew that went to Cape York, each a gun. The others I have settled with. I have a sledge contracted for with Poodloanah for Chopsie and I have a standing offer of a flask of powder for a young bearskin for her. Of the three narwhal heads and tusks on the roof, one is for Emil [Jo's brother], whose kindness I shall always remember, one for Bridgman who is more than thoughtful . . . the other for you.

The papers and records are in the steamer trunk and the two lock tin boxes. These with the ammunition are cached under the floor of our room and the remaining provisions piled over them. There has been no chance to put them anywhere else owing to the constant presence of the Eskimo. After thinking the matter over carefully I felt they would be safer from theft and fire here than anywhere else. Two of the guns are also under the floor, three behind the books and your shotgun in one of the closets. One shotgun and one carbine I have loaned to Nuktah, who will remain here till the ship comes. I have promised him Stokes' house. The other three men who accompany us will summer at Karnah, and I have promised them that portion of the house east of the partition between what was formerly dining room and kitchen and the men's room. Should I not return the rest of the house should go back on the ship. Put on exhibition it will make you independent. All the keys I have put back of the books on the very top shelf.

Good-bye my darling.

Bert

He also left behind a letter addressed to: "Mrs. Peary or my Representative on the Ship," shorter than the other, more impersonal, but on some points more specific:

I shall do all that a man can do. The example of my predecessors who, like myself, have carried in their bosoms the fairest flag the sun ever shone on, will let me do no less. The rest is in His hands.

My movements after reaching Independence Bay and killing and caching as many musk-oxen as possible will depend entirely upon circumstances. It is unnecessary to enumerate possibilities, as once I have put a hundred miles of the Great Ice between me and the Lodge no human help could find or avail us in the event of a catastrophe. I shall return on or before Sept 1st. Nook-tah has a letter for Mrs. Peary. Kindly give the bearer of this a handful of powder.

R. E. Peary

They set out from the lodge with six Eskimos, six sledges and sixty dogs on 1st April, 1895, and at the first moraine two of the Eskimos [not mentioned in his letters] turned back in accordance with the plan, the other four going on as far as the location of the buried cache from where they too were sent back, Nook-tah bearing a letter to "the brave woman waiting in the South." In his book he quotes a paragraph which he says was from that letter, but which in fact is a paraphrasing of part of his letter to his "Representative." His letter to his wife offers only a few comments on the weather, his mileages, and this: "The traveling is good and I shall rush things. I only fear about Lee who is not himself. I believe your prayers have been with me since I started. I know I shall hand you this my darling. Bert."

At that point they had three sledges and forty-two dogs, and slowly, inevitably, as the journey wore on, the suffering party weakened and by the time they had covered five hundred miles, they had only eleven dogs left, all of them completely exhausted, and three of no further use except as food for the others. They had the choice of turning back with insufficient rations, or risking their lives by going on and down into the snow-free valleys where there might be found some game. "Never shall I forget that time and scene . . . I felt . . . that in that cool, deliberate moment we took the golden bowl of life in our hands, and that the bowl had suddenly grown very fragile."

The search for musk-oxen "over a country the roughness of which no one who has not seen it can imagine" now took priority over Peary's dreams of extending his explorations in the area, and their desperate search was rewarded – and their lives saved – when eventually they tracked down a herd of twenty-two musk-oxen, and succeeded in killing six full grown animals and four calves. But the rough terrain had taken its toll on the party and its sledges, and the two weeks in that area, tracking, hunting and packing a supply of meat back up to the ice cap left no time in which to make anything more than a few minor improvements to Peary's previous map. Those two weeks of exhausting and crippling hunting had merely given them a chance of surviving the journey home, a chance for Peary to try again. And so, on 1st June, with only nine dogs left and meat enough for fourteen days, they began their homeward journey.

It was a journey which dragged "life and vital force" out of the men and dogs, a race against death which only one of their dogs survived and which they themselves won only by the narrowest of margins. Lee remarked in his diary that when crossing some of the crevasses near the end of the journey, Peary had taken so little care that it was almost as if he did not wish to survive only to admit that he had failed. And that sense of failure haunted him even more when the *Kite* returned to bring him home, for among the letters he received was one that had been intended as a consoling letter from his mother:

Bertie Mine,

... I need not tell you of my great disappointment last September. Nor of my great anxiety to have you at home. I was sorry for you, my child. I can imagine how much you suffered before you decided to stay another year in that dreary place. I would have borne it for you if I could. I have a mental photograph of you as you turned your face northward away from Jo and baby. I do not often look at it. To have you home again is first in importance with me ... If you have not accomplished all you had hoped to, do not be disheartened; take a cheerful view of your future. *Many* have failed.

His agony was now complete, or so at that time he thought. But then he remembered the meteorites, and an idea that had occurred to him the previous year of shipping them out and selling them on his return to America as a way of raising money for another passage north. By collecting them on his way south in the *Kite*, he would not only have the means by which he might defray some of his expenses; but these trophies he hoped would be well received by the scientific community, and perhaps distract attention from his last two wasted years.

In this move, at least, he was successful. Two of the meteorites (one weighing a thousand pounds, the other 5,500 pounds) were excavated and loaded on board the *Kite*, although two more summer trips in the *Hope* were required in 1896 and 1897 in order to bring out the larger meteorite which weighed, Peary tells us, in the region of one hundred tons. These voyages, recorded in the concluding section of his book *Northward Over the Great Ice*, were "full of incidents ... and one of the most unique episodes in the annals of Arctic exploration."

Of all the great meteorites of the world's collections, as well as the more or less legendary and mysterious celestial visitors, the "heaven stones," "thunderbolt" ... etc, which have elicited the awe and veneration of man since remote antiquity, the "Saviksue" or Cape York meteorites, must, from their exceptional size, their purity, the extreme northern latitude in which they were found, their incontrovertibly celestial origin, and their human associations, be conceded to rank first.

The world's top authorities on meteorites concurred. The Cape York meteorites were a priceless find and eventually Jo was able to sell them to the American Museum of Natural History for the amazing sum of $40,000. Furthermore, the scientific world applauded Peary for making the find that had been one of the objects of almost every expedition which had gone north in that region since Ross's expedition of 1818. He had solved the mystery of the Eskimos' source of iron. They also saluted his ingenuity in shifting that hundred-ton meteorite, known as Ahnighito, from its bed, eighty feet above sea level and some three hundred yards from the coast on to the ship and safely to New York. It had presented Peary with a formidable problem: "The dogged sullen obstinacy and enormous inertia of the giant against being moved; its utter contempt and disregard of all attempts to guide or control it when once in motion; and the remorseless way in which it destroyed everything opposed to it, seemed demonic."

The Eskimos believed it had a soul, and Peary appears not to have discounted this simply as superstition: "if a sledge, ill aimed in the darkness, chanced to strike it, a spouting jet of scintillating sparks lit the gloom, and a deep note, sonorous as a bell, a polar tocsin, or the half-pained, half-enraged bellow of a lost soul, answered the blow." He knew what he was taking. The meteorites had made it possible "for an entire aboriginal tribe, the most northerly one upon the earth, probably the smallest, and perhaps the most interesting, whose habitat is metal-barren, to rise from the stone to the iron age." And yet he took them.

He also took home with him to New York six live Eskimos and the remains of some of their fellow tribesmen whose graves had been desecrated on his orders and their bones shipped out in "five big barrels." Some were the bodies of Eskimos who had recently died, people Peary knew by name. He wrote in his diary: "The ship's men brought off the cask containing Qujaukitsoq and his wife and the little girl together with the accessories of his grave." The museum's records, according to Kenn Harper, the biographer of the Eskimo, Minik, "show that Peary did not donate these specimens to the museum. Instead the museum purchased them from him. Such was also the case over the years with other specimens, both human and artifactual."

Peary was to maintain that he had scientific reasons for bringing the Eskimos back to New York, that he had been asked to do so by Dr. Franz Boas of the museum. But Boas had asked for one, not six. Why then had he brought so many – on the principle, perhaps, that if one would be useful, six would be six times more so? Or was it to attract publicity and further strengthen the goodwill that existed between himself and the museum and, in particular, its president, Morris Ketcham Jesup.

The arrival of the meteorite and the Eskimos in New York certainly attracted attention. Thirty thousand people visited the *Hope* with admission by ticket only. But when all six Eskimos (housed in the basement of the museum) went down with pneumonia, the whole affair became something of an embarrassment for the president of the museum. Peary meanwhile had washed his hands of the whole affair, for as far as he was concerned, his role had been simply to collect and deliver them, and to take any of them back the following summer, should they want to go.

He was, in any case, far too busy to visit the Eskimos or even to spare any thought on the matter, for his time by then was occupied fully with the planning of his next expedition and working on his book, *Northward Over the Great Ice*, throughout which he writes with benign affection of the Eskimos with whom he had lived and travelled during his first three years in the Arctic.

By May 1898, the month in which the last two Eskimos died, he had almost completed his work on the book which included an appendix on the Smith Sound Eskimos, a people he describes as "my uncontaminated, pure-blooded, vigorous, faithful little tribe."

> As I sit here writing now I can see them, already within the shadow of the "Great Night" in their little stone igloos perched upon the shore of the frozen sea, the soft light of their oil lamps glowing into the savage cold and darkness from door and sealskin window. And many a familiar face rises in memory.

He writes of "Old Komonahpik, with his bronzed, impassive face, careful and thoroughly reliable, my bow oar and harpooner." He writes of "Nooktah, my faithful hunter and dog driver," and of "Kessuh, or the 'Smiler,' the walrus killer of Ittibloo." He writes of those who had served him so well as though they were all of them still alive and awaiting for him with that same eager anticipation with which they awaited the return of the sun. And yet two of those hunters he mentions by name, his dog driver Nooktah and the genial Kessuh, were men Peary had brought back to New York, and before he had completed his book, both had died and been dissected and cleaned, reassembled, mounted, cased, labelled and sent to Jesup's museum.

The case against Peary taking the meteorites is that they were a gift from God to that tiny tribe. The argument offered in his defence, and certainly with as much conviction, is that he had always come so well laden with gifts which the Eskimos considered more useful and desirable, that they had no further need for the "irons." As for the Eskimos, Peary later claimed that in bringing them to New York "he was acting on the Eskimos' own suggestion."

But whatever one's point of view on these issues, it is unlikely to be Peary's, for on his mind at that time were issues which he considered of very much greater importance – issues concerning an uncertain future, the most pressing of which was how to raise the support he needed to stay on the payroll as a Civil Engineer in the United States Navy while pursuing an intensely personal ambition to be first to reach the Pole.

Fortunately for Peary, when it became evident that a move was afoot within the Navy Department to post the prodigal Peary to Mare Island on the West Coast, where he would be out of conspiring range of his many new found and influential friends in Washington and New York, the response from Jesup and his wealthy friends was immediate and impressive. They provided the financial muscle, and Lord Northcliffe, the London newspaper publisher, promised Peary the steam yacht *Windward*. With that support, which was later to grow in size and strength and develop tremendous influence as the exclusive Peary Arctic Club, he was given the solid base upon which to build his now publicly admitted dream of planting the Stars and Stripes at the Pole.

But encouraging though these developments were, the credit must go to Charles A. Moore for seeking and winning, on Peary's behalf, the five years' leave the explorer needed in which to secure that prize. The only way that this could be done, since the Secretary for the Navy was determined that Peary would never again abscond from those duties that his Naval commission required of him, was for Moore to go straight to the President himself and request the leave that Peary needed. This he asked as a personal favour in return for the effective political service which he had rendered William McKinley during the Presidential campaign, and McKinley, evidently greatly relieved that the favour which Moore had asked of him would cost only some $14,000 in leave pay for the famous Lieutenant, immediately dictated a memorandum granting the leave requested.

The pressures on Peary were now increasing. He had received in January 1897 the first award of the Cullom gold medal of the American Geographical Society, and in December of the same year, the Patron's gold medal of the prestigious Royal Geographical Society for his explorations in Northern Greenland, which at that time of course were still unchecked. He was also now a public figure whose exploits were known throughout the land, and whose plans for his forthcoming expedition had been published in newspapers and commented upon by the man in the street. The pressures, however, which lay heaviest upon him, were his obligations towards those who now backed him.

A failure now would no longer affect him only on a personal level. He would be publicly ridiculed. No longer could Peary afford to fail – or at least, no longer be seen to.

CHAPTER 8

The Years of Doubt and Suffering

Part 1 "Find a way or make one"

That "Imperial Highway" to the North Pole across the Greenland Ice
Cap, although it had brought him his first two gold medals, a measure of
the fame he so craved, and the admiration of men who were able and
eager to help him continue his search, had, nevertheless, proved to be a
dead end, and had almost taken his life. He needed a new route, and so
he had turned back to that plan which he had outlined in 1885 even before
he had set eyes on the Arctic when he had written in his diary: "Let the
English, the Germans, the Austrians have the Spitzbergen and Franz Josef
and all the other routes, but let us stick to Smith Sound."

Now, thirteen years on, and after so much wasted effort, he had finally
become convinced that he must, like Hall, Nares and Greely before him,
force a ship along that channel which separates Greenland and Ellesmere
Island, and go as far north as possible, perhaps, like Nares, right to the
shores of the Arctic Ocean. Unlike those who had blazed that trail, he
would, however, take on board several Eskimo hunters with their wives,
their dogs and all their equipment as he passed through their territory on
his way north, and after establishing an Eskimo colony at his northern
base, he would wait until the moment was right to "shoot forward to the
Pole like a ball from a cannon."

That route Peary knew could only be forced by a very tough ship,
preferably one specially equipped with engines powerful enough to drive
it through the ice. And so when, in April 1898, he received a cablegram
from Lord Northcliffe informing him that a strike among the machinists
in England was preventing the installation of the promised new engines
in the *Windward*, Peary was crushed, for his plans by that time had been
completed, his financial backing was almost secured, and his men and
equipment selected. Then came a second and far more serious blow.

The lateness of the season was such that I had to make the most of the
Windward as she was. But her extreme slowness (3.5 knots under
favourable circumstances), and the introduction of a disturbing factor
in the appropriation by another of my plan and field of work, necessi-
tated the charter of an auxiliary ship if I did not wish to be distanced.

The *Windward* sailed from New York on the 4th of July 1898, and on the 7th I went on board the *Hope* at Sydney, C.B.

It is interesting to note that in this 1907 quotation from the report to the Peary Arctic Club, he has deleted four words from the same quotation as it was given in the *Bulletin of the Geographical Society of Philadelphia*, in 1904 (Vol. 4, page 5). There Peary had said: "I did not wish to be distanced in my own domain."

Some four months in advance of Peary's first committed decision to launch an expedition "for an extended scheme of Arctic exploration, having for its main purpose the attainment of the North Pole," the veteran Arctic explorer, Captain Otto Sverdrup (who had been with Nansen on the first crossing of the Greenland Ice Cap, and captain of the *Fram* during her epic drift across the Arctic Ocean in 1893–6) had been invited to take command of the second *Fram* expedition in the same region as the Peary expedition, and at practically the same time and for the same duration. Sverdrup's plan also had objectives that were similar. They were, however, not identical, as one can see from the following quote from Sverdrup's book, *New Land*:

> Together with Dr. Nansen and my owners, I agreed on the following route, which was to be up Smith Sound and Kane Basin, through Kennedy and Robeson Channels, and as far along the north coast of Greenland as possible before wintering. From thence we were to make sledge expeditions to the northernmost point of Greenland, and as far down the east coast as we could attain. There was no question of trying to reach the pole.

But although Peary's plan was published in the *Geographical Journal* in February 1898 and Sverdrup's not published until the July issue, it is perfectly clear that both plans had been a long time in preparation. Whether each had been conceived without foreknowledge of the other it is difficult to determine. According to Dennis Rawlins, author of *Peary at the North Pole, Fact or Fiction*, "the US Consul at Bergen was secretly relaying information to Peary about Sverdrup's (and the Dane, Amdrup's) outfit and preparation schedule – via unnumbered correspondence." But as it turned out, the ice was to stop both explorers penetrating the channel, and both were forced to find winter quarters on the coast of Ellesmere Island: Peary's *Windward* at Cape D'Urville where he anchored on 18th August, 1898, and Sverdrup's *Fram* at the northern end of Rice Strait where he found shelter on the 21st of that same month.

Being this close, it was inevitable, sooner or later, that Peary and Sverdrup would meet, and their meeting occurred on 6th October when

Peary and his Eskimo driver chanced upon a field camp occupied at that time only by Sverdrup and one companion. "I had a short and not effusive meeting with Sverdrup," Peary wrote in a letter to Jo. Sverdrup in fact had invited Peary to have coffee, but Peary "had refused, saying that his tent was not more than two hours' drive . . . and that he was going home to dinner." No mention of the meeting is made by Peary in his book. There is, however, an account which supposedly was related to Bradley Robinson by Matt Henson that is interesting, if doubtful, since the events are recorded neither by Peary nor Sverdrup. The story tells of Peary's reaction to a "formal visit" from Sverdrup shortly before Christmas 1898:

> When Sverdrup left, Matt eyed the big man curiously as he strode across the deck and down the gangplank. Peary turned from the deck rail, beckoning to Matt to follow him into his cabin. There he paced the floor with nervous agitation.
>
> "Sverdrup may at this minute be planning to beat me to Fort Conger!" he cried, with marked irritation. "I can't let him do it! I want you to go back to Cape Lawrence immediately, and I'll meet you there in a few days. I'll get to Conger before Sverdrup if it kills me!"
>
> "But, Lieutenant, this is the dead of winter. It's stormy and damned cold on the trail. Wouldn't it be better to wait until spring?" Matt asked.
>
> "No!" Peary cried vehemently. "I can't possibly afford to lose my one chance of a northern base to a competitor."

The expedition had got off to a bad start. The *Windward* had been beset 250 miles south of Fort Conger, Greely's old base, which Peary was hoping to use. Sverdrup had been forced to winter the *Fram* only forty-three miles to the south of the *Windward* and Sverdrup's party of sixteen men, which included a strong scientific element, was better equipped than Peary's party to map the unexplored fjord region to the west of the two beset ships, for on this expedition Peary had reverted to his earlier belief that a small party was more efficient and had brought with him only two companions, Henson and Dr. T. S. Dedrick, to help him direct and encourage his Eskimo support and get him to the Pole. The credit for exploring the fjord country on the east coast of Ellesmere Island would now go to the explorer who produced the best map, and Peary, for all his efforts in the autumn of 1898, was no competition for Sverdrup's men whose mapping made Peary's look amateurish. But far more serious was the threat that Sverdrup posed to Peary's North Pole plan, and the alarming consequences of an illness among Peary's dogs which seriously affected his chances of staying ahead of Sverdrup, for by 20th December the illness had reduced their numbers from sixty to thirty, and the disaster shook the confidence of Peary's Eskimos.

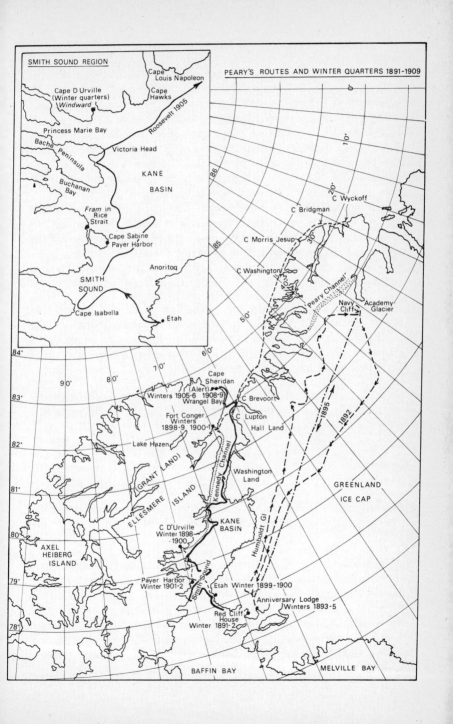

SMITH SOUND REGION

PEARY'S ROUTES AND WINTER QUARTERS 1891-1909

Cape Louis Napoleon
Cape Hawks
Cape D'Urville (Winter quarters) *Windward*
Princess Marie Bay
Bache Peninsula
Victoria Head
Roosevelt 1905
KANE BASIN
Buchanan Bay
Fram in Rice Strait
Cape Sabine
Payer Harbor
Anoritoq
SMITH SOUND
Cape Isabella
Etah

C Wyckoff
C Bridgman
C Morris Jesup
C Washington
Peary Channel
Navy Cliff
Academy Glacier

1895
1892

Cape Sheridan
(Alert)
Winters 1905-6 1908-9
Wrangel Bay
C Brevoort
Fort Conger
Winters 1898-9 1900-1
C Lupton
Hall Land
Lake Hazen
Washington Land
(GRANT LAND)
Kennedy Channel
ELLESMERE ISLAND
KANE BASIN
GREENLAND ICE CAP
C D'Urville Winter 1898-1900
AXEL HEIBERG ISLAND
Humboldt Gl
Payer Harbor Winter 1901-2
Etah Winter 1899-1900
Smith Sound
Anniversary Lodge Winters 1893-5
Red Cliff House Winter 1891-2

BAFFIN BAY
MELVILLE BAY

And so, on Mid-Winter's Eve, with the first light of the returning moon, Peary had set out from the *Windward* with Dr. Dedrick, Matt Henson and four Eskimos on what undoubtedly was the most ill-conceived and badly planned journey he ever made. Peary's own explanation for this winter journey to Fort Conger was that he wanted to be in a position at Cape Hecla on the shores of the Arctic Ocean, "in readiness to start from there with rested and well-fed dogs by the middle of March." But there was no need to expose himself, his men and his dogs to such a journey. He had clearly been driven by panic to attempt it, and driven to push on, in spite of all the warning signs, by an aberration of the rational mind which can only be described as a temporary form of insanity.

On 6th January, after a terrible journey during the final stage of which they had groped "in complete darkness and over a chaos of broken and heaved-up ice," and with their party now reduced in number (two of the Eskimos and nine of the poorest dogs having been left some thirty miles back down the trail to survive as best they could in a snow drift), Henson found the hut and their lives were spared. But in Peary's words:

A little remaining oil enabled me, by the light of our sledge cooker, to find the range and the stove in the officers' quarters, and after some difficulty, fires were started in both. When this was accomplished, a suspicious "wooden" feeling in the right foot led me to have my kamiks pulled off, and I found, to my annoyance, that both feet were frosted.

Brief though Peary's description of this journey is in his book *Nearest the Pole* (the whole journey is covered in only four pages), the horror of that situation comes across:

... awakening, it was evident that I should lose parts or all of several toes, and be confined for some weeks. The mean minimum temperature during the trip was −51.9 degrees F, the lowest −66 degrees F.

Henson's account (as related to Bradley Robinson) offers more detail, but is also strangely incomplete. There is, for example, no mention of Dr. Dedrick:

Matt handed a bucket to Ahnidloo and told him to fill it with snow. Then he inserted the blade of his knife under the top of Peary's sealskin boots. He ripped the boots from both feet, and gently removed the rabbit-skin undershoes. Both legs were a bloodless white up to the knee, and, as Matt ripped off the undershoes, several toes from each foot clung to the hide and snapped off at the first joint.

"My God, Lieutenant! Why didn't you tell me your feet were frozen?" Matt cried.

"There's no time to pamper sick men on the trail," Peary replied tersely. Then he added thoughtfully, "Besides, a few toes aren't much to give to achieve the Pole."

In Peary's account of his ordeal he makes mention of his "faithful Eskimos," but according to Henson they had grown "restless, sullen and discontented," as the storms held them trapped in that cold and depressing hut for weeks on end and, finally, after twelve dogs died through eating the salt pork and beef found at Fort Conger, the two Eskimos decided to eat no more of the white man's food or to risk it even on their dogs. They would abandon the sick man and go home.

It was Henson, and not Peary, who persuaded them to stay. It was Henson who extracted a promise from them that if they found musk-oxen they would remain with Peary and help him back to the ship, and Henson who went out with the two hunters and in the dead of winter tracked down, shot and brought back to Fort Conger two sledge loads of meat which held the Eskimos to their promise, and established Matt Henson as one of the greatest hunters in the folklore of their tribe.

Thus Peary once again was saved by Henson and yet Peary does not mention this hunting episode, or any of the care and concern of his devoted assistant during those dark days at Fort Conger during which Peary (according to his biographer, William Herbert Hobbs) lay on his bunk scratching with a pencil a quotation from Seneca: "*Inveniam viam aut faciam*" – I shall find a way or make one. Nor do Peary or Henson mention that it was Dr. Dedrick who performed the operation at Fort Conger of removing parts of seven of Peary's toes.

What was passing through Peary's mind during that period which he later described as "those interminable black days" it is impossible to guess. But from an undated typescript in the Peary collection we have these words: "though I could not at times repress a groan at the thought that my God-given frame was mutilated forever, still I never lost faith ... I *knew* that I should yet do the work which I had set before myself."

With the need for more surgery on his toes he had, with the returning light, set off for the ship on a journey that must have been one of the most uncomfortable he ever made, and yet the only published record of that ordeal which Peary offered amounts to no more than two short paragraphs, in neither of which does he mention his discomfort or the effort of his companions to minimise the terrible jarring he must have suffered. All he tells us is that "the character of the road precluded riding by anyone but myself. Lashed firmly down, with feet and legs wrapped in musk-ox skin, I formed the only load of one sledge," and that "the mean minimum daily temperature while we were returning was −56.18 degrees F, reaching the lowest, −65 degrees F, the day we arrived at the

Windward." His diary covering that journey (18th–28th February), which was dictated to Dr. Dedrick, does, however, offer a little more information – even the occasional mention of his companions:

> The doctor and Matt, as well as the Eskimos, have completed a by no means slight feat in walking this distance (250 miles) in eleven days. They have had a harder time of it than I, and there could be no more faithful fellows than my two Eskimos, who, walking all day long at the upstanders and driving the dogs, have then turned to at night without a word of complaint to erect or excavate our snow shelters.

Henson says they covered the 250 miles in nine marches, and that in one place: "I bent down and let them guide the sledge over my back as a slide down a drop so as not to jar him too much." He probably did, too. The act would certainly be in character, for Henson was not only a devoted servant to his master, but a very practical and competent polar traveller without whom Peary's ambitions would have faltered and fallen a long way short of any of the successes he claimed.

Unfortunately, Henson's accounts are inconsistent, perhaps a fault of memory, perhaps the fault of his ghostwriters and interviewers. We shall be confronted by more inconsistencies and at a more crucial part of the story; but an example can be found here in the various accounts of the operation carried out on board the *Windward* on 13th March when Peary underwent the "final amputation" of all but the little toe of each foot. According to Bradley Robinson, Henson was not present at this operation – having set off on a hunting trip down the coast "in order to be free of the depressing gloom permeating the *Windward* prior to Peary's subjection to the surgeon's scalpel." The writers Robert H. Fowler and Lin Bonner, however, both state that Henson assisted in this operation, the latter claiming that Henson had said that the ship's surgeon amputated the toes of Peary's left foot, while he, Henson, amputated those of the right foot: "The reason I had to work on one foot was that he (Peary) couldn't stay under the anaesthetic long and we had to work fast. Even as we finished he commenced to groan and kick."

Only on Peary's amazing determination to continue the expedition do all the accounts agree, and no one, however critical of Peary and for whatever reason, can ignore his cold-steel courage and his absolute commitment to fight on. Lieutenant Victor Baumann (Sverdrup's second-in-command) was left with the same impression of Peary after his visit to the *Windward* on 22nd March. At that time Peary was still confined to his cabin and suffering the effects of his operation and yet he left Baumann in no doubt whatsoever that regardless of the fate of the ship, it was Peary's intention "to push northward, in spite of everything."

The Years of Doubt and Suffering

That meeting with Baumann was revealing also of one of Peary's weaknesses. "He further told me that it was on a trip at the end of February last that his toes had been frost-bitten, and that he had been obliged to have them amputated. Upon my expressing my regret at his accident, he answered laconically: 'You must take your chances up here you know.'" Note the date. The journey to Fort Conger in the dead of winter had been a disastrous and almost fatal journey, and its only purpose had been to beat Sverdrup; but this he could not bear to admit even to himself, and certainly not to Sverdrup's second-in-command.

Was it then the fear of failure that drove him on, or his certainty of success? His activities over the next three years appear to suggest the former; but in Peary we are in the company of a man who was motivated on many levels, and the most powerful of these was his deep conviction that it was his destiny to reach the Pole. Without his conviction that he had been chosen, no fear of failure, no craving for fame, no super-human effort of will, or any conceivable concentration of Peary's courage and determination would have been enough to drive him on. The only alternative to this reading is that Peary was a blind fanatic; beyond the reach of all human emotion; beyond the reach of anguish and pain; beyond even the need to return from the Pole, as long as he could reach it. This force, however, as we shall see, although present in Peary to some degree, was not the one that drove him. Such a force would have focused his mind far more sharply upon his objective – as at first reading it appears to have done – but it never could have sustained him.

Only three days after reaching the *Windward* he sent out a messenger across the strait to the Eskimos living on the Greenland side, calling the hunters to come to him with their dogs and sledges in readiness for another journey north to Fort Conger and possibly beyond. Within only five weeks of the operation in which eight of his toes had been amputated, and even before the stumps had healed, he set off on that journey and from Fort Conger attempted to cross over to Greenland. But it was hopeless. The ice-foot proved arduous travelling; the bays filled with broken pack ice were covered with snow almost thigh deep; and the channel "clear across to the Greenland shore, and up and down as far as the glass could reach was filled with upheaved floe fragments, uninterrupted by young ice or large floes." He was a cripple, "a mere dead weight on the sledge," and with the unhealed place on his right foot beginning to "break down and assume an unhealthy appearance from its severe treatment," he abandoned his assault, returned to Fort Conger, and from there went on to the ship.

His published account of this whole period, however, is so thin it is barely possible to follow his activities and one cannot help wondering if, at least to some extent, this may have been his intention. He tells that on returning to Fort Conger from his abortive attempt to cross the channel (probably on 6th May) he sent Henson and an Eskimo out immediately to look for an alternative route, and two hunters in search of musk-oxen. Both of these scouting parties returned two days later, Henson unsuccessful, but the hunters with the report that they had killed sixteen animals. With the skins and beef brought back to Conger, his entire party (except for himself and an Eskimo companion) went out again and brought in another twelve. He then tells us:

> I completed the work of securing the meat and skins obtained; getting the records and private papers of the United States Lady Franklin Bay Expedition together [these being the papers Greely had left behind when he had made his enforced journey south] securing as far as possible collections and property; housing material and supplies still remaining serviceable, and making the house more comfortable for the purposes of my party.

What he does not say is that some time during that period between 10th–23rd May he had his men demolish Greely's old expedition base, which originally was a very sizeable structure of some sixty feet by seventeen, and from the materials build three small Eskimo-style huts, which I was surprised to find still standing when I visited the site in April 1987, a place of ghosts and memories in the soft light of the midnight sun.

Greely had landed here with a party of twenty-five men from the SS *Proteus* in August 1881. He set up his base and spent two years extending the work of the Nares expedition, and conducting a far more creditable programme than is generally believed. Indeed his massive two-volume report on the work of the Lady Franklin Bay expedition is one of the most impressive pieces of work produced by any Arctic expedition prior to Nansen's drift in the *Fram* across the Arctic Ocean.

Peary's reasons for destroying Greely's camp were essentially practical. Smaller huts are easier to heat. But as I approached that place in April 1987, and crawled inside those tiny huts, it was so very tempting to read into Peary's act an attempt to disperse and rid that place of all the spirits that were there reminding him that he was not the first – nor yet the greatest.

Privately Peary was contemptuous of Greely for having abandoned his base at Fort Conger, because, as Greely put it in his book: "Time pressed, our fresh meat and vegetables were gone, our fuel nearly exhausted, and everything in an unsettled condition." In the neighbourhood of Fort Conger Peary had found ample game to support his own party, and this, as far as he was concerned, was proof that he was a more enlightened

Arctic explorer. He does not appear to have made any allowances for the differences in the objectives and the make-up of their parties, or to have been prepared to give any credit to Greely for having brought his party of twenty-five inexperienced men safely through their time at Conger, through, as Greely put it:

> ... the monotony of Arctic life, the depression of months of cold and darkness, the restricted and limited diet, the dangers and extreme privations of winter and spring sledging ... [all of which had been] ... experienced without scurvy, without loss of health or limb, without sickness, and without even a serious frost-bite.

Could it have been this final comment that had hurt Peary's pride and fired the hatred which had later prompted him to write so unfairly of the Greely tragedy?

> The saddest part of the whole story for me was the knowledge that the catastrophe was unnecessary, that it might have been avoided. I and my men have been cold and have been near to starvation in the Arctic, when cold and hunger were inevitable; but the horrors of Cape Sabine were not inevitable. They are a blot upon the record of American Arctic exploration.

But in 1899 the feud had not yet been made public. He had demolished Greely's Arctic base but, not yet being sure of how the public might react, he was only prepared to state in his book that he had "made it more comfortable." What he had, however, already decided was to take home whatever records he could find that might have been left behind by Greely before his enforced trek south, for as Peary later was to say in a private note to Herbert Bridgman, the act would serve as an extra "feather in the [Peary Arctic] Club's cap."

And so, he had finally started south from Fort Conger on 23rd May carrying only "the scientific records of the expedition, the private papers of its members, and necessary supplies." What a pity the gesture had not been a generous and friendly one; but no matter that Greely's Arctic base had served Peary well in his time of need, and was to be useful for years ahead, Fort Conger was now in Peary's "domain" – a "domain" which he had every intention of extending as quickly as possible.

Within two days of reaching the ship he had sent out depot-laying parties back along the trail to the north to establish "a continuous line of caches from Cape Sabine to Fort Conger, containing some fourteen tons of supplies," in readiness for the following spring's sledging, and he had spent the month of July frantically completing his map of the fjord region of Princess Marie Bay, during which time he had made an ascent of the Ellesmere Island Ice Cap to an altitude of 4,700 feet in the hope of seeing new land to the west which he could claim in advance of Sverdrup. But what had all this effort achieved?

His seemingly unshakable and courageous resolution to continue his work in spite of his suffering had set the man in a class of his own. History, it seems, offers no example of a polar traveller the equal of Peary when he felt the need to cram in the miles. But could he not have achieved so very much more if he had directed his energies on one objective? The question, of course, is seldom asked, for in place of results, what Peary had offered was the more admirable record of courage.

It was this courage that had won him the support he needed from the wealthy businessmen back at home, and news of his friend Morris Jesup's success in forming the Peary Arctic Club to support his patriotic ambitions was a tremendous boost to the weary explorer who knew in his heart he had failed yet again. The news had come north with the relief ship *Diana* which had been sent by the Club under the command of its secretary, Herbert L. Bridgman, to make contact with Peary. They had met up with the *Windward* on 12th August at Etah on the Greenland coast. The *Diana* had also brought news from Jo, the happy news that seven months earlier his second daughter, Francine, had been born.

"Never was a man more fortunate in his wife than I," he wrote on 27th August, 1899, after spending almost the entire day at Etah reading and re-reading her letter, "never a wife more loving, tender, delicious, yet with it all, clear and level headed. Your letter was like an exquisite soft warm breeze of spring in this lonely desert."

When the *Diana* came in and I got your valise, I was foolish again as I took the various articles out and thought to myself "she put this in, her touch still lingers on it." Then Sunday, I took my bath, discarded my furs, dressed throughout in your present, put your letter in my inside pocket and devoted the day to you. Ah sweetheart, if only I might really have you if only for a day.

But what poor exchange was his news for her: "My day of trial as well as yours," he wrote, "came on the 7th of January," and yet not until much later in his long letter does he refer to that "trial" again, and then, only in passing from one topic to another:

The past year has been particularly free from annoyances with the exception of the one unpleasant episode which you will have seen noted in the papers before this reaches you, viz the frosting of my toes. This gave the doctor an opportunity to trim them up a little, and as a result when I come back I shall be able to wear a size shorter shoe. The mishap is of no importance. The toes were slow in healing because I did not give them rest. They are well now and cause me no trouble, and no one will be aware of the mishap unless they are told.

In her letter to him, Jo had tried so hard to disguise her true feelings, but they had come through in a comment that life for them both was slipping away. This he had to address.

You are right dear, life is slipping away. That cannot come to you more forcibly than it has repeatedly to me in times of darkness and inaction the past year. More than once I have taken myself to task for my folly in leaving such a wife and baby (babies now) for this work. But there is something beyond me, something outside of me, which impels me irresistibly to the work. I shall certainly come back to you. I believe I shall accomplish my object and then hand in hand we will meet the days and years until the end comes.

... I am neither pessimistic nor optimistic in regard to next year, but I know that affairs are in better condition for coming work than they ever were before and I have a firm deep-seated conviction that I shall accomplish what I came here for. I believe also that I shall do it next spring. All my work of preparation is done, and I have laid out no work for the Fall. Not only the three of us, but the Eskimos and dogs as well, will stay here till February storing energy and eagerness for the work north.

... You can give yourself no uneasiness my darling in regard to the way in which I shall take reverses or disappointments. Either because I am an older man or more of a man than I was once, no ill success will affect me seriously. I am in this work as I would be in any business. I shall do my level best. If I succeed well and good. If not, this is not everything there is in the world by any means.

He goes on, "I sometimes think there is no one thing that I can do well." But this is neither what he believed nor what he was really trying to say. "Certainly I have no business ability as everything in that line goes wrong." The letter offers an insight into his relationship with his two companions:

The doctor [Dedrick] is a faithful, hardworking soul, with some of Verhoeff's characteristics of never admitting that he is cold or hungry or tired, and with the same dogged persistence in doing what he starts on. His great fault is that he is slower (very *much* slower) than the wrath of God; and he has not enough natural mechanical ability to drive a nail. He is learning however. The *Windward* people gave me no annoyance. Bartlett [John] is too nervous a man and a bit too old to take a winter easily, but he never exhibited any peevishness to me and he as well as everyone else on board were always willing and even anxious to do everything I wanted.

The men forward were a particularly nice clean, quiet, decent lot of fellows, and got along finely together. The continuous work throughout the year, and my constant coming and going, broke up completely the monotony of the winter, and the presence of the Eskimos on board helped to liven things for them. But beyond all this the ship's complement I regard as an exceptionally congenial one.

Matt not being confined, and having no drudgery of cooking to perform, had none of his usual winter attack of the blues, but continued as cheerful as the natives. He has worked faithfully and is getting more and more like a husky [Eskimo] every day.

There is also an intriguing and revealing comment on his relationship with the competition – Sverdrup still a threat, but Greely less of one:

I had a short and not effusive meeting with Sverdrup when I stumbled upon his hunting camp in October last. I learned to my delight that the *Fram* was in Rice Strait near Cape Sabine. In March his navigator came to the *Windward* with an offer from Sverdrup to take me and my party north on the *Fram* in the summer and land us wherever I wished. Under the circumstances I was amused at the proposition. It was merely an excuse to see how I was getting along and what I had done.

... Though I have done much more travelling the past year than Sverdrup I imagine he has covered more new ground as he had the entire Spring to devote to the region about the *Fram* and to the westward, while my time was expended in the direction of Fort Conger.

I have distanced him in the amount of game, in every item, and this reminds me, the experience of Sverdrup and myself in the Buchanan Bay, Bache Peninsula region will be a set back for your friend Greely. My party has killed 24 musk-oxen and Sverdrup's some 30-odd in that locality and the waters of which Cape Sabine is the portal. I would ask no better place as far as game is concerned than that region. At Fort Conger things were not exactly as Greely's official report would lead one to believe. I do not think, however, that there will be anything special in any of the private papers.

... The return of the Greely records and valuable instruments may be made, if properly handled, a strong government card.

By now he was into the last two pages of business matters and last minute thoughts, and with these disposed of, a lonely explorer left with nothing more to say than his fond farewells for another year, wrote "God keep you and ours safe and well for me," then climbed back into his animal furs and, like the practical man he was, joined his companions out hunting.

A subtle change in Peary's attitude appears, however, to have crept into his planning at this stage. With the facility of two ships with which to hunt walrus and build up a huge supply of meat to see him through the winter, together with the good news from home, and the certainty that Sverdrup (for reason of the bad ice conditions in Kane Basin) would now move his theatre of operation into Jones Sound and the unknown region to the west and north-west of Devon Island, the pressure on Peary had suddenly eased. He now even had time to make a tour of the Eskimo villages in the *Diana*, recruiting hunters for his next season's work, and settled for the idea of wintering at Etah, instead of Fort Conger. "Two things controlled this decision: First, the uncertainty of carrying dogs through the winter, and, second, the comparative facility with which the distance from Etah to Fort Conger can be covered with light sledges."

He makes no mention of the fact that the ice in the channel that August was impenetrable, and this leaves one wondering if his two other reasons for wintering at Etah, sensible though they were, had been intended to distract the reader from the failure of his original plan. By 4th March, 1900, when Peary set out from Etah, he had a trail blazed all the way to Fort Conger by Henson and the Eskimos, and on arriving at Fort Conger on the 28th, he was greeted with the good news that the advance party had killed twenty-one musk-oxen not far from the hut. He was therefore (and for the first time in his life) now in a really strong position to make an attempt at the Pole; but, once again, it was the fear of failure that changed his course.

On leaving Etah I had not decided whether I should go north from Conger *via* Cape Hecla, or take the route along the northwest coast of Greenland. Now I decided upon the latter. The lateness of the season and the condition of the dogs might militate against a very long journey; and if I chose the Hecla route and failed of my utmost aims, the result would be complete failure. If, on the other hand, I chose the Greenland route and found it impossible to proceed northward over the pack, I still had an unknown coast to exploit and the opportunity of doing valuable work. Later developments showed my decision to be a fortunate one.

His journey around the north coast of Greenland was indeed one of the most worthwhile journeys of his career – and by no means an easy one.

The first sixty miles were particularly tough with "almost continuous road-making through very rough ice," and then came the coastal ice-foot with its "slippery side slopes, steep ascents, and precipitous descents [which] wrenched and strained the men, capsized, broke, and ripped shoes from the sledges." Finally, came the notorious Black Horn Cliffs, off which there is usually open water, or very thin ice. At the time of Peary's outward journey along this stretch of coast, the hazard was the thin ice which "buckled to a very disquieting extent beneath dogs and sledges, and from the motion of the outside pack, was crushed up in places, while narrow cracks opened up in others."

Finally, on 8th May he, Henson, one Eskimo companion, three sledges and sixteen dogs passed the farthest point reached by Lieutenant J. B. Lockwood and Sergeant D. L. Brainard of Greely's expedition, and were now heading into the unknown. To Peary's relief, he discovered that the coastline continued to increase its northing, and eventually, "my eyes rested at last upon the Arctic *Ultima Thule*," which he naturally named after Morris K. Jesup, the man who had, perhaps more than any other, given him his chance to succeed.

He then set off across the pack ice of the Arctic Ocean for the first time; but after only four marches he abandoned all hope of continuing. They were "on the edge of the disintegrated pack, with a dense water sky not far distant." And so they turned back and reached land in one long march – probably about sixteen miles. His first impression of pack ice travel he limits to a few words of simple description, while the impact of that first encounter upon his dream he keeps strictly to himself. It must, however, have occurred to him that the pack ice was a far more formidable adversary than anything he had encountered before, and it must have shattered his theory that he could cross such ice at an average of ten miles a day. It must also have shocked him into realising how vital it now was to travel as far around the coast as possible – to prove the insularity of Greenland. But this he did.

He had pushed on until his provisions were exhausted at a point four hundred miles from Fort Conger which he later named Cape Wyckoff; having discovered about 150 miles of new coastline and, with a part of his flag left behind at Cape Morris Jesup, the northernmost point of land, Peary for once seemed satisfied that he had done enough. Now he could relax. Now he could settle down at Fort Conger and, as his diary notes of 1885 had directed, he could "watch season after season ready to take advantage of a favorable one . . . when the fortunate man waiting on the verge of the unknown region can speed away to the Pole." And a better advance base he could not have had.

The sea, the lakes, the rivers and the valleys were rich with a great variety of game. For over five thousand years this had been the traditional northern migration route of the Eskimo tribes following the so-called "Musk-Ox Way" from Canada across to Northern Greenland, so after a while the natives in the party happily reverted to their far more skilful yet "primitive" methods of hunting, fishing, and snaring birds, and this had suited Peary's plan since they needed to conserve their ammunition for the journeys they would make the following spring.

From the furs and skins of the animals they killed they had repaired or replaced their worn out gear. They made lance heads, harpoons, bows and arrows, traces and harnesses for the dogs, whips, lashings and harpoon lines, all from the animals they had hunted, and with these seemingly crude but effective weapons they moved around that territory with the ease and the confidence of hunters who had thousands of years of experience behind them, and no need for the gun. They even made a couple of kayaks from which they hunted walrus and seal, while others of the party, moving inland as far as Lake Hazen, killed no less than sixty musk-oxen during the months of July and August and returned with stories that the Arctic hares were there so plentiful they had "looked like a vast field of snow."

The "daring decision" that Peary's biographer, Fitzhugh Green, claimed that sojourn at Conger to be, seems therefore to offer the wrong impression. He was, however, right in assuming that it was for Peary an "enthralling period" in his life, for he was, in that time, almost totally dependent on the skills of those hunters, and seeing them for the very first time in that natural state in which they had lived before their lives had been changed by the gun and the white explorer's offer of gifts which had lured them into a form of service they never quite understood. Up at Fort Conger those Eskimos were, in a sense, at home, for all around them were traces of hunters who had lived there before and, apart from missing their families, they were deprived of nothing.

Peary also felt at ease. Having earned himself the right to relax, he had, as his diaries and notes reveal, retreated into his private world and, choosing one of the three huts as a private cabin for himself, lived an essentially solitary existence, cut off from the cares of the world to his south and even the problems of those around him who shared the isolation of those northernmost huts on earth. "Wonderful this cabin," he wrote in his diary on 12th July, 1900, "this mellow life, this warmth." And warm and cosy those three huts were, for there was always plenty of wood for their fires from the debris of Greely's sizeable house, and this they had been able to supplement not only with blubber, but with coal sledged in by Henson from a seam discovered by the Nares expedition not six miles away! "Wonderful", too, Peary wrote, was "this freedom from care or annoyance, this freedom to do as I please." And in his diary entry of 20th December, 1900, he records how he spent his time:

There has never been a time for me in the Arctic before so free from annoyance, worry, or irritation. I have no interruptions, have my place entirely to myself, and can work as I please. No previous winter has my house been so comfortable as is this. I turn out between 5.30 and 6.30 a.m., make my own coffee (one quart) which I can do in fifteen minutes: have my coffee and biscuit, call doctor at eight – devote forenoon to writing or arranging material in most compact form. Doctor gets dinner at twelve, and I go in his place to eat it. Then I get my twenty-four hours' supply of wood, [from the demolished Greely house] ice, biscuit, etc. Then I do whatever is on hand outdoors. Afterwards work on equipment. At 6 p.m., supper, sometimes in doctor's place, sometimes self. Then evening for writing, reading, or planning. About eleven I turn in after preparing my kindling for morning and my coffee kettle.

And yet Peary was having problems. His relationship with Dr. Dedrick was strained and growing worse. With Peary preferring to keep his own company, and Henson preferring to be with the Eskimos, the doctor had found his isolation almost too heavy a burden to bear. He became depressed and at times morose, suspicious of every half-heard comment; and as the polar night dragged on he had cried for help and none of those who heard his cry had made anything more than a token effort to listen and to help him. From his diary it appears he resented the trust which Peary seemed to have in Henson, and confronted Peary with a demand that he should make it clear to Henson that he, the doctor who had saved Peary's feet, was rightfully the second-in-command, and entitled not only to more authority, more respect and responsibility, but also from Henson and his Eskimo friends, more consideration.

In an attempt to pacify his doctor and to keep the peace within his camp, Peary had privately spoken with Henson. But from the notes that he had prepared to remind him of the topics to be covered, it would seem that Peary at this time was also having some problems with Henson and with the Eskimos as well:

I have cleared up some matters with doctor. Now it's your turn, then the Eskimos . . .

I am old enough now and you have been in my service long enough to show me respect in small things . . . I have a right to expect you will say Sir to me always . . . That you will pay attention when I am talking to you and show that you hear directions I give you by saying yes Sir, or all right Sir . . .

I have no fault to find when we are alone together, but when doctor or number of Eskimos present or when we are on board ship you are very different...

Now is there anything which, if different, would make things pleasanter for you?

But the long polar night is never a healer. With the returning light and the doctor pronouncing both Peary and Henson unfit to make their attempt at the Pole, the doctor became even more unpopular, and he in turn very deeply hurt when Peary decided to send him south with the Eskimos to make contact with the ship. So what was really going on in Peary's mind during that long dark winter at Fort Conger? Was he really planning another assault on the Pole in the spring of 1901, or had he somehow lost his faith in the certainty of his destiny?

The published record of this expedition for the period of eleven months from his return to Fort Conger on 10th June, 1900, to 6th May, is almost inexplicably blank.

Apart from occasional hunting trips to Lake Hazen to provide fresh meat for the men and dogs – and only one of these trips he went on himself – Peary appears to have done absolutely nothing to justify staying another full winter and spring at that hut only five hundred miles from his goal. It is almost as though the very proximity of his adversary, the Arctic Ocean, had forced him into submission – a submission of which he was, perhaps, not even consciously aware.

The letter he wrote on the eve of departure is surely the letter of a weary man who cannot bear to admit to his wife, or even to himself, what his heart and mind are telling him.

Conger,
April 4, 1901

My Darling:

We have lived through a year here at Conger, and now, thank God, it is over and I am ready to start.

Never has a winter seemed so long to me, and never have I welcomed back the sun so intensely, and yet in many, in fact most minor ways, I have never had less annoyance. I have been well, have had a comfortable place to live in, have had enough to eat, have been able to live by myself and so avoid all wearying companionship, white or native, have been very successful in getting game.

But night and day, day and night, in my room, in the igloos, at rest or travelling (for we have been in the field most of the time even through the winter) I have had but one thought, an intense unevadable longing for you and my babies. How blind, blind, blind, I was and how clearly you saw it all. A great slice out of our lives, apart from each other, and for what, a little fame. I would exchange it all for a day with you. I am not sick sweetheart, nor worried, nor discouraged. Nothing of the sort, but I woefully overestimated my strength when I thought I could remain away from you three or four years. Two years is the utmost limit, and I should not be equal to that again.

We have been very fortunate in our experiences here. All my efforts have so far turned out well. My letter to the Club will tell you what I did last Spring. We have killed much game here, and I have brought twenty-one dogs through the Winter. Some of us have been more or less worried about ourselves. I have not.

I am starting now with Matt and Ahngmaloktok, to attack my work for this Spring, and do all I can without being rash. I have no misgivings, I have no rose colored hopes. Am going at the job in a very prosaic manner.

I carry the pictures of you, and my babies, and your last letter, with me everywhere. They will be very threadbare when I bring them back to you. Your flag too has been and will be with me constantly. One of its silken stars, and a piece of a red and white stripe are resting now in a cairn on the most northerly land on the globe.

God bless and keep you darling till I come. Kiss my babies for me. Love to the Little Mother.

Always and forever your
Bert

He had on that same eve of departure written a letter to his mother – a letter in which there are indications of that mystical element in his character which he was so careful not to expose in his published writings for fear that his readers might misinterpret this sensitivity as weakness:

... Hardly an hour, certainly not a day, has passed, that I have not longed for you, and Jo, and my babies. I have been *very* foolish. I can see it now when it is too late, and *very very* selfish, and yet I know that you have forgiven me, for you have been with me so many times, and averted trouble [for] me. In my journey of last spring, things happened in which I know you took a part, and yet they seem so strange that were another person telling me of them, I should be incredulous.

Among others the following. In three instances bears passed close to caches of food which I had made for our return, caches which were very important if not vital for our return, without disturbing them. Another time a bear walked over a cache, yet let it alone. Once, open water which barred my passage froze over to let me pass, and twelve hours later was open water again.

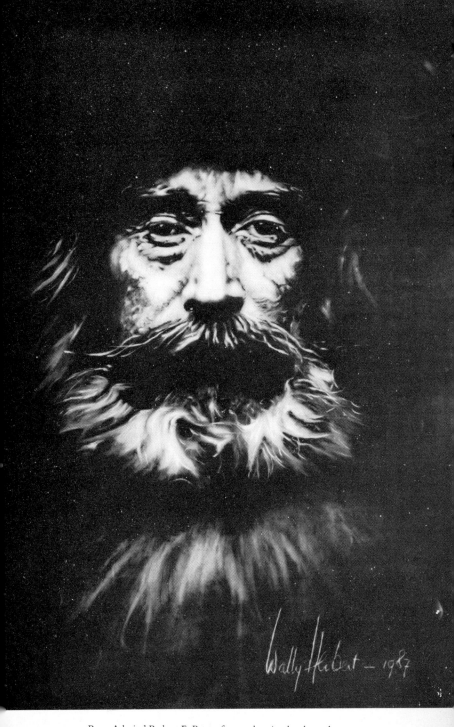

Rear-Admiral Robert E. Peary, from a drawing by the author.

Top left: Nicaragua, 1885 and 1887. Top
right: Josephine Diebitsch Peary. Centre: Jo
goes ashore in North-West Greenland and
(bottom) is as shocked by some of the native
customs as they are amused by her insistence
that they should wash their bodies.

Above left: Jo, her daughter Marie, and Captain Sam Bartlett at Payer Harbor. Above right: Fort Conger. Centre left: Aleqasina, mother of two of Peary's sons. Centre right: Peary and Jo, briefly reunited.

Below: the coastal ice-foot and beyond it the broken ice of the channel.

Top: Matthew Henson (seated centre) among his friends.
Above left: Peary hands out gifts to the seamstresses.

Above right: Peary's companions at their Farthest North, 1906.
Right: the deck load of dogs.

Peary's cabin on board the *Roosevelt* with its
pianola and portraits. Centre: the *Roosevelt*
wintering at Cape Sheridan. Below: hard
going across the pack ice.

Above: approaching the Big Lead. Centre: Camp Jesup (with Peary's inscription edge of frame). Bottom: the moment of truth. Peary reads his sextant.

Opposite page: Top left, Peary; right, Henson. Centre: the flag party. Bottom: Peary's North Pole calculations.

Left: the flag party returning [t]o camp. Centre: riding the homewar[d] trail.

Captain came in *from* 87° 47' in 24 days

Self came in from —— in 20 days (18 marches).

Above: Peary's handwritten memo written after returning to the ship does not say how far north he went. Right: the signpost at Cape Aldrich, Peary's first announcement that he had reached the Pole.

Repeatedly I had the most vivid dreams of you. I know you are watching over me.

I am not sick, mother, not worried nor discouraged. But I am older and I see many things more clearly.

God bless and keep you till I come.

But of that 1901 attempt at the Pole he says very little in his book, so little in fact there are hardly lines enough from which to read a meaning between them.

April 5th I left Conger with Henson, one Eskimo, two sledges and twelve dogs for my northern trip. At the same time the remainder of the party, with two sledges and seven dogs and pups, started south for Cape D'Urville and Sabine, to communicate with or obtain tidings of my ship. On reaching Lincoln Bay it was evident to me that the condition of men and dogs was such as to negative the possibility of reaching the Pole, and I reluctantly turned back.

He had travelled only about forty miles. He had not even reached the shores of the Arctic Ocean and had returned to Fort Conger after an absence of only eight days. Was this the same man who had, the previous year, made that journey around the north coast of Greenland; the courageous and determined explorer who had set his heart on reaching the North Pole, and who had written on the wall of the original Fort Conger hut *"Inveniam viam aut faciam"* – I shall find a way or make one? I believe this was a broken man, a man who had now spent almost a year trying to come to terms with the thought that his goal was unattainable. Peary had written several other letters, memos and instructions on the eve of his departure which it cannot be denied appear to have been written by a man who was setting his affairs in order against the possibility that he might not return. But to assume from these precautions that his attempt on the Pole was a serious one, is to ignore the most feeble effort in his life to achieve his publicly stated ambition, and worse, to ignore his anguish.

The physical problems of reaching the Pole across five hundred miles of the sort of pack ice against which he had tested himself and his theories during his journey of the previous March, cruelly and totally shattered his dreams. He had failed and this time without even feeling he had earned the right to feel proud of his effort, and the only thing that could save him now was the healing love and understanding of those who were most dear to him – those whom he had set aside in his selfish quest for fame. And so, with his dream abandoned, he had started south from his winter quarters with the entire party on 17th April, 1901, and in one short paragraph of his published account he hides much more (or so he had hoped) than his readers would ever imagine:

April 30th, at Hayes Point, I met a party from the *Windward* attempting to reach Conger, and received my mail, learning that the *Windward* was at Payer Harbor with Mrs. Peary and our little girl on board. After a rest at the D'Urville box-house, I went on to the *Windward*, arriving May 6th.

Chapter 9

The Years of Doubt and Suffering

Part 2 "The game is off"

The newly formed Peary Arctic Club, that exclusive band of millionaires who had responded to the call of Morris K. Jesup to assist, promote, and encourage Peary "to reach the Farthest Northern Point" in honour of his country, had dug deep into their pockets to cover the cost of an overhaul to the sluggish old *Windward* and the entire cost of sending her back to the Arctic with supplies to take Peary through another year, and hopefully to a new Farthest North. But in a letter from Jo to Peary dated March 1900 – of which, as was her custom, she had made several copies to send with the whalers in the hope that one of the letters might reach her husband – she had warned him not to expect any improvement in the performance of the ship:

> It will probably be a great disappointment to you to learn that the *Windward* cannot be "re-engined and boilered" this year. The hull is being thoroughly overhauled under Capt. Jack's supervision and she will be fitted up with her old machinery to communicate with you this summer. I do not write particulars, as Bridgman probably will, besides I really don't know them.

And so Peary's gift from Lord Northcliffe was as much a liability as she always had been with her twenty-five horsepower engine that was "not even able to buck the inflowing tide in the East River." A grim prospect indeed for her new skipper, Captain Sam Bartlett, who knew the waters from his previous voyage as skipper of the Newfoundland sealer *Diana*, and knew well enough that his sailing orders not only were totally unrealistic, but that if he attempted to reach Fort Conger he would be putting the lives of his crew and his two very eager passengers at a considerable level of risk.

Sailing from Sydney on 21st July, 1900, both the reputation of the *Windward* and his own fears about her suitability as an ice ship were soon confirmed by the battering she received from the heavy ice in Melville Bay. That battering, however, was only one of the many hair-raising adventures that Jo Peary and her seven-year-old daughter Marie enjoyed during the outward stage of that memorable voyage which everyone had assumed would be simply a summer trip to the Arctic to visit and re-supply Peary. For them it was like an exciting dream, a progression of adventures, all of which were leading inexorably towards the little hut at Etah where they would be reunited with the man whom they had not seen for two years.

But the dream had ended on 19th August, for Peary's personal flag was not flying over the tiny hut – that signal from husband to wife that he was safe and well, and there – and the disappointment of mother and daughter was almost too much to bear. As Marie later was to recall:

My first impulse was to rush to Mother and cry as hard as I could, but one glance at her made me change my mind. She was standing very still, gazing off into the distance with such a strange, frozen look upon her face that I realized at once that she was feeling even worse than I. She was afraid that something had happened to him. Repeated blasts of the whistle brought Eskimos tumbling out of the skin tents that clustered about the house, but there was no sign of a white man. The Captain had a boat lowered at once and went ashore. He returned almost immediately and long before we could hear what he was saying, we could see him waving a piece of paper above his head and shouting. At last we made out the words.

"He's all right, Mrs. Peary," he was calling again and again. "He's just moved across to Cape Sabine and wants the ship to join him there."

My father had never thought that Mother and I might be on board the ship. He pictured Mother at home with a small baby.

They spent a full day at Etah and while the crew were kept busy taking on board provisions from the hut, Jo and Marie went ashore. They found Peary's hut to be "very small and forlorn and dirty" and the skin tents of the Eskimos "fearfully dirty also," but they were as delighted as the Eskimos were when the Captain gave the natives permission to bring all their gear and dogs aboard for a lift across Smith Sound.

All the while, however, Mother and the Captain kept watching the Smith Sound ice with anxious eyes. The season was getting later and later; in order to reach Cape Sabine we would have to go still further north, and the *Windward* had already proved that she was too weak a ship to force her way through the ice. We had congratulated ourselves that we had been able to get as far as Etah.

There was every evidence of an early winter and, aside from all that, sailors are superstitious and there was not a man on board who did not know that Cape Sabine was the spot where the ill-fated Greely expedition had starved to death. No one felt particularly cheerful when, less than an hour after leaving Etah, we encountered the heavy pack ice rushing furiously to the south . . .

Instead of the few hours which it should have taken us to cross Smith Sound, we were eight long days and during all that time there was hardly a minute when the ship was not in danger. Sometimes the big ice fields would hold the *Windward* in so tight a grasp that she could go neither backward nor forward. At other times the floes would crowd in upon the ship so closely that great pieces would break off and pile up against the sides, until some of them toppled over on to the deck and the poor ship trembled and groaned like an animal in pain.

They eventually found shelter in Payer Harbor at Cape Sabine, but Peary was not there either and worse was to come. While everyone was sleeping off the fatigue of the last few days, "a brisk wind had sprung up and blown the ship in against the rocks." Again Marie recalls:

It seemed to me as if I had scarcely closed my eyes when I was wakened by Mother shaking me. She was all dressed in her warmest clothing and, stranger still, the cabin seemed to be turned on its side. The floor was slanted so steeply that Mother could hardly keep her balance.

"Get up, my lamb, and dress just as quickly as you can. I have laid your warm things out for you on the foot of your bunk. The Captain is afraid that he cannot save the ship. It's a sort of joke on us, isn't it?" she added, "after staying up for a week, expecting to be shipwrecked, it happens quietly in the night, with everyone asleep!"

All the time that Mother was talking she was busy packing Dad's important papers into a small bag . . . She seemed quite calm and joked with me as we got ready, just as if things were not serious, but I could tell differently from her face.

Soon we were out in the main cabin, being helped on deck by two strong sailors. The slope of the floor was already so steep that it would have been impossible for us to climb it alone. A boat was waiting to take us ashore, and ashore we went in a blinding snowstorm through which you could scarcely see a foot ahead.

For a while it seemed certain from the screeching timbers that the ship was about to break her back, and with the tide still falling and the blizzard increasing, the crew laboured frantically to lighten their ship and get enough provisions ashore to see them through the winter ahead.

Their relief when the tide at last turned and the *Windward* floated clear of the rocks, was short-lived, for that low tide which had threatened their ship had grounded an iceberg right at the entrance of Payer Harbor and effectively blocked their escape. They thought it would go at the next high tide, but it had merely creeked itself in a bit tighter. They tried blasting the berg with dynamite, but neither blasting, blaspheming nor praying would shift it. They were, as Marie Peary says, "prisoners for the winter."

They were almost three thousand miles from home, and some 250 nautical miles as the sledge travels from Fort Conger. Fortunately the party had Eskimos with them. They could also count themselves fortunate in that they had a woman on board whose two years' experience in the Arctic had given her the inner strength to handle almost any crisis, and who carried the burden of her authority with sensitivity.

Together with Captain Bartlett, Jo soon set about preparing for the winter. The stores were checked and a rationing plan was drawn up to see them through. The ship was bedded down for the winter in the traditional manner by banking snow blocks around the sides and covering the decks with a canopy to conserve the warmth by providing wind-breaks and insulation. And she made sure that every inducement was offered the Eskimos who had come over with the ship, and those who were already there at Payer Harbor, to stay on as support for the party to provide fresh meat, to make fur clothing, and to get a message to Peary.

She was, however, not successful in persuading the Eskimos to make that journey. Marie tells us:

The Eskimos were not used to traveling in unknown territory unless under the leadership of a capable white man ... And so, although at every full moon throughout the winter Mother fitted out a party and offered them great rewards if they reached Fort Conger and brought Dad back with them, the result was always the same.

They would start out in high spirits and travel for a few days; then, completely discouraged and not a little frightened, they would make camp, remain until their provisions gave out, and then return to the ship to report another failure.

One of the Eskimo men finally told Mother that they were afraid to go and look for Peary. He had been gone a long time and had some of the best hunters with him. These hunters had left families behind them and would surely have returned by this time unless they were all dead. And every one knew that it was "pee-ook nah-mee" (very bad luck) for the living to go among the dead.

Only the last of these reasons why Jo was unable to persuade those "frightened" Eskimos to make that winter journey to Fort Conger comes anywhere near to being the sort of explanation the Eskimos would themselves accept, and even this is far from complete. The polar Eskimos survive because of their skill, their caution, and their good sense; because they know when and where to travel, and when to stop and turn back.

The Arctic explorer who needs success invariably takes greater risks, but usually in blissful ignorance not only of his folly but also of his luck.

Jo had no one with whom she could share her anxieties, and with every failure to persuade the Eskimos to make that journey to Fort Conger there had come the crushing waves of despair which she had tried so hard to hide. One senses this in her daughter's writing.

> Just by closing my eyes, I can even now call up the picture of that tiny comfortless cabin on the *Windward* and Mother singing, while tears rolled down her cheeks. I thought then that she was crying because the songs were so sad. But that is the only time that I can remember having seen Mother cry. She was never sad and she never complained. It was as if she had determined that my childhood should not be clouded by griefs and worries which I was too young to understand.

And so for nine months, while Peary had been emotionally frozen in and wasting away his time at Fort Conger, and perhaps not even seriously contemplating an assault on the Pole, Jo and his daughter had been so close, and yet so far away. What a heart-aching waste of nine precious months. What an inconsolable waste of time, time in which they had needed him as much as he now needed them. And yet, his laconic record of that meeting with a hunting party from the *Windward* gives nothing of these feelings away, and we must turn to his daughter Marie for the more endearing version:

> He and his men were out hunting when they met a party of the ship's Eskimos who were also hunting. They stopped to exchange greetings, but Eskimos, like Indians, very seldom volunteer information. They answer the direct question and nothing more. The following conversation took place between Dad and the ship's hunters:
> "Did the ship get up last year?" – "*Yes.*"
> "Who was the Captain?" – "*Captain Sam.*"
> "Who was the steward?" – "*Old Charlie.*"
> "Anyone else on board that I know?" – "*Mitty Peary and Ahnighito.*"
> "Mitty Peary and Ahnighito!" he exclaimed. Wasn't there a little baby? – "*No, no baby.*"
> "When did the ship go back?" – "*Oh,*" said one of the men very calmly, "*didn't go back. Right around the corner here in Payer Harbor.*"
> It was then that Dad, without pausing a moment, struck out for the ship, leaving the amazed and breathless Eskimos far behind. They were completely upset by the tremendous excitement of this man who had always before been calm and self-possessed.

Such eagerness to cover the last seventy-five miles should have taken him to the ship in one long day's march across good sea ice – two at the most. But Peary tells us he rested at the D'Urville box-house (which is twenty-five miles from Hayes Point) and reached the ship on 6th May. He must therefore have spent a great many hours reading and rereading his mail in that tiny hut, caught up in an emotional turmoil of self-doubt and misery; remorse for his foolishness; a desperate yearning for forgiveness; and an even more desperate need somehow to repay the suffering of his family with success.

The most recent letter from Jo was written on board the *Windward*, and dated 23rd January, 1901. Read by a man returning from a wasted winter and a very pathetic attempt at the Pole, it was a letter which surely must have hurt, even though, one may be certain, Jo had never intended anything other than to help him to see himself:

> Should this reach you, you must *not think of coming down* . . . [Aleqasina] has told me how very tender your feet are and you must do nothing that would in any way interfere with your work . . .
>
> You wrote me that *failure* would not affect you seriously. I want you to know that whenever you return your friends, who are many, will think you the bravest, pluckiest explorer that ever went into the field . . . Whatever you do you must take care of yourself . . . Sometimes I think you are a physical wreck. If this is so, come home and let Marie and me love you and nurse you. Don't let your pride keep you back. Who will *even* remember it ten years from now?
>
> . . . Oh, Bert, Bert. I want you so much. Life is slipping away so fast – pretty soon all will be over.

Jo's devotion to the man is truly astonishing. In spite all of her efforts to contact him, she is imploring him to do what *he* feels he must do, and that she will go anywhere, do anything for him. We have no way of knowing in which sequence he read these letters. It is likely, however, that he read the most recent letter first – the one written on board the *Windward* – his first concern being to satisfy himself that all was well with his family. In this case, he still had tragic news to come. There was an uncompromising letter from his mother dated 25th February, 1900, which would have been the first indication:

> Bertie Mine,
>
> . . . Last year I could not write – the attempt excited me so much I felt you would – must come back on the return of the *Hope*. May you never know such bitter disappointment as I experienced when the ship came bringing instead your sad reports of your sufferings and mutilation. It seemed as if I could not bear it. Of suffering and the dreary desolation of your surroundings I know the half has not been told.

Oh my child do come home give up this pursuit – which has resulted in so much suffering and privation to you and sorrow and anxiety to those that love you. Every night dear Marie says dear Lord watch over my dear father and bring him safely home to me. When I was in Atlantic City she said "I miss my little sister but she had to go away." My heart ached for Jo when she had to give up her baby. She needed you in her greatest sorrow. No one could fill your place . . .

But the deepest grief was in Jo's letter dated March 1900:

My Darling, My Husband:
For the first time in my life it seems a hard task to write to you as I ought. If only the time since last August has not been as hard for you as it has been for me is all I ask and pray for nightly. Surely, surely we ought not both to suffer and I have suffered for both. Our little darling whom you never knew was taken from me on August 7th, 1899, just seven months after she came. She was only sick a few days but the disease took right hold of her little head and nothing could be done for her. Emil was more than a brother to me and I don't know what I would have done without him both before and afterward. But oh, my husband I wanted you, how much you will never know. I shall never feel quite the same again, part of me is in the little grave. The news of your terrible suffering came soon after. It nearly prostrated me but you know I am strong and can bear and bear . . . Oh, Sweetheart, husband, together we could have shared it but alone it was almost too much. You too will bear the scars of your suffering all your life and not only physically.

Marie is wild to see you and Mr. Jesup says I must go. He and the Club think it will be for our mutual good. I shall probably come but fear it will make a great disturbance in your domestic life. Our little girl Marie was taken down with the measles Feb 14th, 1900, and for three weeks I watched over her in a darkened room. She came out all right and five days later came home from school with scarlet fever. The crisis is passed in safety and the doctor says nursing and care must do the rest. We are to be quarantined for six weeks longer if all goes well. Surely God will not take her from me too. She is all I have left to live for. I mean the only one to whom it makes any *real* difference.

But eventually Jo shook off her anguish and wrote on subjects of a more general nature – and of polar business:

. . . Wellman's expedition did nothing as was expected and the Italian Duke's relatives are beginning the usual newspaper stories of not having heard from him, whereupon Nansen says he is going to seek the Pole this summer. Perhaps that is why the *Fram* is going round on the East side this summer. However, I do not find anyone to corroborate the above newspaper statement.

... The Belgian expedition is back from the Antarctic. Beyond puffing up Dr. Cook a little more I don't think it has accomplished anything.

... Your mother, Mrs. Jesup and others think I will induce you to return this year if you have not succeeded. But you need have no fears, I am far too proud of my husband to want him to waive duty for inclination. You have involved others in this scheme and as long as you have health and can see your way clearly it is a matter of *duty*. If at the end of your leave you have not succeeded, I know you will gladly return but I know too that you will *never* be satisfied with yourself and it is that which I dread more than your failure. I do wish you could find something with which Greely could be brought low. He makes me *boil*...

Loving, loyal, courageous Jo, so protective of her man, so cunningly supportive that one cannot help but wonder if at times the man deserved it. Without her, that great monument that he was building to himself would never have been strong enough to withstand every setback, every error, every failure. And yet, in spite of her commitment, Jo had found it hard at times to share her husband with that obsession that kept driving him relentlessly, and with his self-destructive dream and tragic need for fame. Nor could it have been easy for her to accept her husband's need for another woman during those years when they were apart.

On board the *Windward* at Payer Harbor was an Eskimo woman, Aleqasina, with Anaukak, her baby boy who, as near as one can guess was born in May 1900. According to Peary's biographer, John Weems, "Ally," as Jo preferred to call her had "innocently boasted of her relationship with Pearyarksuah, not realizing the enormous difference in mores," and Jo had been "stunned by the revelation, but without losing her composure." But from Jo's letter to her husband of 3rd April, 1900, written at the time she was excitedly preparing for her trip north to meet him, there is an indication that she was already aware of this relationship:

I used to brag, sweetheart, that I did not feel married, but I feel very much so now and look it too. You will wish yourself back with your sleek fat Eskimo woman after you have seen me. If you have succeeded everything will look rosy to you for a *little* while and you will even persuade yourself that I am not half bad.

She certainly knew at the time of writing her letter of 28th August, 1900, one of the many written aboard the *Windward* in the hope of making contact with Peary at Fort Conger, but none of which he read until he reached that box-house at Cape D'Urville. In this one she confronted him about his relationship with Aleqasina and her child, and much as she tried to hide her feelings, there is a part of one sentence in her letter that must have found its mark:

> Today I feel as though I should not see you this year and I must put on paper what I had hoped to talk over with you ... You will have been surprised, perhaps annoyed, when you hear that I came up on a ship ... but believe me had I known how things were with you here I should not have come.

On 6th May, 1901, which was Peary's forty-fifth birthday, he reached the *Windward* and was reunited with Jo and Marie after an absence from them of almost three years, and with Jo's encouragement he was soon back on course. But none of this emotional turmoil will be found in Peary's published account, and it is interesting to read the few words he wrote, knowing some of the things he preferred to leave out.

> After a few days' rest the work of establishing new caches along the coast northward, toward Conger, was commenced and continued until the middle of June. Then the preparing of Payer Harbor for winter quarters was carried on till July 3rd, when the *Windward* broke out of the ice and steamed over to the Greenland side. July was devoted to killing walrus, and 128 were secured and transported to Payer Harbor.
>
> August 4th, the *Erik*, sent up by the Club, in command of Secretary H. L. Bridgman, to communicate with me, arrived at Etah. The usual tour of visits to the Eskimo settlements was then made, and both ships pressed into the work of hunting walrus, until August 24th, when the *Windward* proceeded southward, and the *Erik* steamed away to land me and my party and the cache of walrus at Payer Harbor.

He makes no mention of the fact that Dr. Cook had gone north on the *Erik* at the request of the Peary Arctic Club, a fact not generally recorded by Peary's biographers. Representing the interests and the concern of Peary's financial backers, Bridgman had requested that Dr. Cook should examine Peary, and to this examination he had somewhat reluctantly submitted. And Cook's impression of his former friend and commander?

> The first impression was of an iron man, wrecked in ambition, wrecked in physique, wrecked in hope. To the public he was on the way to

reach the Pole, but to himself, no such effort had been made. Peary was worried, anxious, discouraged as I have never seen him before. In desperate overreaching he had frozen both feet. Dr. Dedrick had removed eight of his toes leaving only the two small digits and painful stubs with which he could barely walk.

Cook claimed later to have found Peary to be suffering the early symptoms of pernicious anaemia, and said he had told him to eat raw meat and liver, to which Peary is said to have replied: "I would rather die." This reunion between Peary and Cook had been an uncomfortable one for Peary. Here was a man, nine years younger, who was obviously eager to build upon his reputation as a polar explorer, advising his old leader that he was "through as a traveler." To this, we are told, Peary had not replied.

Nor had Peary shown any outward signs of emotion at the devastating news received in a letter from his cousin Janette Wiley which was brought north by the *Erik*, a letter dated 6th July, 1901, which told him that his mother had died on 2nd November of the previous year while he was up at Conger. "I am sure," wrote his cousin, "that for some weeks before she went away, she felt you were no longer living, and I think a part of her life went out at that time." Is it possible that she had somehow sensed his despair? Perhaps some part of Peary had died during that winter, his belief that the Pole was his for the taking. Certainly he no longer had any illusions. He now knew he would have to fight for it, and concentrate all of his energy on that one objective.

But Peary's grief at the loss of his mother was not the only thing he left out of his published account. On 21st August, three days before the departure of the *Windward*, Dr. Dedrick handed Peary his second resignation, his first having been offered on the day Peary, Henson and the Eskimo Sipsoo had returned to Fort Conger from their northern trip. This time Peary accepted the doctor's resignation gladly, and ordered him to return home on the *Erik*. But this, to everyone's surprise (and to Peary's intense annoyance), the doctor did not do, for he believed he had an obligation to remain in the Arctic in case his services might be needed, and had slipped ashore unnoticed. He then set up home among the Eskimos on the Greenland side of the Smith Sound, while at Payer Harbor on the opposite side (and only some twenty-four miles away) Peary and his ever faithful and indispensable Henson prepared themselves for their fourth consecutive winter in the Arctic, in the company of Charles Percy, the steward from the *Erik*, and several Eskimo families who had, in the hope of great rewards, agreed to help him once again to get up to Fort Conger and possibly beyond.

But soon the winter was looking as black as any of the others had been, several of his Eskimo companions having died as a result of an epidemic of dysentery and the rest too weak or too frightened to be of much help. Dr. Cook's comments on this episode, published in 1911, offer this point of view:

Dr. T. S. Dedrick, who had served Mr. Peary faithfully, was dismissed without the payment of his salary, because of a personal grudge, but Dedrick refused to go home and leave the expedition without medical help. He remained at Etah, living with the Eskimos in underground holes, as wild men do, sacrificing comfort and home interests for no other purpose except to maintain a clean record of helpfulness. As the winter and the night advanced, Dr. Dedrick got news that the Eskimos were sick and required medical assistance. He crossed the desperate reaches of Smith Sound at night, and offered Mr. Peary medical assistance to save the dying natives. Peary refused to allow Dedrick to attempt to cure the afflicted, crying people. Dedrick had been without civilized food for months, and was not well himself after the terrible journey over the storm-swept seas of ice. Before returning, he asked for some coffee, a little sugar and a few biscuits. These Mr. Peary refused him. Dr. Dedrick returned. The natives, in fever and pain, died.

Peary in his letter to Jo dated 5th March, 1902, offers of course a different view of the situation, and how he handled it:

... We got here Sept 16th. Soon after all my natives were stricken down, and six of them died. All but two I buried myself, there being no one else to do it. Matt was down with fever for four weeks. Charlie suffering with a scalded foot all through Dec.

I held my faith all through and have not been sick a day, or missed a meal since we landed.

The cur on the other side turned up as soon as the ice was safe (Jan 6th) anxious to do any kind of work for the Expedition. I told him very plainly that I was done with him, and as soon as he had his things sent him about his business. Since then he has been writing but I have paid no attention to his later letters. He has been no trouble, and has not been able to interfere in any way.

It has been a terrible year for the poor Eskimos. At Cape York they died like sheep in the Fall. Scattered ones died in other places. At Anoritok and other places a throat distemper attacked nearly everyone. At Kookan the meat gave out and they were compelled to eat their dogs. I think half of those now living are crippled or ailing.

The Pole must have seemed much further away than at any other time during those four awful years of privation and suffering; but Peary and Henson, from the very depths of their reserves of will, somehow found enough to drive themselves back up the channel to Conger.

That they were able, in the circumstances, to persuade any of the Eskimos to accompany them is even more amazing, and the explanation for this which invariably is offered by the biographers is that Peary was held in such high regard by his faithful Eskimos, that they would do anything he asked of them. But the folklore of the Polar Eskimos offers no indication of this unreserved admiration for Peary. His journeys, they say, created hardships which through their greater skill and wisdom the hunters would have avoided.

What really impressed them about Peary was in his ships; the rewards he offered to those who went with him; and above all else, the possibility that Peary's spirit was stronger than that of the Tornassuit – the free-ranging and invisible supernatural powers which, in those days, inhabited the world of the Eskimos. This concept was misunderstood by some of the early missionaries so that Tornarssuk (the singular form) was assumed to be the Eskimos' godhead, while by others, Peary and Henson among them, it was assumed to be the devil. In response, Henson had told the Eskimos that "in the south was the greatest and most powerful devil in the sea, the United States Navy." He then let the idea sink in that this devil was feared by Tornarssuk, and that Peary was "the highest honored son of the Navy" and was also feared by Tornarssuk. This was enough, up at Cape Hecla on the shore of the Arctic Ocean, to persuade four of the seven Eskimos to go on to the pack ice, and so, on 6th April, 1902, began Peary's first determined attempt at the Pole. Already he had been on the move for a month, "we had covered not less than 400 miles of the most arduous traveling in temperatures of from −35 degrees to −57 degrees F, and we were just beginning our work, i.e., the conquest of the polar pack, the toughest undertaking in the whole expanse of the Arctic region."

For sixteen days he and his companions fought for every mile they made. It was a hard initiation into hacking a way across drifting pack, from which Peary and Henson presumably gained a great deal more experience than the distance they covered would seem to suggest, for at their Farthest North on 21st April they had covered only eighty-two geographical miles, an average of 5.1 miles a day. All that he could now do was hoist the flag, take his pictures, wonder if he had done enough, and write a few words in his diary: "The game is off. My dream of sixteen years is ended . . . I have made the best fight I knew. I believe it has been a good one. But I cannot accomplish the impossible."

During his weary journey back to Fort Conger (which he reached on 3rd May) he must have been ploughing through a haze of self-recrimination and misery at the poor showing of his final attempt and, as his annual self-assessment shows, he now felt he was past his physical best: "Forty-six. Too old for this kind of work." And then ten days later:

I close the book and turn to others less interesting, but better suited for my years. Were I younger I might feel bitter that my training, experiences, love for the work, and strenuous efforts should be first handicapped by a compulsory start from a low latitude, and then rendered futile by insuperable conditions. As it is, I accept the results calmly. I have put the best there was in me into it. The goal still remains for a better man than I, or more favorable conditions, or both.

As the days wore on, he sank deeper and deeper into the misery of doubt, and that struggle that every failed man knows, a search for explanations and acceptable excuses:

... My feelings are not of the brightest. I think of four years ago when in spite of the setback of not getting my ship farther north, I looked full of life and hope and anticipation at ... what I should accomplish. Now a maimed old man, unsuccessful after the most arduous work, away from wife and child, mother dead, one baby dead. Has the game been worth the candle? And yet I could not have done otherwise than stick to it. I have made my fight as I said I would and I believe a good one, and have missed my goal only because of insuperable obstacles – not because of supineness, or weariness, or carelessness, or mismanagement. I shall be glad to get away from everything here, and yet as I look at the cliffs a feeling akin to homesickness comes over me, but it is for the youthful foolish hopes and dreams with which they have been associated.

His agony was the uncertainty of whether he could have done more, and his thoughts dragged him deeper, until he reached rock bottom:

... As I look about on the scenery that a few years ago would have filled me with enthusiasm, as I think of my high hopes then, and contrast them with my present lack of energy, of interest; as I think of the last four years and what I have been through; as I think of all the petty details with which I have been and am still occupying myself, it all seems so small, so little worth the while that I could cry out in anguish of spirit.

On 5th August, the *Windward* returned, and once again he was reunited with Jo and Marie; but their words of consolation had failed to lift the spirits of the man. All he heard was the disheartening news that Nansen's Farthest North had been beaten by an Italian expedition under the leadership of the Duke of the Abruzzi, and that the record now stood at 86°34′N, 137 geographical miles nearer to his goal than he had been able to reach himself. He would, he must, try again.

Chapter 10

The Weather-Beaten Fanatic

At the time of the first meeting of the Peary Arctic Club on 29th January, 1899, the fourteen founders had resolved not only to unite their considerable influence in helping Peary achieve his objective, but had also each pledged a contribution of $4,000 towards his plan for what he had called "an extended scheme of exploration" which had as its main objective "the attainment of the North Pole."

They had all been impressed by the energy and vision of the man who had twice crossed the ice cap of Northern Greenland and had now set his sights on the ultimate goal. But what had finally sealed their commitment had been the reports and the letters he had written on 12th August the previous year and sent home with his support ship the *Hope*, for so full of confidence had he been on the eve of sailing north from Etah, that Jesup and his wealthy friends had felt it nothing short of their duty to give Peary all the backing he needed to win the Pole for his country.

They were not to know until several months later that the man whom they were intent on supporting had, at the time of the first meeting of the Club, been in Greely's tomb of a hut at Fort Conger, going through what he later described as the "unrelieved blackness" of his ordeal – those forty days and nights of suffering in which he was fighting not only the pain and the horror of the amputations performed with primitive tools by Dr. Dedrick, but also the fear that he might never walk again.

Nor had those friends of his in New York known at the time of their first meeting what sort of relief operation to mount when sending a ship in search of the *Windward*. Was it to be a re-supply mission, or were they to go north to bring Peary out? These were men who were accustomed to seeing results for their money, and yet here they were finding themselves sending out one ship to search for another.

It is perhaps therefore hardly surprising that by the time the chartered *Diana* and Peary's missing and battered *Windward* had returned in the autumn of 1899 bearing the grim news of Peary's condition, and the even more disquieting report that Peary was insisting on staying in the Arctic, the initial enthusiasm of some of his supporters had already begun to wear thin. The determination and courage of their man had not been able to disguise the fact that Peary's original plan was in shreds, nor that he now was a cripple. So what had Peary achieved in his first year – aside from a clearly desperate survey in an area already mapped very much better by members of Sverdrup's *Fram* expedition? Merely a collection of papers and items left behind by others.

They were listed by Peary in his report to his sponsors as the scientific records and personal effects of each officer and man of Greely's expedition, the sextant abandoned in 1876 by Lieutenant Lewis Beaumont, R.N., and various cairn notes left by the Nares expedition. Could it be that Peary had sent them home with Bridgman on the *Windward* hoping that, like the meteorites before, they might distract attention from the failure of his mission? Reading between the lines of Peary's few well chosen words on this subject one might assume that they had: "The personal effects were subsequently distributed by the Club to the survivors and next of kin of the deceased, and the relics of the Royal Navy deposited, through the Lords of the Admiralty, in the Royal Navy Museum at Greenwich."

But although this may have been a small feather in the cap of the Club, for some of the members, at least, the writing was on the wall: they were pledged to supporting a hopeless cause, and the only way of cutting it short was to send the *Windward* back up to the Arctic, this time with Jo and Marie on board in the hope that his sensible wife might succeed where Bridgman had so miserably failed in persuading the maimed and fanatical explorer to pack his bags and come home.

Had it of course been as simple as that they would no doubt have all breathed a sigh of relief. The *Windward*, however, had not returned, and the anxious and press-harassed members of the Club, all of them secretly fearing the worst, had then been obliged to dig very much deeper into their pockets than any of them had originally intended in order to charter the steam whaler *Erik* and outfit a second relief expedition with Bridgman in command and Dr. Cook on board. By this time the faith of Morris K. Jesup must have been strained to the breaking point, for not only had his protégé failed and that glorious plan become a fiasco, but there was now an angry sense of despair among those of his friends whom he had urged to give their support to Peary.

Even with the return of the *Erik* on 15th September, 1901, with the good news that the *Windward* had been found with Peary and his family on board, and the safe return a few days later of Jo and Marie on the lumbering old *Windward* on which they had spent the last fourteen months, the problems of Jesup were as far from over as were those of the man who had insisted it was his duty to make one last attempt at the Pole.

An ardent admirer of Peary though he was, Jesup had been very deeply disturbed by the report which he had received from Cook – that Peary in both the state of his body and of his mind had not appeared in a fit condition to remain another year in the Arctic. These observations had been confirmed not only by Bridgman and some of the other members of the Club who had gone north on the relief ship *Erik*, but had also been the concern of Jo. She had been worried by his determination that Dr. Dedrick should be sent home, by the doctor's refusal to go out on the *Erik*, and the letter he had delivered on the day of the *Erik*'s departure:

> You will never by any voluntary act of mine be deprived of my medical services nor of a helping hand so long as you remain in the Arctic. If I am not to remain at your headquarters, you can depend on my being at the nearest possible point that I can effect a landing and maintain life. My salary of course ceases from date. My full salary, $1,800 a year, being due me, you will please give me an order on the Peary Arctic Club. I shall refrain from making any public and private comment on the chain of circumstances leading to the rupture in our relations until we return to the States, when I shall justify my course for the sake of my family and my honor, if I deem it necessary.

There is no record of how Peary had reacted to this letter from the man whom he now detested – a man who had not only saved his feet, but also perhaps his life. What is, however, threateningly clear from Dedrick's letter is that the ill-feeling between the two men was already irreconcilable and, as Jo and Bridgman must have seen, potentially damaging to Peary's reputation and also to his ambition.

What if Dedrick, cast adrift from Peary's expedition, should not "maintain life," as he put it? Would Peary not be held to blame? What if he did survive a year all alone among the Eskimos – would he, and not Peary, be seen as the hero when he came home to "justify" his course of action? There was another possibility. Supposing in his isolation the doctor should become deranged, and in his bitterness and anger seek vengeance with the gun?

One last effort had been made to persuade the doctor to go home on the *Erik*. Dr. Cook, together with club member Clarence Wyckoff had, at the request of Peary, gone ashore to the Eskimo stone hut in which Dedrick was living and had persuaded him to return with them to the ship to talk the problem through. But Peary had refused to meet him, and Bridgman, acting on Peary's behalf and presumably also on Peary's instructions, had offered the doctor an ultimatum: go home, or go native – or to quote Bridgman's final words on the matter: "You understand that you will not be given one ounce of food from this ship."

"Nor was I," Dedrick was later reported as saying. "I was also told that the $1,800 bonus, which had been acknowledged due to me, was now declared forfeited."

He did in fact leave the ship "with a new rifle, ammunition, furs, and canned goods from the personal stores of Cook and Wyckoff." But even allowing that it was Dedrick's own decision to remain in the Arctic, the casting adrift of Dedrick does follow a pattern in Peary's relationship with some of his men – sad examples being Verhoeff, the even more tragic case of Astrup, and those members of his second wintering crew, all except four of whom Peary had sent home on the *Falcon* in August 1894, disgraced by implication as lacking "the grit and loyalty to remain."

For his wife and only confidant – who had been present on all of those occasions when Peary had reacted so coldly and cruelly towards those who had crossed him, or had lacked, in his view, the will and the courage to do their best – it must have hurt deeply to see this darker side of his nature, and given her cause for the gravest concern as the *Windward* sailed for home.

It is perhaps therefore not surprising that in spite of the very private ordeal of her previous voyage, Jo had felt the need to go north with Marie on the relief expedition of 1902, and to meet Peary at Cape Sabine on 5th August when finally, with his leave almost ended, he had boarded the *Windward* and headed for home, a "discouraged man," according to his daughter, for he was a man who appears to have been blessed with vision, yet cursed with the inability to find an easy way.

He had chosen to cross the Greenland Ice Cap, believing it would be smooth and easy, and had taken that route a second time as though blinded by his first "success" to the lessons it had taught him. It had been much the same with his four-year plan which had returned to his first theory – that dream of which, at twenty-nine, he had been so proud. How many times, at Fort Conger, must he have heard his own words mocking him: "there will come that season when the fortunate man waiting on the verge of the unknown region can speed away to the Pole."

True, he had made a journey in 1900 from Etah, via Fort Conger right around the north coast of Greenland and back to Fort Conger – a journey on which he had established beyond question the insularity of Greenland. But he had already, somewhat prematurely, claimed to have done this on 4th July, 1892, when he had stood on Navy Cliff overlooking the "Peary Channel." He had also, on his attempt at the Pole in 1902, reached a new Farthest North in the western hemisphere of 84°17'N. But this had been only twenty-three miles further than he had previously reached when he had tested himself and his technique against the pack ice north of the Cape that he had named after Morris Jesup, and that record he set in May 1900 had only beaten the Greely record by just over fifty-three miles.

He could, and he should have done so much more, particularly during his last two years. But being obsessed with reaching the Pole he had wasted at least two obvious chances of discovering and mapping new lands to the west, and had lost those lands to his rival Sverdrup who had been in the Arctic for the same length of time. No wonder in his later years he would never willingly speak of that period, those "four lost years" during which the larger, better equipped, and far better organised *Fram* expedition, without the support of Eskimos, had covered a very much greater distance, discovered and mapped (on the whole, commendably) well over fifty thousand square miles, and charted at least two thousand miles of previously unknown coastline. Peary's achievements by comparison (with the exception of course of his north coast journey) appeared to the public as an almost total waste of time, for while Sverdrup was discovering and mapping new land, Peary and his men appeared to have been occupied in nothing more useful than laying out caches, or in trudging dispiritedly back down their trail from one cache to another.

Even to Commander Fitzhugh Green, one of Peary's most devoted admirers, this had been painfully obvious.

For four terrible years he had failed; not gloriously as he had on the Inland Ice, but so dismally that to the end of his life he never wrote more than a few curt pages about that awful period; and he wrote them only because he felt it his duty to make some sort of report to those who had backed him.

The final part of that report Peary had written on his way home and had handed over to Secretary Bridgman on 17th September, 1902, when "after an uneventful voyage" the *Windward* had dropped anchor at Sydney, Nova Scotia. That voyage, however, which in *Nearest the Pole*, Peary so casually dismisses as "uneventful" was, without any doubt, a turning point in his polar career. He had boarded the *Windward* a broken man, a man who had failed himself, his wife, and everyone who had held faith in him over the terrible past four years. And yet by the time that he reached Sydney, not only had Peary regained his strength and come to terms with his wounded pride, but he was confident that by an entirely new plan he would "next time" be successful.

What advice Jo had offered him during their six weeks' voyage home is not on record. We may, however, assume that she had warned him of the growing crisis within the Peary Arctic Club, and the feeling held by several of its members that the Club should be disbanded just as soon as Peary was safely home and before he had any chance of announcing plans for another attempt. We may also assume that the healing privacy of those weeks with a soul mate who could share his burden had saved him on this, as on other occasions.

Certainly by the time they reached Sydney, Peary had drawn enough strength from Jo at least to appear to be what the public expected a polar hero to be: an erect, weatherbeaten, courageous man. But strong though he was, he was rarely direct, and it was simply not in the nature of the man to present his public with anything more than it was in his interest to offer.

On board the *Windward* on the way home, resenting no doubt that he had little choice but to offer Dr. Dedrick a passage, he had not spoken a word to the man. But although it had been Dedrick's own decision to remain in the Arctic for one more year among "savages" for whom, as his diary is evidence, he clearly had more disgust than affection, it had no doubt occurred to both Peary and Jo that he might, as leader, be held responsible for the state of mind the doctor had been in at the time he had made that decision. This being so, Peary must have been greatly relieved when the doctor declined to tell his tale on the grounds that it "might detract from the interest in Peary's exploration."

Not expecting this magnanimous gesture, Peary had safeguarded himself against any embarrassing questions by requesting Bridgman to represent him, offering as an explanation for this, his need to set out immediately for Portland to settle his mother's estate. It was an arrangement which, aside from neatly side-stepping a problem, had also tactically been a wise one, for Bridgman (being himself in the newspaper business as publishing manager of the *Brooklyn Standard Union*) not only knew what the reporters wanted, but also how to cast bait: "Lieutenant Peary has done a great work," he offered, "and has succeeded in going farther north than any American has ever done before." And then, the hint Bridgman knew at least a few of the editors would take and thus give Peary the chance he needed of staying one step ahead of the Club: "As to whether he will ever make another attempt to reach a point farther north in the Arctic than he has, I am unable to say."

Less wise, however, had been Bridgman's statement on returning from the Arctic the previous year when he had been quoted by the *New York Times* as saying that Dedrick was "practically insane, possessed with the mania that . . . he must stay in the arctic regions until the end of the expedition." Had Dedrick not learned of this, he may well have gone home to the bosom of his family and privately nursed his grudge against Peary. But he now felt the need to defend himself, and in a lengthy statement to the *New York Herald* (only a part of which was published) he explained his motives for remaining in the North in terms which cast a different light on the character of Peary:

> They were simply that I would not leave men in the Arctic without a chance for medical aid. The animosity exhibited in the endeavor to brand me [insane] and bring me into disrepute, the refusing of my unpaid salary on such technical grounds, Mr. Peary's almost inhuman treatment of me without provocation during the last year, and his threat

to maroon me for a fifth year ... make reason for my resignation unnecessary ... They would entail a long and, to me, shameful story.

But if this hurt Peary, what hurt him very much more had been the feelings of some of the members of the Peary Arctic Club which he was now, and for the first time, confronting at first hand.

The members having lost hope and faith, we are in a mood of masterly inactivity, if not actually moribund. Peary's experience has definitely taught him that ... Greenland as a route and Etah as a base must be abandoned; that no steamer exists equal to forcing Kennedy Channel and Lincoln Sea.

If he was to have any chance of going north again, Peary had to do something decisive to hold the Club together. He also had to do something to improve the condition of his feet. And so, within a month of returning from the Arctic, he sought out the man known as the surgeon to the four hundred, the distinguished Dr. W. W. Keene of Philadelphia, and on 15th October underwent his third operation. It required that the two remaining little toes which projected beyond the stumps of the others should be dealt with in order to "remove in part the handicap" as biographer Hobbs explained: "The outer joint in each was amputated and, slitting the skin at the front of the feet, the tissue from underneath and behind the toes was drawn forward to make a cushion for the stumps when marching."

And marching Peary was with renewed confidence by 13th November, straight to his place as guest of honour at a dinner given for him by the Peary Arctic Club, and straight to the point: he was ready for another attempt, and he wanted the Club to support him.

He sent off a batch of newspaper clippings the following day to Morris Jesup, all of which supported his patriotic plea that he "ought to have another try," and the delight of Jesup shines right through the exclamation of mock despair which we find in his letter to Herbert Bridgman of 15th November, 1902: "Peary evidently still hankers after exploration," he had sighed almost like the harassed guardian of a brilliantly precocious child. "I do not know what to do."

Neither did Jo. Writing to Peary the day after the dinner, she seems to be trying to hide her own feelings behind those of their nine-year-old daughter Marie and, despite her devotion and sense of commitment, the impression is that she was weeping.

When Marie came home at noon I said to [her] "the *Herald* says the Peary Arctic Club wants your father to go north again."
She just flew to the paper, "let me see it." Then after reading the

paper she burst into a perfect torrent of words. Her eyes flashed and tears rolled down her cheeks. I said "don't you have just as good time when your father is away?" "Yes but I want my father, what's the use of having a father if you only see him in spots."

I said "well the paper does not say that he is going." "Oh, you know very well if they give him the money he will only too gladly go to his beloved huskies." [meaning the Eskimos] All this time I was nearly dying with laughter because she looked so comical. Her flushed tear-stained face, her eyes snapping, her head tossing and all the time her tongue was going. Suddenly she stopped and looked at me in such a curious way, then said "I do believe you are glad he is going – well I am just going to write to him myself."

This she did while I was out this afternoon and I enclose her letter. I also enclose a letter which I will ask you to sign and forward. In looking over the additional checks I find that our balance in the bank is $306.48. I have written to the auditor . . :

Nov 14, 1902

My dear, dear Father:

Of course I know the papers are not always right, but I read that the Peary Arctic Club are trying to get your consent to go north again. I think it is a dogs shame and wish every member of the Club were dead then you would not have to go in the first place. I know you will do what pleases Mother and me and that is to stay with us at home.

I have been looking at your pictures it seems ten years and I am sick of looking at them. I want to see my father. I don't want people to think me an orphan.

Please think this over.

Your loving
Marie

But by now the husband and the father was already far beyond their reach, fretting over how he would raise the necessary money; how he would build the right sort of ship; and how, against impossible odds, he would get another leave from the Navy.

With his five and a half years' leave expired (during which time he had received $14,300 in leave pay), he had reported for duty at the Bureau of Yards and Docks in the Navy Department, Washington, D.C., on 27th November, 1902, feeling, as he put it, as though he "had wandered back like a lost cat."

Here he was, at forty-six, so out of touch with naval routine that he was obliged for a while to walk two paces behind his juniors, and to suffer the silent reproof of those among his fellow officers who had remained faithful to their wedded profession, grown weary with the monotony of it, and envious of Peary's nerve and ability to break free from it and return to its generous bosom just whenever he so chose. And yet there was no outspoken resentment of Peary, as occasionally there had been in the past, for he was seen now as a man who had once had a great idea and had somehow wasted his chance.

But a failure though Peary's four-year expedition had been in his own estimation and also to his great dismay in the opinion of several members of the Club, in the eyes of the President of the United States a failure Peary was not. His thrusting patriotism and his obvious grit and determination were what Theodore Roosevelt liked to see, for a man such as this was a man of his own type: vigorous, bold, and determined to succeed, the very stuff of an American hero. Like Jesup, he believed Peary would win honour for his country given the right opportunity and, with the support of the President, it is hardly surprising that no one in the Navy Department was prepared to take the foolish risk of standing in Peary's way.

A "weather-beaten old fanatic" though he was still being described by some of the more cynical gentlemen of the press, and a man to be "pitied more than derided," according to some of his fellow officers, it was, nevertheless, soon very obvious that Peary was on the move again and simply could not be ignored. Within only two months of returning from his conspicuous failure to reach the North Pole he had, with the results of two examinations confirming his proficiency as an engineer, shot up from the rank of Lieutenant to one more appropriate to his age and his status as an explorer, that of Commander, United States Navy, and sooner than any of his superiors had expected, suggestions were coming from high above to find the man some special assignments.

And this they had done. Within weeks of reporting for duty, he had so impressed the Chief of Bureau with his "superior intelligence and his boundless energy" that he was sent to Europe as president of a naval commission to make a study of the European style of military barracks. It was a task that suited his inquiring mind. More importantly, however, for Commander Peary, the commission offered openings into the society of his fellow explorers and the somewhat more rarefied social heights of some of their admirers.

In England at that time speculation raged over the outcome of Scott's *Discovery* expedition which everyone knew, but no one in authority would publicly admit, had set its sights on the attainment of the South Pole. Peary's own hopes of reaching the North Pole were inevitably rekindled, even though he would require a great deal more backing than he had received on all of his previous attempts put together.

He had of course a stronger base upon which to build than ever he had had before: an unequalled knowledge of the ice in the channel; a hard-earned mastery of the techniques of living and travelling in that hostile region, and the support of that northernmost tribe of Eskimos, the best of whom he was now convinced would be vital to his success. But he knew full well that one false move would scuttle his plan, and it was his recognition of this – the fact that he had honed himself, and acquired, through a great deal of trial and error, a far more effective style of approach – that served him now as his strongest card.

It was a confident form of finesse, and we see it at its very best in the circular letter which Peary sent out on 11th January, 1903, to those who he had hopes would join his exclusive Arctic Club. Its opening sentence sets the tone. He admits to there being "an undercurrent of dissatisfaction in the Peary Arctic Club," but turns the reason for this on its head. He offers a scheme which is patriotic yet seemingly modest in its cost. He offers inducements – their names on the map. In short, he offers a masterful letter which seemingly no self-respecting patriot conceivably could have ignored.

Washington, D.C.,
January 11, 1903

My dear Sir:
Ever since my return from the North last fall, there has been an undercurrent of dissatisfaction in the Peary Arctic Club at letting the work of the Club drop before the Pole was attained.

Correspondence and discussion have now crystallized into the following condition.

I have told the Club that I am willing to throw myself into the work for two more years, and make a supreme effort which shall crown all past efforts with success, if I can have a suitable equipment, and by suitable equipment I mean a *first-class* ship, as this is practically the only expensive item of equipment that I require.

I want no large pay roll, and no expensive and untried items of outfit. My Eskimos and my dogs cost practically nothing.

Given a ship of strength and power sufficient to land me with my party and supplies at or near Floeberg Beach, the *Alert*'s winter quarters, I believe that I am justified in saying that I will answer for the rest.

What I propose is to purchase a strong hulled ship of some 350 to 400 tons net register, bring her to New York, have her heavily reinforced with bulk-heads, struts and sheathing; put into her entirely new engines and boiler of about double the usual power, so that she can exert great pushing power; have trial trips to remedy any minor defects; and let her go north as an American ship and an exponent of American mechanical ability.

I estimate the cost of the work for the two years at $100,000. This is a modest estimate. Other expeditions have cost from $300,000 to $1,000,000.

At a meeting of the Club in New York last Friday some $30,000 were assured provided the entire amount can be raised; but it was not thought quite advisable to authorize me to go ahead and purchase my ship until more money was certain. Another meeting of the Club is to be held on the 19th when the project will stand or fall.

In the meantime a strong effort is to be made to interest other gentlemen in the project. The idea of the present active members of the Club is to increase its membership to fifty gentlemen at $2,000, or one hundred at $1,000 and extend the range of the Club by recruiting from Philadelphia, Boston and Washington, as well as New York. Of course if anyone (as has been the case with some members of the Club) wishes to put in more, so much the better.

In a nutshell the matter stands thus. I know that somewhere the money is waiting to do this work, and I know that between now and July, $100,000 or more can be raised. But the crucial thing is to secure enough money for the purchase of the ship *now*. The time is at best none too long were she ordered this week. I believe if assurances of $50,000 are forthcoming next Monday, the project will go through.

I am after five new members. Members of the Club are after others. This letter is not one of solicitation, it rather offers an opportunity.

It is no figure of speech but cold fact to say that if I win out in this work the names of those who made the work possible will be kept through the coming centuries floating forever above the forgotten and submerged debris of our time and day.

The one thing that we remember of Ferdinand of Spain is that he sent Columbus to his life-work. The one thing we remember of Grinnell of New York, that he sent Kane to his great work.

Very sincerely,

R. E. PEARY

But the response was disheartening. Not only did most of them find suitable excuses for declining to support the proposition, but a good many insulted Peary by simply not taking the time to reply. Even some of the most hopeful prospects turned his proposition down. One of these had been Mr. Henry Bryant, President of the Philadelphia Academy of Sciences, who had earlier been so helpful and supportive – even a privileged passenger on the *Falcon* on the voyage of 1894 which had taken home Jo and her baby and all but two of Peary's men.

Peary's reply to Bryant's letter, which amongst other things suggested that Nansen's concept of a drift was a more effective way of reaching a high latitude, is in parts revealing. So too is Peary's attitude towards so-called scientific projects on polar expeditions:

> I agree with you in a way, in what you say of the drift method. I recognize fully its possibilities ... But this method has several objections.
>
> First, it takes too long (five years at least).
>
> Second, it is in no way fitted for a man of my temperament who can endure almost anything as long as he feels that his own exertions will have some bearing upon the final result; but who would fret himself to death if he were a helpless piece of flotsam, dependent upon the whim of winds and currents, and powerless to work out his own salvation.
>
> Third, it has always seemed a peculiar thing to me that neither Nansen nor Sverdrup has ever moved to repeat his attempt. If the method is such a certainty, why with their experience do they not try it again, and do the thing. You know as well as I that the talk of having secured all the scientific information that is desirable, and not considering the Pole alone of any especial value, is all rot. You and I are no longer chickens, and we both know that no man would give a few facts of so-called scientific information the slightest weight, if balanced against the Pole.

It is clear from these remarks that Peary was simply incapable of understanding a mind such as Nansen's. So deeply rooted was his own obsession with reaching the Pole, he could not conceive of anyone having a greater interest in exploration than in planting a national flag at that point which meant so much to him. So he went on to extol to Bryant the advantages of the Smith Sound route over all others with similar blind-spots in his reasoning resulting from his own investment in the shortest route to fame:

> As to the Franz-Joseph land route, Abruzzi's plucky success, which missed by a hair's breadth being a complete catastrophe, has made people forget that there has been as equally long a list of failures there as by the Smith Sound route. Further I believe Abruzzi's accomplishment marks the limit by that route.

Bryant's reply was typical of the hundreds of letters that Peary received from men he had hoped would help him:

My Dear Captain [sic] Peary:

My delay in answering your letter of January 17th has not been owing to indifference; but because I was turning over the matter in my mind.

Your letter is a strong presentation of the Smith Sound route, and breathes the proper spirit of a leader who believes in himself and his cause. I must confess, however, after hearing your lecture and reading your article in *McClure's* – in both of which the physical obstacles you had to overcome were treated with modest candor – I am more than ever impressed with the almost insuperable obstacles to be overcome by anyone attacking the Pole over the shifting floe ice and open leads which characterize the region north of Cape Hecla (i.e. the Polar Sea). To put the matter briefly in my humble opinion, the chances of success are not promising even under your experienced and resolute leadership.

The disheartening, draining effects of such letters, and the growing threat, as Peary saw it, of being ordered to duty on the West Coast, had surely tested his nerve and persistence as no other period in his life had done, for at this stage he was so close to succeeding in launching his first really viable plan, and yet right on the brink of oblivion. Two more gold medals in 1902, and his promotion to Commander in that same year, had helped improve his status, and so too had the rare distinction (for a serving officer in the Navy) of being elected in 1903 as President of the American Geographical Society. Such honours had, however, only served to remind Peary how far he was still from his dream of fame, and had his admirer in the White House not come to his aid at this critical time there can be very little doubt that his polar career would have ended.

But the man whom Peary had once encouraged with a friendly letter of support from the Arctic was now in a position to return that encouragement, and the orders dated 5th September, 1903, which had come down the line from the Secretary of the Navy read like a blessing to the man who had been almost on the point of quitting.

The attainment of the Pole should be your main object. Nothing short will suffice. The discovery of the poles is all that remains to complete the map of the world ... Our national pride is involved in the undertaking, and this department expects that you will accomplish your purpose and bring further distinction to a service of illustrious traditions.

In conclusion, I am pleased to inform you that the President of the United States sympathises with your cause and approves the enterprise.

He had been granted three years' leave to commence on 9th September, 1903, only a few days after the birth of a son, Robert Peary, Jr. But in spite of his orders which made it clear that it now was his duty to attain the North Pole, the Navy had drawn a line at financing the mission on which they were sending their man. With the Peary Arctic Club still in a state of disarray, Peary had been thrown back once again on the personal support of Morris Jesup, and the advice of Bridgman, the secretary of the Club, who by now had taken over the role of the explorer's personal advisor in all affairs concerning the press and Peary's public image.

Under the street-wise guidance of Bridgman, Peary's image rapidly improved. It was given a further boost on 10th November, 1903, when Admiral Sir Lewis Beaumont, addressing a distinguished audience at the Royal Geographical Society in London, sang Peary's praises loud enough for the wider audience to hear:

> I want you to appreciate how great was the work done by Commander Peary; that, starting from halfway down Smith Sound, 400 miles from the starting-point of the three other expeditions, he has accomplished more than they. I consider it is due first to the man himself, who has shown himself to be every inch a man, not only when such work had to be done, but also when the time of trouble and sorrow came, and he took care of his people at their dying moments.

Generous praise indeed from a man who had wintered in those same regions. But to state that Peary had accomplished more than those expeditions that had gone before was giving Peary more credit than he rightly deserved. More what? More discovered new territory; more scientific results; or was Sir Lewis, caught up in the emotion of his address, simply referring to the miles that Peary had covered? The fact that he admired Peary was all that really mattered, for that admiration was a lift to Peary's reputation at precisely the time he needed it most, and with the presentation of the Livingstone Gold Medal of the Royal Scottish Geographical Society two days later he could return to Washington with some proof that he was the right man for the Club – the man who had earned his chance.

Peary's persistence, and the support of Jo, eventually paid off on 19th April, 1904, when the Peary Arctic Club was given a new lease of life with its incorporation under the laws of the State of New York as a Club "to aid and assist in forming and maintaining certain expeditions to be placed under Commander Robert E. Peary, U.S.N."

But while money was being raised by the Club for the construction of a ship that would be capable of penetrating the ice in the Nares Strait and wintering on the shores of the Arctic Ocean, Peary was collecting drawings and specifications for a very different project, one that was almost as close to his heart as his dream of attaining the Pole.

As early as 1873, when he was only seventeen, he had fallen in love with a thickly wooded island in Casco Bay, off the coast of Maine, which he had promised himself he would one day own. According to his grandson, Commander Edward Stafford, Peary had even known "then and there, where he would build his house: on the bold northeastern bluff jutting out into the bay like the bow of a great ship with the curving, sheltered beach in its lee." He had made more summer visits from Bowdoin College, which is only some fifteen miles or so from the fishing village of South Harpswell – the nearest village to what Peary called his Promised Land – and in 1879, with the first $500 that he was able to set aside, he had bought that island which was named for the eagles that had once nested there.

And it truly is a magical place, its seventeen acres still growing wild with beech, birch, maple and spruce; its underbrush a tangle of berries, its miniature valleys thick with ferns, while in the lee of the island's back which breaks the surface of Casco Bay like one of a school of basking whales, there is still that sloping carpet of grass flanked by two protected beaches, and, all the time, the sound of the sea.

"When he came to the island," his son once told me, "he breathed deeply and relaxed. This was his place. He loved it – and it loved him." And here, in that summer of 1904, he built his house and a smaller caretaker's cottage, completing them by the Fourth of July. And yet, as the family's story goes, he never really completed that house for it was, like his island, something about which Peary could dream in those hours, those days, those months that he was away from home, his family, and his island.

But the interlude of Eagle Island, as his daughter touchingly referred to it, was over all too soon. At a meeting with Morris Jesup, "small as to numbers" as Peary later recalled, "but weighty with importance in the affairs of the Peary Arctic Club," Jesup offered to guarantee the building of the special ship if Peary could raise $25,000 to match his own donation. Generous though the offer was, even with the advice of Bridgman whose skill in "altering public opinion" had recently proved so very effective, there seemed to Peary little hope of raising that much money in time. Fortunately, however, also present at that meeting had been the ship-builder, Captain Charles Dix, and it was this thin and surprisingly gentle-looking man who solved the problem by offering to order all of the timber "on his own responsibility," and to take his chance on Peary raising the money to pay him back.

It was a statement which Peary recorded as being "like a ray of sunlight" both to himself and to Morris Jesup, and with the keel finally laid on 15th October in the McKay & Dix shipyard at Bucksport, Maine, the family set up home in the town's small hotel in order that they might be with Peary, at least for part of the time. "Every morning my father went across the river to Verona, where his ship was being built and remained there all day, personally supervising every step in the construction ... from the time the first timbers of the keel were laid until the finished ship was launched," wrote Marie in her book.

With the *Roosevelt* christened by Jo on 23rd March, 1905, there was now only three and a half months left before the date Peary had set for the departure of the expedition, and every day was spent clearing obstacles that reappeared larger in every dream. It was one mad whirl of meetings, lectures, and status-enhancing public appearances, all of which were a part of his mission and a part of the burden he had chosen to bear. Right from the moment that Peary made the first public announcement of his "final" expedition before a packed house of distinguished delegates at the Eighth International Geographic Congress held in New York on 14th September, 1904, he was constantly in demand by his public and with little time or energy left to devote to his wife and children. This Jo knew she had to accept, as is evident from a poignant sentence in one of her letters to him at this time: "I do feel for you, my dearest; I can't do much or indeed anything except keep quiet."

This was the price they both had to pay if he was to stay ahead of his rivals, and rivals he had, for even though in Peary's view they were not at that time a serious threat, he could see from the comments of the *New York Sun* that he was not looked upon by the press or the delegates as the only American polar explorer present at that Congress: "By far the greater number are men who have met with dime-novel adventures on sea or land. There is Peary, who has journeyed more miles in the Arctic than any other living man. There is Dr. Cook, who came back alive from the frozen Antarctic..."

Peary heard Cook on this occasion deliver no less than three papers on his recent achievements: the first on his attempt in 1903 to climb Mount McKinley; the second, an explorer's "comparative view" of the Arctic and the Antarctic; and the third on the voyage and achievements of the *Belgica* expedition to the Antarctic on which he had been the surgeon. It had, however, clearly been some consolation to Peary that at the dinner which ended that Congress, Peary had been presented by the French delegate with the gold medal of the Paris Geographical Society, for in his speech of acceptance we see him again in his most buoyant and arrogant public role as the only real explorer:

> Next summer I shall start north again after that on which I have set my heart ... Shall I win? God knows. I hope and dream and pray that I may ... If I win, you will have another one of those magnificent tokens [medals] for me, and be proud because we are of one blood – the man blood.

Meanwhile the Peary Arctic Club still needed funds, despite a gift of $50,000 from the banker and director of the Southern Pacific Railroad, George Crocker, another of Jesup's wealthy and influential friends. A well publicised day cruise aboard the *Roosevelt* was arranged by Bridgman for those who might make sizeable contributions. Potential patrons would be able to admire the commodious cabin from which Peary would conduct his final assault, replete with cellarette, pianola equipped to play "popular opera, marches and rag-time," and decorated with an etching of the President. What the would-be sponsors could not know was that it was the cabin in which Peary was to spend a total of two years of his Arctic time, as against only seven months in the field. But for the present all was enthusiasm. According to the *New York Tribune*'s description of the junket, "Every boat in sight, from the ocean grayhounds to the shabby little tugboats, gave three blasts for the *Roosevelt*, as she passed by." And as a result the money came rolling in. Even the world of show business climbed on to the bandwagon with offers of $25,000 from the Hippodrome, and two benefit performances of an African Buffalo Bill spectacle (one of which Peary attended) which raised a reported further $10,000.

And so the relieved and delighted Peary, thanking the American people and newspapers who "had never failed to stand by explorers," boarded his ship at her anchorage off West 34th Street, Manhattan, and at 3.15 p.m. on the blistering hot Sunday of 16th July, 1905, the *Roosevelt* sailed on her maiden voyage bound for a point about as far north as any ship can go.

With his wife Jo, his now almost-twelve-year-old daughter Marie, and his two-year-old son Robert E. Peary, Jr., together with his mother-in-law and some of his friends from the Peary Arctic Club, the explorer stood amidships as the *Roosevelt* steamed down the Hudson River, "bowing to the plaudits that came from all sides of the River" and on across New York Bay where "volley after volley of salutes roared from forts and clubs as the ship passed."

Finally, at a respectable distance from the point of departure, a tug came alongside to take Peary's family and friends back to New York, and in a moving farewell ceremony Bridgman affirmed that the Club would stand by him right to the end. "I am going now in God's name," Peary had replied, "and with the help of God I hope to accomplish the end in view."

But there is no indication in any of his writings that Peary truly believed in God, nor had he any certainty that he would be successful.

CHAPTER 11

Farthest North, 1906?

Part 1 "Nothing short will suffice"

This for Peary was to be his last expedition, or so at that time he thought. He had the experience, he had the right ship, and he now had a commitment so finely honed that seemingly nothing could stop him. But he was also now wiser and more circumspect, and at long last had abandoned the theory (to which he had clung so stubbornly) that the only way to reach the Pole was to travel with a small party. This change to the so-called "Peary System" of supporting parties involving great numbers of men and dogs, being a reversal of his strongly held earlier conviction, was to present him later with several problems, not least of which being how to explain to his many critics why it had taken him so long to devise it.

But on 16th July, 1905, when the *Roosevelt* sailed from New York the black years were at last behind him. Now he had a powerful ship to transport all of his Eskimos, dogs and equipment to the very shores of the Arctic Ocean, and among his hand-picked crew of twenty, at least two men in whom he had implicit confidence, his captain, Robert A. Bartlett, who already at thirty was larger than life, and whose torrent of directions in times of stress was loud and profane enough to burst every bead of sweat on his neck, and the other, of course, was Henson.

Besides these two exceptional men, there were only three others who had been north before: the mate, Moses Bartlett; the boatswain, John Murphy, and Peary's ageing steward, Charles Percy, who had spent two consecutive years in the Arctic, the first with Jo and Marie on the *Windward*, followed by the hard final year with Peary, since when, with his wife, he had held the grand title of "resident in charge of Eagle Island." The other four officers were new to the North: George Wardwell, a man of "phlegmatic temperament" who, having been the engineer in the shipyard in which the *Roosevelt* was built, had expressed himself "deeply interested in her proposed work and anxious to join the expedition"; his assistant engineer, Murtaugh Malone; the surgeon of the expedition, Dr. Louie Wolf; and a twenty-five-year-old engineering graduate from Cornell University, Ross G. Marvin, who Peary described as his "secretary and assistant." Of the rest of his crew, Peary has little to say other than that they were, with one exception, all "natives of Newfoundland [and] of the usual type of sailors and sealers common to that island."

With such a ship and such a crew, unburdened by any commitment to scientific observation or the time-consuming and relatively thankless task of geographical discovery, it can surely be little wonder that he felt the signs were at last propitious, that the time, the man, and the dream were on course for him this time to achieve his goal.

Cape York was sighted at 2 p.m. on 7th August, the run across Melville Bay having been made in twenty-five hours. No ice or ice sky was seen, and on going ashore at the first village he was told that some fifteen families were in hunting camps on Meteorite Island, among them some of his best men. He rounded them up like sheep, in some cases nothing more being needed than the blast of the ship's horn:

> . . . without dropping anchor, shouted to the men to get ready to move . . . At Meteorite Island are three of my old men and, in an hour or two, they are all on board with their belongings, and we steam away, leaving the place deserted. Back to the next settlement and the operation is repeated. Six families move all their belongings on board and desert their village in about three hours.

And so he had gone around the villages of the hunters, collecting Eskimo families, dogs, skins and meat until, on the 16th August, after taking on board coal and walrus meat from the auxiliary steam whaler *Erik*, the *Roosevelt* had "swung out from the harbor of Etah and severed all communication with the civilized world." Peary tells us that:

> Below decks the ship was filled with coal until her plank sheer was nearly to the water; on deck were more than two hundred Eskimo dogs; and on the top gallant forecastle, and the tops of both forward and after deck houses were over half a hundred Eskimos, men, women and children, and their belongings.

Now began the real test of Peary's plan and the "heavy pack ice surging down Smith Sound" soon gave him the opportunity to see how effective his ship could be. A fire, however, had damaged her boilers and reduced by half the driving power which was one of the main features of her design. The ship being also heavy with coal, Bartlett had been somewhat disconcerted by orders from Peary to drive the *Roosevelt* into the ice. Both designer and captain were no doubt relieved when the first test of strength was won by the ship.

But "enthusiastic" though Bartlett became, they failed to carry out Peary's plan of laying a cache of coal and provisions at his old base of Payer Harbor. Indeed, their track was deflected south-west to within some ten miles of Cape Isabella, before they were able to work their way clear and eventually get in at Victoria Head on the thumb end of the Bache Peninsula. There they laid their depot on the 18th, and while the work of unloading was in progress, Peary, with three of the Eskimos, went off to a neighbouring valley which he knew from his previous hunting trips, and brought back "three musk-oxen, a large bull, a cow, and a yearling, the latter being brought aboard alive." This animal, he tells us, "was of the greatest interest to the crew and the 'tenderfoot' members of the expedition, and the arrival of nearly eight hundred pounds of fine fresh beef created a very agreeable impression on everyone." Peary had needed this diversion even more than his men. It was for him a reunion with a part of himself which he had almost forgotten.

> Up to this time the rush of getting on board my Eskimos and dogs, re-stowing the ship and fighting the ice, had left me no time for a thought beyond the demands of each hour. Now as I trod the moss patches besides the murmuring stream whose quieter reaches were crusted with ice, saw the fresh tracks of big game and a little later the shaggy black bulks of the musk-oxen with heads lowered and hoofs stamping, in the way I knew so well, my pulse bounded rapidly and I felt that I had come into my own again.

So many mixed memories came crowding upon him as they weaved their way northwards past Cape D'Urville where the *Windward* had wintered in 1898–9, and the site of the old box-house in which, on 30th April, 1901, he had read those poignant letters from Jo. Now he was heading north, "vigilantly watching the ice" for any opening that might offer a way through to Fort Conger and beyond, and twice they nearly reached Cape Joseph Good at the entrance of the Kennedy Channel, only to be forced back to a shelter behind the massive buttress of Cape Wilkes. From this position he could see that the western coast of the channel was blocked, just as Nares had found it to be at almost this very point on 20th August, 1875: "the ice drifting to the southward on the western side of Kennedy Channel . . . prevented our advance unless I took the ships off into the middle of the strait." And so, Peary tells us: "I determined to test my belief gained in my last four years of work in this region, that the Greenland side of the Kennedy and Robeson Channels offered as a rule more favorable opportunities for navigation than the Grinnell Land side."

But whilst it is true that Peary had the advantage of knowing that coastline like the back of his hand, he had seen the channel north of Cape D'Urville only in that state in which it was passable by sledge. Even during his summer at Fort Conger in 1900, his impression of the movement of ice would have been restricted to a range of only some twenty miles across the Robeson Channel, and from the middle of September into

October, "it being evident," as he says, "that my ship would not reach us," he had set out for Lake Hazen on a hunting trip with Henson and four Eskimos.

Heading his ship across the flow and then boring northward directly against it, he was therefore entering upon a new experience, but he could not admit this without also admitting that his four years of sledging in that region had taught him little or nothing that would help him in driving a ship through that channel. The newness of that experience comes across in the exhilaration of his account:

> In all my experiences I recall nothing more exciting than the thrill, the shock of hurling the *Roosevelt*, a fifteen-hundred ton battering-ram, at the ice to smash a way through, or the tension of the moments when, caught in the resistless grip of two great ice-fields, I have stood on the bridge and seen the deck amidships slowly bulge upward, and the rigging slacken with the compression of the sides.

At Cape Lupton on the Greenland coast, some twenty-five miles across the channel from Peary's three tiny huts at Fort Conger, a sudden swirl of the current swept the *Roosevelt* into the ice-foot and ground her along its vertical wall, twisting the back of the rudder on its stock and almost disabling the gear. They escaped without more serious damage only because the ship had been driven by the ice into a shallow niche in the ice wall where it was protected from the main force of the pack, and there, after hastily securing the ship with every available line, some temporary repairs were carried out.

They moved clear of that ice-foot just as soon as the pressure relaxed, and steamed on around the coast some twenty-five miles to Cape Brevoort, right at the northern end of the channel. This seemed a safer place at which to repair the steering gear, but during the five days they spent mending the rudder they were "crowded out" of their shelter by the ice. For Peary the delay and inaction became unendurable. And so on the morning of the 28th they had set out for one last contest with the channel pack, their objective, Cape Sheridan, a mere thirty miles to their north-west.

It was an ominous start. Within a mile the ship was caught between two old blue floes which "set the *Roosevelt* vibrating like a violin string for a minute or so before she rose to the pressure." But released, they drove her on through ice at times right up to her plank sheer "and frequently of such height that the boats swinging from the deck house davits had to be swung inboard to clear the pinnacles."

"Ah, the thrill and tension of it," Peary exclaims, "the lust of battle, which crowded days of ordinary life into one."

The forward rush, the gathering speed and momentum, the crash, the upward heave, the grating snarl of the ice as the steel-shod stem split it as a mason's hammer splits granite, or trod it under, or sent it right and left in whirling fragments, followed by the gathering for another rush, were glorious.

At other times, the blue face of a big floe as high as the plank sheer grinding against either side, and the ship inching her way through, her frames creaking with the pressure, the big engines down aft running like a sewing-machine, and the twelve-inch steel shaft whirling the wide-bladed propeller, till its impulse was no more to be denied than the force of gravity.

By midnight they were nearer to the western shore than the one from which they had started, but were steadily drifting southward with the pack. Now in desperation they drove the ship until "by sheer brute insistence" they reached the coast at Wrangle Bay, but still thirty miles from Cape Sheridan, and even while they slept the ice and the winter came at them apace, the one nearly twisting the back off the rudder, the other working a more sinister damage on the nerves of the party. "A wild morning," he wrote in his journal on 1st September at Lincoln Bay, ten miles nearer to his goal, "with snow driving in horizontal sheets across the deck, the water like ink, the ice ghastly white, and the land invisible except close to us as we almost scrape against it on the port side. Summer is at an end and winter has commensed."

With the turn of the tide the ice came in again with a rush and forced the *Roosevelt* bodily ashore, and there for a while she had hung at the mercy of a berg that was pressing against her stern, threatening to edge her further and beyond any hope of floating again. Even when the berg released her, she was twice more forced ashore and hauled off before they got clear of Lincoln Bay and crept a few more miles up the coast to a natural dock near a river delta where they had moored with only a foot of water under the keel.

On 5th September they finally made it, with black smoke pouring from the *Roosevelt*'s stack, through to Cape Sheridan, at a point "about two miles beyond the *Alert*'s position," where the ship was moored with her nose facing north.

I have sledged along that coast, and the exposed position of the place has to be seen to be believed; but as far as Peary was concerned, the *Roosevelt* had done her duty.

Since leaving Etah, we had passed the latitudes of the most northern extremities of Spitzbergen and Franz Joseph Land, and now only the northern points of the two most northern lands in the world, Cape

Morris Jesup and Cape Columbia, lay a little beyond us. The northern-reaching fingers of all the rest of the great world lay far behind us below the ice-bound southern horizon. We were deep in that gaunt frozen border land which lies between God's countries and inter-stellar space.

So they started to prepare for the winter. But there was one last test in store for the ship, and for Peary. It came in the form of a large floe of ice:

> Its slow resistless motion was frightful yet fascinating; thousands of tons of smaller ice which the big floe drove before it, the *Roosevelt* had easily and gracefully turned under her sloping bilges, but the edge of the big floe rose to the plank sheer and a few yards back from its edge was an old pressure ridge which rose higher than the bridge deck. This was the crucial moment. For a minute or so, which seemed an age, the pressure was terrific. The *Roosevelt*'s ribs and interior bracing cracked like the discharge of musketry; the deck amidships bulged up several inches, while the main rigging hung slack and the masts and rigging shook as in a violent gale. Then with a mighty tremor and a sound which reminded me of an athlete intaking his breath for a supreme effort, the ship shook herself free and jumped upward till her propeller showed above water. The big floe snapped against the edge of the ice-foot forward and aft and under us, crumpling up its edge and driving it in-shore some yards, then came to rest, and the commotion was transferred to the outer edge of the floe which crumbled away with a dull roar, as other floes smashed against it, and tore off great pieces in their onward rush, leaving the *Roosevelt* stranded but safe.

Peary's plans were vulnerable also from other directions. Fortunate though his hunting parties had been in killing some seventy-three musk-oxen and twenty-seven caribou, his dogs were dying off at an alarming rate. About eighty dogs had died before the cause was traced to the whale meat which Peary had brought north to supplement whatever the hunters could bring in. Peary again:

> This meat to the amount of several tons was thrown away, and I found myself confronted at the beginning of the long Arctic night with the proposition of subsisting my dogs and most of my Eskimos upon the country.
>
> Without my previous familiarity with the region, this would have been an absolute impossibility; even as it was, it possessed elements of uncertainty, but with the satisfactory start already made in obtaining

musk-oxen, and knowing that these animals could be killed by those who knew how, even in the depths of the great Arctic night, I believed there was somewhat more than a fighting chance of success.

On 25th October, portions of four hunting parties from the Lake Hazen region came in, bringing reports of a bag of one hundred and forty-four head of musk-oxen and deer. Following the return of these parties the dogs died rapidly, the number one night reaching ten. It was evident that prompt action must be taken, and in three days one hundred and two dogs, twenty adult Eskimo men and women and six children were sent into the field in addition to those already out. From this time until the 7th February, the dogs and the greater portion of the Eskimos remained in the Lake Hazen region, a portion of the men coming to the ship during the full moon of each month with sledge loads of meat, and returning with tea, sugar, oil and biscuit. With their departure the ship was almost deserted, daylight was nearly gone and the winter may be said to have commenced.

We are here seeing Peary at his best: dynamic, decisive, inspiring, a man who is making full use of his hard earned knowledge and experience, and a man who deserves to win. So great is the difference between this man and the man who spent the winter at Fort Conger five years earlier, it is hard to believe they are one and the same. And yet, he is still a man with a great deal to learn, particularly about the polar pack ice, and the effect of the forces that drive that ice upon the minds of men.

The pack ice was an ominous presence; seldom if ever silent and, when silent, somehow even more foreboding. His experience of travelling on that drifting ice for three weeks in the spring of 1902 presented him now with a mental picture of what was going on "out there"; but its effect went deeper than he was aware, and his anxieties at that deeper level put an enormous strain on the man. Fortunately, he had the presence of mind to keep himself busy during that winter, and to keep all of his men hard at work. They did not, however, need very much urging, for from Christmas Day on, right through to the end of January, the ship was in almost constant danger of either being bodily torn from its moorings and carried away by the drifting pack, or of being forced by the onshore pressure of ice so far inshore that it would prove impossible to re-float the ship and make their escape from that perilous place back south by the route they had come. Peary says of that month:

It was a period of constant anxiety with the ice pack surging back and forth along the shore on each tide and liable to crash in upon us at any time. Every one slept in their clothes, all lanterns and portable lights were kept filled and trimmed ready for immediate use, and provision made for the instant extinguishment of all fires.

Peary's plan for his assault on the Pole was an extremely complex one, involving twenty-eight men and 120 dogs in a shuttle system advancing food and fuel and Peary across 422 miles of drifting and fracturing ice from Point Moss. Peary was estimating that the round trip would take "a hundred days or a little more, an average travel of about ten miles a day", from which it appears that he was expecting to travel an extra 156 nautical miles as detours from his straight line course from Point Moss to the Pole and back. As a percentage, he was therefore estimating 18.5% of his straight line distance as unavoidable extra miles.

But basic plans invariably need some modification, even in Peary's case where he had succeeded brilliantly in getting his ship to the shores of the Arctic Ocean and had, as a result of his leadership and hard earned experience, come through the long polar night with his ship undamaged, and his crew in good heart and ready for action. He had lost a lot of dogs, which was bound to affect his basic plan, and he still needed to fine tune the whole complex scheme. What is really amazing, however, is the basic premise upon which that plan was based. In spite of his discovery in April 1902 that the drifting pack ice is a treacherous surface across which to travel, and his experience of the pack ice during the winter which had given him so much cause for anxiety, he was still basing his plan on the assumption that he could keep his line of supply intact and on the move. He does not, in his written account of this expedition, give us any information about this plan, presumably because the weaknesses in it were embarrassing to admit. But we do have Henson's version of it, and this is the way it was supposed to work:

The expedition would be divided into two parties, the pioneer party would break the trail steadily northward, while the main party followed several days behind. The main body would be broken up into five subdivisions, each with a small group of Eskimos headed by one white man. As the main party advanced over the trail set by the pioneer, one of the subdivisions would drop out at intervals of fifty miles. The sub-party would then return over their trail and pick up supplies relayed forward from Point Moss by the subdivisions behind them, and carry out the provisions north to the next relay team. Thus, when Peary reached a point 250 miles from land, where he would join his pioneering party, he would have an advance base which was being fed constantly by supplies from Point Moss.

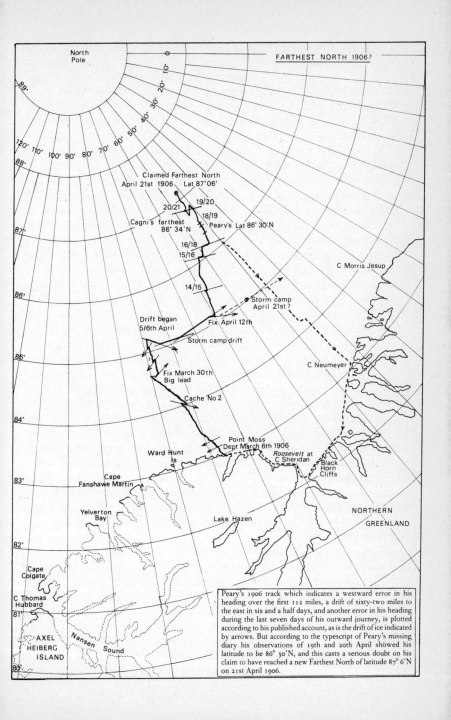

FARTHEST NORTH 1906?

North Pole

89°

120° 110° 100° 90° 80° 70° 60° 50° 40° 30° 20° 10° 0

88°

Claimed Farthest North
April 21st 1906. Lat 87°06'

20/21   19/20
         18/19
Cagni's farthest   Peary's Lat 86°30'N
86°34'N

87°

16/18
15/16

C Morris Jesup

14/15

86°

Storm camp
April 21st?

Drift began   Fix April 12th
5/6th April

Storm camp drift

C Neumeyer?

85°

Fix March 30th
Big lead

Cache No 2

84°

Point Moss
Dept March 6th 1906   Roosevelt at
                           C Sheridan
Ward Hunt   Black
Is   Horn
Cape   Cliffs
Fanshawe Martin

83°

Yelverton
Bay   NORTHERN

                    Lake Hazen   GREENLAND

82°

Cape
Colgate

C Thomas
Hubbard

81°

AXEL   Nansen
HEIBERG   Sound
ISLAND

80°

Peary's 1906 track which indicates a westward error in his
heading over the first 112 miles, a drift of sixty-two miles to
the east in six and a half days, and another error in his heading
during the last seven days of his outward journey, is plotted
according to his published account, as is the drift of ice indicated
by arrows. But according to the typescript of Peary's missing
diary his observations of 19th and 20th April showed his
latitude to be 86° 30'N, and this casts a serious doubt on his
claim to have reached a new Farthest North of latitude 87° 6'N
on 21st April 1906.

"It'll work," Matt Henson is said to have told Peary, "if God, wind, leads, ice, snow and all the hells of this damned frozen land are willing." And one can only wonder, in view of the outcome, if Peary had considered any one of these imponderables. He had certainly not discussed his plan with his black assistant in advance of committing himself and his men to that attempt at the Pole, even though Henson, by this stage in his career, was a more experienced sledger than Peary and, once out on the pack ice, would certainly be the most vital single asset to Peary's chance of success.

Indeed, Peary is reported to have said: "Professor Marvin, Bartlett, Dr. Wolf, myself and two members of the ship's crew [Firemen Clark and Ryan] will form the main party. And to be damned sure we succeed, I'm sending you, Matt out six days ahead of us with the pioneering party."

On Henson now lay the responsibility for breaking a trail across some of the roughest polar pack ice he and Peary had encountered, ice that was cracking up all around them, and certainly much more dangerous to cross than Peary had imagined it would be when he had drawn up his plan. But that was Henson's thankless task, and he set off on 28th February, with the other divisions following his trail on successive days, each improving it by their passage until finally, on 6th March, Peary set out, last in a line of some twenty sledges strung out over the broken pack ice and heading, as he says in his journal, "direct" for the goal.

Out in front, Henson was not only cutting a trail for the rest of the expedition to follow, but increasing his chances with every mile that he pushed farther north, of being cut off from his vital supply of food, perhaps even from any chance of returning safely to land. His was the role, without any question, that required the greatest courage and commitment, and one which Peary (because his journeys on the Arctic Ocean came several years too late in his life) was never fully able to experience, and much less, understand. On the polar pack ice he drove from the rear of his army of men with a frenzied passion to reach his objective, but never with that sense of awe and achievement which only the pioneer can know, and never with that fear and exhilaration which the man in the lead feels in his stomach when he knows he is going right out on a limb.

It is surprising how long it took Peary to realise that his plan could not possibly work. It is almost as though he had taken no account of the fact that he and his men were on drifting ice, although the evidence of this is recorded repeatedly in his diary. Only three days out Peary writes: "At this camp again the floe on which my igloos were built cracked under the terrific pressure, and the igloos shook and trembled as if by an earthquake shock, so that some of the Eskimos rushed out in alarm."

And on the following day (9th March) Peary met Bartlett returning from cache number one for more supplies:

A few moments conversation with him put me in touch with conditions and the location of everyone ahead of me. He reported the ice in motion everywhere, the floe upon which my advance loads were placed yesterday drifted a mile or more to the southeast, and the trail disrupted for a long distance.

But in spite of all the warning signs (first seen as long ago as 1902), he is still indulging in dreams as far into his march as the seventeenth day:

Though I fight against it continuously, I find it impossible under conditions like today not to indulge in some thoughts of *success* as I tramp along, and I get so impatient that I do not want to stop at the igloos but keep right on and on. At night I can hardly sleep waiting for the dogs to get rested sufficiently to start again. Then I think, what will be the effect if some insuperable obstacle, open water, absolutely impossible ice, or an enormous fall of snow knock me out now when everything looks so encouraging? Will it break my heart, or will it simply numb me into insensibility? and then I think, what's the odds, in two months at the longest the agony will be over, and I shall know one way or the other, and then whichever way it turns out, before the leaves fall I shall be back on Eagle Island again, going over the well-known places with Jo and the children, and listening to the birds, the wind in the trees, and the sound of lapping waves (do such things really exist on this frozen planet?)

Can we detect a hint of reality creeping in? If he had been keeping a record of his daily marches up to cache number two which he reached on 22nd March, he would have been aware that he had covered only about seventy nautical miles – an average of 4.1 miles a day over the first seventeen days of the journey. There is, however, no mention in his published account of any daily mileage up to this point. All he tells us is that "four good marches were reeled off from cache number two in good weather," and that each of these four marches was an advance of at least twelve miles. It was in fact slightly less than this because he was losing some miles to the drift, so even with that sudden spurt, his average was only increased to 5.2 miles a day, and this was nowhere near good enough (even supposing he could sustain it) to get him to the Pole. But at the end of that fourth consecutive twelve-mile day, he came up against the obstacle he most dreaded, a great split in the ice – the "big lead." Here, on 26th March, Peary found "three parties banked up" on the south side of "a broad lead extending east and west across our course, farther than we could see."

Realising that he could not afford to feed all of those men and dogs "during what might be a several days' wait," Peary sent two of his divisions (seven sledges) back down the trail on the 27th, and Henson out on a scouting mission in the hope of finding a way across. On the 30th, still held up by the open lead, Peary was able to get a sun observation which gave the position of that camp: it was latitude 84°38'N, longitude 74°W, with a magnetic variation of 107°W. Peary's comment on this was not only unfair, but his magnetic variation points the finger at himself as the cause of the error: "We were somewhat farther west than I intended owing to the constant tendency of Henson and his party to turn to the left in negotiating leads and areas of rough ice."

The implication is that it had come as something of a shock to Peary to discover that his camp at the Big Lead was so far to the west, although there is no reason why it should have done. Henson was travelling on a compass heading and, for most of the time, was way out ahead of Peary; but Peary also had a compass, and it is impossible to believe that he did not check the heading of the tracks he was following, and equally unlikely that he would not have corrected Henson at the first opportunity if he had discovered that Henson was off course. That first opportunity was on 15th March when Henson and Peary were only thirty-seven miles from Point Moss, and of this meeting Peary says:

> On the 15th I overtook Henson and the Doctor with their parties camped together, Henson claiming to be stalled by the weather. I gave him explicit instructions and started him out. I then sent Marvin and his party back to Hecla for additional supplies in order to give Henson a start.

Peary did not meet up with Henson again until they tail-gated on the south shore of the Big Lead on the 26th; but although, as Peary says, "it is not pleasant to be at the rear attending to loose ends," he was still able to communicate and certainly to correct anything as serious as an incorrect heading, as can be seen from this quote from his diary entry of the 18th: "And so the work went on, the parties going and coming, myself in touch with and pushing those ahead of me and pulling those in the rear, so to speak, in a position where I could straighten out any little hitches."

It would appear therefore that Peary had been in ignorance of their actual heading until he had calculated his position on 30th March and done a check on the variation of the compass – at which point, he needed a scapegoat. But there is a more interesting and plausible explanation than Henson's bias to the left and Peary's not having noticed and corrected this sooner. The variation of the compass at Cape Sheridan in 1906 was 95°W, and this same variation had been used when setting a course across the Arctic Ocean from Point Moss. The difference in magnetic variation between those two points taken from modern charts is 11°, and between Cape Sheridan and the position of Peary's camp at the Big Lead on 30th March, 1906, is 20°. If Peary's 1906 expedition had been heading out from Point Moss using the Cape Sheridan magnetic variation, the theoretical track is almost precisely the true bearing that Henson actually took. In other words, it was not Henson's "bias" that took them off course, but Peary's error in using an incorrect magnetic variation when setting his course. He would not have been aware of this error until 30th March, and this explains why he made no effort to correct Henson's heading.

The only other explanation is that Peary had instructed Henson to head in that direction in order to counter the effect of the easterly drift of ice. But if this were so, they over-compensated for the drift, and this would still leave Peary in need of a scapegoat for such a serious navigational error.

On 2nd April, "after a loss of seven days of fine weather," Peary, Henson and their Eskimos took the risk, and by relaying with light loads, crossed the thin ice covering the Big Lead. Peary could have taken Ryan and his party of three Eskimos with him across the Big Lead, but since they had arrived the previous evening bringing with them very light loads (and the disquieting news that the ice back along the trail was badly broken up), Peary had taken only one of Ryan's Eskimos and sent Ryan and the other two back along the trail bearing notes for the other leaders. By crossing the Big Lead Peary had therefore virtually committed himself to an assault on the Pole without any certain support from the south, and without what his critics refer to as "reliable witnesses." From this point on the story takes on a certain air of mystery.

Safely across what Peary believed would be the only major obstacle on his journey to the Pole, Henson and his three Eskimos were sent on ahead to break the trail, while Peary and his three men settled down to another day of "idleness," another "beautiful day," and on the 3rd set off on Henson's trail. They made good progress in spite of the hard going, "going that would seriously discourage an ordinary party," Peary tells us, "but my little brown children of the ice, cheerfully toil their sledges through it with the skill born of life-long experience and habit." On 5th April, travelling in thick weather which Peary found depressing, and a strain he was determined to avoid in future "except when compelled to," he came upon Henson in camp with his party. In his book Peary merely indicates that Henson and his men were all "more or less worried at being so far away, the hard traveling etc." In the typescript of his diary, however, the story is presented somewhat more frankly:

Was not surprised at the end of six hours to come upon Henson humped up in camp with his party "too thick to travel," his men belly aching about being so far away, and the hard traveling, etc. and he as bad as any of them, though of course, he would not admit it . . . He had fallen down badly on his job; and if he does not do better very soon I shall make a change.

Clearly the stress of breaking trail was showing in Henson, but Peary's remark is also indicative of strain. His fear now was that he might not even succeed in bettering the Farthest North of the Italian expedition. Peary's diary for 6th April has the following observation:

The ten days delay of Henson's party, and seven of mine, in fine weather, has been a terrible set back. Without that we would have been beyond Abruzzi today. As it is I am two degrees ahead of four years ago today when I left Cape Hecla. One month today since I left the land, and the delays and Henson's sluggishness have cut our advancement down to five miles per day.

The wind and thick weather which had stopped Henson's party during the 5th, increased to a blizzard by the 6th, and "continued unabated accompanied by a furious and blinding drift" throughout the 7th, another anniversary which drew from Peary a cry of anguish: "On this date Nansen reached his highest, and but for the accursed lead back there, I should be ahead of him today. As it is I am some 70 to 80 miles behind him and stalled again." And so the blizzard continued, its "infernal howling" an accompaniment now to thoughts which always started hopefully, only to be cursed by the weight of the wind:

I cheat as much of the time away as possible planning what I will do when I get back; the various islands; the house in Cleveland Park; the Geographical Society, etc., etc., and then I run against the blank wall, unless I win *here*, all these things fall through, success *here* is what will give them existence. Then I go over again what I shall do in the various contingencies, if it ever clears, but that does not take long. I know pretty well what I shall do in every contingency I can think of. And always through the black shadow of impending failure shows the steady light of so many days nearer my island and its people.

Finally, on the 12th, Peary was able to get some "approximate meridian observations with the transit, in the face of continued vibrations." These observations are not recorded in the diary, but in Peary's book he gives the position as latitude 85°12′N, "and our longitude but slightly west of the ship at Sheridan." They had drifted almost due east sixty-two miles in six and a half days. But Peary gives no indication of how he arrived at his longitude, and if he had simply calculated it from the time of the highest altitude, one must regard it as extremely dubious.

Peary was now faced with a choice between playing it safe and turning for home, or risking his life and the lives of those who travelled with him, by heading north in an attempt to establish a new record. His critics, and there are many, generally follow Captain Thomas F. Hall, whose book *Has the North Pole Been Discovered?* develops the theory that on 14th April, when the storm abated, Peary abandoned all hope of setting a new Farthest North record (having already, back at the Big Lead, abandoned any hope of reaching the North Pole), and had set out for the *Roosevelt* at Cape Sheridan which, because of the eastward drift of Storm Camp over the last eight days, now lay almost due south. Hall's explanation for how Peary ended up on the north coast of Greenland is given in ten words: "he unavoidably was carried by the drift to Cape Neumeyer."

But let us look at Peary's options as though we were in Peary's position. He desperately needed to set a new Farthest North record as the culminating achievement of his final expedition and as some consolation for failing to reach the Pole. On the evidence of what he had done to date, such a feat would take at least nine days' hard travelling, for his best seven days' travel from cache number two to Storm Camp (not including the delays) had only produced a northing of seventy miles, or an average of ten miles a day. In his favour, however, Peary tells us that the storm which robbed him of so many days' travelling had improved the surface across which he was now so eager to march: "On the old floes where it had not scoured the snow off entirely, it had packed it harder, and the patches of rough ice, and the pressure ridges were now filled with snow hammered in until it would bear a mule." Hall contests the improvement in the surface as a result of the storm by quoting Peary's comments on the effects of the previous storm: on 4th April Peary had found that the rough ice had "served as nets to catch all the snow blown off the level places, and there it lay soft and deep. It was going that would seriously discourage an ordinary party."

The issue, however, is not the surface. The question is: faced with a choice of making one desperate bid to beat the record northing set by Commander Cagni of the Italian expedition of 86°34′N – a distance in a straight line due north from Storm Camp of only eighty-two nautical miles – would Peary have had a go for it, or would he have quit and headed for the ship? Here is his answer to this:

It was evident that I could no longer count in the slightest degree upon my supporting parties, and that whatever was to be done now, must be done with the party, the equipment, the supplies which I had with me. Unfortunately the party was larger than it need be (eight of us in all), and the supplies much smaller than I could have wished. I gave my men their supper and turned over for another nap while they obtained a few hours' sleep. I had no occasion to think or worry, I knew already what I should do in this contingency.

Of course he went north! No other conclusion carries any credence, for no other explorer in Peary's position would have done otherwise.

How far north he went is another issue entirely.

CHAPTER 12

Farthest North, 1906?

Part 2 "The first day of dark"

At 2 p.m. on 12th April, Peary sent Henson and his two Eskimos ahead to break a trail northward. One hour later, he sent two other Eskimos south in the hope of making contact with Marvin and re-opening his supply line from the ship. With the return of his two Eskimos from the south his worst fears were confirmed: beyond the first igloo on the homeward trail "they had been stopped by open water and completely shattered ice extending as far as they could see from the highest pinnacles."

Peary and his seven companions, cut off from their supporting parties and with less supplies than he could have wished (he does not say how many days' supplies he was carrying), now had another of those familiar death-defying struggles on his hands, and after "abandoning everything which [they] did not absolutely need," they set out on Henson's trail at 9 a.m. on the 14th and "bent every energy to setting a record pace." Peary's handwritten original diary of his journey is missing. But I came upon the typed up version by chance amongst Peary's galley proofs and draft manuscripts at the National Archives. It was Peary's practice in his sledging diaries to head each entry with the journey's day number, followed on the line below by the full date of the record, and in the typescript version above the entry "40th day. Saturday. April 14th, 1906" are the puzzling words: "First day of 'dark.'"

Only a sight of the original would give a clue as to whether this was added later or not. There is no astronomical significance in this remark. So what then does he mean? The remark does not appear in the published account; but then neither do so many others which he made in his diary but presumably considered too personal to be published. Indeed, the whole journey from this point on becomes mysterious. His mileages are far exceeding anything he has ever done before; but there is a lack of consistency. On the mysterious 14th, for example, he claims in his book:

> The first march of ten hours, myself in the lead with the compass, sometimes on a dog-trot, the sledges following in Indian file with drivers running besides or behind, placed us thirty miles to the good; my Eskimos said forty.
>   At the end of the march I was a tired man. Had raised blisters on

the bottom of both feet, and soft as I was after the days in camp, was sore in every bone with the rapid pace, which was not less than three miles an hour. My Eskimos insisted it was nearer four.

But the typescript of his diary says they only travelled for nine hours "at nearly three miles an hour." Then on the 15th we find in the typescript another of those personal remarks which Peary chose not to publish:

> Started at 8 a.m. Twenty minutes later came upon Henson's igloo (these two igloos two hours apart!!) and find his record giving a yarn about a lead etc., etc. Four and one half hours after starting came upon him camped beside a *closed* lead, where he had been for some twenty hours. He claimed that it had just closed, but that is a lie, and if I had not come up, he would be there still. The truth is, he is worse than the Eskimos in being frightened to death with these leads. We have crossed eleven today with no trouble, a little detour always giving us a chance to cross.
>
> Travelled ten hours, then camped in very thick weather. Traversed several large level old floes which my Eskimos remarked at once looked as if they did not even move in summer.
>
> Also noted berg-like pieces of ice discoloured with sand, my Eskimos also remarking that these looked as if we were near land.
>
> Have travelled at a good pace again today and feel that we must have covered twenty-five miles. I hope it is more.

In his book Peary says that on this day they "covered thirty miles" and that on the 16th their pace on the march was "not less than two and one-half [nautical] miles per hour," whereas in the diary he says "we have come at a rate of two miles an hour at least, and am sure we did as long as it was clear."

What is becoming clearer as the two accounts approach the date on which he reached his Farthest North is that there has to be good reason for these differences, and why, in the case of his published account, he makes no mention of how many hours they travelled on the 16th or how many miles they made good on that day. He is evasive also in his book about the activities of 17th April, a day on which they did not travel. Why then does he not say so?

> Our stay in camp was longer than usual owing to the continuance of the wind and snow. While here, six worn-out dogs were killed and fed to the others to save our small store of pemmican, and the skeleton condition of these dogs as shown when they were skinned, threw my men into a temporary panic, as they said that the entire pack might

give out at any time and they wanted to turn back from here, but I told them I was not ready to turn back yet, and should not be until we had made at least five more marches to the north.

Why did he still feel compelled to make "five more marches" if, since leaving Storm Camp, he had travelled at least sixty miles (as he states in his book) on his first two days and, by implication, at least twenty on the third, a total that would have put him only some two miles short of Cagni's record? Could it be that he had not travelled as far as he claimed and knew that at his rate of progress he still had a struggle on his hands to pass the Italian record, or was he genuinely aiming to go as far north of the previous record as he could before turning back?

In his diary entry for 18th April, the first entirely calm day since leaving the Big Lead, Peary states that they travelled ten and a quarter hours, which is "thirty-six hours in all from storm camp, and if our rate has been two and one half miles per hour, we are close to Abruzzi's highest."

He actually would have passed the Italian record if he had travelled thirty-six hours from Storm Camp at a rate of 2.5 miles per hour, and yet he seems to imply that he is still south of it. Whether he was or not we shall never know. What can, however, be seen by comparing his published account with the previously unpublished typescript of the missing diary, is that he makes no mention of 19th April and the impasse they met that day, choosing instead to expand on the momentum of the 18th.

For three or four miles, Peary tells us, the dogs "struck such a pace that I found it difficult to keep ahead of them." The character of the ice was improving – the floes becoming "larger and the rafters more infrequent." And even though the cracks and narrow leads were increasing, they were at right angles to their course. The dogs that could not keep the pace were fed to the others. Nothing here to indicate any real problem. And yet a problem they had on 19th April, according to the typescript of that missing diary:

A fine calm night and morning, giving promise of another good day. I turned out before 5 a.m., made tea, and we were under way at 6.45. Perhaps a mile from camp crossed a narrow lead.

The snow softer and deeper, my feet sinking in several inches at every step. A little later came upon leads on either side but hoped to run them out. At 9.30 found ourselves in a network of leads between two large ones, and the ice in motion. Backed out of this as quickly as possible, in two places barely getting sledges over leads, in time to escape being caught on detached floes. I then stopped to get an observation before an advancing bank of cloud from the north should obscure the sun. Set up transit and got one uncertain ante-meridian sight before sun disappeared.

We then followed the [missing word] by big lead south for a mile or two to see if we could cross, but found it slowly widening and so camped. Thick bank of fog and light snow with wind began at same time.

Saw three seals in the lead and Sipsu shot one but it sank. This turned the Eskimos a good deal.

Had I been slower this morning, the lead would have opened before we got to it, and I should have followed along the west shore, and as it seems now, been alright.

Peary's track according to his diary for 19th–20th April

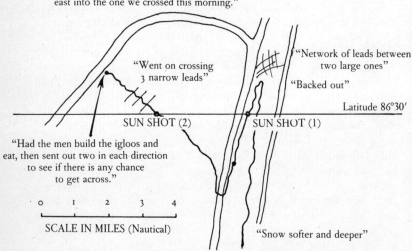

"Lead some 200 yds wide, trending N.E. & S.W. (true) and crossing around to the east into the one we crossed this morning."

"Went on crossing 3 narrow leads"

"Network of leads between two large ones"

"Backed out"

Latitude 86°30'

SUN SHOT (2)　　SUN SHOT (1)

"Had the men build the igloos and eat, then sent out two in each direction to see if there is any chance to get across."

0　1　2　3　4

SCALE IN MILES (Nautical)

"Snow softer and deeper"

"Yesterday's position (19th April) was east of today's (20th April)"

Clearly from his diary entries his party and his dogs were just about spent and the conditions for travel becoming more difficult all the time. And so to the 46th day, Friday, 20th April, 1906 – the day before his Farthest North:

Turned out early and sent two men in opposite directions along the lead to see if any changes during the night had made it possible for us to cross. Sipsu found a place and at 9 a.m. we got under way. At this time sun visible through drifting fog or frost smoke. An occasional glimpse of blue sky and cirrus clouds overhead, showed that it was clear above, and made me hope that at noon I might have a clear sight.

But his entry for 20th April ends with the words: "We are in a perfect mesh of leads." And so too at this point ends the typescript for, inconceivable as it may seem, the crucial final page is missing.

What then happened on that final day? Did they escape from that "perfect mesh of leads" and go on to gain a new Farthest North? According to the published account, and the accepted (but un-checked) verdict of history, it would appear they did:

April 20th we came into a region of open leads, trending nearly north and south, and the ice motion became more pronounced. Hurrying on between these leads a forced march was made. Then we slept a few hours, and starting again soon after midnight, pushed on till a little before noon on the 21st . . .

When my observations were taken and rapidly figured, they showed that we had reached 87°6′N latitude, and had at last beaten the record, for which I thanked God with as good a grace as possible, though I felt that the mere beating of the record was but an empty bauble compared with the splendid jewel on which I had set my heart for years, and for which, on this expedition, I had almost literally been straining my life out.

It is perhaps an interesting illustration of the uncertainty or complexity of human nature that my feelings at this time were anything but the feelings of exultation which it might be supposed that I should have. As a matter of fact, they were just the reverse, and my bitter disappointment combined perhaps with a certain degree of physical exhaustion from our killing pace on scant rations, gave me the deepest fit of the blues that I experienced during the entire expedition.

As can perhaps be imagined, I was more than anxious to keep on, but as I looked at the drawn faces of my comrades, at the skeleton figures of my few remaining dogs, at my nearly empty sledges, and remembered the drifting ice over which we had come and the unknown quantity of the "big lead" between us and the nearest land, I felt that I had cut the margin as narrow as could reasonably be expected. I told my men we should turn back from here.

My flags were flung out from the summit of the highest pinnacle near us, and a hundred feet or so beyond this I left a bottle containing a brief record and a piece of the silk flag which six years before I had carried around the northern end of Greenland. Then we started to return to our last igloo, making no camp here.

That Farthest North, Peary claims, was reached at local noon on 21st April, 1906, but no record remains of the observation he made at that point, and no distances or total hours of travelling are given in his book for the last three marches. The typescript of his missing diary offers some intriguing information which casts a different light upon the climax of that 1906 assault. The crucial passage is dated Friday, April 20th:

> Have re-checked yesterday's and today's sights and they give very similar results, the mean of which is 86°30′ (the places are in the same latitude only yesterday's position was east of today's) but I fear that both altitudes are a little low, one before meridian, the other after it. Since the observation, we have come about two miles.

Since Peary was looking for a latitude check, it is unlikely that the observations would have been taken much more than say one hour off local noon. Keeping this in mind, let us seek an explanation for that expression: "but I fear that both altitudes are a little low."

Peary does indeed have reason to feel despondent. At latitude 86°30′, the altitude of the sun one hour before or after the sun's transit of the meridian on 19th and 20th April, although lower than the meridian altitude only by a few minutes, does put Peary's actual latitude on those two days still some distance short of the Farthest North record, perhaps by as much as twelve miles.

So how does this affect his claim? Let us first extract and summarise the information he offers in his book on their mileages during the first four marches (or first five days) from Storm Camp. He tells us they travelled for ten hours on the 14th at "not less than three miles an hour" which placed them "thirty miles to the good" – the Eskimos estimating forty. He claims also to have travelled for ten hours on the 15th "at a good pace," and that during this march "felt that we had covered thirty miles or more." He does not tell us how far, or for how long they travelled on the 16th, offering only that their pace "was not less than two and one-half miles per hour"; does not actually *say* that they travelled on the 17th (although he does imply they did), and on the 18th offers only that they travelled for ten hours. From this of course it is impossible to get any idea of how far he travelled – and this we must assume had been his intention.

In the typescript of the missing diary, however, he made that revealing remark on the 18th about the total number of hours they had travelled, from which it is possible at least to work out what distance he believed they had covered during those four marches. "Travelled till 5 p.m. 10 1/4 hours. This is thirty-six hours in all from storm camp, and if our rate has been two and one half miles per hour, we are close to Abruzzi's highest."

Thirty-six hours at an average rate of two and a half miles per hour is ninety miles. We can also fill in from this remark the hours and distances he covered on the 16th and 18th – these being six hours of travel on the 16th covering fifteen miles, and on the 18th (at a rate of two and a half miles per hour) a total of twenty-five miles. The missing total from the book now stands at one hundred miles, and the typescript estimate at ninety.

But those two sun altitudes he took on 19th and 20th April, being as he tells us "a little low," would have given him a latitude somewhere in the region of 86°22', making his camp on the 18th only about sixty-two miles north of Storm Camp, since on the 19th (according to the diary) he had travelled for only three hours on a northerly heading before being forced to back out of a dangerous area. Confusing? No more so than it must have been for Peary.

He had either overestimated his mileages, or he had travelled the ninety miles and lost twenty-eight of them in detours – and he must have made detours, since no journey across drifting pack ice is possible without these additional, heart-breaking miles. But Peary avoids the issue of detours in his book, preferring to mention only the straight line or "latitude" distances he has covered, and then, as we have seen, only when it suits him. He also avoids any mention in his book of those two sun sights which placed him on 19th and 20th April still some twelve miles south of the Italian record.

Let us now take a closer look at those last two and a half days of his northward march. One is struck first by the fact that on the 19th, in spite of desperately trying to make progress north and to get beyond the Italian record, he succeeded only in running into a cul-de-sac and having to back out, and by noon on the 20th, he was no further north than he had been twenty-four hours earlier. So what was his situation at camp on 20th April? The diary typescript tells us that after his sun sight (they had stopped at 11 a.m. and had not got on the move again until 12.15 p.m.) they had crossed three narrow leads:

> ... and at 1 p.m. brought up [against] a lead some two hundred yards wide, trending N.E. & S.W. (true) and crossing around to the east into the one we crossed this morning. Had the men build the igloos and eat, then sent two out in each direction to see if there is any chance to get across. I do not care to tax the strength of the dogs by making them do useless travelling, and to go into what is apparently another "cul-de-sac" would be useless.

Peary then writes about re-checking his sights – a passage already quoted above – and concludes: "We are in a perfect mesh of leads, the under-stream from which keeps the sun obscured and doubtless has much to do with this incessant wind." This hardly sounds the sort of area from which he is about to extricate himself and make a final northward march of somewhere between thirty-eight and forty-three nautical miles in a straight line – and one should add, at the very least, twenty-five per cent for detours. This is the distance he would have to cover from the camp in the close vicinity of which he had taken two sun sights for latitude, up to the latitude he claimed as his Farthest North. So what does he say of this final push north in his book: " . . . a forced march was made. Then we slept a few hours, and starting again soon after midnight, pushed on till a little before noon of the 21st."

This is all he tells us, no mention of the travelling conditions or their pace. There is, nevertheless, some information here of interest. From the camp at which they "slept a few hours" to their Farthest North was a journey of almost twelve hours, some thirty miles if they were travelling at the pace he claims they had been since leaving Storm Camp. It should also be noted that this was only half of the latitude distance they travelled on that date for, as his book states, they did not camp at that place, but began their hazardous journey home just as soon as he had completed his observations: "We had already made a good day's march. Now we had to duplicate it without rest or food. When at last we stumbled into camp I was nearly blind from the effects of the cutting snow and wind, and completely done up with the long continued exertion."

In the light of the information provided by this typescript of his diary we are left with two questions to answer: did Peary succeed in passing the Italian record and setting a new Farthest North; and, if so, how far north did he go?

His average latitude distance per march from Storm Camp to his camp on 20th April (assuming that camp was only a couple of miles south of his observed latitude of 86°30', thereby giving Peary the maximum possible benefit of the doubt) was seventy-six nautical miles in six marches – an average of 12.7 miles per march. But in the twenty-four hours between noon on the 19th and noon on the 20th he had succeeded only in moving a few miles to the west, and had made no northing at all. His camp of the 20th was on the wrong side of a two-hundred-yard-wide open lead, and that camp he knew to be some miles short of the Italian record – how many, he did not know exactly, and neither do we. Of one thing, however, we may be certain: Peary was the sort of man who would have made a super-human effort to beat the record, and he probably did reach a new Farthest North, beating the standing record of 86°34' by a few miles.

So what about that claim of Peary's that he reached latitude 87°6'? I find it almost impossible to accept that from the camp of 20th April he travelled a minimum of seventy-six nautical miles on that return journey to the claimed Farthest North and back to that same camp – this being the straight line distance without any additional miles for detours. Such mileages are not uncommon under perfect surface and weather conditions in the Thule District of North-West Greenland with the men and dogs in excellent condition. But on 21st April, 1906, Peary's "few remaining dogs" and his companions were nearing the limit of their endurance. They were travelling across pack ice that was broken up and in motion, and some of the leads they crossed on their northward march had "moved to such an extent" that on their return march, Peary and his companions found "some difficulty in picking up [the] trail on the southern side of them."

Why did he not simply state how far he had actually gone? Any increase in a Farthest North record of less than twenty miles (on the evidence of Cagni's increase on Nansen's record by a mere twenty miles), would almost certainly be regarded in some quarters as suspicious. Even a new Farthest North that was twenty-five miles beyond the standing record would still be in the 86° range and therefore bracketed with the records of Nansen and Cagni. Once clear above latitude 87°, however, the new record would somehow seem more valid and less likely to be questioned. But here, of course, I am only presenting a view of the dilemma which might have crossed Peary's mind. There is no firm evidence to show that it did – no more evidence than there is to show that Peary really did reach latitude 87°6′ on 21st April, 1906.

One more navigational issue needs looking at before turning south: we need an explanation for the shift of the track to the east during the journey from Storm Camp to the Farthest North (which Peary later *guessed* to be longitude 50°W). At first glance this might appear to be a deflection from the true north heading caused by the drift of the ice to the east. But surprisingly, Peary does not appear to have countered that drift by setting a course to the west of north. His experience at Storm Camp, when he drifted due east sixty-two miles in six and a half days, must surely have been a warning that with the wind still blowing from the same direction he would need to make frequent checks on his longitude if he was to stay on course for the Pole. And yet this he did not do.

Now supposing that he had set his course to the west to counter the drift. What explanation are we left with that might account for that shift to the east? Could it possibly be a reversal of his previous error over the magnetic variation – that in setting his course for the Pole from Storm Camp he was using the magnetic variation he had calculated on 30th March at the extreme western reach of his track? The difference in magnetic variation between those two camps is almost exactly the angle that his course is offset from true north to the *east* as he heads north from Storm Camp. One cannot therefore ignore the possibility that this was a navigational error, and not simply the effect of drift. Indeed, either way, it was an error in heading which both could and should have been corrected by taking longitude observations on the northward march. As we shall see later, in the discussion of Peary's 1909 journey, longitude observations are essential in any attempt to reach the Pole. To the polar explorer, a knowledge of one's longitude is far more useful in practical terms even than an exact knowledge of the variation of the compass; but it would appear in this instance that Peary had no knowledge of either.

The journey back to land was one of the most harrowing and close-run escapes of Peary's polar career; but re-tracing that journey from data provided in the published account is impossible. He offers not a single date or position fix from his Farthest North through to 2nd June, the date he left the *Roosevelt* on a journey westward along the northern coast of Ellesmere Island, and according to the ship's log, he set out on that journey only one week after his arrival at the ship. Some of Peary's critics maintain that his vagueness about the events of his return journey are not the result of his exhausted state, but had a deliberate purpose – namely, to suppress or to "remove every scrap of evidence that could be used by scientists to check, and thereby prove or disprove, the authenticity of latitude 87°6′N."

He tells us that with two Eskimos (whose dogs had been eaten and whose sledges had been discarded) he scouted ahead of the party along the faulted homeward trail south to Storm Camp and that they frequently "ran for considerable distances" in order to stay ahead of the dogs. He tells us that their last march into Storm Camp was reached "God only knows how ... in the teeth of another blinding western blizzard with driving snow, through which none but an Eskimo, and a very good one at that, could have kept the trail for five minutes."

He tells us that from Storm Camp he had set a "bee line" course for the nearest part of the Greenland coast, and says: "I alone of the party knew how far we had drifted and that our salvation now lay in the direction of the Greenland coast and its musk-oxen." And sure enough, by the time of his return to Storm Camp some time around 27th or 28th April, the westerly winds would have drifted it into a position which was on a straight line between Peary's Farthest North and Cape Neumeyer, and almost straight down the meridian as far as the Big Lead. There is, however, no indication that he knew this for a fact for, with the exception of his observations at the Big Lead on 30th March, he makes no mention in any of his writings of having taken observations as a check on his longitude and the extent of his eastward drift. Initially he even offered his new record Farthest North only as a latitude, his longitude 50°W only appearing later when it was found necessary to have a longitude in order to plot his track and his Farthest North point on a map. So was he really heading deliberately for "the Greenland coast" or simply guessing that by heading due south (fast enough to beat the drift) that is where he would end up?

On the third march south of Storm Camp they had crossed the scar of the Big Lead and for a while he had allowed himself to be encouraged by the thought that this obstacle was at last behind. But on the second march south of the scar they had found what they had been dreading: a broad black lead of open water, some half a mile or so in width, lying directly across their path and reaching as far to the east and west as the eye could see. Turning east, Peary had sent out scouting parties searching for a way across, but after surviving some lucky escapes they had resigned themselves to wait, and had remained (for how many days Peary does not say) "drifting steadily eastwards, watching the lead widen," their chances increasing with each day that passed of being carried into the Greenland Sea. It was a fearful prospect:

> Now as we lay in this dismal camp, watching the distant southern ice beyond which lay the world, all that was near and dear, and perhaps life itself, while on our side was only the wide-stretching ice and possibly a lingering death, there was but one appropriate name for its black waters – "the Styx."

Dogs were being fed to dogs and sledges broken up for fuel to cook the meat of those that they themselves were eating. But eventually (how many days later we are not told) two of his scouts had come "hurrying back breathless, with the report that a few miles from camp there was a film of ice extending clear across the lead – now something over two miles wide." All of them, convinced because of the lateness of the season that this would be their only chance of getting across, put on their snowshoes and set out, sixty feet between each two men, each of them some distance behind the dogs and sledges, and the tension in the adventure – which was evidently Peary's first encounter with such a wide stretch of thin ice – comes strongly across:

> Once started, we could not stop, we could not lift our snowshoes. It was a matter of constantly and smoothly gliding one past the other with utmost care and evenness of pressure, and from every man as he slid a snowshoe forward, undulations went out in every direction through the thin film incrusting the black water. The sledge was preceded and followed by a broad swell. It was the first and only time in all my Arctic work that I felt doubtful as to the outcome, but when near the middle of the lead the toe of my rear kamik as I slid forward from it broke through twice in succession I thought to myself "this is the finish," and when a little later there was a cry from someone in the

line, the words sprang from me of themselves: "God help him, which one is it?" but I dared not take my eyes from the steady, even gliding of my snowshoes, and the fascination of the glassy swell at the toes of them.

Their problems, however, were by no means over, for the ice on the southern side of the lead was a frozen "conglomeration of fragments from the size of paving stones to literally and without exaggeration the dome of the Capitol."

It had not seemed, wrote Peary, as though any creature other than a bird would be capable of getting beyond it, but on turning to his weary men to offer a few encouraging words he had caught that familiar "glint in their eyes" which had told him that no words were needed. They had finally scented land and were as determined as he was to reach it. And so they "stumbled desperately southward" for one march, two, and part of the next; but with never a direct mention of date from the day they had reached their Farthest North, nor ever a mention of how many miles or how many hours they had travelled.

He tells us that on the day after they had emerged from the southern edge of the zone of shattered ice, they had been able to make out the distant snow-clad summits of the Greenland mountains, and that this had improved the spirits of the men. Finally, "I headed directly for the rolling bit of shore at Cape Neumeyer, where I was positive we would find a few hare and hoped that we might find musk-oxen round in Mascart Inlet."

But my old friend, Inuutersuaq, from the Thule District of North-West Greenland, offers a different version of these events – the version of Oodaaq who had been with Peary on that journey:

One day at last they caught sight of land after they had passed through the freezing fog from the large holes in the ice ... Their spirits were high because they knew that they would reach the ship before any of them died of starvation ...

There was now hardly anything left of their provisions, but fortunately it was not too far to land. At last the sun broke through and its rays shone down on them. They were looking forward very much to reaching land. They knew of course how many provisions there were at Cape Columbia. Piulersuaq [Peary] got busy. Now finally he could read the sun's altitude. His followers were very anxious because they did not know exactly where Cape Columbia lay. When Piulersuaq had finished looking at the sun the others could see how his spirits had dropped. He turned to them and pointed with an outstretched arm in a direction where there was no land to be seen and said: "The ship is that way." The constant west wind had driven them towards the northern part of Peary Land.

Piulersuaq insisted that they should head for the ship. But for once Oodaaq contradicted him.

. . . "If we set out today for the ship we will certainly die gradually like dogs within three or five days. Die of starvation!" said Oodaaq to the others. "Today we must eat what is left of our food, even if it does not satisfy our hunger! We have to reach land now. If there are animals here, they are our only hope for survival." The others agreed and Peary brightened up.

Where the full truth lies it is no longer possible to be sure. The Eskimos believe the story told by the great hunter Oodaaq who, they say, had no need nor reason to lie. But regardless of whose decision it was to head for the nearest land, Peary's problems were soon increased, for a mile or so from Cape Neumeyer (which they reached some time between 9th–12th May) his own exhausted men had crossed the fresh tracks of three emaciated dogs and four men who were moving east, "slowly and with irregular steps." The dispirited party, which proved to be Clark's, was found only a few miles further on in a camp which would probably have been their last had Peary's Eskimos not found and fed them, for already they had eaten their spare seal skin boots and were about to kill their last dogs.

The meeting of these two parties was, however, to arouse far more suspicion in the minds of Peary's critics than any other issue of the 1906 assault, for it was advanced as some sort of evidence that Peary had not gone north from Storm Camp, but had abandoned his attempt at a new Farthest North and set out for the ship from the camp. Indeed, Captain Thomas F. Hall's interpretation of this fateful meeting is that these two parties had "travelled together or nearly together over the same route all the way from the big lead camp to Neumeyer." This is not only a totally improbable theory, but ludicrous in the extreme. So what is the explanation? I would suggest the one that Peary offers: that Clark arrived at the Big Lead shortly after Peary and Henson had crossed it heading north, and with the lead now open again, wisely decided to turn back. Caught in the same storm that had carried Peary's party to the east, Clark's party also drifted east; but unlike Peary, Clark had no way of calculating his position, and so on setting out to return to the ship on 13th April, he took the wrong heading by assuming he was still west of Cape Sheridan, and this wrong heading, together with the continuing eastward drift, took him to a landfall on the north coast of Greenland.

It was a fortunate meeting, beyond any doubt, but for Clark and his men, not for Peary. With the addition of Clark's party, Peary now had responsibility for the lives of twelve men, four of whom in their weakened condition were barely able to walk. Had Peary and Henson, and the three Eskimos who had been with him in 1900, not known that coastline and the likely places where game might be found, Clark's party would almost certainly have perished, and Peary's would have reached the ship only by the narrowest of margins.

In this situation, as during the crisis of the previous winter, we see Peary at his best: responsible, concerned, defiant in the face of near disaster, drawing upon his experience and his last reserves of confidence. His assault on the Pole may have been a failure; but no man who has travelled those desolate coasts, or who is prepared to think himself into that utterly desperate situation which Peary faced on reaching the coast, can come to any other conclusion than that he had saved the lives of those men. It is through this sort of incident (and there are many of them) that Peary won the respect of the Eskimos, and the respect also of his fellow explorers which no amount of armchair criticism can diminish.

Consolation enough for some perhaps; but not enough for Peary. His diary entry for the day following his return to the *Roosevelt* already indicates his need, his duty, to do more:

What a delicious thing rest is. With Jo's picture on the wall above my head, with my face buried in Ahnighito's pillow of Eagle Island fir needles, and its exquisitely delicious fragrance in my nostrils, I for the moment echo from the bottom of my heart Ootah's [Oodaaq] remark, "I have got back again, thank God!" Yet I know that a little later I shall feel that I might have done more and yet got back, and yet again still deeper down I know that we went to the very limit.

CHAPTER 13

Farthest North, 1906?

Part 3 "Crocker Land"

Peary quotes from the entry he made in his diary on the day after he returned to the ship, but there are no quotations in his book from his entries on those last three days of his outward journey; no mention of those latitude sights which placed him still a few miles south of the record that he had to beat; nor does he offer a single date, a definite distance, or any reliable information from which his homeward track might be plotted from his Farthest North to his landfall on the coast of Greenland – not even the date he returned to his ship.

So what was really going through his mind during those "delicious" hours in his cabin on his first night back on board? Would not the pictures above the pianola of his dear friend and mentor Morris Jesup, and those of President Roosevelt and Charles H. Darling, the Assistant Secretary of the Navy have been frowning down on him? Would he not have been reminded by that picture of Judge Darling of the orders signed by him – the orders releasing him from naval duties "to complete the map of the world" and that directive: "The attainment of the Pole should be your main objective. Nothing short will suffice."?

He had been convinced that with the right ship, the right crew to get her to the right winter quarters, and the right men to accompany him, nothing would stop him from reaching the Pole. He had written to the Secretary of the Navy on 2nd September, 1903, that from his proposed winter quarters at Cape Sheridan he would travel "due north over the polar pack [expecting] to accomplish the distance to the Pole and return in about a hundred days or a little more, an average travel of about ten miles a day. This plan is the result of some twelve years of almost continuous experience in these latitudes."

But from Point Moss he had headed in the wrong direction. His much publicised system of supporting parties had all too obviously broken down, and assuming that his Farthest North was not much beyond that "mesh of leads" which had stopped his advance on 20th April a few miles short of the Italian record, he had gone no more than half way to the Pole, and at five miles a day on his outward march had averaged less than half the rate which publicly he had predicted.

There were of course excuses to hand, but excuses were not the answer.

He needed a way of diverting attention away from his failure to reach the Pole – a new Farthest North that was far enough from the previous record that he would not be challenged to prove it, and a stretch of coastline on the prominent features of which, as promised, he could place the names of all of the principal members of his Club, in the hope that they would continue to support him, perhaps even give him another chance.

No other explanation makes sense of Peary's compulsion to set out again, only a week after reaching his ship, on a journey westward "to fill in the unknown gap in the coast" which lay between the farthest point west reached by Lieutenant Aldrich of the British expedition under Sir George Nares in 1876, and the farthest point reached by his old rival Captain Otto Sverdrup. The unseen region between these two points was a stretch of coast which in a straight line extended no more than sixty-five miles, so his only hope must surely have been that he would find that coastline deeply indented, thereby offering a lot more features, enough perhaps to justify what was bound to be a hazardous journey, since the season already was far advanced and his men and dogs were exhausted.

Amazing though it is that Peary should even have considered this journey, exhausted as he was from his previous trip, it is even more amazing that he was able to persuade three Eskimos (Egingwah, Kooloot-ingwah and Ooblooyah) to suffer the journey with him. What incentives he offered he does not say; but he had boasted in his circular to the Peary Arctic Club in January 1903 that "my Eskimos and my dogs cost practically nothing," and explains in his book *Secrets of Polar Travel* that:

In exchange for dogs, skins, or other supplies necessary for my work, or as rewards for services rendered, I have always given them the very best articles and materials which could be brought ... [and that] ... as a result of my various sojourns among them, the entire tribe has been raised from the most abject destitution to a condition of relative affluence.

They were, however, all relatively inexpensive items when considered against almost any other part of his expedition budgets, since what he had given them, as he tells us himself, had been "an ample supply of cutlery, knives, hatchets, saws, cooking-utensils, and needles ... repeating-rifles and breech-loading shot-guns and plenty of ammunition, and [for every hunter who served him well] ... wood for his sledge, lance, harpoon and spear."

Besides these gifts which had increased their efficiency as hunters and ensured a more abundant food-supply and better clothing, he tells us that he had "tried to help and instruct them to cope more effectively with their inhospitable surroundings," how to treat wounds and other accidents, and how to treat simple diseases, most of which, although this he does not say, had been brought to them by ship. And in return he "used" them. Indeed, he boasts: "I have used the Eskimos to a greater extent than any other explorer."

Using their country as a base for my work, I have lived among and worked with them . . . made a thorough study of their language, their mode of living, the food they ate, the houses they built and the clothing they wore. I have made these people my friends, training them in my methods, and directing the modification and concentration of their own methods in order to make them more useful and valuable in my work . . . In my last expedition it was in my power to utilize the entire energy and concentrate the entire resources of the tribe on my work and objects.

He expands on the question of language further on:

The language of the Eskimos is not difficult to acquire, one season spent among them being sufficient to gain a working knowledge of it. It is necessary for explorers to learn it, as the Eskimos have little or no desire to speak English, and consider it far simpler for the white man to speak their language.

Bartlett, who was with Peary for a total of three years in the Arctic spanning a period of eleven years through to the conclusion of Peary's last expedition, was a devoted admirer of the man, "because I knew he was already the greatest Arctic traveler alive." But he tells us that:

Peary never pretended he could talk Eskimo. I know he says in his book that it is easy to pick up the language. It was easy to pick up enough words for us to get along. But we never talked more than a jargon – just a rough grouping of nouns and verbs and adjectives without any attempt at grammar. It may sound impossible that we could get along with so little speech. But don't forget that in the North you get down to brass tacks.

How then did Peary manage them? The answer of course is Henson. He became the bridge between the white man and the Eskimo through his eventually fluent knowledge of their language and his very much deeper empathy with those "simple" people. Peary did not admit this in any of his published writings as it would have detracted from the impression he wished to create; but the relationship between Henson and the Eskimos is there in that letter to Jo from Etah in which he commented that, "Matt, not being confined ... [is] ... as cheerful as the natives ... and is getting more and more like a husky [Eskimo] every day."

In his book, *Secrets of Polar Travel*, Peary does, however, offer a few suggestions which give us an insight into his own relationship with the Eskimos:

> One must make a psychological study of these people properly to manage them. They are people of peculiar temperament, very much like children, and should be handled like children, firmly, but gently.
>
> ... In firmness, tempered with love and gratitude, I have found the best method of dealing with them, and their faithfulness has abundantly attested its efficacy.
>
> Some may get the idea that the Eskimos would serve as faithfully as they did me, almost anyone who offered them gifts, but the record of arctic exploration shows that such is not the case. They have not only known me for almost twenty years, but I have saved whole villages from starvation, and the greatest hope and ambition of the children have been to become hunters or seamstresses who would some day be rewarded by "Pearyaksoah."

But they certainly did not share or understand Peary's desperate need to bridge those sixty-five miles. They took him on that western trip (since Peary at this stage in his career never drove a team himself) simply out of native curiosity to see that northern coast.

And so the four of them set off on 2nd June, their leader's feet and legs still swollen from the battering of his last great trip, and six days out, with Peary feeling "much below par," they reached Cape Columbia and climbed 1,800 feet to the peak of a steep conical pile of loose stones which formed the northern of the twin peaks. In his diary that night Peary wrote:

> Today has seen the accomplishment of what I planned last fall, almost as soon as the *Roosevelt* reached Cape Sheridan: the building of a cairn, the display of the Stars and Stripes and the placing of my record and a piece of the flag, on the summit of Cape Columbia, the northern extremity of North America.

The cairn was found and Peary's record retrieved in 1953 by Dr. Geoffrey Hattersley-Smith while on a dog sledge reconnaissance of the northern coast. Written on a scrap of note paper, it had been placed in a cocoa tin together with a piece of the flag Jo had made (and which Peary always wore next to his skin). The note at first glance seems ordinary enough – a typical cairn note, traditionally brief, factual, and intended simply as a record:

> June 8, 1906
>
> Arrived here midnight June 7th from the Peary Arctic Club's S.S. *Roosevelt* which wintered at C. Sheridan.
>
> Am on my way west along the coast with 3 Eskimos and 3 sledges. Last night I killed 6 muskoxen just east of here.
>
> There is nearly continuous water along the icefoot; a lane running directly north from here, and several lakes to the N.E. and N.W. (true).
>
> In April of this year I reached the highest north yet attained going north on the meridian of this Cape and returning upon the Greenland coast a little east of 50°W Long.
>
> I build this monument and leave this record, with a portion of my U.S. flag as a permanent mark of my visit.
>
> R. E. Peary, U.S.N.

His statement that he went north on the meridian of Cape Columbia was not true. But far more surprisingly, he gives neither a date nor a latitude for his claimed Farthest North. Does this perhaps suggest that Peary had not yet decided whether to present the story of the last eight days of his outward journey exactly as he had written them in his diary, or whether to ignore those two latitude sights of 86°30′, and produce an entirely different version that would place his record Farthest North safely out of range of dispute above the eighty-seventh parallel?

The terrible strain of that homeward trek during which, at times, the pain in his feet had been so severe that his jaws, Peary tells us, "were actually aching" from the "viciousness" with which he had ground his teeth, was hardly conducive to the sort of thinking that would, in exchange for one more chance to reach his goal, leave him with a burden of conscience. Such a deception, in any case, was almost too dreadful to consider, unless of course he was to find the "deception" was only a minor one and could be entirely justified by a successful end result. But he needed time to think this through. Preferably the peace and quiet, and comfort of his cabin where he could in total privacy review his whole achievement and decide what he should do.

In the meantime, he had his "duty" to consider and some reward was surely due, for no other explorer before him or since has put in so much self-punishing effort right at the end of a travelling season, to extend by only a few miles a map which could far more easily have been completed on another occasion by another explorer.

His reward came on the sixteenth day out from the *Roosevelt*. Peary recorded in his diary entry of 17th June, at 10.30 a.m.: "A day's march (8 hours) beyond Aldrich's Farthest, and what I see before me in all its splendid, sunlit savageness, is *mine*, mine by the right of discovery, to be credited to me, and associated with my name, generations after I have ceased to be."

He now began his survey, pacing the miles of his traverse until his brain was numb with the incessant counting, and as the coastline took shape on his map, he was able to start distributing the names of his friends and supporters upon those features that were his by right of discovery. And fortunately there were some indentations. From his journal entry of the 18th: "In today's march we passed the mouth of a black precipitous-walled bay, some eight to ten miles wide at its mouth, with apparently several interior ramifications. Mine!!"

But how little had been left on that northern coast for the greatest polar traveller to discover, and how sad it is to see in his diary those truly pathetic cries of delight as he is reduced to picking up the crumbs that others, with much less hunger for fame, had left behind on that coast.

By the 24th he had come to the end of his traverse across the gap between the two known areas, and in one last bid to look around for any land his rivals might have missed, he had climbed the two-thousand-foot mountain behind Cape Colgate. In his book *Nearest the Pole* he briefly describes what he saw to the east, to the west and south, and then, finally to the north: "North stretched the well-known ragged surface of the polar pack, and northwest it was with a thrill that my glasses revealed the faint white summits of a distant land which my Eskimos claimed to have seen as we came along from the last camp."

But strangely, the diary makes no mention of this sighting of land to the north-west, and the directions of those features he does mention are unaccountably all forty-five degrees in error.

Four days later, on the evening of 28th June, they turned out after a fruitless attempt to sleep owing to the "swarms of big blue flies which, attracted by the meat, swarmed round and into the tent and over us," and hitching all their dogs to one sledge, drove to an altitude of six hundred feet up the hill behind Cape Thomas Hubbard, the more prominent of the two capes at the northern tip of Axel Heiberg Island and the extreme western limit of his journey. From there they went on to the summit at about 1,600 feet, where a cairn was built similar to that on Cape Columbia, in which (as was his custom) he left a brief record and a piece of his flag. In his book he tells us:

The clear day greatly favored my work in taking a round of angles, and with the glasses I could make out apparently a little more distinctly, the snow-clad summits of the distant land in the northwest, above the ice horizon.

My heart leaped the intervening miles of ice as I looked longingly at this land, and in fancy I trod its shores and climbed its summits, even though I knew that that pleasure could only be for another in another season.

Again the diary makes no mention of this new land to the north-west, his entry mysteriously stopping dead, and continuing on the next page with the words: "With the completion of my work on the summit and the building of the cairn, we came down to the sledge and dogs from whence I returned to camp . . ." – the same words which he uses in his book. The cairn records (all of which have since been recovered) are equally reticent about his discovery. In 1914 Donald B. MacMillan went in search of the land that Peary claimed to have seen, but there was no land.

If Peary had seen anything, it would have been a mirage similar to the one which had produced the "Croker Mountains" reported to have been seen by Ross in Lancaster Sound and named by him after the First Secretary of the Navy. But if Peary thought he had seen land, why did he not mention it in his diary, his cairn notes, and in the telegrams he sent out on his voyage home informing his sponsors of his achievements?

It does seem strange that "Crocker Land," which was named by Peary after George Crocker, one of the contributing members of the Peary Arctic Club, does not make its appearance until the publication of Peary's *Harper's* article in February 1907, and later that year with the publication of his book *Nearest the Pole*. Is it not conceivable, then, that however strongly one may wish to ignore it, both Crocker Land and his claim to a new Farthest North may have been forced upon Peary by his desperate need to be given one final chance?

His work completed, and with the fine weather coming to an end, he turned for the ship, but first added three lines at the bottom of a page, as though writing faster than normally: "I have no reason to complain. It has lasted long enough for me to get and see what I wanted." What meaning lies in those words we shall never know; but after an enforced rest of two days while a storm raged at this his most westerly camp, he set off on the three-hundred-mile trek to the ship confessing to a feeling of "sadness and regret at leaving this last camp."

It was a striking picture, the deer and hare, feeding in the brilliant sunshine under the high bluffs, the call of the birds, and the sound of running water. And the picture will be repeated again and again, summer after summer, but I, to whom it belongs, should never see it again.

The remark is sad from a man who knew from Sverdrup's map that he himself had not discovered the land that he was leaving.

As for his journey back to the ship, it was another ordeal, but this time of ploughing through "the devil-inspired labyrinth of lakes and rivers set in a morass of knee-deep slush." His clothes were rotting, the stench of wet skins was as disagreeable as they were uncomfortable to wear, and the going was getting harder all the time:

> With open water and shattered ice on one side, and the entirely impracticable ice-foot lake and Cape Henry cliffs on the other, our only possible route was the crest of the stupendous and now doubly ragged and chasm-intersected ice-foot. Along this, after I had dug out a tortuous road with a pickaxe, the sledges, one at a time, were pushed, dragged, hauled, hoisted and lowered by all of us, and sometimes unloaded and backed over the roughest places.

From the camp at View Point near Cape Joseph Henry, Peary sent Egingwah ahead with a letter for Bartlett asking him to send out men and dogs to help bring them in, but one march further on Peary had met up with Marvin and his three Eskimos bearing disturbing news:

> The *Roosevelt* had broken out from winter quarters at Sheridan on the 4th of July, and had squeezed down along the shore past Cape Union when she was smashed against the ice-foot just south of the cape, tearing another blade from the propeller, and breaking off her stern post and rudder. She was now lying at Shelter River just south of Cape Union effecting repairs.

Finally, on 30th July, with heavy pieces of tin cut from pemmican containers serving as insoles in his footgear to protect the soaked and softened stubs of his amputated toes, his fifty-eight days of minor triumphs and massive doses of misery came mercifully to an end. "My kamiks," he says, "were cut through, my tin soles broken in dozens of pieces, and my feet were hot, aching, and throbbing, till the pain reached to my knees."

The very next day after his return to the ship, seeing the trouble she was in, Peary had gone up to Bartlett and said: "We have got to get her back, Captain. We are going to come again next year."

"I should have thought he wouldn't have wanted ever to see the place again," comments Bartlett. "But it was like him when he was lowest to be still planning for the future. Already he was thinking of his next attack on the Pole."

From where did this defiance come, this unbelievable courage and almost crazy determination? Surely now we are seeing obsession, and not simply a craving for fame. Surely a man as committed as this must eventually break the curse of failure which so unfairly had been laid upon him and stride on to success. This he must have believed in his heart, for how else could he have read, and rejected, the closing words of the letter Jo had written on 18th March and sent north with the whalers.

> Oh, I pray you will return in safety to your ship and come home. Think of it *home* and to *stay* for I shall not let you get away again. You probably smile but I mean it this time. I have waited in vain for you to show me some consideration, now I shall demand it. I can't live this way any longer besides, your children have some claim upon you also. My Husband, my sweet heart. I want you so much. Just think life is nearly over and we have missed most of it.
>
> ... God bless you my darling and bring you in safety *next* Fall, to
> Yours with love – Jo
>
> P.S. My Bert, this is just like saying goodbye over again. Do, do come to me soon. Jo

The story of the *Roosevelt*'s voyage home from the shores of the Arctic Ocean is a story of brilliant seamanship and one of the classic tales of the sea. For seventy-five days, Bartlett tells us, they were battling their way in a sinking ship through the ice floes south to Etah:

> I used to go on deck and decide that we would sink in a few minutes and then go down and make a last entry in my diary. Then I'd come up again and we'd still be afloat and I'd try to explain how it was possible for a wreck like ours not to sink ... All the time the jury rudder we had rigged was being punished worse and worse and the bottom was getting more holes punched in it. Most of our men had given up hope long ago. Only Peary was at all optimistic.

They managed to beach the ship at Etah to make repairs. But when they had "packed stuff into the holes in the bottom of the ship and nailed canvass over them," Peary would not entertain the idea of putting all of his Eskimos ashore and sailing immediately for home. Bartlett explains:

> ... Peary had promised them that, before leaving them, he would get enough fresh walrus meat. He had also promised to land them with the meat at any place they wanted, either with their friends or at some village that they chose. Some of them were homesick. They hadn't seen their families for over a year, so they were brought to the place where their relatives lived. We had lots of good reasons for not doing this. We were short of coal and food and in a crippled condition, with

winter upon us and a long stormy route to follow. Peary knew this better than anyone on board. But 'Pearyakshwa' had given his word and he never broke it, so the thing was done. It is no wonder these people loved and respected Peary. No other man in the past or future can or will get these people to do what he did.

They finally got away from Cape York in a blinding snowstorm on 26th September, heading across the notorious Melville Bay. Bartlett tells us "it wasn't a nice feeling there in the driving snow and the darkness. But Peary was not at all dejected and continued to talk about his plans for the next voyage," even though they had not enough coal to get them home (the firemen were "sweeping the bunkers to fill shovels") and were finally reduced to "cutting away beams and loose timbers for fuel" in their effort to reach Hebron, Labrador.

There, with no coal available, they took on green wood and blubber for their furnaces and limped on to Hopedale from where, on 2nd November, Peary sent out two telegrams: one to his wife, the other to his mentor, Morris K. Jesup – the second being the longer of the two:

Cablegram *Called* No. 2

Morris K. Jesup,
195 Madison Ave,
N.Y. City.

Roosevelt wintered North Coast Grant Land somewhat north Alert's winter quarters. Went north with sledges February via Hecla and Columbia. Delayed by open water between 84 and 85 degrees. Beyond 85 six days' gale disrupted ice, destroyed caches, cut off communication with supporting parties, and drifted me east. Reached 87°6′N. Latitude over ice drifting steadily eastward. Returning, ate dogs, drifted eastward, delays by open water, reached north coast Greenland in [word unreadable] condition.

Killed Muskoxen and returned along Greenland coast to ship. Two supporting parties driven on north coast Greenland. One rescued by me in starving condition. After one week recuperation on *Roosevelt* sledged west completing north coast Grant Land, and reached other lands near 100th meridian.

Homeward voyage *Roosevelt* incessant battle with ice to Etah and with storms and head winds C. York to Labrador Coast.

Roosevelt magnificent ice fighter. No deaths or illness in Expedition.

Peary

On they crept, down the coast and it was not until they reached Chateau Bay, Quebec, on 15th November that Peary was able to send out his five-thousand-word story to the *Boston Herald*, the one which offered no dates for his northern journey except the date of his claim to have reached a new Farthest North. By this time the wheels had already been set in motion by the National Geographic Society to present him with the first Hubbard Gold Medal at the annual banquet of the Society on 15th December, and messages were fairly singing down the wires between Peary and Jo who was waiting for him in Sydney. "If my wishes were horse power the *Roosevelt* would steam thirty knots," Peary said in one of his cables.

In the early dawn of 23rd November, out of the blackness of a south-west storm, the *Roosevelt* crept into Sydney Harbor where the *Boston Herald* had hired a tug to take Peary ashore. Their correspondent records him eagerly scanning the windows of the quayside hotel as they drew up to the wharf.

There was a quick flutter of a handkerchief from one of them, barely discernible in the first gleam of the dawn. It was Mrs. Peary's window.

Jumping like a flash, Peary broke off in the midst of his conversation, sprang six feet from the tug's rail to the dock and sprinted up the slippery wharf to his brave, hopeful wife's arms.

Hopeful that he would not go north again? Such a hope would have been in vain. Even before he had come ashore, that burning question had been asked, and non-commital though his reply was said to have been, everyone who knew the man also knew the answer. For Jo, Peary's obsession with the Pole must have been as hard to bear as her husband's love of another woman. This, in so many words, she admitted: "In this affair, if you win I shall lose all love of life – if you lose, life will hold no happiness for you."

This was her burden. His was his need to reach the North Pole, made heavier now by a deception which Peary could not even share with the woman who understood him.

CHAPTER 14

The Threat of Dr. Cook

There was to have been a public banquet to welcome home and honour the explorer; but with plans for a very much greater banquet developing in the capital city at which he would be the guest of honour and presented with a special gold medal by the President himself, and with a dinner also being arranged by the Peary Arctic Club in New York, Peary politely let it be known that he needed to start for New York right away. And so the obliging dignitaries of Sydney settled for a very much simpler reception which had left the explorer and his wife free to set out by rail the next day, leaving Bartlett the task of getting the almost rudderless *Roosevelt* through all the hazards that bedevilled the final thousand miles of that incredible voyage. As Bartlett later recalled:

> Going through St. Peter Canal in thick weather I ran the *Roosevelt* into a fence which was built down into the water, and jammed her nose hard and fast into the bank. This happened because our rudder could not operate fast enough to let us maneuver in narrow waters. I remember a girl was milking a cow behind the fence. When she saw the *Roosevelt* headed straight for her she grabbed the stool on which she was sitting and dashed screaming up the hill. The cow galloped after her. The poor old *Roosevelt*, as well as ourselves, was ready for the insane asylum or the dump heap.

Peary of course did not share this view. The ship which he himself had designed had brought them through experiences that no other ship afloat would have survived. As for the general morale of the party, he assured us that it could not have been better: "Personally, I have never spent a year in the Arctic regions so entirely free from the petty annoyances and friction which are usually a most disagreeable feature of an Arctic expedition."

He had said much the same thing in 1900 when he was having trouble not only with Dr. Dedrick, but also with Henson. This time, however, although he had failed to reach the North Pole, he was returning with far more impressive results. He was claiming to have reached a new Farthest North. He was claiming also to have determined "the existence of a distant new land," and since no one was likely to have the temerity publicly to dispute these claims, he was confident they would serve as proof that next time he would be successful – if he was given a chance.

This then had been his assertive, buoyant, triumphant mood on 13th December, 1906, when he had attended a dinner of the Peary Arctic Club in New York. For almost a month the members of that exclusive Club had been waiting for a first-hand account of what he and their ship had been able to achieve against the most appalling odds. For Peary too it was a crucial meeting. Among the men attending that dinner there were more than enough who might, if their names were put on the map, be willing to support a final attempt. There were even a few, as Peary knew, who were actively working behind the scenes to establish him as a public hero, a move considered essential to the plan, since judging by the scorn of the press, the public were yet to be convinced that they needed Peary to reach the North Pole and leave there, as it was his custom, a piece of his silk flag.

But that was soon to be changed, for Peary had then headed on to Washington with his friend and advisor Herbert Bridgman (and with Grosvenor and Moore of the National Geographic who had both been guests at the homecoming dinner) to attend that banquet at the Willard Hotel at which he was presented with the highest award that the National Geographic Society could bestow, and by none other than his greatest admirer, the man after whom he had named his ship and whose support he could now rely on.

No longer could the press deride his ambition. He had, through that medal and the added distinction of accepting it at the hands of the President, been raised to the status of a national hero, and had more than met the expectations of every newspaper editor in America with his impassioned speech of acceptance. Here I am, he seemed to be saying. The only man who has the right. The only man who knows the "way." The one man who can do it. "To me the final and complete solution of the Polar mystery is the thing which should be done for the honor and credit of this country, the thing which it is intended that I should do, and the thing that I must do."

In the *tour de force* he had spelled out a warning to every other polar explorer who might have set his sight on the goal that was clearly reserved for Peary. They should stay well clear of his chosen route. They should stay well clear of his Eskimos and dogs. Above all else, they should stay well clear of that track which destiny had laid out before him twenty or maybe more years ago.

There had been words too in that powerful speech for every American, and in particular for those with money enough to invest in a project that would become part of the heritage of their children's children: "Should an American first of all men place the Stars and Stripes at that coveted spot, there is not an American citizen at home or abroad, and there are millions of us, but what would feel a little better and a little prouder of being an American."

These were the sort of stirring words that President Roosevelt liked to hear and Peary clearly knew it.

Small wonder that with the friendship and admiration of the man in the highest office in the land, Peary was granted three more years' leave from the Navy to follow on without a break from his previous three years' leave. Nor does it come as any surprise that Peary, in his letter of thanks to his friend in the White House, now felt able to confide, "I believe that I shall win this time, and I believe that this is the work for which God Almighty intended me."

But the *Sunday Herald*'s story of 16th December with its banner headlines: "Peary awarded gold medal – President Roosevelt makes the presentation address," and its read-on headline, "Peary, in response, asserts that the Pole can be gained by methods used by him," had caught the eye not only of millions of new admirers, but the attention also of a few of the *Herald*'s readers who intensely disliked the man and his methods. One of these was William Wallace, a former employee of the American Museum of Natural History in New York, and the guardian for the past ten years of Minik, the youngest of six Eskimos Peary had brought back from the Arctic in 1897. Four of those six Eskimos had died of tuberculosis within a few months of arriving in New York, including Qisuk, the father of Minik, and what the boy was not to discover until several years later was that his father's body, having been dissected by students at Bellevue Hospital, had been put through a macerating plant for a process of bone-bleaching before being handed over to the American Museum of Natural History. There the skeleton of Qisuk, mounted and preserved, had eventually rejoined the remains of some of his fellow tribesmen whose bones had been brought back to New York by Peary in 1896 and 1897.

William Wallace had read Peary's book, *Northward Over the Great Ice*, and so in time had Minik. But Wallace had kept from his foster son the awful secret of Qisuk's fate and his own involvement in the affair, for it had been at Wallace's macerating plant that the Eskimo's skeletons had been prepared for their journey to their last resting place – the museum in New York. Gruesome though the whole story is, Minik was loved by the Wallace family and, at the suggestion of Morris Jesup who seemed genuinely to want to help the boy, Wallace and his wife had taken him in with Jesup offering to contribute towards the cost of his upkeep. It had also been on Jesup's suggestion that the boy was eventually given the name Minik Peary Wallace.

The relationship between Wallace and Jesup had, at that time, been a trusting one. But Wallace had broken that trust by embezzling and Jesup had insisted the man should resign. Wallace had then made a few veiled threats that he might disclose his knowledge of "transactions that had taken place – and continued to take place – between the museum, Peary, and the Peary Arctic Club." Jesup washed his hands of Minik, and the world of a now bitter William Wallace began to fall apart. For six years Wallace had nursed his grudge, but seeing that article praising Peary he went on the path of revenge.

"GIVE ME MY FATHER'S BODY" the sensational headline screamed out at the readers of the *New York World* on 6th January, 1907. There were pictures of Minik all over the page, one of him dressed in polar furs. There was an artist's drawing of the kneeling boy with his pleading arms outstretched towards the American Museum of Natural History, and a sub-title which read: "The pathetic story of Minik, the Esquimau boy, who is growing up in New York and is going to find the North Pole some day, but who now wants most the bones of his father from the Museum of Natural History."

The shock waves of that tragic story would have had a more damaging effect on the reputations of Jesup and Peary had it not been for the fact that the majority of readers, whilst sympathetic towards the boy's pleas for his father's bones, "that he might put them in a quiet grave somewhere," felt also that Minik had reason to be thankful for the opportunity to grow up in America.

The scandal nevertheless hit Jesup hard, not only as one of the founders of the museum in 1868 and its president since 1881, but as a deeply religious man he had felt the implication of inhumanity as an unfair and direct attack on his Christian ethics. He had been one of the founders and a one time president of the Young Men's Christian Association; had founded and funded the Society for the Suppression of Vice for Saint Anthony, and with the fortune he had made in railroad supplies and banking he had, on retiring from business, devoted himself as a philanthropist to causes which reflected his passion for moral rectitude, education, science and patriotism. The Minik affair cast a grotesque shadow across his impeccable reputation as a man who espoused the principles of love and concern for one's fellow man and the respect of human dignity.

The scandal must also have worried Peary, not so much for what it said, but for what it might lead on to. It was a well-known and accepted fact among those who had been North with Peary (and certainly among all the Eskimos) that Peary had been enamoured of Aleqasina since first meeting her during his first winter at Anniversary Lodge, at which time she had been about ten years old. This first meeting is even on record in the form of some rough notes in Peary's distinctive hand:

When I came to take the ethnological photos of the family, the girl, then just beginning to develop into a woman, evinced extreme reluctance to having her picture taken, and only a direct order from her father accomplished the desired result. Later Alakahsingwah (this was the girl's not unmusical name) brought some trifling presents for little Ahnighito.

He had described her as "the belle of the tribe" in 1896 when she was still only thirteen, and was known to be sharing her with her husband Piugaatoq in 1898. Indeed, she had borne two children by Peary: the first son, Anaukak, in May 1900, and the second son Kale in May or June 1906. By 1900 even Jo had known about this relationship and, no doubt with much reluctance, had come to accept it. But Peary could certainly not afford to have his devout and uncompromising friend and mentor Morris Jesup learn of such things and, surprisingly, he never did.

The following March the Peary Arctic Club agreed to put the *Roosevelt* in dry dock for refitting and Peary once more embarked on a programme of lecturing and fund raising with never the time he wanted to spend at home with his wife and children. His notes to Jo became fewer and briefer, until finally even "my darling Jo" was cut down to the letters "M.D." Then came the setback. The contractors failed to complete the repairs to the *Roosevelt* by the agreed date, 1st July, and Peary was forced to postpone the expedition for one whole year. It was a vicious blow for a man in his fifty-second year who knew that the balance between age and experience would not remain in his favour much longer.

In January 1908 he was dealt another blow with the death of his chief supporter and backer, Morris Jesup. Coming on top of the delay, this at first seemed "an absolutely paralysing defeat." And yet, he says, "when I gathered myself together and faced the situation squarely, I realized that the project was something too big to die; that it never, in the great scheme of things, would be allowed to fall through."

Jesup was to leave an estate valued at almost $13,000,000 of which over $9,000,000 went to his wife and another million to the American Museum of Natural History of which he was president. But he had made no provision either for Minik or for Peary's expedition. His death also threatened to jeopardise the protracted negotiations which had been going on since 1897 between him and the Pearys over the sale of the meteorites which Peary, contrary to popular belief, had only lent to the museum, pending the finding of a purchaser willing to put down the $50,000 asking price Peary had placed on the famous stones.

The Pearys needed that money badly as security, since practically everything that Peary earned went into his expeditions. This Jo had made very clear in her letter to the museum's new president, Henry F. Osborn, a respectful two months after the death of Jesup.

> I think it only fair to state that the meteorites are my property, and that the money obtained for them will not be expended in Arctic Exploration. It is all I have with which to educate my children in the event of anything happening to my husband. Of this Mr. Jesup was cognizant and he approved entirely my keeping the proceeds as a nest egg.

The sale eventually went through in 1909; but in the meantime, Morris Jesup's widow's donation of $5,000 set an example which others soon followed and, with General Thomas H. Hubbard as the new president of the Club, preparations went ahead for Peary's final expedition.

But not all of the problems that appeared at this time were short-term crises which money or influence could solve, and one such problem for the ageing Peary was the growing ambition, and with it the threat, of Dr. Frederick Cook.

He had arrived on the scene by a different route – by a series of polar expeditions upon which he had built a reputation as a man of extraordinary resourcefulness. Peary had himself described the surgeon of his first expedition to North-West Greenland as a man of "unruffled patience and coolness in an emergency . . . a helpful and an indefatigable worker." He had won the admiration also of the fare-paying passengers on the "summer pleasure cruise to the Arctic" which he had organized in 1894 in an effort to raise funds for his proposed Antarctic expedition. That pleasure cruise of the *Miranda* had been an ill-fated one, as had also been his voyage in the *Zeta* the previous year; but as Prof. G. Frederick Wright, one of the passengers aboard the *Miranda*, was later to write:

> When our ship was injured upon the rocks, the courage and skill which he showed in venturing 100 miles northward along the rugged coast of Greenland in a small boat to get relief, prepared me for believing that he would accomplish any daring enterprise that was within the reach of human effort.

Even Herbert Bridgman had supported Cook's plan for an Antarctic expedition, stating that: "The work of unlocking the great mystery of the South ... could be entrusted to no more competent hands than Dr. Cook's ... those who know him know that he combines the patience, judgement, and zeal of the explorer."

The greatest praise, however, was still to come. Having failed to raise the funds for his own expedition to the Antarctic, he had joined the

Belgian Antarctic expedition in Rio de Janeiro in September 1897 on its way south for a summer scientific cruise down the west coast of the Antarctic Peninsula; but the *Belgica* had been caught in the ice some three hundred miles south of the Antarctic Circle and forced to winter in the pack. There is no question that Cook's optimism and quietly persuasive manner held that expedition together. Presented with the prospect of scurvy among the crew, he had insisted, over the protests of his companions, that they should eat fresh meat – seal and penguin. Presented with a crew who were suffering from a severe form of depression which Cook called "Polar anemia," he sought to get at the cause and not merely treat the symptom but to raise the spirits of the men. Presented with the alarming prospect that they might be held captive by the pack ice through a second winter (which it is unlikely they would have survived), Cook proposed digging trenches from the ship to the nearest open water, his theory being that, by removing the snow cover and exposing the "darker" ice beneath it, the heat of the sun would weaken the ice along the line of the trenches, so that if the ice fractured at all, it would more probably do so along that line. The three days' work on this scheme was abandoned as a failure when it was realised that they had started work on it too late in the season to be effective, but the idea in principle had been sound. Cook then proposed sawing a canal through the ice to the nearest open water 2,200 feet away – a desperate project which occupied the entire crew for a month. Amundsen was mate on the *Belgica* and observes that their escape from the ice was "due first and foremost to the skill, energy, and persistence of Dr. Cook."

He returned as the hero; was knighted by the King of the Belgians, and awarded the Gold Medal of the Royal Geographical Society of Belgium. Some years later a newspaper was to attribute to Amundsen the opinion that Cook was "a genius . . . the finest traveller I ever saw." An extraordinary comment (if it was true) coming from a man of Amundsen's calibre, for the only time he ever saw Cook sledging had been on a five-day outing from the ship in the spring of 1899, during which they had travelled only fourteen miles. It had, moreover, been the only ice journey that Cook had made since the year he had spent in the Arctic with Peary, on which he had made not a single sledge trip further than 130 miles from their base in McCormick Bay.

His fine reputation as an explorer notwithstanding, there can be no escaping the fact that Cook, in terms of experience as a polar traveller, was simply not in the class of Peary. By the summer of 1907, he had spent only two and a half years living in those trackless regions to which he had now set his heart on returning.

As Cook put it: "I waited, and fortune favoured me in that I met Mr. John R. Bradley." He was exactly the sort of sponsor that the loner Cook was looking for: a wealthy big game hunter who needed the expertise of Cook in organising a summer expedition to the Smith Sound region in search of bear, and a gambler whom Cook could depend upon to enter into the spirit of the quest that Cook now had in mind. With seemingly unlimited funds provided by the wealthy Bradley, Cook (with the help of Captain Bob Bartlett who was later bitterly to regret that he had offered him advice) bought a Gloucester fishing schooner of 111 tons, and had it converted within a month into a luxurious floating hunting lodge with her hull sheathed with oak, her power increased, and her holds stocked with two years' supply of provisions against the possibility that she might be held by the ice. Finally, Cook appointed as master of the *John R. Bradley*, Bob Bartlett's cousin, Moses, who had three times been mate of Peary's ships, the last time with the *Roosevelt*.

Unlike Peary, who was meeting setbacks at every turn, Cook, blessed with a run of good fortune, was ready to sail by 3rd July, 1907 and, without announcing his intentions, he had quietly slipped away.

An Arctic expedition had been born without the usual clamor ... no press campaign heralded our project, no government aid had been asked, nor had large contributions been sought from private individuals to purchase luxuries for a Pullman jaunt of a large party Poleward. For, although I secretly cherished the ambition, there was no definite plan to essay the North Pole.

He admits five pages on in his book that he and Bradley had talked of the possibility of an attempt at the Pole. He also says that "without any conscious purpose," they had taken on board all the extra supplies he might need should he decide to leave the ship. A definite plan he may not have had; but even by the amount he admits, this voyage was clearly a "hunting trip" unique in the annals of history.

Bradley's version confirms this. One day in early June, after all the preparations to the schooner had been completed, and the two men were lunching together in New York, Cook had said quite simply: "Why not try for the Pole?" Bradley was somewhat alarmed at this; but having discovered that all Cook wanted was his approval of the idea, and his permission to take some extra equipment aboard the schooner for the "extension" of the cruise, Bradley had agreed saying:

"We'll fit this expedition for the Pole and say nothing to anyone about it" ... We figured it this way: in case we got up to Etah and found the natives were not well or the dogs scarce or any other conditions unfavourable, we could call it a hunting trip and return quietly home again.

As things turned out, the conditions were to prove favourable for Cook, and leaving the *John R. Bradley* at Etah, they had pushed on twenty-five miles up the coast to the tiny settlement of Anoritoq, and here Cook was convinced he should stay:

> Ordinarily, Annoatok [Anoritoq] is a town of only a single family or perhaps two, but we found it unusually large and populous, for the best hunters had gathered here for the winter bear hunt. Their summer game catch had been very lucky. Immense quantities of meat were strewn along the shore, under mounds of stone. More than a hundred dogs, the standard by which Eskimo prosperity is measured, yelped a greeting, and twelve long-haired, wild men came out to meet us as friends.
>
> It came strongly to me that this was the spot to make the base for the Polar dash. Here were Eskimo helpers, strong, hefty natives from whom I could select the best to accompany me; here, by a fortunate chance, were the best dog teams; here were plenty of furs for clothing; and here was unlimited food. These supplies, combined with supplies on the schooner, would give all that was needed for the campaign. Nothing could have been more ideal.

And so from Etah, as a gesture perhaps of courtesy, he had sent a letter to Herbert Bridgman, Secretary of the Peary Arctic Club. The letter, dated 26th August, 1907, and mailed by Bradley on his return to Sydney on 1st October, brought news which, in spite of all the warning signs that had been seen, was to shake Peary to the core.

> I have hit upon a new route to the North Pole and will stay to try it. By way of Buchanan Bay and Ellesmere Land and northward through Nansen Strait over the Polar Sea seems to me to be a very good route. There will be game to the 82nd degree, and there are natives and dogs for the task. So here is for the Pole. Mr. Bradley will tell you the rest. Kind regards to all.

Peary's reaction is not on record. We do, however, know that he was approached by several well-meaning friends over the next few months who expressed concern (for Peary's sake) that Cook was in Peary's rightful territory and might well, judging by the McKinley affair, be tempted to fake an attempt at the Pole. The Arctic explorer, Vilhjalmur Stefansson, was one of these advisors. Belmore Browne and Herschel Parker, who had been with Cook on his controversial ascent of Mount McKinley in 1906, had also expressed their suspicion about Cook strongly and in person to Peary. They even pressed for the Explorers' Club to conduct an investigation into their president's claim, but Cook had sailed for the Arctic without submitting any evidence, and without giving notice to the Club of his intention to remain in the Arctic for at least a year.

Peary's response on being asked by the Explorers' Club to succeed the absentee president was tempered by the wise counsel of his wife who advised:

> They are all fakes. But in view of present conditions it might do you considerable harm to antagonize these people. Harm in this way – that they would assist Cook in every way just to annoy you. Of course if you become their president it would increase your popularity in that direction (not that I should care for that very much) . . . Whatever you do, do it in a dignified manner as becomes the *greatest Arctic explorer of the age*.

As a result, Peary is reported by the *New York Times* to have replied that: "He did not care to serve unless the club would give him the assurance that, in the event of Dr. Cook returning and claiming to have found the North Pole, proper proofs would be demanded of him . . . Mr. Peary was prevailed upon to accept the presidency, the club acquiescing to the demands he made concerning proofs from Dr. Cook."

Another indication of Peary's seething indignation is the 1,200-word indictment of Cook which he dated "May, 1908" and sent to the Editor of the *New York Times*, a part of which read:

> I beg to note that Dr. Cook has located himself at Etah; which has been my rendezvous and depot for years; that he has about him my Eskimos and dogs assembled at Etah with the expectation of meeting me there last summer; that he is appropriating to his own use the services of the Eskimos whom I have trained in methods of protracted, serious arctic sledge work and is utilizing their intimate knowledge of the routes and game resources of the land to the north, which they have gained under my lead and guidance . . . I wish to say that I regard Dr. Cook's action in going north "sub rosa" . . . for the admitted purpose of forestalling me as one of which no man possessing a sense of honor would be guilty.

But aside from the sense of outrage he felt at Cook's violation of polar ethics, Peary regarded Cook's plan of travelling alone with the Eskimos (and presumably out on the Arctic Ocean without the use of supporting parties) as an implied insult to his own record as an explorer. Had he not, after all, tried, tested, and hopelessly failed to get any further than eighty-two miles out onto the pack ice in 1902 by persisting with his original theory that a small party was the only way which offered any chance of success? Had he not, even with a large and well equipped expedition, using the best men and dogs, and with the *Roosevelt* positioned less than forty miles from the northernmost point of land, still failed to get any further north than 87°6'? Was it not also an insult to suggest that there could be such a thing as a "new route" which would be better than anything he had found in all the years he had been travelling in that region?

Not only was Cook, in Peary's view, unethical and insulting. He was also rash and absurd. He was proposing to start from about the same latitude as Payer Harbor (Peary's starting point in 1902); but would be taking this "new route," as he called it, a longer and possibly more difficult route than Peary's which would bring him to the shore of the Arctic Ocean at the northern end of Nansen Sound. From this point to the Pole he would have two hundred miles more pack ice-travelling to do than from Cape Hecla, and on this so-called "new route," which had been discovered, mapped and travelled by Sverdrup's expedition, although there would be a good chance of game, hunting it would delay them.

The man, in Peary's view, was a fool, but that did not make him less of a threat as is evident from the "driving spur" of his rival's stated passion for the Arctic, his obvious craving for fame.

During those dizzy hours on deck I thought of those who had preceded me; of heroic men who for three centuries had braved suffering, cold and famine, who had sacrificed the comforts of civilization, their families and friends, who had given their own lives in the pursuit of this mysterious, yea, fruitless quest. I remembered reading the thrilling tales of those who returned – tales which had flushed me with excitement and inspired me with the same mad ambition. I thought of the noble, indefatigable efforts of these men, of the heart-sickening failures, in which I too had shared. And I felt the indomitable, swift surge of their aweful, goading determination within me – to subdue the forces of nature, to cover as Icarus did the air of those icy spaces, to reach the silver-shining vacantness which men call the North Pole.

Different though the two men were, almost it seemed from different worlds, for more than forty years the destinies of each had been converging and only now were they aware that only one could win. Which man then had the advantage? Both at this time would have said the other did not stand a chance – but neither man believed it.

Cook's advantage of course was that he was one full year ahead. With his sole white companion, Rudolph Franke, and the entire population of

Eskimos from Etah, Cook had moved up the coast on the schooner and set up their winter quarters at Anoritoq at the end of August 1907. Already he had sent word around the settlements that Peary was not coming, but that he, Daagitkoorsuaq, was intending a journey across Ellesmere through the musk-ox grounds. This news had delighted the Eskimos, and soon Cook's persuasiveness had the entire tribe of 250 people employed in the service of the expedition.

They were soon to realise that this expedition was very different to one of Peary's. For a start, Cook's schooner (which had sailed for home on 3rd September) was very much smaller than Peary's ships, and there were less materials brought ashore; but they were happy enough to be with Cook – he was an easy man to live with. They enjoyed also getting involved in new ideas, and Cook had plenty of these. He had brought with him a good supply of hickory already cut to approximately the right sizes for sledge construction, together with the necessary tools, and as soon as the long polar night descended, the box-house in which Cook and Franke lived was converted into a workshop and he set his Eskimos to work building a sledge which he claimed combined the durability of the Eskimo and the lightness of the Yukon sledge.

> From eight to ten men were at work at the benches, eight hours each day, shaping and bending runners, fitting and lashing interchangeable cross bars and posts, and riveting the iron shoes. Thus the sledge parts were manufactured to possess the same facilities to fit not only all other sledges, but also other parts of the same sledge.

These sledges, the joints of which were lashed with seal-thong, were twelve feet long, thirty inches wide and had a runner width of an inch and an eighth. He tells us in a footnote in his book that the Peary sledge:

> ... is a copy of the Eskimo sledge, a lumbering, unwieldy thing weighing over a hundred pounds and which bears the same relation to a refined bent-hickory vehicle that a lumber cart does to an express wagon. In this "Jesup" sledge there is a dead weight of over fifty pounds of useless wood. The needless weight thus carried can, in a better sledge, be replaced by fifty pounds of food. This fifty pounds will feed one man over the entire route to the Pole.

Cook's own sledges weighed only fifty-five pounds, and the Eskimos must have been amazed and amused – as invariably they are when a white man with very little experience in the Arctic insists that he knows best. But Cook offers this comment:

After a careful study of the art of sledging – traveling from the earliest times to the present day, after years of sledging and sledge observation in Greenland, the Antarctic and Alaska, I came to the conclusion that success was dependent, not upon any one type of sledge, but upon local fitness.

Cook, one should remember, had at this time spent just over one year in the Arctic, had done some travelling on the ice cap, a little local sledging in the region of McCormick Bay and fourteen miles on the Antarctic pack ice, whereas most of the Eskimo hunters of the Smith Sound tribe (the Thule, or polar Eskimos, as they are usually called) have, by the time they are about forty-five, travelled over 60,000 miles across all types of ice. Some of those Eskimos he was employing to make his sledges had also been with Peary out on the Arctic Ocean, which at this stage Cook had not even seen. And yet he claims in his book that his sledges were right for the job.

He was convinced also, having read of Peary's many hold-ups on the wrong side of an open lead, that his party would need some form of boat. "Foolish indeed," he says (and Nansen and Johansen would have agreed with him), "is the explorer who pays slight attention to this important problem." And so after some research he had selected a twelve-foot collapsible boat with a wooden frame.

The slats, spreaders and floor-pieces were utilized as parts of the sledges. The canvas cover served as a floor cloth for our sleeping bags. Thus the boat did useful service for a hundred days and never seemed needlessly cumbersome. When the craft was finally spread for use as a boat, in it we carried the sledge, in it we sought game for food, and in it or under it we camped. Without it we could never have returned.

He made a few other improvements to his equipment: using canvas to replace the seal-skin dog harnesses, and cotton cord to replace their edible traces, and he had brought with him lightweight tents and pemmican, the sledge travellers' staple diet when the supply of fresh meat runs out. He had also, wisely, gone out with the hunters on a six-day hunting trip to the north at the end of October, and with the November moon had made a five-hundred-mile round trip to the settlements to the south, thus increasing his experience since returning to the Arctic by a total of about three weeks.

Eventually, on the morning of 19th February, 1908, Cook set out with eleven sledges, eleven men and 103 dogs, each in prime condition.

My heart was high. I was about to start on the quest which had inspired me for many years! The natives were naturally excited. The dogs caught the contagious enthusiasm, and barked joyously. At eight o'clock in the morning our whips snapped, the spans of dog teams leaped forward, and we were off.

My polar quest had begun!

Two days later, while Cook was at Greely's camp at Cape Sabine, with Payer Harbor tucked in behind it, and musing on what a "curious whim of fate [it was] that this ill-starred camp of famine and death, in earlier days, should have marked the very outset of our modern effort to reach the Pole," Peary, three thousand miles to the south, was writing a cryptic note to his wife: "Just a line. Shall start early in the morning. Matters are apparently 50% better than three years ago, more dogs, ice more stable . . ."

CHAPTER 15

The Final Arrow

After a bitter delay of one full year, the *Roosevelt* had finally sailed from New York on 6th July, 1908, to the swelling tide of well-wishers' cheers and the whistles, the sirens, and even the guns of the river's saluting ships.

"Surely," Peary was later to write, "no ship ever started for the end of the earth with more heart-stirring farewells than those which followed the *Roosevelt*." But he had been seeing that memorable send-off from New York in the company of a hundred of his wealthiest supporters. Henson had seen it differently: "Men in the streets brawled among themselves over the degree of disaster the expedition would meet. Gamblers accepted fabulous odds on success, while women wept for no reason. It was tense and exciting, yet it was ugly and vicious."

It had been for Henson a relief to get away, to leave the hurtful world behind and steam on up to Oyster Bay, the summer home of President Roosevelt, where the following day Peary and Jo were guests of the President at a private luncheon before all going on board, the President eager to inspect the ship that Peary had named after him. And he had evidently inspected her rather more thoroughly than Captain Bob Bartlett had been expecting: ". . . nothing escaped his piercing eyes. He went into the lower hold and into the engine room. He inspected Peary's quarters and the living spaces of the sailors . . . and demanded to know the names of every one of us."

But the great man's verdict had been "Bully!" and as he and Peary were standing on the deck shaking hands, Peary had uttered his now famous words.

"Mr. President, I shall put into this effort everything there is in me – physical, mental, and moral."

"I believe in you, Peary," the President had replied, "and I believe in your success – if it is within the possibility of man."

Thus Peary was committed to return with the prize – or not return at all.

The *Roosevelt* sailed on to New Bedford where the whale boats were collected, then on to Peary's beloved Eagle Island in Casco Bay where a massive, steel-bound spare rudder was taken on board as a precaution against a repeat of the misfortune of 1906, and finally at Sydney on 17th July, Peary parted from his wife and children: "Another farewell – and there had been so many! Brave, noble little woman! You have borne with me the brunt of all my Arctic work. But, somehow, this parting was less sad than any which had gone before. I think that we both felt it was the last."

Henson, now a married man, knew also in his heart that this would be his final voyage. He sensed it in his slowness to respond to being on his way to share again the simple life with those who accepted without prejudice the colour of his skin. He sensed it in his need to seek the company of men he knew well from the previous voyage: "Captain Bob," as he was affectionately known by his men; George Wardwell, the chief engineer; John Murphy, the boatswain; Charles Percy, the steward, and, particularly, Prof. Ross Marvin who had been on Peary's last expedition. Of the quiet, earnest Marvin (who was listed by Peary as his secretary and assistant) Henson wrote: "he has taken great interest in me and, being a teacher, has tried to teach me ... navigation, my knowledge so far [consisting] only of knot and splice seamanship."

And so for a few days he stayed well clear of Peary's three excited new men who, in their eagerness to please, were tiresome to bear. He had seen it all before. College men, all three of them; as self-assured as all the others who had found the life too hard, or Peary too obsessive. And yet, in spite of all their noise, he came to like those three: the powerfully built doctor, John W. Goodsell; the thirty-four-year-old teacher, Donald B. MacMillan, a graduate of Peary's own alma mater; and George Borup, the handsome and boisterous "kid" (as Henson called him), who was only one year out of Yale "but well set up for his age."

They were all three in awe of Peary, and two of the three were to remain so. But if they had expected to get to know Peary during the voyage up to the Arctic, they must have been disappointed, for the Commander preferred to keep his own company, and to leave Bob Bartlett to run the ship with his own profane brand of encouragement. And so on through the gateway into Peary's "domain," which began at Cape York, the *Roosevelt* weaved its way northwards to Etah, while Peary and Henson, who had transferred to the support ship *Erik*, went into the fjords to collect more Eskimos and dogs.

On board the *Roosevelt*, speculation as to the whereabouts and intentions of Dr. Cook was given free rein, and from the letters Ross Marvin wrote to his friend L. C. Bement, we can get some idea of the feelings of Peary's party towards the man who, for all they knew, may already have forestalled them. In a letter dated 30th July, two days before the *Roosevelt* reached Cape York, he wrote that Peary had spent all of one meal "explaining to his men just how he felt about Dr. Cook." The intensity of Peary's hatred was an uncompromising introduction to the rivalry between these two for MacMillan, Borup and Dr. Goodsell, and left them in no doubt where their loyalties were expected to lie. The Arctic, he told them, "is a great test of character . . . that brings a man face to face with himself and with his companions; if he is a man, the man comes out; and if he is a cur, the cur shows as quickly."

From Etah on 7th August Marvin wrote:

> Dr. Cook seems to be the whole topic of conversation here, but whatever I will tell you I wish you would consider it as confidential. He sent all but two of his natives back from Cape Hubbard, where the Com. [Commander] had been last summer, and said he was going on to Crocker Land but not the Pole.
>
> . . . Dr. Cook and his two natives are not back yet, they had a canvas boat big enough for three on the sledge with them. All we know is what we have picked up from the Eskimos. Perhaps we will see this white man before we leave here.
>
> . . . I would not dare write this about Dr. Cook if I did not feel sure that you will keep it to yourself.

Marvin wrote again on the 11th, by which time there had been some dramatic developments:

> . . . The Dr. Cook affair grows more complicated every day. His man Rudolph Frankie [Franke] arrived here yesterday in a boat from North Star Bay. He is real anxious to leave here and wants to go home on the *Erik*.

His reception had not been friendly. According to one of the sailors on the *Roosevelt*: "The man could hardly walk, but I tell you, sir, that the steward on board would not give him a drop of coffee or anything to eat. So he went on shore to sleep with the Eskimos." The following morning Bartlett went ashore and apologized to Franke for the way his crew had treated him, and brought him back on board to be fed. Franke then told his story to Bartlett and Marvin, and showed them a letter sent back by Cook with Koolootingwah and Inugito from the Arctic Ocean. It was dated 20th March and written at the end of their third day out from Svartevoeg which is some ten miles down the coast from the northern tip of Axel Heiberg Island.

> Dear Rudolph:
>
> . . . To present we have seen nothing of Crocker Land, and I am taking a straight course for the Pole. The boys are doing well, and I have plenty of dogs . . .

While I expect to get back to you by the end of May, still I wish you to be ready to go to Acponie, the island off North Star, where the whalers' steamers come, by the fifth of June; and if I am not back, go home with the whalers. I think however we will be back.

Gather all the blue-fox skins you can. These must be our money on the return trip. If you can get a few bear skins, take them, also narwhal and walrus tusks, but do not give much for them . . .

If Kudnu, the Dane [Knud Rasmussen], is still there, urge him to wait for our return either at Annoatok or at North Star, for I am anxious to go to Upernavik at once on our return, and he can be of much use to us . . .

I have regretted many times that you are not with us, but at the moment it seemed best to send you back . . . I trust you are of the same opinion.

So goodbye, and now for the Pole.

Bartlett had no authority to offer Franke a passage home on the *Erik*. For that permission, Franke had to wait for the return of Peary from his trip around the settlements and camps. On this, Peary's fears that Cook had already taken the best men and dogs had proved to be unjustified, for he and Henson, as he says, "obtained all the Eskimos and dogs we needed – two hundred and forty-six of the latter, to be exact." He also tells us that there was for him "a strange mingling of pleasure and sadness in this gathering together of our brown-skinned helpers, for I felt that it was for the last time." Henson, however, offers a different picture of this trip, for not every hunter who responded to Peary's call met with his approval.

Commander Peary gave me explicit instructions to get Nipsangwah and Myah ashore as quick as the Creator would let them, but to be sure that their seven curs were kept aboard; these two huskies [Eskimos] having exalted ideas as to their rights and privileges . . .

But that was Peary's view, not Henson's. Being fluent in their language and much closer to them than Peary, he could see how unfair this was:

Acting under orders, I obeyed, but it was not a pleasant task. I have known men who needed dogs less to pay a great deal more for one pup than was paid to Nipsangwah for his pack of seven. The dogs are a valuable asset to this people and these two men were dependent on their little teams to a greater extent than on the plates and cups of tin which they received in exchange for them.

In 1967, one of the old men in Siorapaluk, the northernmost present-day village in the Thule District, had told the French eskimologist, Jean Malaurie, about Peary – "the great tormentor," as the old man called him.

> I was very young, but I will never forget how he treated the Inuit. It was in Uummannaq [Thule], in July 1908, and this voyage was to be his last. His big ship arrives in the bay. He is hardly visible from the shore, but he shouts: "Kissa Tikeri-Unga! – I'm arriving, for a fact!" The Inuit go aboard. Peary has a barrel of biscuits brought up on deck. The two or three hunters who have gone out to the ship in their kayaks bend over the barrel and begin to eat with both hands. Later, the barrel is taken ashore, and the contents thrown on the beach. Men, women, and children hurl themselves on the biscuits like dogs, which amuses Peary a lot. My heart still turns cold to think of it. That scene tells very well how he considered this people – my people – who were, for all of that, devoted to him.

The *Erik* was reunited with the *Roosevelt* at Etah on 11th August, and started transferring three hundred tons of coal and fifty tons of walrus and whale meat, some fifty tons of coal being left ashore for the return voyage. Franke went to Peary to ask permission to go out on his support ship. "He showed me a letter from Dr. Cook," Peary says in his book, and after an examination by Dr. Goodsell showed the man to be suffering from incipient scurvy and in a serious mental state, "I had no alternative but to give him a passage home on the *Erik*."

Again, Henson offers a different version, this time with the help of Bradley Robinson:

> Pushing his way through the crowd, the white man rushed to Peary and seized him by the arm.
>
> ... "Please, dear God, take me away. I can't stand it. I can't!" he sobbed hysterically. He held out a black, grimy fist and, slowly opened his clenched fingers, revealing a grubby wad of paper nestled in his dirt-smeared palm.
>
> "Look," he screamed. "Look! I can go away. I have permission from Dr. Cook ..."
>
> At the mention of Cook's name Peary scowled and snatched the crumpled paper from the man's trembling hand. As Peary unwadded the sheet, the man covered his face with his hands and sobbed convulsively.
>
> When Peary had finished reading he looked up at the others. "This man is Rudolph Franke," he announced tersely. "Cook left him here in charge of a cache of supplies, with permission to go home on the first boat."

Dr. Goodsell led Franke away, and Peary started to follow. He hesitated, and then turned back to his men. "That, gentlemen," he said sombrely, "is an example of what can happen to a white man in the Arctic."

Franke was later to maintain that he was given passage only on the condition that Cook's furs and ivory were handed over, "just as the enemy has to hand over their arms to the victorious party." The other side of the story, which was offered to the press by the Peary Arctic Club in the form of a letter from Peary, stated that Franke had been given the option of turning the furs and ivory over to Peary, or leaving them where they were. Franke chose to hand them over, but on examination "the skins were wet, mildewed, and rotting, and the horns broken from knocking about." And so the Club, deciding that the furs and ivory were practically worthless, billed John R. Bradley $100 for "sending Franke home for 'humanity's sake.'" Cook was later to counter this with a claim that, "one narwhal tusk worth to me at least $1,000 was polished and sent as Peary's trophy to President Roosevelt." Either way, the furs and tusks had not been the trophies of Cook's own hunting, but merely the better side of a deal (common in those days among explorers) in which valuable furs and ivory were exchanged for useful items which the explorers had obtained cheaply from any quayside chandlery before setting out.

With Rudolph Franke disposed of, Peary addressed himself to making sure Cook's supplies did not fall into the hands of the Eskimos and thereby devalue his own gifts. He sent his boatswain John Murphy and cabin boy Billy Pritchard ashore with Harry Whitney, a wealthy sportsman who had taken passage north on the *Erik*, to man Cook's hut as a well provisioned and discrete sub-base as a precaution against the loss of the *Roosevelt* and, at the same time, to lay the foundations for any future claim he might care to make of having set up a relief station for his inexperienced rival.

His next move still to this day remains something of a mystery. He ordered the following notice to be posted on the door of Cook's shack: "This house belongs to Dr. F. A. Cook, but Dr. Cook is long ago dead and there is no use to search for him. Therefore, I, Commander Robert E. Peary, install my boatswain in this deserted house."

He then wrote to his more influential friends warning them to be on their guard against the reappearance of the doctor and to discount any claims he might make. Such a precaution would suggest that Peary was assuming that Cook had survived, so what was the thinking behind the notice tacked on the shack door? Marvin knew, but could not risk telling even his friend Bement:

... the Dr. Cook affair has become a tangle and a hard nut to crack. I am writing Peary's confidential letters concerning the matter, and so my lips must be closed. So you see how I stand. I know more about it than anyone else, but I can say less. The others can write what they know; with me it would be a breach of trust.

It is certain that Peary had not the slightest fear that the doctor had succeeded. He had learned from the Eskimos that Cook had set out from Cape Thomas Hubbard with only two hunters and twenty-six dogs, on a two-way journey if the Pole really was his intended objective, totalling over one thousand nautical miles if he was to travel in a straight line – and this Peary knew from his own experience to be impossible across the polar pack. Peary also knew that by adding on those extra miles Cook would be obliged to travel to find a passable route, he would find himself faced with the utterly unachievable feat of covering, at a minimum, 1,300 miles of polar pack ice with only the food he could haul on two sledges and the flesh of the dogs that were hauling them.

In order, however, for Peary to focus the mind of every member of his party on the awesome task that lay ahead, it was not enough simply to point out these facts. Cook had to be totally removed from the scene and given up for dead. This can be the only explanation for the assertive wording of that strange notice which Peary had ordered nailed to the door of Cook's deserted house at Anoritoq. Whether Peary actually believed what he had written, we have no way of knowing. But the gesture was effective enough, for there was no further mention of the hapless doctor, and once again the whole vast area from Baffin Bay right up to the Pole became the exclusive preserve of Peary, with no one around to steal his prize or to rob him of the glory which his suffering had earned him. All that now remained to be done before departing was to write a farewell letter to Jo:

Peary Arctic Club
North Polar Expedition

S.S. Roosevelt,
Etah,
Aug. 17, 1908

My Darling:
    Am nearly through with my writing. Am brain weary with the thousand and one imperative details and things to think of.
    Everything thus far has gone well, too well I am afraid, and I am (solely on general principles) somewhat suspicious of the future.
    The ship is in better shape than before; the party and crew are

apparently harmonious; I have 21 Eskimo men (against 23 last time) but the total of men women and children is only 50 as against 67 before owing to a more careful selection as to children. Two only of my last farthest north are on board now, Ootah and Panikpah. Sipsu I have left because of his numerous children, Ahngmaloktok because his wife is not well, Ahngodoblaho did not want to go, and Pewahto* and his family I left on general principles.

The Cook circumstances have given me a good deal of extra work and trouble; but have worked out satisfactory.

I have landed supplies here, and leave two men ostensibly on behalf of Cook. As a matter of fact I have established here the sub-base which last I established at Victoria Head, as a precaution in event of loss of the *Roosevelt* either going up this fall or coming down next summer.

In some respects this is an advantage as on leaving here there is nothing to delay me or keep me from taking either side of the Channel going up. The conditions give me entire control of the situation.

Added to this, Whitney is going to stay here through the winter to hunt muskoxen in Ellesmere Land and he and his friend Norton are going to have a ship come up next summer. This insures me against having to stay here another year in event of loss of *Roosevelt*. It is fine. Whitney's sister, Mrs. Charles Dickey, 37 E. 51st Street, New York, who has large means like himself will help him. Will suggest you write and tell her not to worry about Whitney, and later make her acquaintance.

You have been with me constantly, sweetheart. At Kangerdlooksoah I looked repeatedly at ptarmigan island and thought of the time we camped there. At Nuuatoksoah I landed where we were. And on the 11th we passed the mouth of Bowdoin Bay in brilliant weather, and as long as I could I kept my eyes on Anniversary Lodge. We have been great chums dear.

Tell Marie to remember what I told her; tell "Mister Man" [Robert Peary, Jr.] to remember "straight and strong and clean and honest," obey orders, and never forget that Daddy put "Mut" in his charge till he himself comes back to take her.

In fancy I kiss your dear eyes and lips and cheeks sweetheart; and dream of you and my children, and my home till I come again.

Kiss my babies for me.

Aufwiedersehen. Love, Love, Love.

Your Bert

P.S. August 18, 9 a.m. . . . Tell Marie that her fir pillow perfumes me to sleep.

---

* Piugaatoq (Pewahto), was the husband of Aleqasina, the mother of two of Peary's children.

Now, at last, he could move on. He put ashore those Eskimos he did not want, and when the *Roosevelt* headed out of Etah fjord on 18th August, 1908, and turned north to face the ice of the channel, she was loaded almost to the water's edge with the coal she had taken on board from the *Erik*; some seventy tons of whale meat from Labrador; the meat and blubber of some fifty walruses; twenty-two eager Eskimo hunters together with all of their hunting equipment; seventeen well fed and chattering women, with ten children of various sizes and 246 dogs.

"Ahead of me," Peary wrote, "lay – my dream, my destiny, the goal of that irresistible impulsion which had driven me for twenty-three years . . . Should I succeed? Should I return?"

And so, once again, the *Roosevelt* and the men who drove her through the ice of Kane Basin and the Robeson Channel, were put to their toughest test, and at 7.15 a.m. on 5th September, 1908, only fifteen minutes later than their time of arrival in 1905, the *Roosevelt* returned to Cape Sheridan.

With her first winter still fresh in the minds of Peary and Bartlett, a safer place was found for her second winter on the shore of the Arctic Ocean, inside a reef and as far up the beach as they could take her on the tide. And while she was being prepared for the winter, the hunting parties were sent out to the Lake Hazen region. Depot-laying journeys along the coast to Cape Columbia also got under way to take advantage of the remaining light, and to break in and train the new men. Such trips, however, no longer had any appeal for Peary:

> I had planned from the beginning to leave most of the hunting and other field work to the younger members of the expedition. Twenty odd years of Arctic experience had dulled for me the excitement of everything but a polar-bear chase; the younger men were eager for the work; there was much to do on board ship in planning for the spring, and I wished to conserve my energies for the supreme effort. There was no systematic training, because I do not believe in it. My body has always been able thus far to follow my will no matter what the demands might be, and my winter's work was largely a matter of refinement of equipment, and of mathematical calculations of pounds of supplies and miles of distance. It was the lack of food which had forced us to turn back at 87°6'. Hunger, not cold, is the dragon which guards the Rhinegold of the Arctic.

And so, in comfort, and this time with only one encounter with the pack ice which terrified the Eskimos and threatened the ship, Peary spent his last winter in the Arctic planning and reading while his eager crew worked, trained, blazed the trails and prepared the way for their master. Finally, one by one, his "divisions" set out for Cape Columbia until, by the 21st of February, 1909, Peary alone of the polar party was left on board the ship.

That last day was one of perfect quiet and rest, free from interruptions. The morning I devoted to going over carefully the details of the work already done, to see that no slenderest necessary thread had been overlooked, and to considering again, point by point, the details of the coming journey. When I had satisfied myself . . . that everything was in its place and every possible contingency provided for, I had a few hours in which to look the situation squarely in the face, and to think of those other times when, as now, I was on the eve of departure into the void and unknown North.

This was my final chance to realise the one dream of my life. The morning start would be the drawing of the string to launch the last arrow in my quiver.

At 10 a.m. on the morning of the 22nd – "Washington's Birthday" as Peary reminds his readers – he set out with two young hunters, Arco and Kudlooktoo, with their two teams of dogs, to follow the hard packed trail ninety miles north-westward along the coast to Cape Columbia. Before him lay a journey, he states, of "nearly a thousand miles" – a strange total since he also tells us a few lines further on in that same chapter entitled "Arctic ice sledging as it really is" that "From Cape Columbia we were to go straight north over the ice of the Polar Sea – four hundred and thirteen geographical miles."

He cannot be referring to the total from the ship to the Pole and back, as this would total 1,006 miles, 180 of which, in any case, is coastal ice. His "nearly a thousand miles" (which he later calls "some nine-hundred odd miles") must therefore be twice the distance from Cape Columbia to the Pole which means that he is allowing for some fourteen per cent of his total distance to be extra miles as detours. This is worth bearing in mind, as it is one of the few references anywhere in his published writings in which he offers a clue as to the actual total distance he travelled on his final journey – and to those unmentionable extra miles.

And why set out from Cape Columbia? There is a stretch of ninety miles along that coast from any point from which he could have chosen to set off without increasing his distance to the Pole by more than ten miles, and in 1909 there may well have been (as there usually are) places along that coast which offered an easier way on to the pack.

True, Cape Columbia is the northernmost point of land. But he had not set out from there on his two previous attempts. So could there have been some other reason, one he was not prepared to admit because it was too personal and might have been misinterpreted by some of his readers?

Is it not curiously appropriate that Cape Columbia lies on almost exactly the same longitude as his Eagle Island home, where the latitude and longitude of the house is inscribed over the door of the porch? Is it not at least a possibility that Peary on this final attempt to reach the Pole had chosen to project his dream along the very same meridian of his beloved Eagle Island, through Cape Columbia and on to the Pole – a line so straight that he had no need to check his longitude as he headed towards his goal?

The suggestion appears at first glance absurd. Peary, after all, had certainly had enough experience of the polar pack ice by this stage in his career to know that the entire mass of floating ice that forms the skin of the Arctic Ocean – all five-million square miles of it – is moving under the influence of winds and currents; constantly forming new ridges of pressure, fracturing, splitting, and breaking up. He knew well enough from experience that there is no surface on the face of the earth (capable of bearing the weight of a man) that is more unstable than the drifting pack ice, and that travelling in a straight line to the Pole across this broken, moving surface is absolutely impossible. And yet he implies that he did.

He tells us also (with an emphasis that points a derisive finger at his rival, Dr. Cook) that without the "Peary System" of pioneer and support-ing parties it would be "a physical impossibility for any man to reach the North Pole." His supporting parties would serve also to keep the trail open for the rapid return of the main party. "Twenty-four hours – or even twelve hours – of strong wind," he says, "even in the depth of the coldest winter, will set the big floes grinding and twisting among themselves, crushing up into pressure ridges in one place, breaking into leads in another place." So a party starting back over the outward trail is able to "knit together all faults and breaks in the trail that have occurred during that period by reason of the movement of the ice."

So he does admit to there being a movement of the ice. He could hardly do otherwise, having drifted some sixty-two miles almost due east in six and a half days as a direct result of the wind which was from "a little south of true west." There had, during that eastward drift, been "no detectable disturbance in the ice" and it had, he said, been "moving eastward as one mass." And yet he is proposing to go straight up the meridian of Cape Columbia to the Pole, presumably keeping his course by countering the drift to the east.

But when he awoke before dawn on 1st March, the wind was whistling about the igloo, and "this phenomenon," Peary tells us, "appearing on the very day of our start, after so many days of calm, seemed the perversity of hard luck."

The wind was from the east – a direction from which I had never known it to blow in all my years of experience in that region. This unusual circumstance, a really remarkable thing, was of course attributed by my Eskimos to the interference of their arch enemy, Tornarsuk – in plain English, the devil – with my plans.

Some parties, he says, would have considered the weather impossible for travelling, and would have gone back to their igloos, but not Peary's:

One by one the divisions drew out from the main army of sledges and dog teams, took up Bartlett's trail over the ice and disappeared to the northward in the wind haze. This departure of the procession was a noiseless one, for the freezing east wind carried all sounds away. It was also invisible after the first few moments – men and dogs being swallowed up almost immediately in the wind haze and drifting snow.

I finally brought up the rear with my own division . . . An hour after I left camp my division had crossed the glacial fringe, and the last man, sledge, and dog of the Northern Party – comprising altogether twenty-four men, nineteen sledges, and one hundred and twenty-three dogs – was at last on the ice of the Arctic Ocean, about latitude 83 degrees.

When they were far enough out onto the ice to be away from the shelter of land, they got the full force of the violent east wind. And the going was rough. Two of the Eskimo-style sledges were smashed completely – another badly damaged.

On their second day out they met their first serious obstacle. With the wind continuing to blow from the east "with unabated violence," they came to open water about a quarter of a mile wide, which had formed since Bartlett had passed the day before. Peary exclaims: "The wind had been getting in its work!" He has the evidence before him – the wind is moving the ice.

Before daylight on the 3rd they heard the "grinding of the ice," and with the first light thrashed across the raftering young ice, which was "moving, crushing, and piling up with the closing of the lead." But on the other side there was no sign of Bartlett's trail. "This meant," Peary says, "that the lateral movement (that is east and west) of the ice shores of the lead had carried the trail along with it." He sent out scouting parties, and they found Bartlett's tracks a mile and a half to the west. But if the wind had moved the northern floe, it might also have moved the southern one – the whole area moving westwards, some floes faster than others. This possibility Peary admits in his account of the 1906 journey, but never in 1909.

Two marches further on they came upon Bartlett, held up, as they were now themselves, by a lead that extended as far east and west as they could see from the highest pinnacle of ice. It was at that time about a quarter of a mile in width with a dense cloud of vapour hanging in a sullen canopy above it and occasionally sinking to obscure the opposite shore.

For the next six full days the lead continued to widen, and Peary to become more desperate. And yet in spite of his experiences in 1906 he had stubbornly and foolishly refused to take any form of boat, and even faced with the very same problem three years later, his pride would not permit him to admit to his companions that he now wished that he had one! All he would admit to was that "more mental wear and tear was crowded into those days than into all the rest of the fifteen months we were absent from civilization" – and this is about as close as he came to ever admitting that he was wrong.

If the lead did not close, then Peary's final attempt would have failed after only four marches out from the coast. If it closed or froze over and let them pass, it might open again and cut off their return to land. In Peary's view it was a test of nerve to wait there in the hope of going on. To many of the Eskimos, however, it was beginning to look like the proof of foolishness and they began to fret. Peary writes:

> I would see them talking together in twos and threes, just out of earshot. Finally two of the older men, who had been with me for years and whom I had trusted, came to me pretending to be sick. I have had sufficient experience to know a sick Eskimo when I see one, and the excuses of Pooadlonah and Panikpah did not convince me. I told them by all means to go back to the land just as quickly as they could, and to take with them a note to Marvin, urging him to hurry. I also sent by them a note to the mate of the ship, giving instructions in regard to these two men and their families.

The note to the mate, according to Dr. Goodsell, had instructed him "to give them a reasonable amount of provisions so they and their families could leave immediately on a long [600-mile] trip to Etah. In effect, he was dismissing them for their grumbling." Peary's diary entry for the 7th confirms this. It also suggests he might not have been as polite as the book version of the incident implies: "In evening Pooadlonah came to me whining he was sick and I packed him and Panikpah back for the land at once. Am done with these two."

This heavy-handed treatment of two of the most experienced men in the party – Pooadloona being Bartlett's best man, and Panikpah having been one of those who went with Peary to his Farthest North in 1906 –

far from putting a stop to the "whining," as Peary called it, had a demoralizing effect on the other hunters which came very close to getting out of control. Peary himself admits this in so many words: "Two of them were rendered unconscious by the fumes of the alcohol cooker in their igloo, frightening all the rest of the Eskimos half out of their wits, and I was seriously puzzled as to what I should do with them."

He does not say that the accident occurred while MacMillan was preparing tea; or that it took the Eskimos fifteen to twenty minutes to revive and that when eventually they did, MacMillan tried to convince them that there was nothing wrong with the stove, that they had merely been asleep. Nor does Peary mention that, had the results been fatal, the others would have quickly deserted and that would have been the end of his dream – that he needed those Eskimos far more than they needed him. That information comes from Dr. Goodsell. Peary does, however, admit on this occasion to the situation being saved by someone else's initiative.

> MacMillan was invaluable to me during this period. Seeing the restlessness of the Eskimos, and without waiting for any suggestion from me, he gave himself absolutely to the problem of keeping them occupied and interested in games and athletic "stunts" of one kind or another. This was one of those opportunities which circumstances give a man silently to prove the mettle of which he is made.

By the evening of the 10th the lead had almost closed, but Marvin had still not arrived with a load of vital supplies, a situation similar to the predicament that had faced Peary on the south side of the Big Lead on 2nd April, 1906. Should he cross it and take a chance on Marvin crossing it also? After a clear night with the temperature at $-40°F$ and with the new ice now thick enough to bear their weight, he committed himself to the bold decision and left a note for Marvin:

> 4th Camp,
> March 11, 1909

> Have waited here (6) days. Can wait no longer. We are short of fuel. Push on with all possible speed to overtake us. Shall leave note at each camp. When near us rush light sledge and note of information ahead to overhaul us.
>
> Expect send back Dr. and Eskimos 3 to 5 marches from here. He should meet you and give you information.
>
> We go straight across this lead East-South-East.
>
> There has been no lateral motion of the ice during 7 days. Only

open and shut. *Do not camp here.* CROSS THE LEAD. Feed full rations and speed your dogs.

It is *vital* you overtake us and give us fuel.

Leaving at 9 a.m., Thursday, Mar. 11.

PEARY

They made four marches from the Big Lead before, in the latter part of the afternoon of the 14th, "Marvin came swinging in at the head of the rear division, men and dogs steaming like a squadron of battle-ships, and bringing in an ample supply of fuel." By this time, Henson and his Eskimos had taken over the lead as the trail-breakers and the morale of the whole body of men had improved. Now at last had come the time for some good hard sledging, and on the 15th, undaunted by temperatures in the minus fifties, by the "loud reports and rumblings among the floes," and by a lead which cut right across their path and on the north side of which they could see the ice moving, they pressed on.

That night was one of the noisiest that I have ever spent in an igloo, and none of us slept very soundly. Hour after hour the rumbling and complaining of the ice continued, and it would not have surprised us much if at any moment the ice had split directly across our camp, or even through the middle of one of our igloos.

Then on the 16th, after passing two of Henson's igloos in the space of six hours of following a cut trail, we find Peary commenting ungenerously, as he had done in 1906:

I knew, from experience, that yesterday's movement of the ice and the formation of leads about us would take all the spirit out of Henson's party until the main party should overtake them again. Sure enough, the next march was even shorter. At the end of a little over four hours we found Henson and his division in camp, making one sledge out of the remains of two. The damage to the sledges was the reason given for the delay.

The damage was real and very obvious. But Peary had no conception of the strain of breaking a trail across moving and breaking pack ice way out ahead of the main party, and was not at any time in the rest of his career to experience it. On the 18th he put Marvin in the lead to "try to make two long marches to bring up the average," as he says in the book, but in his diary he says it was "to make up for Henson's three short marches." And yet, at the end of the following day's march, he was expressing the hope that "with good weather, and the ice no worse than that which we had already encountered, Borup might get beyond 85 degrees, Marvin beyond 86 degrees, and Bartlett beyond 87 degrees."

Goodsell and MacMillan had already taken the home trail, so this meant that already, at latitude 85°23', less than one third of the way to the Pole from Cape Columbia, Peary had decided to take Henson (who was unable to take sun sights) on the final stage of his journey in spite of his evident disappointment with Henson's recent performance in breaking trail.

He now sent Bartlett and his two Eskimos out to break trail northward early on the 20th; Borup with three Eskimos back down the homeward trail; Henson with two Eskimos he sent out in Bartlett's tracks to improve the trail, and set Marvin to work with his men making a sounding, while he himself, "in order to give Bartlett one march the start of us," and to conserve his energy, spent the day resting. By this arrangement, the "main party" (by which he means himself and his Eskimos) would arrive at the igloos of the pioneers, get them on the move again, and then sleep off their much lesser fatigue in the igloos that had been vacated. It was an arrangement, Peary tells us, that "kept the parties closer together, relieved the pioneers of all apprehension, and reduced by 50% the chance of separation of the parties by the opening of a lead." This way he was also able, as his diary suggests, to keep pushing from behind anyone he felt was slacking:

Sunday, March 21 ... A fine day ... I left camp 4 a.m. Arrived Captain's camp 11 a.m. Found Henson and party there and one of Captain's men with broken sledge. Got them all off ...

Monday, March 22 ... Another fine day. Got started soon after midnight. Reached Captain's camp 10.30. Henson still in his igloo as usual. One of Captain's men still there. Gave him a good sledge and took his broken one. Fixed up a snow shelter and had Marvin take a latitude sight. Result 85°48'.

This observation showed an average of eleven and a half miles "*made good*" (Peary's emphasis) for each actual march. And then he comments: "Included in these marches had been four short ones resulting from causes the recurrence of which I believe I could prevent in future." His "urging" of his men, combined with generally improving conditions, did bring results. By the 25th – Marvin's Farthest North – they had reached latitude 86°38', and two days after Marvin had turned back, when Peary staggered into Bartlett's camp at the end of their "hardest march for some days," they were already across the 87th parallel.

But even now, Peary tells us, "on reaching my highest record with every prospect good, I dared not build too much on the chances of the white and treacherous ice which stretched one hundred and eighty miles northward between me and the end." And sure enough, ahead of them the following day there was "a thick, smoky, ominous haze drifting over the ice" and they only made twelve miles before coming upon Bartlett's camp beside an open lead. It was one of those camps which every traveller on the polar pack ice sooner or later is bound to experience and never thereafter forgets. First there is the creaking and groaning of the ice; then a strange feeling in the pit of the stomach – an eerie feeling that *this* one is different to all of the rest – then the yapping of dogs and the yelling of men, and all of the chaos and confusion that follows as the floe cracks up like an egg shell:

> ... on the opposite side of the lead stood one of Bartlett's men yelling and gesticulating with all the abandon of an excited and thoroughly frightened Eskimo.
>
> Awakening my men, I kicked our snow door into fragments and was outside in a moment. The break in the ice had occurred within a foot of the fastening of one of my dog teams, the team escaping by just those few inches from being dragged into the water. Another team had just escaped being buried under a pressure ridge ...
>
> Bartlett's igloo was moving east on the ice raft which had broken off, and beyond it, as far as the belching fog from the lead would let us see, there was nothing but black water ...
>
> Our two igloos, Henson's and mine, were on a small piece of old floe ... [and] ... it was clear that it would take very little pressure to detach us and set us afloat also like Bartlett's division.
>
> I routed Henson and his men out of their igloo, gave orders to everybody to pack and hitch up immediately.

And so it goes on. The Eskimos who have been travelling and hunting on moving ice all their lives are now suddenly "excited and thoroughly frightened," and Peary is giving "orders to everybody" to do what is perfectly obvious.

They had the whole of the following day to reflect upon their night's adventure, while from that lead there rose a cloud of black sea smoke so dense that they were unable to see the northern shore, and were even beginning to wonder if such a shore existed. By the morning of 30th March, however, the lead had closed to let them pass, and all that day they had travelled together, constantly crossing areas of ice "which had only recently been open water." One six- or seven-mile stretch was so thin that the ice buckled under them and although they got in "a good twenty miles," their fears were now increasing:

The entire region through which we had come during the last four marches was full of unpleasant possibilities for the future. Only too well we knew that violent winds for even a few hours would set the ice all abroad in every direction. Crossing such a zone on a journey north is only half the problem, for there is always the return to be figured on.

They were also, on Bartlett's final march north of the 31st, now heading directly into a wind, and here for the first time (on this trip) Peary admits that the wind *is* having an effect on the ice:

This northerly wind, though hard to struggle against, was better than an easterly or westerly one, either of which would have set us adrift in open water, while, as it was, the wind was closing up every lead behind us and thus making things easier for Bartlett's supporting party on its return. True, the wind pressure was forcing to the south the ice over which we traveled, and thus losing us miles of distance; but the advantage of frozen leads was more than compensation for this loss.

Peary claims that, had the weather been clear on the 31st, "we should undoubtedly have covered twenty-five miles . . . but it is difficult to break a trail in thick weather as rapidly as in clear, and this day netted us only twenty miles." He tells us also:

Our latitude was the direct result of the northerly wind of the last two days, which had crowded the ice southward as we traveled over it northward. We had traveled fully twelve miles more than his [Bartlett's] observation showed in the last five marches, but had lost them by the crushing up of the young ice in our rear and the closing of the leads.

He is here noticing the effect of the wind on the ice because he is able to measure it against the latitude observations taken by Marvin and Bartlett. But no observations for longitude have been taken on the entire journey – they have had no checks on their lateral drift, and with the exception of that northerly wind of the last two marches, all the strongest winds during the journey have been from the east.

On the morning of 1st April Bartlett set out to walk five or six miles to the north in the hope of reaching latitude 88°; but on returning to the camp and taking his meridian observation to determine their latitude, his results gave 87°47', and he was a disappointed man. He had broken trail on nineteen days of the northward march, as against Henson's four and Marvin's two. He had earned the right to go on to the Pole. But this was not to be. Peary wanted Henson:

In this selection I acted exactly as I have done on all my expeditions for the last fifteen years. He has in those years always been with me at my point farthest north. Moreover, Henson was the best man I had with me for this kind of work, with the exception of the Eskimos, who, with their racial inheritance of ice technique and their ability to handle sledges and dogs, were more necessary to me, as members of my own individual party, than any white man could have been. Of course they could not lead, but they could follow and drive dogs better than any white man.

Henson, with his years of arctic experience, was almost as skillful at this work as an Eskimo. He could handle dogs and sledges. He was part of the traveling machine . . .

The second reason was that Henson . . . would not have been so competent as the white members of the expedition in getting himself and his party back to land. If Henson had been sent back with one of the supporting parties from a distance far out on the ice, and if he had encountered conditions similar to those which we had to face on the return journey in 1906, he and his party would never have reached the land. While faithful to me, and when *with me* more effective in covering distance with a sledge than any of the others, he had not, as a racial inheritance, the daring and initiative of Bartlett, or Marvin, MacMillan, or Borup. I owed it to him not to subject him to dangers and responsibilities which he was temperamentally unfit to face.

Peary of course owed Henson far more than this claimed "concern" for his safety. He *needed* Henson. In one of those rare moments in his life when he had spoken to a companion as a man and not as master, he had admitted to MacMillan: "I can't get along without him."

"I felt a keen regret," Peary says, "as I saw the captain's broad shoulders grow smaller in the distance and finally disappear behind the ice hummocks of the white and glittering expanse toward the south. But it was no time for reverie, and I turned abruptly away and gave my attention to the work which was before me."

Only 133 miles now lay between him and his dream of fame, and with his last reliable witness gone, he paced the ice impatiently and divided off the distance in days:

Every nerve must be strained to make five marches of at least twenty-five miles each, crowding these marches in such a way as to bring us to the end of the fifth march by noon, to permit an immediate latitude observation. Weather and leads permitting, I believed I could do this. From the improving character of the ice, and in view of the recent northerly winds, I hoped that I should have no serious trouble with the going.

If for any reason I fell short of these proposed distances, I had two methods in reserve for making up the deficit. One was to double the last march ... the other was, at the conclusion of my fifth march, to push on with one light sledge, a double team of dogs, and one or two of the party, leaving the rest in camp. Even should the going be worse than was then anticipated, eight marches like the three from 85°48′ to 86°38′, or six similar to our last one, would do the trick.

Underlying all these calculations was the ever present knowledge that a twenty-fours' gale would open leads of water which might be impassable, and that all these plans would be negatived.

... This was the time for which I had reserved all my energies, the time for which I had worked for twenty-two years, for which I had lived the simple life and trained myself as for a race. In spite of my years, I felt fit for the demands of the coming days and was eager to be on the trail. As for my party, my equipment, and my supplies, they were perfect beyond my most sanguine dreams of earlier years. My party might be regarded as an ideal which had now come to realization – as loyal and responsive to my will as the fingers of my right hand.

A little after midnight, on the morning of 2nd April, and after eight hours (according to his diary) of sound, warm, and refreshing sleep, and a hearty breakfast, Peary set out ahead of the others on foot.

Up to this time I had intentionally kept in the rear, to straighten out any little hitch or to encourage a man with a broken sledge, and to see that everything was in good marching order. Now I took up my proper place in the lead. Though I held myself in check, I felt the keenest exhilaration, and even exultation, as I climbed over the pressure ridge and breathed the keen air sweeping over the mighty ice, pure and straight from the Pole itself.

CHAPTER 16

The North Pole – Or Not

On 2nd April, 1906, when the Big Lead had effectively severed all contact with his supporting parties, Peary's speeds had suddenly increased. A coincidence, perhaps, but the same good fortune appears to have recurred on exactly the same date three years later:

> It was a fine marching morning, clear and sunlit, with a temperature of minus 25 degrees, and the wind of the past few days had subsided to a gentle breeze. The going was the best we had had since leaving the land, with patches of sapphire blue ice (the pools of the preceding summer).

Some of the pressure ridges surrounding these pools were all of fifty feet high, he tells us. But they were "not especially hard to negotiate," Henson usually finding a gap or a ramp of hard packed snow up which the dogs could haul the sledges to the top. The feeling that they were now "well started" on the final stage of their quest for the Pole affected him like wine.

He is encouraged by the results of their first march from the camp where Bartlett turned for home, for they had travelled for ten hours without stopping and covered, he believed, some thirty miles, although "to be conservative," he called it twenty-five. He is optimistic to the extent of indulging in some wishful thinking:

> ... we were well over the 88th parallel, in a region where no human being had ever been before. And whatever distance we made, we were likely to retain it now that the wind had ceased to blow from the north. It was even possible that with the release of the wind pressure the ice might rebound more or less and return us some of the hard-earned miles which it had stolen from us during the previous three days.

But he feared the moon and its power to stir the tides and open new leads in the ice fields.

> The moon had been our friend during the long winter, giving us light to hunt by for a week or two each month. Now it seemed no longer a friend, but a dangerous presence to be regarded with fear. Its power, which had before been beneficent, was now malevolent and incalculably potent for evil.

They put in another ten-hour day on 3rd April, the weather "still clear and calm." But on this day (their second march north of Bartlett's farthest) they had only made twenty miles because of an "early delay with the pickaxes and another brief delay at a narrow lead." They were now half-way to the 89th parallel, and Peary is now working so hard he tells us he was "obliged to take up another hole in my belt."

> All day long we had heard the ice grinding and groaning on all sides of us, but no motion was visible to our eyes. Either the ice was slacking back into equilibrium, sagging northward after its release from the wind pressure, or else it was feeling the influence of the spring tides of the full moon. On, on we pushed, and I am not ashamed to confess that my pulse beat high, for the breath of success seemed already in my nostrils.

On the third march he tells us they hit the trail a little before midnight between 3rd and 4th April. The temperature at the beginning of the march was −40°F; but aside from that, the weather and going were even better than the day before.

> The surface of the ice, except as interrupted by infrequent pressure ridges, was as level as the glacial fringe from Hecla to Cape Columbia, and harder. I rejoiced at the thought that if the weather held good I should be able to get in my five marches before noon on the 6th.
>
> Again we traveled for ten hours straight ahead, the dogs often on the trot and occasionally on the run, and in those ten hours we reeled off at least twenty-five miles.

Near the end of that third march, they crossed a lead that was about a hundred yards wide on a skin of ice that sagged beneath them as they glided across it, two of the men "on all fours." Peary had watched them with his heart in his mouth; but then admits that this is all part of the game, that "a man who should wait for the ice to be really safe would stand small chance of getting far in these latitudes."

They were all tired that night; but by dead-reckoning they were within sight of the 89th parallel, and Peary was satisfied with the progress: "Give me three days more of this weather," he had written in his diary. How long they slept he does not say either in the book or the diary, offering only that "early in the evening of the same day, the 4th, we struck on again."

The temperature at the start of that fourth march was −35°F, and with the slight rise the sledges were hauling a little more easily and for much of the time the dogs were on the trot. Then came a stroke of good fortune:

Toward the end of the march we came upon a lead running north and south, and as the young ice was thick enough to support the teams, we traveled on it for two hours, the dogs galloping along and reeling off the miles in a way that delighted my heart. The light air which had blown from the south during the first few hours of the march veered to the east and grew keener as the hours wore on.

I had not dared to hope for such progress as we were making. Still the biting cold would have been impossible to face by anyone not fortified by an inflexible purpose.

At the end of each day's march, while the igloos were being built, he had time for reflection on their utter remoteness in that "trackless, colorless, inhospitable desert of ice," and one cannot help wondering if Peary was also sensing that one day more, or even perhaps a single hour of heading further from the land, might be that one too many.

I knew of course that there was always a *possibility* that we might still end our lives up there, and that our conquest of the unknown spaces and silences of the polar void might remain forever unknown to the world which we had left behind. But it was hard to realize this. That hope which is said to spring eternal in the human breast always buoyed me up with the belief that, as a matter of course, we should be able to return along the white road by which we had come.

But this is clearly retrospection. The passage may even have been written for him by A. E. Thomas, the dramatist and novelist who later admitted to having ghostwritten some eighty per cent of the book that was published under Peary's name. It was what the readers expected to read. It was also as much as Peary could be persuaded to write, or in those sections ghosted for him, as much as he would endorse. His silences speak louder.

Sometimes I would climb to the top of a pinnacle of ice to the north of our camp and strain my eyes into the whiteness which lay beyond, trying to imagine myself already at the Pole. We had come so far, and the capricious ice had placed so few obstructions in our path that now I dared to loose my fancy, to entertain the image which my will had heretofore forbidden to my imagination – the image of ourselves at the goal.

But the "notes" in his diary have already been indicating his expectations of success since 26th March, and over this crucial stage of his outward march the upper pages of his diary are packed with memos which offer a rare glimpse into that private world where Peary spun his dreams of duty and, through his duty, fame.

Gavel of Order of the N.P.

Meteorite Star
and diamond.
Pendant
N.P. flag gold
and enamel proper
colours.

Have Borup take a 5″ x 7″ 3½ to 4 ft. focus portrait of me in deer or sheep coat (face unshaven) with bear roll, & keep on till satisfactory one obtained. Have Foster color a special print of this to bring out the gray eyes, the red sun burned skin, the bleached eyebrows and beard, frosted eyebrows, eyelashes, beard.

Have "Harpers" take entire matter, book, magazine articles, pictures & stories (100) Kane got 75 from his book, Nansen 50 for his.

Name the camps from Columbia to Pole after Arctic explorers (home & foreign, being sure to remember each nation) & members of the Club and others. Put camps of Markham, Lockwood, Nansen, Fram, Abruzzi, etc at their respective latitudes. Alternate members of Club with the explorers. Put Camp Jesup at top . . .

Purchase Haskell I. if entire island can be secured?

Mark 1. monument for Mausoleum? Faced with marble or granite, statue with flag on top, lighted room at base for 2 sarcophagi? Bronze figures Eskimo, Dog, Bear, M. O., Walrus, etc, etc or bronze tablets of flag on Pole & suitable inscription. Bust.

Photos & hundred words or so of text in re N. Pole to all publishers of geography. Prepare & furnish plate for entire page in geographics.

Senior Rear Admiral on retired list (with full pay ?) R- Ad- pennant with diagonal white bar.

Work done while under special orders counter-signed by the President therefore in line of duty. Has cost Govt. nothing; while it gains all the prestige. At head of list of such names as Franklin (?) McClintock, Ross, Parry, Kane, Hall, DeLong, etc, etc.

England promoted & knighted dozens & paid thousands in rewards. Note promotion Greely, Schley, Melville. Pres. Am. Geo. Soc. & 8th Int. Geog. Cong. Hon. Mem. & Gold Medalist of principal home & foreign Geog. Socs. Navy record a good one. Nicaragua Canal. Slated for bureau [top job] by everyone but Pres. R——

There are others which follow after a gap of a few blank pages, but all of the above are in a straight run and come before the key entry of his log which was written on a loose-leaf page on which there is no date. Clearly the writer of these notes is already travelling in a haze of self-congratulation.

At their camp on 5th April, he gave his party a little more sleep, as they were all "pretty well played out and in need of rest." And there, he tells us in his book, he took a sun sight which gave a latitude of 89°25′, thirty-five miles from the Pole. In his diary, however, he does not mention this observation on the day he claims to have taken it, which is surprising. He mentions it only as a margin note on the 6th.

The thick weather gives me less concern than it might, had I not been forehanded yesterday and fearing a cloud bank in the south took a latitude sight (89°25′). This is 2 miles ahead of my dead reckoning and indicates that I have been conservative in my estimates as I intended, or that the ice has slacked back, or both.

There is no record of this observation among the main body of the Private Papers of Admiral Robert E. Peary at the National Archives, nor is it to be found among the small body of special documents presented to the National Archives for safe-keeping on 10th April, 1970, by Commander Edward Peary Stafford, U.S.N., although all of the other original observations made on that 1909 journey were among that accretion which included Peary's original diary. I did, however, find a mysterious note in Peary's hand when going through those special papers for the first time on 26th April, 1985.

The records show that this note had been in an envelope on the front of which (in Jo's handwriting) was written: "Original Observations made by R. E. Peary, U.S.N. at 90 degrees N. Lat. April 5 & 6, 1909," and on the back, "Opened & observations copied August 1, 1935. Marie Peary Stafford." This envelope and its single folded sheet of notepaper had been kept in a larger registered mail envelope, together with twenty-five sheets of observations, notes, affidavits, and sketches, and an envelope containing a certificate signed by Peary stating "the movements of the Expedition from April 1st 1909, to Apr. 7th 1909." On this envelope (with a letterhead return address "First Portland National Bank") Jo had also written: "Original North Pole Observations."

Most of the contents of the larger envelope at one time or another had been published, facsimiles of some of the original observations having appeared in Peary's book. But what was to be made of that single sheet of observations? An indication of Peary's sensitivity regarding those figures is the fact that they were never published and were kept in a separate envelope. According to the notes of Peary's trusted friend and advisor, Isaiah Bowman, President of the American Geographical Society, that single sheet of observations had been given to Jo by Peary "with the remark that she should treasure it as her most precious possession and never let it out of her hands unless it was to silence 'that G-d-m s-o-b Cook.'" He had advised Jo in 1935 that she should send him a copy of the document, which accounts for the note on the back of that envelope stating that it had been opened and the observations copied on 1st August, 1935, by Marie Peary Stafford.

But although that document records three altitudes of sun together with the times of those altitudes, there is no indication of which limb of the sun Peary shot, nor is there a date of the observations. The note in Jo's hand on the envelope does not help since she states that the observations were made on 5th and 6th April when clearly all three altitudes were shot in one session over a period of only three minutes. Peary had, in any case, added further confusion by writing on the upper left of that sheet the word "Betelgeux" – the name of one of the brightest stars, yet one which it seems unlikely he would have been able to pick up with a sextant at that time of the year.

So why had Peary kept this document separate from the other observations and told Jo it was "her most precious possession?" The mystery remains unresolved. There is an indication that Peary was assuming a sun's declination of $6°35.20'N$, which would suggest he took those observations on 7th April, and from those three altitudes it appears that the sun was ascending, which it should not noticeably have been had those observations been made at the Pole. But although this seemed suspicious, there was, in my judgement, simply not enough information on that document from which to calculate a latitude with any certainty and it was therefore inadmissible as evidence.

Since there was no proof from the note of the sun's declination that those altitudes had been taken on the 7th, I had even considered the possibility that they might have been shot on the 5th or 6th, as stated on the envelope. But Henson in his article in the *Boston American* of 17th July, 1910, said that Peary made "no observation in the five days" after Bartlett turned back. Even Peary himself, under oath the following year during his questioning by the Congressional Naval Affairs Subcommittee, had denied taking any observations on the 5th. This raised another question. If he had not taken any, why then had he claimed in his book that he had? Could it be that he had inserted this margin note in his diary later, realising that his critics might be suspicious of a claim to have travelled by dead-reckoning alone the entire distance from Bartlett's farthest to his own life's objective?

And what of that final march? They set out before midnight on the 5th, the weather overcast, grey and shadowless, "a colorless pall gradually deepening to almost black at the horizon, and the ice ... ghastly and chalky white." But the going was even better than before with hardly any snow on the hard granular surface of the old floes, and the "sapphire blue lakes" larger than ever. The temperature had risen to −15° and with less friction from the sledges, the dogs "caught the high spirits of the party ... tossed their heads and barked and yelped as they traveled." Now at last they were within striking distance of the goal, and despite the melancholy aspect of the surrounding world, Peary tells us that:

> ... by some strange shift of feeling the fear of the leads had fallen from me completely. I now felt that success was certain, and, notwith-standing the physical exhaustion of the forced marches of the last five days, I went tirelessly on and on, the Eskimos following almost automatically, though I knew that they must feel the weariness which my excited brain made me incapable of feeling.

They covered what Peary estimated to be a total of thirty miles in twelve hours, and Henson's weary bones confirmed that they had come the right distance from Bartlett's camp. He does not, however, recall the Eskimos following Peary. On the contrary:

> I, who had walked, knew that we had made exceptional distance in those five days. So did the Eskimos, for they also had walked. Lieutenant [sic] Peary was the only surprised man. He, because of his crippled feet, had ridden on the sledge the greater part of the journey up, as he did upon the return. Riding, one cannot so well judge of distance traversed.

What Henson says is perfectly true; but in Peary's book there is no indication of any doubt on his part: "The last northward march ended at 10 o'clock of the forenoon of April 6th. I had now made the five marches

From Bartlett's Farthest North Camp to Camp Jesup and back

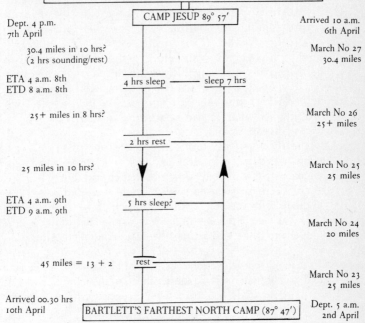

At Camp Jesup Peary slept approximately four hours after taking the 6th April "noon" observation (although the galley proof states only "two or three.") Peary claims that he then travelled a total of thirty-six miles with a light sledge and a "double team," and had a maximum of two hours sleep after making these trips, completing his observations/computations, and conducting the "flag ceremony" before setting off on the homeward journey.

CAMP JESUP 89° 57'

Dept. 4 p.m.
7th April

Arrived 10 a.m.
6th April

30.4 miles in 10 hrs?
(2 hrs sounding/rest)

March No 27
30.4 miles

ETA 4 a.m. 8th
ETD 8 a.m. 8th

4 hrs sleep ——— sleep 7 hrs

25 + miles in 8 hrs?

March No 26
25+ miles

2 hrs rest

25 miles in 10 hrs?

March No 25
25 miles

ETA 4 a.m. 9th
ETD 9 a.m. 9th

5 hrs sleep?

March No 24
20 miles

45 miles = 13 + 2

rest

March No 23
25 miles

Arrived 00.30 hrs
10th April

BARTLETT'S FARTHEST NORTH CAMP (87° 47')

Dept. 5 a.m.
2nd April

NOTE: Total distance covered (straight line nautical miles) from the time Peary left Bartlett's Farthest North Camp at 5 a.m. 2nd April, to his return there 30 minutes past midnight on 9th April was 130 × 2 = 260 + 36 miles he did in the vicinity of Camp Jesup = Total 296 nautical miles. This gives an average of 37.94 nautical mpd for 7.8 days.

ALSO: From 5th April to Camp Jesup and back to Bartlett's Camp Peary covered 196.0 nautical miles in 4 days at an average of 49.0 mpd.

No percentage for detours added to any of these figures – add 25% minimum

NOTE: Some historians have assumed from Henson's statement in his *Boston American* article of 17th July, 1910 that Camp Jesup was reached on the evening of 6th April. But this is not what Henson said. Polar explorers travelling on a night routine invariably refer to the end of the day's march as the evening, and we therefore take it that the arrival time at Camp Jesup was between 10 a.m. and 10.30 a.m. on the 6th.

planned from the point at which Bartlett turned back, and my reckoning showed that we were in the immediate neighborhood of the goal of all our striving."

According to two of Henson's accounts, he arrived forty-five minutes ahead of Peary and probably had his igloo built by the time that Peary came in. Peary himself tells us that during the last five marches, he would break trail on foot only at the start of each march. In Henson's article in *World's Work* he says that Peary "was usually the first to leave camp, for he had no sledge to drive; I was the last, in order to be sure that nothing was left behind. The Commander's trail was easy to follow, and I usually caught up with him in an hour or two, and then generally went ahead."

In an interview in 1953 (two years before his death) Henson is reported to have said much the same thing: "Peary, he stayed back while I broke trail. I never would see him until the end of the march." And yet in this same article he said: "I know the last 133 miles he didn't walk," which appears to contradict what he had said in the *World's Work* article. So what are we to believe?

Probably the *World's Work* story, since it was published only a year after the events that Henson is recalling, and while Peary was overseas collecting medals, so it is the only article at that critical time which Peary did not censor. The best balanced verdict would therefore be that Peary was only in the lead for the first few miles of each of the last five marches north and rode the sledge the rest of the way, while Henson went on, out in front, finding the route and setting the pace – and a cracking pace he set.

From this it would therefore seem likely that Henson did, as he claims, reach the end of that final outward march ahead of the Commander. What then, if anything, was said by Peary when eventually he arrived at that northernmost camp, and what was the true sequence of events during the time they spent in that region? Peary's diary offers no comment, not even the time that the last march ended, and his ghostwriter evidently had a hard time in trying to persuade the busy explorer to release any information. On 3rd May, 1910, he had written to Peary:

I am not at all satisifed with the extent of the material you gave me concerning what you did at the Pole ... That thirty hours at the Pole is what we have been working up to ... I wish you would send me an account of every single thing you did there. What the others did. What you said ... And there is one more thing I wish respectfully to urge on you and that is the importance of scrutinizing all the proof with the utmost care, remembering that every enemy you have in the world [is] sure to go over your book with a fine-tooth comb for the purpose of picking flaws in it. And only you yourself, can prevent . . . technical errors or misstatements . . .

Many years later in a letter to Andrew Freeman, author of *The Case for Doctor Cook*, Thomas was to comment that *The North Pole*, on which he worked for eleven weeks, "was a dull book, because Peary was a dull man and it was impossible to get much lively human material out of him." But Peary did eventually offer this concerning his arrival at his northernmost camp, and his first crucial observation:

After the usual arrangements for going into camp, at approximate local noon, on the Columbia meridian, I made the first observation at our polar camp. It indicated our position as 89°57′.

We were now at the end of the last long march of the upward journey. Yet with the Pole actually in sight I was too weary to take the last few steps. The accumulated weariness of all those days and nights of forced marches and insufficient sleep, constant peril and anxiety, seemed to roll across me all at once. I was actually too exhausted to realize at the moment that my life's purpose had been achieved. As soon as our igloos had been completed and we had eaten our dinner and double-rationed the dogs, I turned in for a few hours of absolutely necessary sleep, Henson and the Eskimos having unloaded the sledges and got them in readiness for such repairs as were necessary.

Henson, at the end of that fifth march (and before Peary had come in) was already, by his own dead-reckoning, pretty confident:

In fact, I believe that the full distance had already been covered. One can tell to within a mile or so how far one walks on the northern ice, and I reckoned that we were even now at the very Pole.

Henson, in his interview at the age of eighty-eight, admitted that Peary had told him he wanted him to stop before the end of that last northward march, so that he could go on ahead with one of the Eskimos.

"Don't you want me to be with you?" Henson had asked.

"I meant *we'll* take one of the boys," Peary had replied. But Peary had "let it slip out what he was thinking," and Henson had been hurt: "Shoot, I had been with him up there nearly twenty years. Freezing my hands. I saved his life when a musk-ox tried to gore him. I helped amputate his toes. Of course I wanted to be there side by side with him."

And so Henson had gone on without stopping, and was so far ahead of Peary by the end of his march that he had his igloo built by the time Peary came in. At this point in the story, according to the 1953 interviewer Henson became agitated, and "unable to stop until he had told it all." Here is Henson:

"I said, 'I think I've overrun my mark two miles. I think I'm the first man to sit on top of the world.' "

" 'What?' he said. Then, 'We'll see tomorrow.' "

The interviewer asked if Peary was angry because Henson had not stopped and waited for him.

"Oh, he got hopping mad. No, he didn't say anything, but I could tell. I didn't know what he would do. I took all the cartridges out of my rifle before I went to sleep. Took them out and buried them in the snow."

Here of course we must allow for the possibility of an old man being fed leading questions by a journalist with his sights on an exposé. According to the account in Henson's book, *A Negro Explorer at the North Pole* (which carries a short and not particularly effusive foreword by Peary and was clearly vetted by him), Henson first realised the importance of Camp Jesup when Peary "fastened the flag to a staff and planted it firmly on the top of his igloo."

He goes on to say, however, that "As prospects for getting a sight of the sun were not good, we turned in and slept, leaving the flag proudly floating above us." Henson's article in *World's Work*, published two years earlier than the book, says much the same thing. From this we may assume that Peary's first observation on the 6th was not witnessed by Henson. Indeed, he was probably not even aware that Peary had made one.

But it was Henson's turn now to feel hurt and angry, for one of his Eskimos (Oodaaq) came and told him that Peary was planning on leaving him in camp and going on the last few miles with two Eskimos, a light sledge, and a double team of dogs. So just how much further away was the Pole?

Peary wrote two full pages of diary entry under the date 6th April, together with some additional comments on the observation he claims to have made the day before which ran on into the margins, and both pages, judging by the contents, were written on arrival at Camp Jesup, before he had taken his first observation on the 6th. At the bottom of the second page he writes: "Can I wait to cover those other five." By dead reckoning, he was therefore assuming he was five miles short of his goal.

Shortly after Henson had turned in, there was a break in the cloud, and Peary was able to snatch a sun sight, by his own admission (during the later Peary Hearings) the first since leaving Bartlett's farthest camp. It was one shot only of the lower limb. The time was 12.50 p.m. If the shot was as he actually read it, then they were still three miles short of the Pole, but he could not know in which direction the Pole lay because he did not know his longitude. He needed more observations to confirm his position, and if his latitude was actually as he stated, then he needed ideally to get a bit closer to his objective.

But why leave Henson behind at Camp Jesup? Peary offers no explanation in his published accounts or in the Peary Hearings, and, oddly enough, was never asked to explain this action. Henson tells us he was left behind "repairing a sledge and in charge of the camp." But the

Peary's diary entry for 6th April, 1909

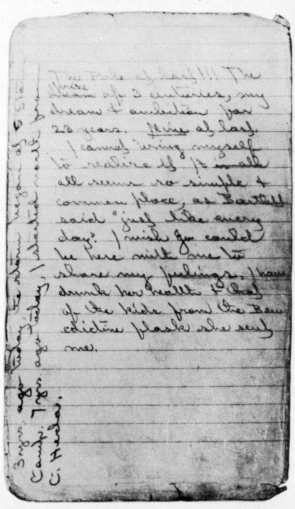

Eskimos could have done that work had Peary really wanted to share the Pole with the man who had helped him attain it.

We must now consider the possibility that Peary's observation at 12.50 p.m. on 6th April was his first indication that he was still a long way short of the Pole, so far from the Pole that, at least for a while, nothing seemed to make sense.

I would suggest that he argued for hours with himself, as I did when faced with a similar problem a mere seven miles from the same goal sixty years later, and that eventually Peary's exhausted mind insisted that his sun sight was wrong – and that he truly *was* at the Pole.

How long he slept the sleep of exhaustion he does not say. He does tell us, however, that on awaking, the first thing he did was to write in his diary – and then misquotes what he wrote. The original diary version reads:

> The Pole at last!!! The prize of 3 centuries, my dream and ambition for 23 years. *Mine* at last. I cannot bring myself to realize it. It all seems so simple and common place, as Bartlett said "just like every day." I wish Jo could be here with me to share my feelings. I have drunk her health and that of the kids from the Benedictine flask she sent me.

But this is a loose-leaf page inserted at page sixty-six in the diary. There are four blank pages between his entry for 6th April and his next entry of the 9th. So when was this written? Perhaps he wrote it at the time he says it was written, and was writing what he needed to write – not a statement of his certainty that he had reached the Pole.

At 6 p.m. Columbia meridian time, with the sky still overcast, but with indication that it would "clear before long," Peary set out with his own two Eskimos (Egingwah and Seegloo), a light sledge and a double team of dogs, and claims that they "pushed on an estimated distance of ten miles." Peary then says he made a series of observations at Columbia meridian midnight and returned to Camp Jesup in time to take another set of observations at 6 a.m. on 7th April. He then set off again, at right angles to his previous course, and travelled another eight miles, this time with Egingwah and Ootah (one of Henson's Eskimos), before returning to make his final observations at Camp Jesup at noon.

Henson was not involved in any of this activity, having been left at Camp Jesup throughout; but he had been aware of the coming and goings, and his recollections of the events are very different from Peary's. In his 1953 interview he had said that Peary "was gone about one and a half hours, long enough to take observations." In the *Boston American* article, he says that Peary and two Eskimos set out on the morning of the 7th (which would have been Peary's second trip – this one of eight miles each way), and again, according to his recollections, Peary was away only a short time:

> In about an hour the Commander returned. His face was long and serious. He would not speak to me. I quietly learned from the boys accompanying him that he had made observations a few miles further on.
> "Well, Mr. Peary," I spoke up cheerfully enough, "we are now at the North Pole, are we not?"
> "I do not suppose that we can swear that we are exactly at the Pole," was his evasive answer.
> "Well, I have kept track of the distance and we have made exceptional time," I replied, "and I have the feeling that we have now just about covered the 132 miles since Captain Bartlett turned back. If we have traveled in the right direction we are now at the Pole. If we have not traveled in the right direction then it is your fault."

To this Peary had made no reply. Nor did he reply to the offer of congratulations which Henson mentions in his book, although Henson seems confused over when this event occurred, since he dates the event 7th April, and yet goes on to describe being awakened later by the return of Peary and "his" boys from their overnight journey of twenty miles. The gesture and the response, whether it occurred on the 6th or the 7th, is nevertheless revealing:

> ... I was sure that he was satisfied, and I was confident that the journey had ended. Feeling that the time had come, I ungloved my right hand and went forward to congratulate him on the success of our eighteen years of effort, but a gust of wind blew something into his eye, or else the burning pain caused by his prolonged look at the reflection of the limb of the sun forced him to turn aside; and with both hands covering his eyes, he gave us orders not to let him sleep for more than four hours.

So what is the meaning of all of this? Henson's explanation is simply that Peary had worked himself into a silent rage on account of Henson's having reached the Pole ahead of him. In his 1910 article he wrote:

It was my boy Ootah who disclosed to me that Peary was to leave me behind in the final few miles to the Pole, and with Egingwah he witnessed the disappointment of Commander Peary when, a few miles from the camp, his observations told him that he had overstepped and gone past the Pole, which we had reached the night before.

The trip on which these two Eskimos had been together was the shorter of the two – the sixteen-mile round trip which Peary claims to have made in the forenoon of the 7th – and no observations were made by Peary on that trip, at least, none was claimed to have been made. But Egingwah had been with Peary on the first trip also, the one during which Peary had done the crucial set of observations at "midnight" which either confirmed that Camp Jesup was only a few miles from the Pole, or was some considerable distance from it – at least fifty miles, and probably more than sixty.

Supposing that Henson's interpretation was essentially true, there is no reason why Peary should have shown "disappointment" with that observation if its result had been as he claimed, for by his extra trips Peary had been closer to the Pole than Henson. If on the other hand those observations had confirmed Peary's worst fears of 6th April, namely, that they were nowhere near the Pole, then the "disappointment" witnessed by Egingwah was very real and justified.

Which are we to believe? Peary did not prove by his altitudes of the sun that he had, beyond doubt, reached the North Pole, for the simple reason that Pole observations can very easily be faked. So how could Peary have proved he had been to the North Pole if there was nothing he could bring back from that spot that would serve as evidence of his hard won achievement? The short answer is a well kept log. His diary could, and should have been a convincing narrative account of his daily struggle with the polar pack. It should have included a detailed record of weather and ice, and a steady progression of position checks by altitudes of the stars, the planets or the sun for latitude and longitude, as well as checks for the variation of the compass along the route to the Pole. And all of these observations should have been recorded in notebooks in which, not only were there no blank pages that could not readily be explained, but also from which no pages had been removed. If these notebooks had then been examined by handwriting experts to determine that they had, as claimed, been written in the field and each entry on a different day, and had then been very thoroughly studied by an impartial and international committee made up of eminent geographers and scientists and the record accepted by them, Peary's claim would have been established beyond dispute. But Peary's diary and observations do not measure up to these requirements or stand up to these stringent tests.

We are thus forced back to the possibility that Camp Jesup was off course to the west of his assumed heading and that he was at least fifty miles from the Pole. Let us look more closely at his dilemma. He had enough food on his sledges to make that correction and, at the rate they had been travelling over the past five days, they could reach the Pole in two days – or three at the most. But the pull to return safely was now a strong one and, as he says in his book: "All the plans for the expedition were formulated quite as much with an eye toward a safe return from the Pole as toward the task of reaching it."

That plan was also based on the principle that the return would be faster than the outward journey because they would be sledging along a blazed trail and using igloos already built. If they were now to correct their course and head directly for the Pole, they would have to return along their tracks or risk missing that trail which had been kept open by the returning supporting parties, and that two or three days' extra travelling to reach the Pole would therefore be doubled to a round trip of some five or six days north of their Camp Jesup.

But there was another factor in that dilemma. To reach the Pole now he would have to admit first to his five bone-weary companions who had risked their lives to get him to that point, and later to his supporters and public, that "the greatest Arctic explorer of the Age" (as Jo had proudly called her husband) had made an error of navigation that would certainly stain his reputation.

How much sharper now seems that remark which Henson had made "cheerfully enough" in his innocence of their true position: that if they had not travelled in the right direction, it was *Peary's* fault! How much more poignant too now seems that moment when Henson had ungloved his right hand and gone forward to congratulate the man whom he served on the success of their eighteen years of effort, and Peary, "with both hands covering his eyes," had turned and walked away.

Could it be that the heart-broken Peary could not bear that Henson might read the misery in his eyes and suddenly know the cruel truth that they had come the right distance – but in the wrong direction?

Could it be that Peary had left Henson behind at Camp Jesup because he needed time to think, time perhaps to adjust himself to that heartless, mocking truth? If this was the truth of Peary's discovery, then there were no thirty hours in the life of this man that were blacker than those at his Farthest North.

But is it right to read his mental anguish in those nine blank pages in his diary? They were a space which presumably Peary left clear in order that he might later record his activities at and around Camp Jesup and during the first eighty miles of his journey back along the homeward track – nine blank pages, and a loose-leaf page on which he had written, "The Pole at last!!!"

Perhaps he is hiding nothing at all.

Details of how he spent those hours at that place which Henson believed was near enough to be called the North Pole are certainly to be found in the book. They had, according to Peary, travelled at least thirty miles on their last march north. He himself had then snatched "two or three" hours' sleep before travelling a further thirty-six miles and taking altitudes of the sun "at four different stations, in three different directions [and] at four different times," and was planning on travelling thirty miles more before allowing his body and mind another four hours of sleep. He must surely have been in a daze of both physical and mental exhaustion by the afternoon of 7th April when he looked around for a suitable pinnacle on which to perform the ritual his five companions were all expecting – for they were, after all, at the Pole.

The original draft of his book's description of this historic and memorable event somewhat surprisingly still exists. It was written by his ghostwriter, A. E. Thomas, whose plea to Peary for more information on what he actually did at Camp Jesup had evidently not elicited much, for he has clearly been obliged to guess, as can be seen by Peary's corrections and additions which are written in his own distinctive hand. The following is the text of that draft with Peary's deletions shown in square brackets, and his additions in italics:

Of course there were some more or less informal ceremonies connected with our arrival at our difficult destination, but they were not of a very elaborate character. We planted [four] *five* flags at the top of the world. The first one was a silk American flag which Mrs. Peary gave me fifteen years ago. [I daresay that] That flag has done more traveling in [low] *high* latitudes than any other [that has ever been manufactured] *ever made*. I carried it [with me] *wrapped about my body* on every one of my expeditions northward after it came into my possession, and I left a fragment of it at each of my successive "farthest norths."

(Margin note: *Insert all this here* – Peary listing his achievements)
By the time it actually reached the Pole, therefore, it was [a] somewhat [battered] *worn* and [fragmentary ensign] *discolored*.

(Margin note: *Is Mr. Thomas right in this?* – Editor's note referring to the next nine lines of the draft manuscript, all of which Peary deleted)
[But the fragments were lashed to a stout tent-pole which was stuck

in the top of a hummock of ice that rose at the back of our igloo. There it flapped idly in the gentle wind that blew lazily all the thirty hours we spent at the Pole, and when we turned our backs upon that long-sought desolate spot the last thing we saw was the battered flag. Its mission had been accomplished, its travels were over, it was fitting we should leave it behind us.] *A broad diagonal section of this ensign would now mark the farthest goal of earth – the place where I and my dusky companions stood.*

... After I had planted the American flag in the ice [Henson addressed the Eskimos in their native tongue and proposed three cheers] *I told Henson to time the Eskimos for three rousing cheers,* which [the natives gave with the utmost good will] *they gave with the greatest enthusiasm.* Thereupon I shook hands with each member of the party – surely a sufficient unceremonious affair to meet with the approval of the most democratic. The Eskimos were childishly delighted with our success. While of course they did not realize its importance fully, or its world-wide significance, they did understand that it meant the final achievement of a task upon which they had seen me [and others] engaged for many years.

(Margin note: *How did they show it? What did they say?*)

Peary added nothing about the Eskimos, but one cannot help admitting his stylistic corrections were an improvement, and he did endorse and may even have written himself the following conclusion:

It is not easy to write about such a thing, but I knew that we were going back to civilization with pretty nearly the last of the great adventure stories – a story the world had been waiting to hear for nearly four hundred years, a story which was to be told at last under the folds of the Stars and Stripes, the flag that during a lonely and isolated life had come to mean for me a symbol of home and everything I loved – and might never see again.

Finally, he wrote a note on a United States postal card, addressed to Mrs. R. E. Peary, South Harpswell, Maine, which he was later to hand deliver at Sydney.

My dear Jo,   90 N. Lat (North Pole) Apr 7th
    I have won out at last. Have been here a day of the finest weather. I start for home and you in an hour. Love to the "kidsies."

                                                        Bert

At about four o'clock on the afternoon of 7th April (after only a few hours' sleep) they set out on the homeward trail. Peary says of that moment:

> Though intensely conscious of what I was leaving, I did not wait for any lingering farewell of my life's goal. The event of human beings standing at the hitherto inaccessible summit of the earth was accomplished, and my work now lay to the south, where four hundred and thirteen nautical miles of ice-floes and possibly open leads still lay between us and the north coast of Grant Land. One backward glance I gave – then turned my face toward the south and toward the future.

But what did the future hold for him if he did not return successful? Had it not been his duty to succeed, his duty to his wife and family; his duty to those who had financed this, his last expedition, and all of the others that he had made; his duty also to his fellow countrymen to plant the Stars and Stripes at the Pole and to bring back a tale of which his countrymen would be proud for as long as the stories of human endeavour still stirred the heart of humankind and inspired the young to succeed? If these were some of the thoughts on his mind, small wonder he was a stranger to Henson:

> From the time we knew we were at the Pole Commander Peary scarcely spoke to me. Probably he did not speak to me four times on the whole return journey to the ship. I thought this over and it grieved me much. I thought of the years we had worked together for the one great aim. I remembered his many acts of kindness and naturally I did not forget what I had done for him ... It nearly broke my heart on the return journey from the Pole that he would rise in the morning and slip away on the homeward trail without rapping on the ice for me, as was the established custom.

In sixteen forced marches during which the Commander, according to Henson, had ridden the sledge the entire way, they reached Cape Columbia. They were marches during which they had strained every nerve to keep up the almost killing pace in order that they might save their lives and "return to tell the story."

They were marches during which the mind of Peary, exhausted by the endless stress, had occasionally sought some comfort in those soothing realms of fantasy, but whereas those fantasies on his way north had nourished Peary's most cherished belief that he had been chosen, that he had a mission, that it was his destiny to be the discoverer of the North Pole, those fantasies only offered him now the conviction that he had earned, through suffering, the right to his reward.

"My life work is accomplished," he wrote in his diary on the morning of 23rd April a few hours after reaching the igloos at Cape Columbia.

The thing which it was intended from the beginning that I should do, the thing which I believed could be done, and that I could do, I have done. I have got the North Pole out of my system after twenty-three years of effort, hard work, disappointments, hardships, privations, more or less suffering, and some risks. I have won the last great geographical prize, the North Pole, for the credit of the United States. This work is the finish, the cap and climax of nearly four hundred years of effort, loss of life, and expenditure of fortunes by the civilized nations of the world, and it has been accomplished in a way that is thoroughly American. I am content.

But was he really? This he would have his public believe; but the note in his diary above his entry for 10th April tells a different story:

. . . U.S. made Melville & Schley Admirals & Greely Brigadier General for their Arctic work. England knighted James & John Ross, Parry, Franklin, Nares, McClintock, Richards (?), Beaumont, etc, etc. Paid Parry $125,000 – Phipps (?) 25,000 – etc, etc. for their Arctic work.

The entries in his diary span exactly the same number of days in his life as his life at that time had spanned in years, and there at Cape Columbia for practically two whole days they slept before going onto the ship.

In one march on the smooth, hard-packed land-fast ice of the coast they reached Cape Hecla, a run of forty-five miles, and in another "of equal length" they reached the *Roosevelt*. "My heart thrilled," Peary says in his book, "as I saw the little black ship lying there in its icy berth with sturdy nose pointing straight to the Pole." But as he approached the ship and saw Bartlett coming out to meet him, he says "something in his face told me he had bad news even before he spoke."

"Have you heard about poor Marvin?" he asked.
"No," I answered.
Then he told me that Marvin had been drowned at the "Big Lead," coming back to Cape Columbia. The news staggered me, killing all the joy I had felt at the sight of the ship and her captain.

Bartlett remembers this differently:

Peary reached the ship on April 27th. I happened to be up on deck when the Eskimos shouted that he was coming. I ran out on the ice to meet him. He look haggard but not weak. He grasped my out-stretched hand while I exclaimed: "I congratulate you, sir, on the discovery of the Pole."

"How did you guess it?" he asked, laughing at my excitement. I then told him the news of Marvin's death.

Bartlett had returned to the ship on 24th April, only three days ahead of Peary and his party, who had travelled an absolute minimum of three hundred nautical miles further than Bartlett, although more realistically (by adding twenty-five per cent for detours) about 375 miles further. And yet Bartlett accepted without question that Peary had reached his objective – even more readily than Henson.

It seems strange also, even allowing that Peary was exhausted, that he appears to have had no desire to celebrate his success on arrival at the ship or even to share his triumph with his crew. He told no one. It was simply left for them to guess. Henson's sad commentary on his relationship with Peary after returning to the ship merely adds to the mystery:

> From the time of my arrival at the *Roosevelt*, for nearly three weeks, my days were spent in complete idleness. I would catch a fleeting glimpse of Commander Peary, but not once in all of that time did he speak a word to me. Then he spoke to me in the most matter-of-fact way, and ordered me to get to work. Not a word about the North Pole or anything connected with it.

Only Dr. Goodsell put the question to him directly, and to this Peary had merely replied, "I have not been altogether unsuccessful." He was equally evasive in the letter he sent by messenger to MacMillan and Borup who were at Cape Morris Jesup doing tidal observations. Its opening words simply said: "Arrived on board yesterday. Northern Trip entirely satisfactory. No need of Greenland Depots . . ."

Peary's diary offers very few details on how he spent his last eighty days at Cape Sheridan. His crew and Eskimos were, as usual, kept busy, and the organisation of all this activity clearly occupied much of his time. But with his last journey over and no longer any real *need* to do any more "it remained only to arrange the results."

There was time now, at last, in the peace of his cabin, to think through carefully what he had done, and what he had been seen to have done by those five men who had travelled with him north of Bartlett's farthest camp. There was time now to study what he had written, and to look with a very much clearer eye at the darker side of what for him was still a cruel dilemma.

But what evidence is there to suggest that Peary, having reached the ship, had still not decided whether he could go through with his claim? Among the Peary Papers at the National Archives in Washington, D.C., I discovered two loose-leaf memos in Peary's hand which, on the evidence of the dates mentioned in the notes and the type of paper used, were written on his return to the ship.

The first of the two pages notes:

Goodsell returned to ship from 84°29' in 12 days. MacMillan in 11 days including establishment of depot at Ward Hunt Island. Borup returned from 85°23' in 23 days including establishment of depot at C. Fanshaw Martin. Marvin's men came in from 86°38' in 23 days.

The second page concludes the list:

Captain came in from 87°47' in 24 days. Self came in from —— in 20 days (18 marches).

Why has Peary not written in how far north he went?

On 12th June, fifty-six days after returning to the ship, he signed a statement which he had written outlining the achievements of the "Peary Arctic Club North Pole Expedition, 1908." It was to be framed behind glass to "protect it from the weather" and fastened beneath the four arms of a "guide-post" which was constructed from sledge planks on board the ship. This, Borup and two Eskimos took back along the trail and erected, as instructed, at Cape Aldrich, as "a permanent monument" to the expedition. The signed statement, however, oddly omitted to mention the date the North Pole was reached, this part of the statement reading simply:

S.S. Roosevelt
June 12th, 1909

This monument marks the point of departure and return of the sledge expedition of the Peary Arctic Club, which in the spring of 1909 attained the North Pole . . .

On each arm of the guide-post there is a copper plate with an inscription punched in it by hammer and nail. Each arm gives the name, the date, and the distance to Peary's key points of achievement. On the eastern arm: "Cape Morris K. Jesup, May 16, 1900, 275 miles." On the southern arm: "Cape Columbia, June 6th, 1906." On the western arm: "Cape Thomas H. Hubbard, July 1st, 1906, 225 miles." And on the northern arm: "North Pole, April 6th, 1909, 413 miles."

Here then was Peary's first public announcement that he had reached the Pole and, although it might be several years before it would be seen again by a human eye, Peary was now committed.

CHAPTER 17

The Onus of Proof

The onus of proof lies with the explorer and Peary knew this well enough, for he himself was always assessing and comparing the claims of his principal rivals against the actual achievements of those with whom he was competing. In his lifetime, however, he failed to provide conclusive evidence that he and his companions had reached the North Pole, and the burden of his unproved claim had therefore to be carried by those who had taken Peary at his word or had a vested interest in defending his success.

So with whom now lies that burden of proof – his biographers or the historians? Both claim to speak with the voice of scholarship, some even with authority. But what chance have either, eighty years on, of getting under the skin of the truth when the man whose records they have been studying was clearly being driven by the conviction that the Pole was his and that he had not only the right to reach it, but also to reap "the rewards of priority" and take his place in history? Let us, however, take a closer look at Peary's astonishingly casual attitude towards the problem of finding his way across 413 nautical miles of drifting pack ice to his objective.

Certainly the greatest single strength in his 1909 plan was the sum total of his polar experience, and in particular, his experience of 1906. The fact that he was able to place the *Roosevelt* in almost precisely the same prime position that he had used as a winter quarters in 1906 was also a tremendous advantage, for not only was Cape Sheridan about as close to the Pole as he could winter a ship and stand a reasonable chance of breaking free the following summer, but he knew that coastline and all the areas where his hunting parties were likely to find game. He had also, in 1909, a stronger, more experienced, and more committed party, and no winter crises to distract his eager men from their mission. In short, on this final expedition, he had his first real chance to succeed and he knew it. And yet, instead of building upon the foundations of his past experience, we find not only a repetition of some of his errors of 1906, but new ones which in certain cases can only be described as astonishing.

In spite of the fact that the west-south-west winds had carried him way off course to the east on his attempt at the Pole in 1906, he appears, in

1909, to have completely ignored the possibility that he might have been blown off course to the west by the easterly and north-easterly gales he experienced during the early stages and the mid-point of his outward journey. Why would a polar traveller of this man's undoubted calibre have risked the entire success of his journey, and his last opportunity of reaching the Pole, by simply assuming he knew which way the pack ice was drifting from the movement he could see locally? Every opening lead and every grinding sound of ice under pressure is an indication that the ice is moving. Even ice floes that appear to be motionless may be drifting intact – the whole vast area in motion. Peary knew this from past experience.

What then gave him the crazy idea that he could strike out across the drifting pack ice, and without any observations for longitude or any checks on the variation of the compass, could aim for and hit the Pole? It is simply not acceptable to assume that Peary set his course to counter the drift of ice, for there is no way of knowing which way the ice is drifting, or at what speed, without frequent position checks by solar observations.

Is it not also amazing that in spite of the near fatal encounter with the Big Lead in 1906, he took no boat, or any material from which to make one? He knew that Nansen and Johansen on their attempt at the Pole in 1895 had taken kayaks, and would not have survived without them. Even Cook, whose experience as a polar traveller Peary disparaged, had been wise enough to take with him a folding canvas boat.

The presence of Cook in Peary's "domain" also shows up another weakness in Peary's planning of his final attempt. In spite of being suspicious that Cook might fake a claim to have reached the Pole ahead of him, Peary appears to have totally ignored this threat by making no provision to secure conclusive proof of his own route, or even of the attainment of his life's ambition, and his published intention of providing a line of soundings (with samples of the ocean bed) along the outward track of his journey, he only half-heartedly carried through.

Peary's plan, first published in the *New York Herald* and in part repeated in his book, stated:

First, I shall follow the north coast of Grant Land as far west as Cape Columbia, and possibly beyond, instead of leaving this land at Point Moss as I did before. Second, leaving the land, my course will be more west of north than before, in order to counteract or allow for the easterly set of the ice between the north coast of Grant Land and the Pole, discovered on my last expedition.

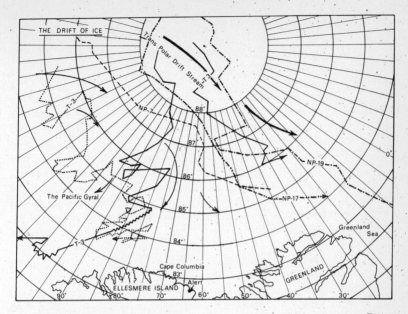

It is entirely reasonable therefore to assume that in March 1909, Peary did set his course to the west of north in order to counter the expected eastward drift and stay on the Columbia meridian, and that this he believed he succeeded in doing. In his letter to Acting Superintendent F. W. Perkins of the US Coast and Geodetic Survey, dated 3rd March, 1910, he states that his soundings "were made on the meridian of Cape Columbia, and plotting on that meridian at the latitudes which I think are noted in the table on the profile sheet will give their position." During the Peary Hearings he also confirmed that his longitude "was not far removed from the meridian of Columbia," the point from which he had set out across the Arctic Ocean.

But of course it is inconceivable that Peary's route followed this meridian directly to the Pole, and equally difficult to believe that Peary and his companions covered in a dead straight line the 296 nautical miles from Bartlett's camp to the Pole and back to Bartlett's camp in 7.8 days – an average of 37.9 nautical miles a day. Even allowing a very modest twenty-five per cent for detours, this increases the distance they more probably covered to 370 nautical miles at an average of 47.4 miles a day. Converting this to statute miles, we find that they must have averaged 54.5 miles a day for those 7.8 days. Across flat sea ice this is not unreasonable; but across polar pack ice this sort of average is nothing short of phenomenal.

But harder still to believe: from his 5th April camp to the Pole and back to Bartlett's Farthest North, he claims to have covered 196 nautical miles in four days, an average of forty-nine miles a day. This works out (after adding twenty-five per cent for detours) at an average of 61.2 nautical miles a day (or 70.4 statute miles a day). No explorer, before or since, has claimed to have covered these sorts of distances across polar pack ice over the same number of consecutive days, and even the most successful expeditions in the last ten years have taken longer to reach the North Pole than Peary claimed it took him to reach that elusive spot and return to his point of departure.

In May 1985 the Steger International Polar expedition stated in a press release that one of their goals was "to accomplish at least one 30-mile day as part of their effort to examine Admiral Peary's disputed claim of having accomplished similarly high daily averages on his expedition." So what was the outcome? In *North to the Pole*, Will Steger's account of his successful journey in 1986, he says:

> ... our expedition was shedding light on the question raised about his mileage – the contention that one simply can't travel thirty-five to fifty miles a day on polar ice, as Peary claimed. Our dogs had started this journey pulling payloads that weighed nearly three times those on Peary's nineteen sleds. Surely, by the time we reached 88 degrees, our dogs were far more exhausted than Peary's were when he started his final dash from nearly the same point. Yet the average mileage for our last five marches – just under thirty-four miles – was virtually the same as what he clocked on his final dash.
>
> ... Thus, while the jury is still out on his navigation claims, I find his mileage claims to be plausible. Whether Peary's crew stood at the North Pole on April 6, 1909, can never be proven beyond doubt, but I believe it's possible they could have done it.

This, coming from a man who has travelled by dog sledge to the North Pole virtually along the same outward route as Peary, seems conclusive. But it is clear from the table of mileages at the back of his book (compiled by Paul Schurke, his co-leader and navigator) that Steger has made a mistake. Their average mileage over their last five marches was not, as he states, thirty-four miles, but twenty-five *statute* miles, or 21.7 nautical miles. Steger is evidently referring to his route miles (the distance he actually travelled) and is giving that "average" in *statute* miles. The Steger expedition had a satellite fix of their position on the morning of 23rd April which gave their latitude as 87°50' (only three miles north of Bartlett's farthest), so we may make a direct comparison between Steger's and Peary's journey from that point to the Pole.

From the table of distances at the back of Steger's book giving the "net gain towards the Pole each day" in statute miles, we find that they travelled 146 statute miles in seven days (they reached the Pole on 1st May), an average of 20.85 statute miles, or 18.13 nautical miles. Peary covered that same distance, since he set out from a point three miles south of Steger's latitude and, according to Peary, Camp Jesup was three miles short of the Pole. The difference, however, is that Peary claims to have covered that distance in four days and five hours – an average of 30.95 nautical miles a day, as against Steger's 18.13 nautical miles.

It is very clear from this that the performance of Steger's party, admirable though it was, can in no way be regarded as a vindication of Peary's claimed speeds or distances. On only one day on Steger's entire journey did he better the average of Peary's four days' northward march from Bartlett's farthest, and Steger's best latitude distance in one day – thirty-two miles, being 27.82 nautical miles, on 26th April – is only half Peary's average during his homeward run from Camp Jesup to Bartlett's farthest.

Naomi Uemura, whose fifty-five days' solo trek with dogs in 1978 also took the shortest, or so-called "Peary route," to the Pole, reached the North Pole on 29th April. His time over the distance from Bartlett's Farthest North to the Pole (with satellite fixes at each end of the run) was seven days at an average of eighteen nautical miles a day, almost exactly the same as Steger's. His best day's net gain was 32.37 nautical miles, better than Steger's but a long way short of Peary's. In 1968–9 my own expedition's best day during the 3,800-mile journey with dogs from Alaska via the North Pole to Spitsbergen was only twenty-six nautical miles, and we were at that time travelling with very light loads. So how is it that Peary was able to make such incredible marches?

In his diary entry for 9th April, after the march which returned him to Bartlett's Farthest North camp, Peary offers an explanation: "From here to the Pole and back has been a glorious sprint with a savage finish. Its results due to hard work, little sleep, much experience, first class equipment, and good fortune as regards weather and open water."

His good fortune as regards to weather includes the "wild day" of 9th April when they benefited from a strong north-north-east wind which increased to a gale, and for the last half of the march the ice was raftering all around them and beneath their feet under the "pressure of a howling gale."

Fortunately we were traveling nearly before the wind, for it would have been impossible to travel except before the gale and following a trail with the gale in our faces. As it was, the dogs scudded along before the wind much of the time on the gallop. Under the impact of the storm the ice was evidently crushing southward and bearing us with it. I was strongly reminded of the wild gale in which we regained "storm camp" on our return march in 1906.

There are certainly similarities, and aside from those that were pounced upon immediately by Peary's critics, it will be noticed that the following wind which was bearing them south, and thus reducing the overall distance they had to cover, was *not* reducing those suspect averages for the obvious reason that the camp for which Peary's party was heading was also drifting south.

But let us now look at some of the navigational errors that may have affected his outward journey, any one of which, had it gone unnoticed or uncorrected over the full length of his outward march, could have robbed Peary of the Pole. Firstly, there is the possibility that Peary made an error in his heading, an error caused by the drift of ice carrying him off his assumed meridian by an unchecked amount and in an unchecked direction.

In recent years a great deal of data has been collected on the effect of wind on the drift of pack ice. For the purpose of this assessment, however, I am inclined to think that Nansen's empirical law of drift is adequate, since the data provided by Peary is too vague to justify a more scientific study. This empirical law, which is based upon an analysis of the *Fram*'s drift and that of other vessels, states that: "ice fields drift at 1/50th of the speed of the wind that moves them, while the direction of the ice drift in the northern hemisphere deviates from the direction of the wind by 28 to 30 degrees – to the right."

Apply this law of drift to the first three days of Peary's outward journey and the track is deflected by over twenty nautical miles to the west of the Columbia meridian by the time the party reaches the Big Lead at latitude 84°. It is possible that the track was deflected further than this. Peary states in his diary and his published accounts that the wind was "violent" and "continued with unabated violence." At no point, however, either in his diary or his published accounts, does he ever give an estimated wind speed. It was the same with the 1906 journey: "violent" winds; "furious and blinding drift"; winds which continued their "infernal howling" all night; and at what Peary called Storm Camp, a frequent use of the word "gale," which according to the 1805 Beaufort Wind Scale is a wind average of between thirty and forty knots. During our sixteen months' crossing of the Arctic Ocean in 1968–9, we recorded no wind speed over forty knots, and from weather observations at various locations on the Arctic Ocean over the past forty years we now know that true "gales" are unheard of, and "storms" virtually impossible.

So what wind speeds was Peary really experiencing? The only check we have is offered by his 1906 drift at Storm Camp. Here he drifted sixty-two nautical miles in six and a half days and, by applying Nansen's

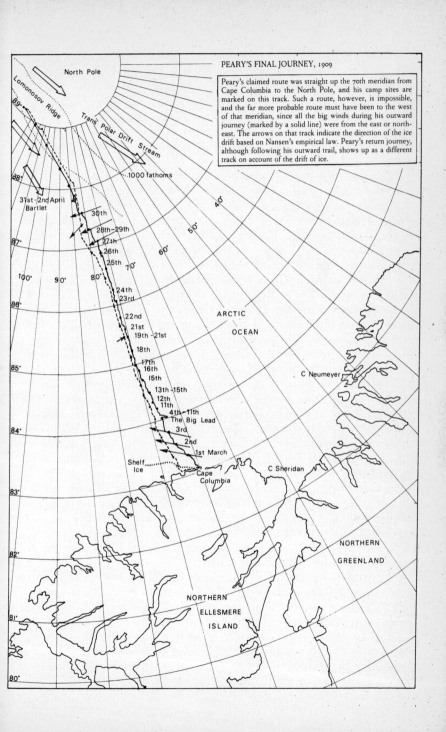

PEARY'S FINAL JOURNEY, 1909

Peary's claimed route was straight up the 70th meridian from
Cape Columbia to the North Pole, and his camp sites are
marked on this track. Such a route, however, is impossible,
and the far more probable route must have been to the west
of that meridian, since all the big winds during his outward
journey (marked by a solid line) were from the east or north-
east. The arrows on that track indicate the direction of the ice
drift based on Nansen's empirical law. Peary's return journey,
although following his outward trail, shows up as a different
track on account of the drift of ice.

North Pole

Lomonosov Ridge

Trans Polar Drift Stream

···1000 fathoms

31st–2nd April
Bartlet
30th

28th–29th
27th
26th
25th

24th
23rd

22nd
21st
19th–21st

18th
17th
16th
15th

13th–15th
12th
11th
4th–11th
The Big Lead
3rd
2nd
1st March

Shelf
Ice

Cape
Columbia

ARCTIC

OCEAN

C Neumeyer

C Sheridan

NORTHERN

GREENLAND

NORTHERN

ELLESMERE

ISLAND

law and working backwards, so to speak, we find that the wind driving the ice during that period must have been averaging just under twenty knots – a "fresh breeze" on the Beaufort Wind Scale. This does not sound as dramatic as a "gale" but, in fairness to Peary, I am bound to say that a strong wind on the Arctic Ocean is more dramatic than a strong wind anywhere else in the world because of its effect on the pack ice and on the nerves of the men who are helplessly drifting on those fracturing floes of ice.

There are two tracks plotted on the chart. The right-hand track is the outward track plotted from information extracted from Peary's diary and his published accounts which shows an approximation of the detours mentioned, and the effect of the wind drift and other factors which would have affected this track. The left-hand track is the homeward route which shows that although Peary and his party were following the trail of their supporting parties, the ice has drifted, and the arrows indicate the direction of that drift calculated from Nansen's law. It will be noticed that every major blow that Peary experienced on his outward journey drifted his track further west of his assumed meridian of 70°W. He seldom mentions any break in the trail, and is clearly assuming (and occasionally states) that there was no indication of any lateral drift. But of course, if the whole vast area was in motion and drifting to the west, this drift would not be noticeable except by doing an observation for longitude.

Had Peary made no other directional errors on his outward journey than the error of not checking his lateral drift, he would, by the time he reached Bartlett's Farthest North, have been on longitude 80°W, or about twenty-three nautical miles to the west of his assumed longitude. There is the possibility that he may have been even further west than this, for in plotting the right-hand track I have deliberately underestimated his wind speeds in order to give him the benefit of the doubt, assuming he was exaggerating them for literary effect. Clearly Peary's need to reach the North Pole distracted him from his obligation as an explorer to observe and to record, and this is a charge against him that cannot be ignored.

Now consider the error that would have affected his course as a result of a false assumption of an easterly drift of ice, and Peary's consequent compensation for this non-existent drift.

Here again, I have given Peary the benefit of the doubt, and assumed that he did not (as he had originally planned) set his course to the west of north. I am assuming that a man of his experience would have realised that the predominantly easterly winds would have carried him west, or at least, would have had the effect of countering the drift he assumed was normal for that region. If, on the other hand, he *did* stick with his original plan, then the position of Bartlett's Farthest North camp would have been perhaps ten nautical miles further west than I have plotted it.

The error in his heading would have been further increased if he had assumed he was on the Columbia meridian, and set his course according to the position of the sun at local noon "Columbia meridian time," when in fact he would have been west of that meridian. For example: if at 16h 52m 26s on each day when the sun was visible (this being the time the sun transits the Columbia meridian, using the 1909 almanac and calculating for longitude 70°W) Peary had assumed the sun was due south, and had headed precisely in the opposite direction (or directly for the head of his shadow) he would not have been heading due north, as he believed, but to the west of it. At the Big Lead on 11th March, his error would have been 5°25'W, at the latitude shot of the 22nd, his error would have been 7°08'W, and at Bartlett's Farthest North on 1st April, his error in heading would have been 14°22'W.

An error in Peary's chronometer would also have affected his heading, and on his return to civilisation it was found that his chronometer had indeed been ten minutes fast during the period he was making his journey. When his chronometer told him that the sun was on the Columbia meridian, the sun was therefore short of the transit by ten minutes, or 2.5° of arc. An error of 2.5° in aiming over a distance of 413 nautical miles would have put him west of the Pole by eighteen nautical miles.

Magnetic variation is another key navigational issue in which Peary appears to have been in error. During the Peary Hearings he was asked if "in using a compass in the northern regions you use it with a calculated variation?" To this Peary had replied: "You use it, checking it by observations wherever you can." He then volunteered that there was some knowledge of the variation on the compass along the north coast of Grant Land, data collected on previous expeditions which had been plotted on published charts: "They have the lines of certain variations, but, of course, the greater the number of observations, the more accurate the data." Peary had then been asked if he had taken such a chart with him, and surprisingly, he had not only admitted that he had not, but also, and less excusably, had not taken any observations on his last expedition to determine the variation of the compass. At this point in the questioning, Peary appears to have been embarrassed, for he promptly changed the subject by describing his activities while in the vicinity of the Pole.

I have, however, found one reference in the Peary Papers at the National Archives which seems to indicate that he did make one check on his compasses. This is mentioned on a loose-leaf of paper, identical to several other loose-leaf notes which, on the evidence of dates mentioned, must have been written on his return to the ship. The memo reads: "The sun setting due E & W Mar, 21 & 22 gave accurate check on compasses also just touching northern horizon Mar, 26 & 27." At this latitude, in my experience, such a method of checking the compass variation would not have been accurate. In fact, it would not even have been accurate enough to arouse any suspicion that he was off course to the west.

By not taking observations for magnetic variation, the steering error would have increased the further north the party travelled, and as with all the other errors, they would have been drawing the party further and further to the west. By the time they reached Bartlett's Farthest North camp, the variation of the compass would have been 135° or 27° west of the Columbia variation, and as Peary went north of latitude 88° on this incorrect heading, he would be crossing isogonals more often and his error would have been increasing all the time, throwing him ever further and further to the west.

If we give Peary the benefit of the doubt, and assume that his crude compass check of 22nd March may have given him a rough idea of his error, and he corrected his heading accordingly, then his accumulation of error due to his uncertainty of the variation of the compass would have started from 22nd March, and the most probable position of Camp Jesup would be position B on the map on page 265. If he did not do any checks for variation of the compass on his 1909 journey, then the most probable position for Camp Jesup would be position C.*

The irony of this particular error is that had Peary not been drifted off his meridian to the west but had managed to stay on the Columbia meridian, he would have had little problem with his compass variation as the isogonal runs very nearly along that meridian. Paul Schurke, the navigator of the Steger expedition, found the variation changing only ten degrees from land to the Pole.

But just as checks should have been made on the compass at regular intervals, so too should position fixes have been made (latitude and longitude) to check the direction and extent of their detours. Although it is clear from Peary's written accounts that the course was not that impossible straight line, he at no time in his published record mentions what percentage of additional miles he had to cover in order to get around the obstacles of pressure ridges or open leads.

He has written two notes on detours, both in the form of loose-leaf memos which, like the one on his compass check, were probably written on his return to the ship. The first states: "Distance traveled in excess of distance made good, say 10% to 87 or 4 degrees i.e. 28 naut miles (nearer 50′)." His first estimate is clearly impossible, and this he knows, hence the comment. If we take his more realistic estimate of 50′ of latitude over a distance of 4°, this works out at a percentage for detours of 20.8. In his second memo (and there is no way of knowing which was written first),

---

* See also my comment on Peary's soundings in Appendix II, page 343.

he states: "Up to and including the 20th March the distance actually traveled was probably 25% in excess of the distance made good." Both Borup and Goodsell agree that the percentage for detours was of this order.

During the sledging stages of the trans-Arctic journey in 1968–9 our detours were in the region of seventy-five per cent, very close to the figure that the Plaisted expedition arrived at during their one-way trip to the North Pole with Skidoos in 1968. The Steger expedition estimated fifty per cent for their journey. The Frenchman, Jean-Louis Etienne, who manhauled solo to the North Pole in 1986 estimated forty-five per cent. Is it not therefore extremely unlikely that Peary's 1909 expedition travelled only an additional sixty miles as detours during the first 240 miles, the roughest part of the journey by all accounts?

It is, in any case, not simply a question of how much further Peary had to travel, but in which direction. Over a long journey, the diversions to the left and right of an ideal course tend to balance out; but this cannot be assumed for all journeys. If they were mainly to the west, his general steering error would have increased as he would be moving further from his assumed meridian. If to the east, however, his steering error would have decreased. There is therefore an element of uncertainty in this question of detours which must not be overlooked for, even giving Peary the benefit of the doubt once again, and accepting his estimate of an additional sixty miles up to latitude 87°, this is sixty miles which he would also have to cover on his return journey (since he was following the outward trail), and this affects his overall daily average which is already at the extreme limit of credibility.

As well as all mileages being "latitude distance" between two points, not the miles actually travelled by men and dogs, we should remember that the mileages given by Peary (both in his diary and in his book) are, for the convenience of the navigator, nautical miles, not statute. Convert Peary's nautical miles to statute miles and add on a realistic percentage for detours, and suddenly Peary's distances seem truly incredible!

There is also the human bias to consider, a smaller issue, but one, nevertheless, which cannot be discounted. No matter what method of steering is being used by the dog driver (a compass course or steering by the sun), there is always a possibility of human bias, a tendency with some trail-breakers consistently to edge to the left or right. If this error goes undetected by those who are following the trail, it can increase to a sizeable amount.

There is yet another problem for the traveller heading along Peary's route. As he gets to within two degrees of the Pole he will begin to notice the effect of the Trans-Polar Drift Stream. The track of the trans-Arctic expedition from our winter quarters to the Pole was very strongly affected by this current, and we were constantly being drifted to the right and countering it as best we could. The rate of drift varied, and was further complicated by the wind drift; but the general ice drift on calm days in the vicinity of the Pole was between two and three nautical miles a day in the direction of longitude 30°W. This estimate, based on personal experience, is supported by data from the drifting stations, and even Peary admits to its existence. He was losing ground by "treadmilling" on his five marches north from Bartlett's Farthest North camp, and ended up some twelve nautical miles short of the distance he claimed he had physically covered practically in a straight line.

It is my guess that the distance made good during those five marches was reduced not only by the "treadmilling" misery of going against the drift of ice, but also by detours. Even allowing Peary, yet again, the benefit of the doubt, and accepting his claim that he travelled 125 nautical miles in those five outward marches, the most probable position for Camp Jesup (at position B) is still some fifty-five nautical miles from the Pole.

And what of the Pole itself? Matthew Henson makes an interesting comment in his article for *World's Work* in April 1910: "The sun in that latitude does not cross the sky by traveling overhead. It goes around the horizon in a circle, starting low down and gradually rising for a little distance, and then sinking back towards the horizon, but never reaching it."

True, he does not specify which latitude he is referring to, and the implication is that he is writing about the apparent behaviour of the sun during the period shortly after Bartlett turned for home in latitude 87°45'. It is, nevertheless, surprising that he chose to describe the sun's apparent motion a few score miles short of the Pole when he could, with much more effect and general interest, have described its motion at the North Pole itself, thereby giving an eye witness account of having actually been there. The alternative explanation is of course that he was describing the motion of the sun as he himself saw it from the Farthest North point of their final journey – the camp which Henson had reason to believe from Peary's actions, and the ceremony of planting the flag, must surely be the Pole.

This raises the question of whether, at that position on 6th and 7th April, it would have been obvious to Peary even in advance of taking an altitude of the sun that he was not at the Pole. Let us, for the sake of argument, assume that position B on the map on page 265 was the position of Camp Jesup on the 6th and 7th – namely, latitude 89°05'N, and longitude 135°W. At this position, the difference in the sun's altitude between noon and midnight on the 6th would have been 1°38', or three sun's diameters, and this *would* have been noticeable since the sun's altitude at upper transit (local noon) was only slightly over seven degrees.

Without even doing an observation, Peary would therefore have realised that he was not at the North Pole. But as we have seen, the last day before reaching Camp Jesup on which the sun was visible both at noon and at midnight was 4th April, and at that time he was still far enough from his goal to have other things on his mind.

Three latitude shots were all that were taken on that final journey between Cape Columbia and Bartlett's Farthest North. Not a single observation for longitude. Not a single reliable check on his compass. If a polar traveller does not know both his latitude *and* his longitude, that traveller does not know which way to go!

Will Steger maintains that it is possible to keep a rough heading by observing the sastrugi – the wind-chiselled surface of the snow.

> . . . their value as navigation tools for polar travelers became increasingly apparent as I considered the error I had made on the day we traveled off course. Surely, Peary and Henson had come to understand thoroughly the value of the sastrugi over their years of travel. Though we took frequent longitude readings to fine-tune our bearing of travel, I now realized it was possible for polar travelers to carry on for days without sun sights and feel reasonably assured that they were headed roughly northward through careful observation of the drifts.
>
> This knowledge, it seems to me, must have been part of the "sixth sense" Peary and Henson had developed through their vast experience. Having been an explorer and navigator for more than twenty years and a professional navigator for thirty-five, Peary was an exceptionally well-seasoned judge of direction and distance.

Steger's empathy with Peary I share. His assessment of the usefulness of sastrugi on the polar pack as an indication of direction I do not. In certain areas of the Arctic where the wind direction is fairly constant, sastrugi is an invaluable guide – indeed at times, in my own experience, it has been a life saver. But the risk of relying upon it in an area where the winds are not from a constant direction is obvious, and the winds were not constant on Steger's expedition (as can be seen from the table at the back of his book), nor were they on Peary's.

Allan Gill, with whom I have made all of my most miserably enjoyable journeys in the Arctic, and who has spent nine and a half years to date out of a total of nineteen years in the polar regions, including fifteen high latitude winters, merely chuckled at the suggestion that one could navigate on the Arctic Ocean by using the sastrugi as a guide, since one of the most common features of the icescape of the Arctic Ocean is the star sastrugi caused by winds from different directions.

Aside from the changing winds, there is also the risk that the sastrugi the traveller might be tempted to use as his guide is on a floe which has gyrated since the sastrugi was formed. The traveller who is making a dash for the Pole by the shortest route is seldom long enough in one place (and making precise observations of the movement of the ice) to be aware of any changes in the orientation of the floes.

As for the sixth sense, it would be nothing less than irresponsible for a leader of a polar expedition to rely on this to guide his party to the Pole, and judging by Peary's deflection of twenty degrees to the west of true north when heading out from Point Moss in 1906 as a result of using an incorrect compass variation, I find it hard to accept that Peary had this sixth sense.

The test of a navigator is his ability to reach his objective, the test of the explorer, to bring back proof to support his claims. We may take it as certain that Peary on his final journey went north of latitude 88°, perhaps even north of 89°, for here was one of the most determined polar travellers ever to set his sights on the Pole; a man of sharp and refined intelligence, of iron hard concentration and courage; a man who at the time of setting out from Cape Columbia already had a total of ninety-two days' experience of travelling on the polar pack, and who knew that this would be his final attempt to reach the North Pole. And yet, almost unbelievably, he set out on that crowning achievement of his polar career with apparently nothing more than the certain direction of his destiny to guide him across the drifting pack ice to his goal! And where was his proof he had been to the Pole?

The answer – he had none.

CHAPTER 18

The Gold Brick

In 1906, when Peary had returned from the Arctic claiming a new Farthest North record, his claim had not been challenged. No one had asked to see his proof. No one, not even out of curiosity, had requested that Peary should show them his diary or permit them to check his observations before saluting the man's achievements and honouring his claim. His word was accepted, as also had been the word alone of every other polar explorer who had claimed an advance on the previous best, and rightly so, for explorers are ethically bound to be truthful and they were all honourable men.

Some of course were more honourable than others, and certainly some more deserving. It must, however, be said of Peary that, apart from believing his own name headed both of these lists, he was invariably convincing. Recall the occasion Peary received his special gold medal at the hands of the President of the United States. He had won the respect of almost all of those who were at the banquet with his seemingly genuine statement in praise of the virtues of the man who is true to his vocation. "The true explorer does his work not for any hopes of reward or honor, but because the thing he has set himself to do is a part of his being, and must be accomplished for the sake of the accomplishment."

Why then had Peary any reason to suppose that he might now, less than three years after making that speech, be faced with the burden of producing some proof that he had been to the Pole? The answer of course lies in the emergence of what Peary regarded as a serious threat to his exclusive right to attain it.

The rapid ascent of Dr. Frederick Cook from obscurity in 1891, to sharing the distinction of being guest of honour with Peary at that National Geographic Society banquet in December 1906, could not be seen by Peary, or his friends and his supporters, from any other point of view. Cook had, in Peary's opinion, deceitfully taken advantage of the delay in preparing the *Roosevelt* for her final battle with the ice, and taken advantage also of Bob Bartlett's innocence, trust and expertise. Bartlett had helped Cook and Bradley over the choice of the sloop in which they were to go north, and was later to write:

Every time I met Dr. Cook he inquired solicitously about plans and the details of our preparations ... I expanded under the Doctor's amenities and like a fat fool told him everything. No wonder the trusting sailorman gets into hot water ashore!

Another thing: Peary had so little money at that time that I was paying my own salary and that of our crew out of some money I had in the bank in St. John's. To ease the strain, and with Peary's permission I acceded to the request of Dr. Cook to let his schooner have some of the men we were holding for the *Roosevelt*. These were picked sailors used to ice navigation.

Thus while Peary's hands were tied, Cook had, in Peary's view, planned and prepared an expedition with the thoroughly underhand intention of stealing the prize upon which he had set his heart, and for which he had already paid all but the last ten per cent of the price. To such charges, of course, Cook had answers.

Mr. Peary's attitude that the Eskimos, because he had given them guns, powder and needles, belong to him, is as absurd as his pretention to the sole ownership of the North Pole. Although Mr. Peary had spent about a quarter of a century essaying the task by means of luxurious expeditions, he had done little more than other explorers and did not, in my opinion, either secure an option on the Pole or upon the services of the natives ...

The Eskimos belong to no one. For ages they have worked out their rigorous existence without the aid of white men, and Mr. Peary's pretention becomes not only absurd but grotesque when one realises that following the arrival of ships with white crews, the natives have fallen easy victims of loathsome epidemics, mostly of a specific nature, for which the trivial gifts of any explorer would ill repay them.

Peary had, in any case, prepared the rod for his own back when he was reported in the *New York Times* as having made it a condition of his accepting the presidency of the Explorers' Club that "in the event of Dr. Cook returning and claiming to have found the North Pole, proper proofs would be demanded of him." He said the same to the International Polar Commission in Brussels.

Peary appears, however, to have been so convinced at the time of sailing north from Etah that Cook was "long ago dead," that he relaxed on the need to bring back with him conclusive proof of his own achievements, and this was probably the greatest mistake he ever made in his life. The shock of learning, on his return to Etah, that Cook not only had reappeared, but was making the astonishing claim that he had reached the Pole on 21st April, 1908 (almost a full year ahead of Peary) meant that not only was he now faced with the need to disarm and discredit his most dangerous rival, but he was suddenly confronted by the alarming certainty that he would himself be "compelled" to produce convincing proof that he had reached the North Pole.

In his book, he made no mention of Cook's claim whatsoever. He merely stated:

> We stopped at Cape Saumarez, the Nerke [Neqe] of the Eskimos, and a boat's crew went ashore. It was there I first heard of the movements of Dr. Frederick Cook during the previous year while absent from Anoratok. We arrived at Etah on August 17. There I learned further details as to the movements of Dr. Cook during his sojourn in that region.

This casual reference of Peary to his rival was seen by his friends as a dignified and even eloquent disdain for the stated achievements of the man who, without any supporting proof, was claiming to have forestalled him. It also hides the anger and the frustration that Peary was feeling – a bitterness and sense of hurt which because he was unable to express it may already, up at Etah, have started turning in on Peary to become that cancer in his soul which by slow degrees destroyed him.

Bartlett speaks more bluntly of their reaction upon hearing of Cook's amazing claim:

> It was good to find Peary was not especially concerned. He and I with our years of Arctic experience knew how utterly impossible it was for Cook to have crossed a thousand miles of Polar Sea ice without supporting parties; especially since he had taken the Ellesmere Land route, which meant hundreds of miles of stiff travel before he even set foot on the Polar Sea.

Henson's recollections in *Dark Companion* offer us, through Bradley Robinson, some emotional quotations which are clearly Robinson's inept attempt to imagine what Peary might have said, had he still at that time been on speaking terms with his Negro assistant. We are also offered in Henson's *A Negro Explorer at the North Pole* an opinion about Cook which, if it is true, makes one wonder why Peary invited Cook to return to the Arctic with him on his 1893–5 expedition:

> To us, up there at Etah, such a story was so ridiculous and absurd that we simply laughed at it. We knew Dr. Cook and his abilities . . . and, aside from his medical ability, we had no faith in him whatever. He

was not even good for a day's work, and the idea of his making such an astounding claim as having reached the Pole was so ludicrous that, after our laugh, we dropped the matter altogether.

Professor MacMillan and I have talked to his two boys and have learned that there is no foundation in fact for such a statement, and the Captain and others of the expedition have questioned them, and if they were out on the ice of the Arctic Ocean it was only for a very short distance, not more than twenty or twenty-five miles. The boys are positive in this statement, and my own boys, Ootah and Ooqueah, have talked to them also, and get the same replies.

But far from being the casual conversation that Henson's comments seem to imply, the information gathered from Cook's two Eskimo companions had, under Peary's direction, been very carefully extracted and logged, and was later presented as an eight-page signed statement of their testimony that was sworn to and registered by the Notary Public of New York on 23rd November, 1909.

In Peary's introduction to this testimony he says that the Eskimos at Neqe had told him "in a general way where Dr. Cook had been ... but that the boys who were with him, I-took-a-shoo and Ah-pe-lah, said that this was not so. The Eskimos laughed at Dr. Cook's story."

The signatories of this document – Peary, Bartlett, MacMillan, Borup and Henson – state that the testimony of the two boys "was unshaken by cross-examination, was corroborated by other men in the tribe, and was elicited neither by threats nor promises." It states also that "the bulk of the boys' testimony was not taken by Commander Peary, nor in his presence, a fact that obviates any possible claim that they were awed by him." During the taking of the testimony the boys had said that "Dr. Cook had threatened them if they should tell anything."

The first part of their testimony confirms the information given in Cook's letter to Franke dated 17th March, 1908, except for the distinctive addition which bears the hallmark of Peary's ego, namely, that they had "crossed Ellesmere Land through the valley pass at the head of Flagley Bay, indicated by Commander Peary in 1898, and utilized by Sverdrup in 1899, to the head of Sverdrup's 'Bay Fjord' on the West side of Ellesmere Land."

According to the testimony, a cache had been left at Svartevoeg, and four of the Eskimos had stayed there while "two others, Koolootingwah and Inughito, went on one more march with Dr. Cook and the two boys, helped build the snow igloo, then returned without sleeping." Cook was later to claim this last support party had made three marches from Svartevoeg. But the crucial part of the testimony comes at the head of page four:

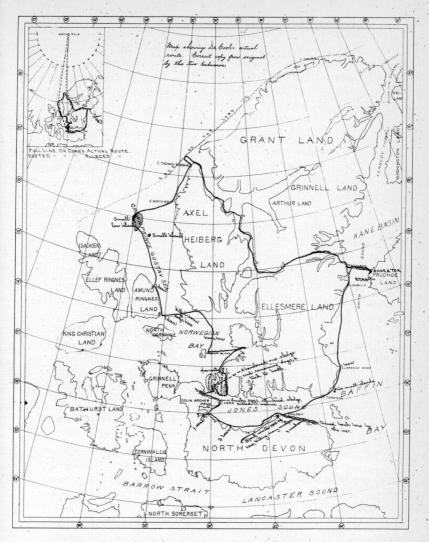

On this copy of Captain Otto Sverdrup's 1904 map Cook's two Eskimo companions were persuaded by Peary's men to plot the route they had taken. Aside from the main differences between the route marked on this map and that marked on Cook's, they have plotted Meighen Island (on latitude 80° west of Axel Heiberg Island). This island, which they plotted correctly, was not marked on Sverdrup's map, and Cook, surprisingly, makes no mention in his book of having seen it.

After sleeping at the camp where the last two Eskimos turned back, Dr. Cook and the two boys went in a Northerly or Northwesterly direction, with two sledges and twenty odd dogs, one more march, when they encountered rough ice and a lead of open water. They did not enter this rough ice, nor cross the lead, but turned Westward or Southwestward a short distance, and returned to Heiberg Land at a point West of where they had left the cache and the men had turned back.

In the original notes taken by Borup, he writes that both boys stated emphatically that "they did not go out of sight of land," and that both also said "they saw cairn built by Peary" on the hill overlooking Cape Thomas Hubbard. Cook later denied he had seen it and stated, "I doubt very much if Peary ever reached this point, except through a field-glass at a very long range." For a further analysis of the testimony of Itukusuk and Aapilaq, see Appendix I.

Angry and bitter though Peary must have been, it is evident from the taking of this testimony that he was already preparing his counter-attack, and now armed with the testimony of Cook's two companions and with a tracing of Sverdrup's map on which they had marked the route they had taken, he breathed a sigh of relief. Fortune now proceeded to play into his hands. Cook had left his "instruments, notebooks and flag" with Harry Whitney, who had spent the winter hunting with the Eskimos in the Smith Sound region, on the assumption that they would be safe with Whitney and could be carried back to New York on the *Erik* which Whitney was hoping would collect him. Meanwhile, Cook, after a few days spent in recuperating from his arduous journey from Jones Sound, where he and his two Eskimo companions had spent the winter in an "underground den," set off with dog teams on a seven-hundred-mile journey to Upernavik on the west coast of Greenland, from where he was hoping to find a whaler, or to take a passage on a supply ship to Copenhagen. But Whitney's relief ship had not arrived, and Peary agreed to take Whitney home on the condition that none of Cook's property was brought aboard.

It was a tough decision for Whitney. If he did not take passage on the *Roosevelt*, it was likely that he would have to spend a second winter in the Arctic living with the Eskimos. And so he packed Cook's instruments, notebooks and flag in his own trunk. Suspecting this, Peary confronted him with it and Whitney submitted. Cook's property was taken ashore at Etah and cached, by whom, no one seems to be sure, for although, according to Henson and Whitney, this task was performed by Whitney and Bartlett, the captain later denied it.

As it turned out, the *Roosevelt* was to meet up with the schooner *Jeanie* at Saunders Island, and together the two ships had gone into North Star Bay in order that coal brought north for the *Roosevelt* could be transferred. Whitney also transferred ship and, according to Peary, he was at that time only one day's sail from Etah and there was clear water along the eastern shore of the sound. So what did the man do?

Did Whitney run back to Etah for those immensely valuable records and instruments? He did not. He sailed directly west, where the ice was packed against the western shore. He wanted a bear. He cared more about a bear than he did about Cook's property. He would not cut out two days of his hunting to go back for what he says now he knew was Cook's proof of the discovery of the Pole.

The article by Barton W. Currie of the *New York World* from which this statement is quoted goes on to comment that:

... whereas Dr. Cook had left his polar flag, his instruments and records to the mercy of a stranger at Etah, he [Peary] had sewn his flag into his undershirt, sewn his records into his clothing and taken every precaution to guard his instruments against destruction.

Cook was returning to the world with insufficient proof that he had been to the Pole. But so too was his rival, Peary.

The schooner *Jeanie* brought him a letter from Jo written on 16th July, 1909, before she could know the outcome of his last journey. It was a letter she had copied six times and sent out, each with a different whaler, in the hope that at least one would reach him and find him safe, and well, and finally successful:

If you have succeeded then you are happy and nothing will matter to you, but if you have not, oh my dearest and best of sweethearts try to content yourself with us. We will try our best to make up in a measure for your disappointment. We love you and would sacrifice anything to give you your desire, but if it is not to be, won't you try to be happy with us. I have spent my best years in waiting for you. What is left of my life I should love to spend in waiting upon you if I can only please you and have you love me a little bit. I try to believe that in two months from now I will hear from you. What if you should not return? I simply could not face another winter without you, the last one is a horrible nightmare ... My nerves are all gone. You must, *you must come home.*

Peary read this letter at North Star Bay on 23rd August. With it was a letter from his six-year-old son Robert:

July 15, 09

My own dear dad,
    I hope you will be home soon. Eagle Island is great and I want you very much. I salute you every night. And I have tried to be straight, and strong, and honest. Mut is pretty well but you must come and take care of her yourself because she wants you badly. I send you my best love and a bushel of kisses.

Remember to Mat
Your loving, Mugs or
Robert.

Jo had written again the following day, and speaks in one part of her letter of a premonition, or is it merely the natural anxiety of a waiting wife: "The suspense this time seems worse than ever and I feel all the time as if something aweful were coming to me."

But besides a whole batch of letters from Jo with news and warnings about his rivals, Captain Sam Bartlett of the *Jeanie* had also delivered a thick letter from Bridgman giving Peary "a complete run-down of everything that had transpired to date in the matter of Dr. Cook's pre-emptive polar expedition as well as informing him of the events that had led to the repatriation of Minik," the orphan whom Peary had taken from the Arctic at the age of seven and who was now a thoroughly disoriented, discontented and bitter young man of nineteen who had completely forgotten his native tongue.

Minik's guardian, William Wallace, had written to Peary in June 1908 asking the explorer to take Minik home, but Peary had declined, regretting that his ship was too crowded, and the issue had finally come to a head on 9th May, 1909, when the *San Francisco Examiner* had run a sensational article on the plight of Minik under the heading: *"Why Arctic Explorer Peary's Neglected Eskimo Boy Wants to Shoot Him."* The article, illustrated with photographs of both Minik and Peary's daughter Marie dressed in their polar furs, and with a sketch of the boy gazing in horror at his father's skeleton "grinning" at him from a glass case in the New York Museum of Natural History, quoted Minik as saying: "I can never forgive Peary, and I hope to see him, to show him the wreck he has caused," and concluded with the veiled threat: "And if he does meet Peary, what then may follow?"

The article had not only incensed Jo, but had also deeply disturbed her. Clearly the only way to silence Minik was to ship him off to Greenland. But on the *Jeanie*? It was a risk in view of the state of mind of the boy and his publicly stated threat. It was a risk, nevertheless, that Bridgman and Jo had decided to take, and Minik on the eve of his departure had shot his final blast of abuse:

You're a race of scientific criminals. I know I'll never get my father's bones out of the American Museum of Natural History. I am glad enough to get away before they grab my brains and stuff them into a jar!

You Americans never will discover the North Pole ... Only an Eskimo can live for any length of time up there. When I get back to Etah in the north of Greenland, I am going to organize an expedition of my own and go in search of the Pole myself.

Minik's threat that he would shoot Peary was of course not carried through. Bridgman's carefully laid plans had seen to that. But up at North Star Bay Peary was certainly hurt and enraged, and glad to be rid of this thorn in his side in order that he might now turn his thoughts to ridding himself of the other.

He was, however, still unconvinced that the threat of Cook was as serious as the letters delivered by Sam Bartlett had warned him, and the full shock did not come until two days later at his final place of call. At Cape York, he had collected three boxes of mail left fifty feet above sea-level at the extreme end of the cape by Captain Adams of the whaler *Morning*, and with them, a letter marked "urgent" from the Captain informing him that Cook was in Upernavik claiming to have reached the Pole on 21st April, 1908, and was hoping to take passage on the first ship south. When that might be, Peary could not guess. But the implications were obvious. In his refusal to take Cook seriously, he had underestimated his rival's determination to announce his achievement ahead of him.

This letter from Adams must have been the first definite indication that Peary had of Cook's intention for, had Peary taken the Cook threat seriously at Etah, there can be little doubt that he would have broken with his normal habit of using his ship, his boats, and his crew to get in an ample supply of meat to see the Eskimos through the winter. We may also take it as a certainty that he would have cut short the emotional farewells with those who had helped him over the years, disembarked all of his Eskimos and dogs at points convenient to him, and then headed at full speed for North Star Bay and on to the nearest wireless station at Indian Harbor, Labrador, 1,500 miles to the south.

If only Peary had done this, it is surely more than likely that the *Roosevelt* would have reached Indian Harbor ahead of Cook reaching Lerwick in the Shetland Islands.

But instead one full day was spent at Cape York, then they were forced to take shelter in the lee of the middle pack in Baffin Bay for two days in a howling gale, and as a result of these delays the *Roosevelt* did not reach Indian Harbor until the evening of 5th September, only one day after Cook's tumultuous welcome in Copenhagen, and three days after Cook's claim had made the front page story of the *New York Herald* on 2nd September, 1909.

Strangely, Peary did not go ashore immediately upon arrival to telegraph the news of his claim, though the station was open twenty-four hours a day. According to the postmaster, Peary filed nothing until the following morning when he and Bartlett rowed ashore. He sent a few triumphant words to Jo: "Have made good at last – I have the D.O.P. [damned old Pole]. Am well. Love. All well. Wire again from Chateau. Bert."

Next, as Peary puts it, "the message 'Stars and Stripes Nailed to the North Pole' was sent flashing over the world." This had been followed in rapid succession, by one from Bartlett to his mother; the cipher signal "Sun" to Bridgman meaning "Pole reached, *Roosevelt* safe," and at least twelve others to supporters, agencies, publishers and clubs. Among them were two that are particularly revealing, the one to Bridgman which clearly indicates Peary's need now for recognition: "Kindly rush following: wire all principal home and foreign Geographical Societies of all nations including Japan, Brazil, etc., that the North Pole was reached April sixth by Peary Arctic Club's expedition under Commander Peary." And the one to Henry Romeike, a newspaper-clipping agent in New York: "Clip all editorials, illustrations, cartoons, and jokes on my work and hold till further instructions."

Out on Eagle Island, the afternoon of 6th September had been a quiet one, Jo having gone up to her room to rest leaving her now sixteen-year-old Marie on the front porch reading. That peace, and Jo's very private anxiety, were soon to be disturbed by the noise of a motor boat and a man bearing a telegram. Marie writes:

With one hand I pulled open the screen door, and with the other I seized the poor man by the coat and dragged him inside, and, snatching the telegram from him, I dashed upstairs to Mother.

She was not nearly as excited as I was when she read: "To the Associated Press, New York City. Have nailed the Stars and Stripes to the Pole. Peary." She had lived through so many false reports and rumours that she did not dare to let herself believe the good news.

"I will come down and talk to this man who has been kind enough to take the trouble to bring us the news," she said, "but you know as well as I do that if your father had reached the Pole and sent a message to the press there would be a personal message for me, too."

Peary's message for Jo was delivered only a few minutes later by the store keeper from South Harpswell, and for the rest of the day the cove was choked by hired boats and the island overrun by reporters.

That same evening, four thousand miles across the Atlantic, a farewell dinner was being given at the Tivoli in Copenhagen for the visiting newspaper reporters who had been covering the North Pole story. The guest of honour was of course Dr. Cook, and with him on the top table, Captain Otto Sverdrup, Peary's old rival, who had come over from Christiania (now Oslo) to honour the man who had beaten Commander Peary to the Pole. It had been a marvellous story told by a modest man, who was sitting there with a great garland of roses around his neck which he wore, according to Hearst Newspapers editor W. T. Stead, "as if he had been crowned with roses all his life." They were all of them, however, in for a shock which stampeded the guests for the exit.

It came soon after the very first speaker of the evening had got to his feet to address his audience. A messenger tiptoed in and handed the Danish newspaper host an envelope, the contents of which so greatly surprised him, he handed it over to Stead to read out.

"In a wire from Indian Harbor, Labrador, dated September 6, 1909," Stead announced, "Peary says: 'Stars and Stripes nailed to the Pole.'"

The guests were both bemused and stunned, as is evident not only from their reports, but also from the photograph taken a few seconds after that announcement was made. Some suspected it was a hoax and all eyes were on Cook.

"I am proud," he said when asked to comment, "that a fellow American has reached the Pole. As Rear Admiral Schley said at Santiago, 'There is glory enough for us all.' He is a brave man, and I am confident that if the reports are true his observations will confirm mine and set at rest all doubts."

Cook's composure at that testing moment greatly impressed Stead, who saw him as "a naive, inexperienced child" in the furore that followed. "Everything that a clever rogue would do instinctively if he wished to hoax the public, Dr. Cook did not do."

Stead had got the impression from Cook's earlier book, *To the Top of the Continent*, that it must have been tougher getting to the top of McKinley than it had been to reach the North Pole. "No, said Dr. Cook. The whole ascent at the last was so soon over – up and down in a rush. I was only four days up and four days down when we found the road. The North Pole was a very different matter."

Stead had been impressed by the fact that Cook had not started out for the Pole "with a procession of brass bands," and had taken a new route. He also approved Cook's assessment of the Eskimo:

Compared with our best men, he is not on a level, but compared with many of our civilized people he is their superior ... They have their limitations, but their love of berg and their skill to read the face of the sky and the face of the sea are very remarkable. They are also in their way loyal to their employer.

... On all Arctic questions an Eskimo is a better expert than the best American or European. We white men are all but amateurs compared with the Eskimo, who is the professional.

"And Etukishuk and Ahwelah, where are they now?"

They are probably in the neighborhood of Annotok, where, rich in the weapons and stores I handed over to them, they will be regarded as Arctic millionaires.

"Do you think they could be depended upon?"

Yes, I think so. They are not, of course, scientific witnesses, in the modern sense. But they have the science of the Polar Sea at their finger end – the natural science of the man who is the evolved product of the Arctic region. I would much rather trust a good Eskimo to give a clear, intelligible account of the polar region across which he has traveled more than any ordinary European. I do not know whether they will be found, but their report of my journey will be very good evidence – Eskimo evidence no doubt. But I only wish I had them here with me to tell you our story in their own way.

From his interviews and observations, Stead had concluded that, mistaken though Cook may be, he was not "a fakir, a liar [or] a deliberate scoundrel who set forth to make a fool of the whole human race." And his reason? Because Cook was "both too honest and too limited to have conceived so colossal a fraud."

This appears to have been the impression not only of the majority of Stead's fellow reporters, but the consensus also of the Council of the Royal Danish Geographical Society whose president, in the presence of the royal family, presented the Society's silver medal to Cook after his lecture at the Concert Palais on 7th September, and the following evening, after Cook answered satisfactorily some questions put to him by Professor Stromgren of the University Department of Astronomy, it was announced that King Frederick, President of the University, had given his assent to the award of an honorary doctorate to the explorer. So generous indeed had been the voices raised in support of honouring Cook that the *"J'accuse"* articles of Philip Gibbs, a feature writer on the London *Daily Chronicle*, and the outspoken disgust of Peter Freuchen, the Danish polar explorer, were simply brushed aside.

Meanwhile, Peary was still at Indian Harbor, Labrador, keeping the wires busy before sailing on to Battle Harbor. There was a message to his wife which read:

Indian Harbor via Cape Ray
Sept. 8, 1909

Mrs. R. E. Peary,
   Good morning. Delayed by gale leaving early this morning. Don't let any Cook's lies disturb you. I have him nailed.

Bert

Another he sent out to the Associated Press on 7th September: "Cook's story should not be taken too seriously. The two Eskimos who accompanied him say he went no distance north and not out of sight of land. Other members of the tribe corroborate their story."

He sent one also to his sponsoring newspaper, the *New York Times*, which they printed on 11th September, advising:

Do not trouble about Cook's story or attempt to explain any discrepancies in his statements. The affair will settle itself. He has not been at the pole on April 21st, 1908, or at any other time. He has simply handed the public a gold brick.

These statements are made advisedly, and I have proof of them. When he makes a full statement of his journey over his signature to some geographical society or other reputable body, if that statement contains the claim that he has reached the pole, I shall be in a position to furnish material that may prove distinctly interesting reading for the public.

Robert E. Peary

He even sent one to Cook's sponsoring newspaper saying: "Do not imagine *Herald* likely to be imposed upon by Cook story," followed of course by the same denunciation he had sent to the *New York Times*. All of these messages took precedence over his own eagerly awaited report, much to the dismay of Bridgman in New York who was frantically trying to get a message through to Peary urging him to hold fire as his attack on Cook was doing more damage to himself than it was to the man he was attacking.

It was one of the most sensational news items in the history of journalism. Within a space of only nine days, the "Goal of Centuries," as the *New York Times* called it, had been claimed by two men and one of these heroes by implication was calling his rival a liar. The public could not get enough of the story, but not until 9th September did Peary send out any information of his own achievement, and even this was only a "brief summary," as he described it, some 270 words to be "printed exactly as written." He had on the same day filed the first part of his full story which ran to some 7,300 words; but it was to take two days to transmit it all, and the full, unabridged and unedited version was not to appear in the *New York Times* until 12th September, by which time Jo and her children and Herbert Bridgman were all at Sydney awaiting the arrival of the *Roosevelt*.

"Her happiness was clearly evident to all," said the *New York Times*; but in her confusion she had let her guard slip by admitting, " 'We have been married twenty-three years.' And after a pause, 'we have lived but three.' "

Her letter to Peary of 12th September from Sydney expressed the hurt that she was hiding:

> Sweetheart, Sweetheart, after all your privations and sacrifices now when you should be showered with honors and have everything your own way, this miserable creature causes a disturbance which can't help but annoy you and take from the pleasure of your success. I am nearly crazy and have been since Sept. 1st when the news first came. If you only can keep still and not discuss this creature until you have had an opportunity to see what he and others have said it would be far better. Oh to know what is best.

That letter was carried on what Barton W. Currie, the Staff Correspondent of the *New York World*, was to describe in his despatch of 19th September as "probably the most unusual voyage of newspapermen to any given point in this hemisphere to obtain an interview." Thirty-two journalists had set out from North Sydney on an 850-mile voyage to Battle Harbor, aboard the cable-laying steamer *Tyrian*. It was eight o'clock on the morning of 16th September when, as Barton Currie describes it:

> Three whaleboat loads of reporters and photographers swept down on the *Roosevelt* like so many boarding parties of pirates, swarming over the sides by ladders or ropes or anything handy, and one little chap from Boston taking a header into icy waters.
>
> Peary was in his cabin when the boarding parties arrived. As he stepped out on to the broad afterdeck he faced the muzzles of a dozen cameras, and what might have appeared to him as the onslaught of an eager band come to strip him of his secrets and tear down the wall of resistance he had erected against certain mysteries involved in his dash

to the North Pole, and his denial that Dr. Frederick A. Cook had beaten him to it.

But as Peary stepped out from his cabin and squared his broad shoulders back against the mizzenmast of the *Roosevelt*, the eyes of all the boarding journalists were suddenly drawn to the American flag that fluttered above. This seemed to have an electrical effect upon both cameramen and scribes, and before a word was spoken to Peary three rousing cheers were sent up for him. He bowed to this and smiled from ear to ear, showing every one of his big strong teeth, that are almost wolfish in their set and grip as he talks.

Peary's appearance and attire were not wanting in picturesqueness. Indeed, he looked a good deal like a dramatized miner, in his square cut blue flannel shirt, rough black trousers and huge brimmed sombrero. His sandy mustache bristled out on both sides like two rough brushes twisted to a point. There was a two days' growth upon his cheek. But his skin was as clear as a woman's and remarkably smooth for a man of his years. Every inch of him, every ounce of him was hard as Bessemer steel; his muscles danced and squirmed under his shirt as he moved and breathed. Whenever he spoke he heaved out his great chest, gestured slightly with his freckled, well kept hands, and made a peculiar gurgling sound in his throat, his Adam's apple sticking out in the loose flesh as if it had been a lump of coal.

Peary greeted each of the boarding party, but then "begged to be excused while he read a dozen letters that had been brought to him," promising that he would grant an hour's interview later. This took place in the loft of Trader Croucher's store. There were no chairs, only one small bench, and piled around were casks and heaps of cod nets and trawling traps.

Peary entered the room with Capt. Dickson of the *Tyrian* and Capt. Robert A. Bartlett, skipper of the *Roosevelt* and, sitting between them, enthroned himself on a pile of nets. A deep circle of reporters perched themselves on other piles of nets and on casks, and squatted on the floor. The room was filled to capacity, and no smoking was permitted because of the inflammable character of the merchandise heaped about . . .

The sunlight that streamed into the low windows of the loft was as brilliant as the concentrated rays of a spotlight, cutting out vivid paths on the floor and giving a peculiarly stagey effect to the first general interview that the discoverer of the North Pole had granted. Peary's big, sandy head, his ever pulsating muscles and constantly working nostrils stood out in a shaft of this vivid sunlight with cameo sharpness. A Labrador gale, uncanny in the brilliant sunlight, whistled and groaned and snarled with wolfish howls at the eaves. The scene was one that cut itself indelibly into the mind.

Commander Peary puffed out his chest with a deep inhale of breath as he squared off for the first question of the interview. His smile vanished for a moment as he noted the reference to Cook in the first sally:

"Commander Peary, after you left Cape Sheridan, did you see anything to indicate the existence of 30,000 square miles of land?"

Peary's jaws opened and shut with a snap, and he replied:

"I have not said that in my statement."

"Then there is no land there?" was asked.

"I did not see any. I have said that I saw none."

Peary was then asked if he had found any evidence of Cook having been there before him.

"There was not the slightest indication of Cook or any one else."

This was said with a vehemence that approached a snarl.

"Is it possible," broke in another of the interviewers, "that Cook might have been there and you not have found any evidence of him?"

"Yes," said Peary with another snap of the jaws, then checked himself suddenly and put up his hand. "Wait a moment. I said yes – but let me put it this way. Without reference to Cook, I will say that there are hundreds of routes outside of mine any one of which could have been taken by a reputable explorer with a well-equipped expedition, and have left no traces which I would have noticed."

As Peary settled back with a grim smile this question was suddenly sprung:

"Is it possible to fake observations of the Pole so as to deceive scientists?"

Peary stood up, and while the muscles of his face worked convulsively, snapped back:

"In the opinion of Admiral Sir George Nares of the British Navy, Admiral Melville of the United States Navy, and myself, it would have been possible for a skillful man to fake observations of the Pole, even to the extent of deceiving scientists."

Just as another question was being put Commander Peary broke in with a nervous gesture and said:

"Now we are getting on this question of Cook, and I want to tell you where I stand so that you won't ask me any more questions of this kind. I repeat what I have said that Dr. Cook had not been at the Pole ... Now, I do not propose to answer that any further or to produce my proof until there is a properly authorized statement by Dr. Cook himself before a reliable disinterested party."

Top: Dr Cook at the banquet in Copenhagen on 6th September, 1909 moments after the announcement that Peary had reached the North Pole. Captain Otto Sverdrup is left of Cook. Left: Cook's summit picture of Mount McKinley with the tell-tale peak showing mid-right of picture. Bottom: the Mount McKinley massif with the fake Peak in mid-foreground. Bottom right inset: Cook in 1906.

Frederick A Co

Top: the picture Cook claimed was taken at the North Pole on 21st April, 1908, but the Eskimo on the left is wearing muskox skin Kamiks [boots] which were made during the following winter.

Right: Cook's picture of a "submerged island of Polar Sea" 120 miles from the North Pole, as it appears in his book. Above: same picture printed to the edge of the original plate shows it to be a glacier with land on the right.

Above: Cook's "Bradley Land" is not an ice island, but a photograph taken on the west coast of Axel Heiberg Island.

Above: portrait of Dr Frederick A. Cook, from a drawing by the author.

Above: Cook's winter den at what he called
Cape Sparbo.

Above: Cook's two boys hunting musk-oxen
near their winter den.

Inset: Jo greeting Peary on board the *Roosevelt* at Sydney.
Below: Peary later addressing a crowd.

Above: Peary presenting his proofs to the National Geographic Society's subcommittee (left to right: Grosvenor, Tittmann, Moore, Peary, Gannett and Chester).

Pictures taken during Peary's triumphant medal collecting tour of Europe. Top right: the special gold medal presented to Peary by the Royal Geographical Society.

Peary's home on his beloved Eagle Island—his "sanctuary" as he called it. Bottom: the Peary family.

Peary was to leave behind him in the Arctic two sons, the younger, Kali, being the father of Peter (above) who sledged to the North Pole twice.

Rear-Admiral Robert E. Peary – explorer. Born 6th May, 1856, died 20th February, 1920.

Peary was asked about his own observations at the Pole, and replied that he was not prepared to discuss them beyond a certain point, that point being his observation at 89°57'. "I took other observations beyond that point, but I am not at liberty to say just what I observed when I made sure I was at the Pole."

Currie tells us that Peary indulged in a peculiar smile before explaining that "under the peculiar circumstances" he did not feel inclined to give any information as to what he had observed of the conditions at the Pole "until other statements as to the conditions at the Pole have been submitted." He was asked if one of his marches of forty miles in twelve hours was not exceptionally fast travelling for the Arctic, to which Peary with "his usual click of the teeth, as if biting off the subject forever" had replied: "The speed from the eighty-eighth parallel to the Pole was not fast for me, but would have been very fast for any other expedition."

In the same edition of the *New York World* was printed a statement from Dr. Cook on board the *Oscar II* bound for New York, which read in part:

> Why should Peary be allowed to make himself a self-imposed dictator of my affairs? In justice to himself, in justice to the world and to guard the honor of national prestige, he should be compelled to prove his own case; he should publish at once a preliminary narrative, to be compared with mine, and let fair-minded people ponder over the matter while the final records by which our case may eventually be proved are being prepared.
>
> I know Peary the explorer. As such he is a hero in Arctic annals and deserves the credit of a long and hard record. To Peary the explorer I am still willing to tip my hat, but Peary's unfounded accusations have disclosed another side to his character, which will never be forgotten.

The *Oscar II* dropped anchor on the morning of 21st September. For Cook it was the start of an extraordinary day. New York and Brooklyn paid homage with ten thousand people at the dockside to greet him, a motorcade of three hundred cars, a reception at the Bushwick Club and a banquet that evening. It was, as the report in the *Herald* said, a "demonstration of popular confidence and enthusiasm without parallel in the history of this city." Even the *New York Times* conceded that the sincerity of the welcome "could not be doubted," that New York was proud of him.

On that same day, after a delay that no one has ever satisfactorily been able to explain, the *Roosevelt* reached Sydney. Marie Peary recalls:

> Some friends of Mother's took her, with Robert and me, on board their yacht, the *Sheelah*, and we steamed out to meet Dad.
> I will never forget our first sight of the *Roosevelt*, silhouetted against

the brown cliffs of the shore. She was dressed in all her signal flags; the flag of the Peary Arctic Club flew from the foremast; my father's personal flag was at the stern; the Stars and Stripes at the main mast; and from the mizzen top flew a huge red, white and blue flag with the words "North Pole" diagonally across it.

The *Sheelah* lowered a boat and we were set across to the *Roosevelt*. I can't remember any of the details of that day except that everyone was in wild spirits and Dad was here, there and everywhere, looking happier and prouder than I had ever seen him look.

And yet from Barton Currie we see a different Peary, an angry and bitter man, muzzled and weakened, in his view, by the counsel of Hubbard and Bridgman. "'What I have to say,' said Peary with an inflection that was almost a snarl, 'will not be long delayed, you may rest assured on that score.'" But then dutifully he had dictated to the disappointed journalists the wisely prepared announcement:

> Acting on the advice of General Hubbard and Mr. Bridgman, the president and secretary of the Peary Arctic Club, I wish to express my thanks to all my friends for their kind offers and invitations, and also to beg to say that I prefer to accept no invitation to a public reception or ovation until the present controversy has been settled by competent authority.

Through the eyes of his daughter the train journey home to Eagle Island was "a triumphal tour." But through Peary's eyes, the cheering crowds on the station platforms who had gathered to see the hero pass by, and even the fifty thousand people who in Portland, Maine, had "lined the streets and yelled themselves hoarse," were blurred by the bitterness which in the privacy of his home was finally to engulf him.

CHAPTER 19

The Tarnished Prize

On the very same day that Peary sent his triumphant message from Indian Harbor, Labrador, there had appeared in the *New York Sun* a story from a place which to most New Yorkers probably seemed as remote:

> Butte, Mont,
> Sept. 5

> Fred Printz, a well-known guide and resident of Darby, Mont., takes the present occasion to charge Dr. Cook with fraud. In part of his allegations he is supported by Ed. Barrim [Barrille], another guide . . . Both men allege that Dr. Cook did not place a foot on Mt. McKinley, but that lower peaks were climbed and photos taken of smaller mountains in order to deceive the public. Printz in an interview says:
>
> "I am just as sure as I'm living that Dr. Cook never saw the North Pole. Any man who would make the representations he did as to his alleged ascent of Mt. McKinley is capable of making statements credited to him in the press about the North Pole achievement."

The timing and wording of the story had, however, aroused a certain amount of suspicion that Printz, who was an "untutored horse-packer," had probably been inspired and helped by someone with a vested interest in casting doubt upon the integrity of Dr. Cook, and it may well have been, as Cook's biographer Freeman implies, that Printz had made his attack on Cook at the suggestion of General Thomas H. Hubbard. He may even have been offered a financial inducement to tell his story to the *New York Sun*.

Being a shrewd observer of the public mind and seeing the public response to Cook, Hubbard had not the slightest doubt that this was a contest that would have to be fought solely on the word of each man. Peary had offered him and the Club no other weapon with which to fight, or so at least they had thought at that time. From the first report their man had sent out which had given the names of those he had taken on his final heroic dash to the Pole, it was obvious to all of Peary's supporters that his claim was no stronger than that of his rival, since the only proof that either man had was the observations they had taken themselves. Indeed, Peary's case, in the minds of many, was already regarded as the weaker of the two as a result of his somewhat unfortunate comment that the party he had chosen to go with him to the Pole was "as loyal and responsive to [his] will as the fingers of [his] right hand." The comment, absurdly proud though it was and entirely in character, naturally attracted suspicion.

Faced with this problem, Hubbard had no choice but to silence Peary with the threat that the Club could only help him win his laurels if he resisted every public temptation to speak his mind. In the meantime they would rebuild his image as an honest, strong, and silent hero, while at the same time, and in great secrecy, working upon the weaknesses and the record of his rival.

It was a tactic which Fitzhugh Green described somewhat euphemistically as a control of the "proper sort of publicity necessary to present the dignity of the truth." But although the tactic effectively restricted Peary's public appearances, it had not protected him from the remarks that almost daily hurt his pride when his mail brought packages of newspaper clippings and abusive letters from total strangers, nor had that tactic provided Peary with any outlet for the rage which his family and his closest friends were alarmed to see was threatening to destroy him. Even with Hubbard and Bridgman now in control of affairs, the situation had to get worse before their actions had any effect. Aside from which, as they both knew, the timing of the destruction of Cook was absolutely crucial.

Accordingly, Hubbard made the following impartial-sounding pronouncement in the *New York Times* on 24th September:

> Concerning Dr. Cook, I would say, let him submit his records and data to some competent authority, and let that authority draw its own conclusions from the notes and records taken in the field ... All that is wanted is the data and records made in the Arctic. Competent authority will determine from them where Dr. Cook has been. I may say that Commander Peary will also be expected to turn over his data and observations for the same purpose.

Nothing could sound fairer than that. Hubbard knew, however, at the time, that this would put Cook at a disadvantage since the doctor had laid much stress on the fact that his "proofs" were on their way home with Whitney, and Hubbard had been informed by Peary that this was most unlikely.

Cook was still riding the crest of his wave on 26th September when he had received a telegram from Whitney sent from Indian Harbor:

"Started for home *Roosevelt* . . . Peary would allow nothing belonging to you on board. Said to leave everything in cache Etah."

This news, coming close on the heels of the attacks of Peary and the horse-packer Printz, hit Cook hard. He had promised the University of Copenhagen that he would send them proofs of his claim in order that they might have the privilege of examining and confirming them, but he was to confess later that, "disturbed by the growing uncertainty of proving such a claim to the point of hair-breadth accuracy by any figures, despair overcame me." He confesses also that in that state of mental depression he had "desperate premonitions." And yet, asked at the time if he feared that his claim might be rejected by the Danes if he was unable to submit all of his data, he had been calmly evasive. "The scientists are the ones to say. It would not do for me to offer an opinion."

The sportsman Harry Whitney almost immediately upon returning had plunged into seclusion. "This young hunter," as Barton Currie tells, "who would think nothing of pursuing a family of polar bears up the icy steeps of a glacier, palpably trembled at the mention of either Cook or Peary."

Whitney was in a position to clear up a good deal of controversy over what had happened up at Etah and had already stated that he considered Dr. Cook "the gamest sort of explorer and believed his story." His manner, however, had also revealed "an undefined fear of Commander Peary." He was desperately anxious to come down to New York to see Peary about the disposition of his trophies, but feared he might bump into Dr. Cook before he saw Peary, and he did not want Peary to think he had gone first to Cook. "If only something else will turn up that will make them forget me," said the young man, "I will be happy. I have been dragged into this thing by the neck. If any one will show me a quick way out of it I will take it – provided that way does not lead north again. Hunting Arctic game is great sport, but I've had my fill of it."

Peary was quick off the mark with a signed statement to counter and silence the charge that he had been aware of the nature of the material belonging to Cook that he had ordered should be put ashore:

> I cannot conceive it possible for a man under the circumstances to have left such priceless things out of his sight for an instant. As he went across Melville Bay to Danish Greenland with three or four sledges and teams of dogs, his instruments, his records, and his flags would scarcely have added a feather weight to the burden.

So outraged, however, was the general public by the seemingly churlish behaviour of Peary in refusing to take Cook's property aboard, they did not question which of these two explorers was the more responsible. They saw only a loser demeaning himself by shouting "fraud," a distinguished explorer demanding "proofs" from his dignified rival, knowing full well that the proofs demanded could not be produced. Peary's popularity at this point was just about at its lowest ebb, and the strain of preparing for the ordeal of presenting his diary and observations to a "competent authority," as Hubbard had suggested, and frustration at what he was reading about his rival, was driving him dangerously close to the edge.

Vilhjalmur Stefansson, a friend of the family, confided much later to Walter Sullivan, the Science Editor of the *New York Times*, that:

Peary had suffered a mental breakdown, and his condition, which in those days would have been considered a disgrace, was kept secret. Much of the subsequent controversy would have been prevented had Peary's illness been acknowledged, but Peary's wife had extracted a promise of silence from Stefansson in her lifetime, and according to Stefansson, her daughter Marie "practically exacted the same pledge."

Stefansson did not say when this breakdown occurred, but the statement does have a ring of truth, for Peary undoubtedly was under great stress, and there was probably only one occasion over the next two years when he was under a heavier strain than during those three weeks after sending his triumphant message flashing over the world.

He was, we know, deeply hurt by the poll conducted by the *Pittsburgh Press*, the results of which were published on 26th September. Over 76,000 readers responded to the call from the editor to send in their votes on which of the two explorers they believed, and an astonishing ninety-six per cent had given their vote to Cook. Even more disheartening for Peary was that seventy-six per cent of those readers did not believe he had reached the Pole, an indication if ever there was one of the public's preference for a hero who either has no axe to grind, or grinds it out of sight. Maybe it was the way the questions were posed, but it is interesting that it did not even cross the mind of a single one of those 76,000 voters to challenge the claims of both men. It was simply one or the other.

Three days after that poll was published, a letter addressed to Herbert Bridgman was released for publication. It was from Prof. Ralph Stockman Tarr who had been with Peary on his 1896 summer meteorite expedition, but it was in response to a request on another matter:

I have your letter of September 22 and shall gladly do what little I can to further the inquiry regarding Cook's claim to have climbed Mt. McKinley . . . I was informed by a number of people that the prospector, Ed Burrill [Barrille] . . . admitted to his friends that they never got above 5,000 feet and that he jokes about the way in which the public has been fooled.

The public, who do not like being fooled, were suddenly aroused and eager for more information from Barrille, and from anyone else who might throw more light on the claims of the now enigmatic Dr. Cook, and they did not have long to wait. On 4th October, Barrille's affidavit was notarised and brought to New York by General James Ashton, a lawyer retained by Hubbard "to obtain all information possible regarding the disputed ascent of Mount McKinley by Dr. Cook." On 29th September (the same day that Bridgman had released Tarr's letter for publication) the Board of Governors of the Explorers' Club passed a resolution to appoint a committee "to secure and consider all evidence obtainable bearing on the claim of Dr. F. A. Cook, that he had reached the summit of Mt. McKinley, and that the committee ascertain if possible whether or not Dr. Cook reached the summit of Mt. McKinley as claimed." At the first meeting of that committee, and in spite of their decision "that no information respecting the work of the committee be given out," the *New York Times* reported that they had "perused a 'batch of letters' showing that Cook had falsified his claim to have ascended Mount McKinley, and announced that Hubbard had 'been working on this line of evidence.' "

Then came the two devastating releases of the Peary Arctic Club, their trump cards, so to speak. The first, published in the *New York Times* on 13th October was the statement of Cook's two Eskimo companions that they had, while on the so-called journey to the North Pole with Cook, never been out of sight of land. The second, published the following day in the *New York Globe*, Hubbard's paper, was the Barrille affidavit which stated:

1 That at no time did Cook and he get nearer than 14 miles in an air line from the top of Mount McKinley.
2 That the photograph of the summit published in *To the Top of the Continent* was a peak 8,000 feet high and "not less than 20 miles in an air line distance from the top of the mountain."
3 That he [Barrille] kept a diary and in the part covering the ascent Cook forced him to leave a blank space which Barrille filled in with false entries dictated by Cook.

Cook had boldly and publicly challenged this statement and announced that he would himself finance an expedition to return to Mt. McKinley and retrieve the record he had left on the summit. This was, however, an idea born of desperation. Even his friend the Arctic explorer Anthony Fiala had declined to support it, as had also Prof. Herschel Parker, the co-organiser of the 1906 attempt, who was already on record as saying that "Cook has not made a satisfactory explanation of Mount McKinley." Parker in any case was at that time planning with Belmore Browne an expedition to the same mountain to locate the peak which Cook had photographed and claimed as the summit. Then came the affidavits of Printz and Miller who had also been with Cook on the McKinley expedition, and a statement by Russell Porter supporting them. All of Cook's men were against him, and so too now was the press:

"Smashed is Dr. Cook by the sworn narrative of Edward N. Barrille," stated the *Globe*, "The similarities between the Mount McKinley hoax and the North Pole hoax are readily discernible." And from the *New York Times*, "this witness to whom Dr. Cook appealed for support in his Mount McKinley story testifies against him, just as the Eskimos to whose testimony he appeals testify against him."

Cook presented himself at the Explorers' Club to defend his claim on 17th October; but it was an ordeal he felt obliged to cut short, declining to testify on the grounds that "his hardships in the long polar night had affected his memory." He had requested a month's time in which to get together his records, and had then returned to the lecture trail. But by now he was beginning to feel persecuted:

> On every side I sensed hostility; the sight of crowds filled me with a growing sort of terror. I did not realize at the time that I was passing from periods of mental depression to dangerous periods of nervous tension. I was pursued by reporters, people with craning necks, good-natured demonstrations of friendliness that irritated me. In the trains I viewed the whirling landscape without, and felt myself part of it – as a delirious man swept and hurtled through space.
>
> . . . Really, as I view myself from the angle of the present, I marvel that a man so distraught did not do desperate things.

But he did. In one last bid, as Freeman says, to "stem the tide that was about to engulf him," he arranged while on a western tour to give a free lecture in Hamilton, Montana, on 28th October, and through an agent had publicly announced that he would give his version of the Mount McKinley story, and then meet Ed Barrille "face to face and answer any charges which his former guide cares to make." It was a disastrous and naive misjudgement.

That evening in the packed Opera House proved to be one of the most incredible and bizarre events in the history of the town. People had come from miles around to see the steam rise from the contestants, for no one had come just to hear Cook's North Pole lecture. But at the end of this Cook appeared to be ducking out of a confrontation. He professed his veracity, taxed his accusers with accepting "more than thirty pieces of silver," then concluded: "For the present I am willing to trust my case to the citizens of Montana as a jury. After you have read the mass of testimony my counsel has collected, I am ready to abide by your verdict."

To cries of outrage from the audience, Cook had then prepared to leave the platform. But Barrille and Printz, in the company of their lawyers, had come to see action and, prodded by his friends, Barrille got to his feet and asked for permission to contradict the explorer. Cook's idea of a trial was evidently very different to that of his jury, for he turned and angrily replied to his former climbing partner: "I've got the Opera House tonight, and if you want to talk tomorrow night, you can hire it."

There was uproar. Several of the audience demanded that their man should be heard, and in no time "there were twenty people ... on the stage, each trying to talk at once." But Cook had refused to debate with a rabble and, clearly shaken by the experience, retired back-stage, a tragic man, and now a frightened and a trapped one, for there was no back door by which he could escape. Meanwhile the editor of the *Anaconda Standard* called for a resolution condemning the doctor, and the Senator for Montana, Joseph A. Dixon, went back-stage to talk with Cook and persuaded him to come out on to the platform to face the men who were accusing him. "If I were Dr. Cook," the Senator declared, coming out ahead of Cook, "I would not leave the State of Montana without cross-examining these men."

And so began a brawl of abuse and accusations which, at the insistence of Barrille and the loud support of all of his friends, produced a statement from Cook, written out there and then and submitted to the hostile crowd: "I have stated," he said, holding the note up for all to see, and shouting now to make himself heard. "I have written it out, made an affidavit that we have been at the top of Mount McKinley. After I have said that, the evening is at an end and I do not care to stay any longer."

But the crowd were wanting more than this and even the Senator commented accusingly: "If he doesn't care to hear the other side, why certainly he can retire. But if it were me and my reputation was at stake, I would stay here until morning." Cook, however, had no choice, and although he fought to the bitter end, the final resolution of that assembly was crushing.

We, the people of Ravalli County, Montana, assembled at Hamilton, after patiently listening to the charges and counter-charges that have been exchanged by the parties to the Mount McKinley controversy, do declare our belief in the veracity and statement of Ed Barrille and Fred Printz.

It had been a black month for the doctor with only one small ray of light which had appeared in the form of a letter in the *New York Times* on 21st October, a week after the publication of the shattering statement of his two Eskimo companions. That letter from the Danish explorer, Knud Rasmussen, appeared at first to repudiate the statement taken from Cook's two boys, and even today it is still considered to do so by the devout supporters of Cook on the grounds that Rasmussen, who spoke the language fluently, was the first explorer to visit the tribe after Cook had set off on his journey south to Upernavik.

"No one in the world can name him a swindler," Rasmussen had stated. But he also said that during his stay in the Cape York region "I did not meet Dr. Cook's two companions ... and the information I could get from the other polar Eskimos was therefore only second hand." So how far north was he told Cook and his two companions had gone by the Eskimos at Cape York?

> The Eskimos, of course, cannot give the distance in figures, but they say that on the journey over the ice field from the shore the sun began to appear and stood high in the sky, and at last did not disappear at all, so that it was almost Summer before they reached land again.

But this is merely a reference to the phenomenon of the midnight sun. Had Cook and his two boys been at the Pole, his companions would have told a different story for they would have noticed what no other men had seen before, that they had reached a point where the sun appeared to remain at the same altitude throughout its full journey "around" their camp.

Rasmussen's intervention had therefore done little materially to support the claim of Cook, or to check the alarming pace at which Cook found himself, by the end of October, heading directly towards disaster.

Peary meanwhile, having pulled back with the help of his friends from the brink of a very similar disaster, was now feeling safer and far more confident in his guides, for although at a meeting on 1st October the Board of Managers of the National Geographic Society had stated the Society "could accept the personal statements of neither Commander Peary nor Dr. Cook that the pole had been reached, without investigation by its Committee of Research or by a scientific body acceptable to it," moves were already afoot in the Peary camp further to embarrass Cook by publicly accepting the suggestion of the National Geographic Society that *both* explorers should "speedily submit their observations to a competent scientific commission in the United States." One of these moves was a telegram from Hubbard to Prof. Ira Remsen, President of the National Academy of Sciences, which was of course published in the *New York Times*: "Peary willing and desirous to submit all his records and data to National Academy Committee or other scientists impartially selected."

As expected, Cook had declined this invitation on the grounds that he had already promised that his data would be sent first to the University of Copenhagen. As was also expected, Prof. Remsen found a suitable excuse for not involving himself and the National Academy of Sciences which was not due to meet until late November. His off-the-record reason was that there was too much bitterness and temper swirling around the Cook–Peary affair. Thus the way was now left clear for the National Geographic Society to act, and their justification for doing so on the face of it seemed reasonable:

In view of the fact that Commander Peary had been waiting since his return in September to submit his records to a scientific commission in the United States, the National Geographic Society believed it should receive his papers without further delay in order that his claim of having reached the pole might be passed upon.

They also sent off a telegram to the University of Copenhagen on 15th October requesting a waiver of their first claims to Cook's observations, a request which, not surprisingly, was rejected by the Danes. On the same date they also sent a telegram to Peary: "Board of National Geographic Society wishes to act on your expedition at regular meeting next Wednesday [20th October]. Can you not immediately forward us sufficient records to justify action then?"

Peary replied immediately: "Will have material in Washington by Wednesday. That I trust will serve the Society's purpose." But he did not send the "sufficient records" requested. He merely sent a Portland attorney with certain papers which, as it was later recorded during the Peary Hearings, "brought the record up to the time that Bartlett left him." Whether Peary had really been hoping that information would be sufficient we have no way of being certain. The *New York Times* of 21st October stated that Peary would not be asked to appear in person "unless some unforeseen tangle over the records should arise." The National Geographic Society's record of the meeting of their Board of Managers on 20th October appears to foresee no such tangle: "the records and observations and proof of Commander Robert E. Peary that he reached the Pole April 6, 1909, were submitted to the Society."

From this it would appear that the Society had already decided that his proofs were acceptable in advance of seeing the crucial data. The Society did, however, appoint a three-man "sub-committee of experts" to study Peary's records and observations, and in a press release they were named as Mr. Henry Gannett, Chairman of the Committee on Research, Chief Geographer of the US Geological Survey; Rear-Admiral Colby M. Chester, "who has been known for many years as one of the best and most particular navigators in the service;" and Mr. O. H. Tittmann, Superintendent of the US Coast and Geodetic Survey.

What the press release did not mention was that all three men were admirers of Peary; all three had been members of the dinner committee of the 1906 banquet at which Peary had been awarded the first Hubbard Gold Medal of the Society; all three had been members of the Committee of Research when, in 1907, $1,000 from the Society's Research Fund was voted as a token contribution towards the very expedition the claims of which they were now appointed to assess, and that Rear-Admiral Chester was a member of the Peary Arctic Club and an outspoken critic of Cook. Moreover, they all believed that Peary had reached the North Pole in advance of seeing the crucial data. Mr. Gannett was challenged on this very point during the Peary Hearings and had replied: "Every one who knows Peary by reputation knows he would not lie; I know him by reputation."

They had nevertheless felt obliged to ask Peary to submit the remainder of his "proofs" in order that they could present "a complete and impartial report," material which Gannett seems to have believed that Peary would have sent in the first place had he been able "to leave his home at that time in order to attend the committee." So why had he been unable to attend? He does not appear to have been too busy, judging by his letter of 28th October to Gilbert H. Grosvenor of the National Geographic Society:

> Mrs. Peary and I are not worrying or being disturbed to the extent that you and others doubtless imagine. As you are aware, I never was in this thing for money, so that Cook's reported success in that direction is not troubling me. Nor is his apparent hold on the illiterate public . . .
>
> The quiet, undisturbed time which I am now having is very pleasant to me. It is particularly agreeable to have this opportunity after so many years of effort, of being with my wife and children in our island home, with no thought of the future to disturb either of us, and with the feeling of intense satisfaction and content that results from having done the thing that one has started out to do.

But was he really enjoying a "quiet and undisturbed time" on Eagle Island? His daughter Marie tells us: "It was hard to get Dad to talk much about his feelings when he reached the Pole." It was surely hard also to prepare himself for that crucial meeting in Washington on 1st November at which his diary and his observations at Camp Jesup would have to be shown.

He need not have been anxious about the outcome, for those three men who had been appointed to the embarrassing task of questioning him were totally in awe of the man. Here is Gannett's account of their meeting, as recorded at the later Peary Hearings.

> Mr. Peary came from his home near Portland, Maine, and brought his records in a gripsack and his instruments in a trunk. First he met the committee at the office of the Geographic Society and we appointed a meeting at the house of Admiral Chester, who was a member of this committee. We simply sat down with him and read his journal from his original records; he had an original record made in a little book, a notebook, you know, at that time, and it had all the earmarks of being the original. He read the journal over two or three days before Bartlett left him, we all read it together; we included in the reading two or three days which Bartlett was with him, and from that time on to the Pole and all of the way back to Cape Columbia. We also had his astronomical observations recomputed, examined them, not recomputed, for he had already computed them on these sheets. He had one sheet for a set of observations, and Admiral Chester recomputed them; I do not know whether Mr. Tittmann did or not, I do not remember; we had this line of soundings; the tidal observations I never saw.
>
> I saw no longitude observations, and my understanding is he didn't make any; I do not see why he should. He kept his direction by the compass and the direction of the sun at noontime, and his purpose was to go north.

Both Gannett and Tittmann had admitted that the North Pole observations could have been faked, and that their "belief in the personal honesty of Peary" had entered into the findings of their committee. It was also admitted that "no effort was made by [their] committee to interrogate Henson to verify in any way the statements made by Peary," and that the instruments had been "examined . . . down at the station that evening without moving the trunk." And so it would appear, as Mr. Roberts pointed out during the Peary Hearings, that the explorer had presented his case "in the house of his friends, so to speak," and that the committee appointed to examine his data "were prejudiced in his favor." Indeed, their decision to approve Peary's claim had almost certainly been made before Peary caught his train that very evening, since out of respect for the man they would clearly have had no desire to keep him in suspense over a matter of such immense concern to him personally. And their official verdict? This was received by the Board of Managers of the National Geographic Society on 4th November:

> Commander Peary has submitted to this subcommittee his original journal and records of observations, together with all his instruments

and apparatus and certain of the most important of the scientific results of his expedition. These have been carefully examined by your subcommittee, and they are unanimously of the opinion that Commander Peary reached the North Pole on April 6, 1909.

They also feel warranted in stating that the organization, planning, and management of the expedition, its complete success, and its scientific results reflect the greatest credit on the ability of Commander Robert E. Peary and render him worthy of the highest honors that the National Geographic Society can bestow upon him.

> Henry Gannett
> C. M. Chester
> O. H. Tittmann

The report was of course unanimously approved, and it was resolved that a special gold medal be awarded to Peary. It was also resolved that another "sub-committee of experts" should immediately look into the question of whether or not anyone had reached the North Pole prior to 1909. To this end the Society sent off a telegram to the University of Copenhagen which read:

The National Geographic Society is about to send representatives to Copenhagen. As our committee has access to the original records of Commander Peary, we respectfully request the University of Copenhagen to grant them the courtesy of being present at the official examination of Dr. Cook's papers.

The Danes, however, were not impressed, since according to their inquiries the National Geographic Society "had no scientific standing whatsoever" which led them to regard the offer "as little less than an insult."

Cook was now faced with the seemingly impossible task of persuading a special commission of the University of Copenhagen to pronounce favourably upon his own claim, and on 20th November, in a now desperate effort to hold off rejection, he had written to Prof. Torp, Rector of the University, requesting that his material should be considered as a preliminary report, pending the return of his instruments and notes from Etah. In the meantime he had become entangled in a web of problems created by two men who later were to claim that Cook had employed them to fake a set of observations which he could send to Copenhagen. Cook maintained that George Dunkle and August Loose had merely been employed to recompute his own observations as a check, and that when they came up with a completely new set of faked observations, he had thrown the men and their observations out of his hotel room. But this incident, together with his absolute conviction that he was being followed by private detectives, and the numerous letters, "all telling in more or less plausible form of plots to steal his records and even murder him if possible," had cracked his nerve.

On 24th November, he found himself with a chance to escape. Cook's loyal secretary, Walter Lonsdale, tells the story:

On arriving in New York, we were successful for the first time in shaking off our shadowers, and the doctor suddenly exclaimed to me:

"Lonsdale, here is a chance of getting away unnoticed, and I'm going to take it."

We ran for a streetcar which was already in motion, boarded it, and went with it as far as Thirty-third Street, where we got off and entered the subway, making sure that we were not being followed. We left the train at Bleeker Street, slipping out just before the last door was closed, and from there we made our way up a circuitous route to the Pennsylvania Station.

I bought en route, at the request of Dr. Cook, a pair of scissors, a safety razor, and some black paste for touching up the face. Entering a cafe, the explorer took off his mustache, and we then proceeded to a barber shop, where we had his hair cut short. In the meantime I had bought a black slouch hat and, entering a second cafe, the finishing touches were put to the disguise.

The two men finally parted company at the Pennsylvania Railway Station, Lonsdale to sail to Copenhagen with Cook's report and papers in a black iron box, and Cook into an ignominious and deeply tragic exile.

"If the hounds are still pursuing you," he wrote to his wife a few days later, "put my original records in a safe deposit box and leave the key with Mr. Wack [his attorney]; if they are not following you, bring the records with you. My life is of more importance than the polar matter, which can wait if necessary." The letter, postmarked Toronto, Canada, offered no address. Even his instructions that she should sail for Europe at once and meet him in Algeciras offered no suggestion of a meeting place, a date, or even his name. The man whom the world had hailed as a hero, the man who could only escape through the indignity of a disguise, and whose own name he now could no longer use, had gone.

In Copenhagen in September Stead had asked Cook:

"Do I understand that although you divided your documents into two parts, the loss of either would still leave adequate material to make good your claims?"

"That is true," answered the explorer. "The calculations would have to be worked out over again, but the material would be all there."

This response may have for the time being satisfied Stead who believed he was dealing with an honourable man. But data of this nature, if genuine, does not need time for preparation. If the observations and diary are genuine it is because they are made in the field. If Cook had been to the Pole as he claimed, he could have handed over the relevant data then. But he knew well enough that the material he was sending to the University of Copenhagen after three months' delay would not be acceptable as proof of his claim. He also knew that what he had left behind with Whitney at Etah would not have made the slightest difference. His only hope had been that his claim to that Etah data being crucial would hold off the inevitable decision a little longer. But the strain of it all had become too great.

On 9th December, the day after Lonsdale arrived in Copenhagen with the iron box containing copies of Cook's records, the *New York Times* published the affidavits of Dunkle and Loose, another sensational denunciation of the integrity of Dr. Cook which filled seventeen columns and continued the following day. In their sworn statements they had declared that Cook had agreed to pay them $2,500 for a set of fake observations which could be used to support his claim, and a bonus of $1,500 if the observations were accepted by the University of Copenhagen. "Why was Captain Loose employed to fabricate this set of records of observations?" the *Times* asked. "Are these the records that are now in the hands of the faculty of the University of Copenhagen – if not, then for what purpose were they prepared?"

These questions were answered by Lonsdale in a long telegram to the *New York American* in which he stated that Loose had been employed by Cook:

> ... for the purpose, not of fabricating records, but merely checking observations taken by the doctor ... Loose, however, did not inspire confidence and was told by Dr. Cook that he did not want his services or figures, and he was discharged.
>
> Any figures worked out by Loose have not been used in the report sent to Copenhagen, for with Dr. Cook I have compared originals with all copies made. I can safely repeat that no alterations in the originals have taken place.

Self-confessed participants though Loose and Dunkle were in an attempted fraud, their accusations created a stir, and the timing of the publication of their affidavits in the *New York Times* was clearly intended to cast further doubts on the claims of Cook in advance of the Copenhagen Commission's assessment of those claims. The iron box which Lonsdale had handed over to the Commission contained only two typewritten documents: a sixty-one-page report of the expedition which, as the Commission noted, was "essentially the same that was published during

September and October of this year in the *New York Herald*," and a sixteen-page copy of Cook's notebooks which contained "*no* original astronomical observations *whatsoever*, but only results."

The papers presented were not accompanied by a letter from Dr. Cook, but Lonsdale assured the Commission that the second document "was a complete and accurate copy of all the information contained in the note-books, which, according to the opinion of Dr. Cook, could be of any use for the University's examination." He had also assured them that the "original note-books, which for safety's sake had been sent to Europe by another route, would be turned over to the University in the course of a few days."

The notebooks, however, had still not arrived by 17th December when the Commission met to prepare their report, and all the embarrassed Lonsdale could offer was a letter he had received from Cook, on the envelope of which there was the postmark "Marseilles, 14 December, 1909" – a letter in Cook's own hand, but with neither a mention of the place nor the date of writing. As the Commission noted, the letter offered nothing. It was in fact more in the nature of a plea: a reminder that since his instruments and "most of his astronomic observations had been left behind at Etah," it might without these "seem unwise and impossible" to pass final judgement upon his journey. The Commission did not agree. The outcome of their study, published in Copenhagen on 21st December, 1909, stated:

> The data in the documents submitted to us are of such an unsatisfactory character that it is not possible to declare with certainty that the astronomical observations referred to were actually made; there is likewise lacking details in practical matters – such as sledge journeys – which could furnish some control. The Commission is therefore of the opinion that the material transmitted for examination contains no proof whatsoever that Dr. Cook reached the North Pole.

COOK'S CLAIM TO DISCOVERY OF THE NORTH POLE REJECTED; OUTRAGED DENMARK CALLS HIM A DELIBERATE SWINDLER. That page-one headline of the *New York Times* (only part of which has been quoted) was typical of most of the headlines in newspapers of the western world on 22nd December, 1909, for although in the precise language of the Commission's report they had not, in so many words, branded Cook an impostor, the press were now convinced that he was: a "monster of duplicity," an "infamous wretch," a "shameless swindler," one of the most "audacious and memorable imposters in the annals of science," and a man whose "flight was a confession."

Many newspapers quoted Knud Rasmussen, since he had been an

advisor to the Commission and had reason to feel an even deeper sense of outrage, having previously stated his belief in Cook's claim: "The papers Cook sent ... are almost impudent. No schoolboy could make such calculations. It is a most childish attempt at cheating. Cook has killed himself by his own foolish acts."

And that, it seemed to almost everyone, he had, thus ending, as the *New York Times* put it "one of the most audacious attempts upon record to obtain by false pretenses, an attempt which was the more disgraceful because its success would have deprived a heroic fellow-countryman of his hard-won laurels."

The reaction to the news of Cook's downfall from that heroic fellow-countryman, surprisingly, is on record, for it happened that on the evening the news broke he was the guest of honour at the annual banquet of the New England Society in Manhattan. The president of that society was General Thomas H. Hubbard, to whom fell the honour of introducing the "discoverer of the North Pole." To "prolonged cheers" Peary had bowed graciously. Now at last he was free to speak with the authority of an explorer whose claim, as the *New York Times* that morning had said, was finally "incontestable throughout the civilized world."

> The greatest of the earth's trophies has been won for the United States and for New England ... And now it would seem a fitting sequel to that if ... the Stars and Stripes might wave at both ends of the earth's axis ... I would be glad to aid in any way in the promotion and organization of an American Antarctic Expedition.

But if Peary had seen new horizons that evening, he must surely also have noticed the cloud that appeared above the northern one early the following day. It was in the form of a simple comment published in the *New York American*, a "call" from Rear-Admiral W. S. Schley for Commander Peary "to submit his proofs that he had reached the North Pole to some scientific body other than the National Geographic Society ... The University of Copenhagen should ... examine the Peary proofs, for in that way they would be submitted to the same test that was applied to those of Cook."

And there was another, in the *New York Sun*: "Cook was too hastily acclaimed as the discoverer of the North Pole. Let us not be too hasty in acclaiming him the prince of imposters ... Insane delusions are caricatures of the time and place where they are developed."

But did this not apply as much to Peary as it did to his rival? Were not both explorers acclaimed too hastily, and might not both be the victims of a delusion that they had stood at the Pole?

CHAPTER 20

The Burden of Truth

With the Copenhagen verdict having gone so decisively against Cook, it was only to be expected that the Explorers' Club, of which he had been a founder member and president for a few months in 1906–7, "having found no evidence" to support Cook's claim to having reached the summit of Mt. McKinley, resolved at a special meeting on the eve of Christmas 1909 "that the name of Dr. Cook should be dropped from the rolls of the Club." Anthony Fiala, one of Cook's oldest and closest friends, had put his signature to that decision, and when other old friends, many of whom who had been members of his own ill-fated *Miranda* expedition of 1894, took similar action a few days later and expelled Cook from the Arctic Club of America, the demise of the doctor had seemed complete.

"His flight was a confession," the *New York American* had scornfully stated. "He has been his own worst enemy," was the later verdict of Fiala, "for he did much by his flight towards confirming the opinion that he was a fraud." And this, sure enough, is the risk Cook had taken. Cook was now a hunted man, the victim, as he firmly believed, of a conspiracy to discredit him.

Few men in all history, I am inclined to believe, have ever been made the subject of such vicious attacks, or such malevolent assailing of character, or such a widespread and relentless press persecution, as I; and few men, I feel sure, have ever been made to suffer so bitterly and so inexpressibly as I because of the assertion of my achievement. So persistent, so egregious, so overwhelming were the attacks made upon me that for a time my spirit was broken, and in the bitterness of my soul I even felt desirous of disappearing to some remote corner of the earth, to be forgotten. I knew that envy was the incentive to all the unkind abuses heaped upon me, and I knew also that in due time, when the public agitation subsided and a better perspective followed, the justice of my claim would force itself to the inevitable light of truth.

It was to become Cook's theme, one which shifted the focus of interest away from the issues he could not win to those which appealed for sympathy and compassion. It also stirred in some a sense of outrage at the way in which he had been hounded and so shamelessly abused by those who had the power and the objective to destroy him. It was the conspiracy, Cook argued, that had robbed him of his rightful prize and, but for that conspiracy, he would have been acknowledged as the first to reach the Pole.

There were a few who still believed that Cook had told the world the truth and truth is indestructible. Cook would return, they had warned Peary, and next time he would win. But from where did they draw this firm assurance? Simply from the word of the man?

There were, they argued, too many questions still unresolved. How, for instance, had Cook been able to describe so exactly the nature and the drift of the ice at the Pole if he had not been there and seen it himself? There were also of course those notebooks at Etah which the supporters of Cook are still to this day determined to believe would have proved his claim if only they had been retrieved.

But no explorer in his right mind would have left his original notes with a stranger, particularly a stranger who was sharing a hut with two men who were loyal to his rival and one of them openly hostile. It is my view that Cook had left nothing at Etah that was crucial in proving his North Pole claim, and this was clearly the opinion of the Danes who had found themselves in the embarrassing position of having to reject his claim.

The plain fact is that neither explorer had anything more that he could offer other than a detailed account of the journey, and neither man at that point in time was ready or in the right frame of mind to take on the task of writing his book, Peary because he was far too busy lecturing and collecting his laurels, and seeking (with the help of his friends) to speed the passage of a bill through Congress that would give him the recognition and status that he believed his achievement had earned him, and Cook because he needed time to come to terms with the forces of evil that he was convinced were ranged against him to rob him of his rightful honours and break his will to fight.

And so the laurel wreath for both already had become the noose, for there was no escape for either from the claims that they had made, nor from their obligation now to carry with them to the grave the burden of the truth. In Peary's case, as we have seen, his choice had been between admitting that he had gone in the wrong direction and had failed to reach his goal, or looking back along the trail at all those years of suffering and convincing himself that he had earned the right to claim it.

In the case of his rival, the decision to fake the claim had come earlier, for if the story of the Eskimos is true, Cook had abandoned his attempt at the Pole as early as two days into his journey across the pack ice of the Arctic Ocean, and had not felt his claim under serious threat until after his McKinley claim had collapsed and he was about to send his data with Lonsdale to Copenhagen. He could at that time have gone with Lonsdale, or even taken a different route and presented himself before the Commission. But this, significantly, Cook had not done, and the reason goes deeper than his need to withdraw to "allow the atmosphere to clear of the stench stirred up by rival interest."

Consider his situation. Had his claim been genuine, he could have settled the issue at the time of his triumphant return to civilisation, for on 5th September after a luncheon at the American Legation in Copenhagen he had the perfect opportunity when closeted in the Chancery with Prof. Torp, *Rector Magnificus* of the University, and Prof. Elis Stromgren of the University Department of Astronomy. As a result of their private questioning of Cook they had recommended that the faculty award him an honorary doctorate, and at that meeting the explorer had offered to submit his data to the University for their examination as soon as Whitney had returned with the instruments and the notebooks containing "the rough material upon which [his] results were based."

His misery and confusion are obvious from the route he took after parting from Lonsdale at Pennsylvania Railway Station. First he went to Quebec in the hope of finding Captain Bernier, the skipper of the Canadian government ship that had taken supplies up to Etah in 1909. But it was a dazed idea, a pointless journey. Not only did he fail to find the captain, but he was in the wrong season of the year, since no attempt to reach Etah could be made until the following August. So what was that impulse to seek out the captain – a fear perhaps that the Peary supporters might send someone up there to rob the cache and then swear that they had found nothing there, or was Cook perhaps much closer at that time than his admirers believe to losing control of his mind?

His actions point to a nervous man, a man on the run, seemingly frightened by his own shadow and moving and thinking behind a disguise. Under an assumed name he had sailed for Liverpool and on from there to Marseilles. But this we only know from the undated, unaddressed letter Cook wrote from there to the Commission who were about to decide on his claim. "It has been impossible to establish communication with Dr. Cook," the report of the Commission duly noted, his "address is unknown even to his secretary." Small wonder they had so little confidence in the material he had sent them.

From there he had gone on to Algeciras at the southern tip of Spain where he and his wife were reunited. According to his biographer, Freeman:

Since she had no address for him and did not know his assumed name, they wandered around the streets looking for each other. Finally they met in a small park. Mrs. Cook had brought one of Cook's arctic diaries and when they had sent it to Lonsdale ... they sailed for South America.

Together they spent a month in Buenos Aires, and then made a voyage south through the Straits of Magellan and up the west coast to Santiago. But there, being recognised, Cook moved on, across the Andes back to Buenos Aires from where his wife returned to New York to rejoin their children, leaving Cook for a while to wander alone through Paraguay before sailing on to London.

Cook was in London when Peary was passing through on his grand tour of the European capitals, delivering his lectures and collecting his medals, and attended Peary's lecture before the Royal Geographical Society in disguise. "I stood twenty yards from Peary, and none recognized me," he told the *New York World* reporter, with bitter relish. That lecture, however, rekindled his own need for fame and, according to Freeman, "still under an assumed name, Cook settled down at the Hotel Capitol, 1 Pall Mall, to complete his book on the attainment of the Pole, and to wait for the public to take a calmer attitude toward his case." But there was little chance of that, for no sooner had he broken cover on 2nd October, 1910, than the hounds were on his trail again.

By then, two expeditions to Mount McKinley which had set out with different objectives had returned to tell their tale. The Explorers' Club expedition, supported by funds from the Peary Arctic Club, had set out to locate the peak which Cook had stated was the summit. On this expedition were Prof. Herschel Parker and Belmore Browne who had been with Cook during the exploratory stage of the 1906 climb, and both were convinced that Cook's claim was false. The objective on the other hand of the Mazama Mountaineering Club's expedition, to which the *New York Herald* had made a sizeable donation, was to vindicate the claim of Cook by retracing his route to the summit.

The Explorers' Club party positively located the "fake peak" as a small knoll at an altitude of only 5,300 feet. It was four miles off the obvious route up the main course of the Ruth Glacier on an insignificant ridge, and some nineteen miles from the true summit of Mount McKinley, and there is no mention by Cook in his book or in his *Harpers Magazine* article of his having made this detour. The Mazama party, who had been concentrating their efforts on retracing Cook's route, eventually reached a point where, as Terris Moore puts it, Cook's map "abruptly departs from reasonable accuracy into complete fantasy." At this point they reached the unhappy conclusion that Cook could not possibly have scaled the mountain by the approach route he claimed to have used. They also located most of the places from which Cook had taken the photographs that appeared in his book and all of them had been taken between ten and twenty miles from the summit, and not high on the mountain as his picture captions state.

There was no longer the slightest doubt in the mind of any member of the Mazama expedition that the claim of Cook was false, and they had all been believers in Cook before following his trail. One can sense the hurt of this in the words of their leader C. E. Rusk:

> Dr. Cook had many admirers who would have rejoiced to see his claims vindicated, and I too would have been glad to add my mite in clearing his name. But it could not be. Of his courage and resolution there can be no doubt ... His explorations around Mount McKinley were extensive ... And that one trip alone – when with a single companion he braved the awful solitude of the Ruth Glacier and penetrated the wild, crag-guarded region near the foot of McKinley – should have made him famous. But as we gazed upon the forbidding crags of the great mountain from far up the Ruth Glacier at the point of Cook's and Barrille's farthest advance and realized how utterly impossible and absurd was the story of this man who, carrying a single pack, claims to have started from Tokositna on the 8th of September, and to have stood on the highest point of McKinley on the 16th of the same month.
>
> The man does not live who can perform such a feat. Let us draw the mantle of charity around him and believe, if we can, that there is a thread of insanity running through the woof of his brilliant mind ... If he is mentally unbalanced, he is entitled to the pity of mankind. If he is not, there is no corner of the earth where he can hide from his past.

The climb was attempted again in 1956 by Walter Gonnason and three companions on an expedition sponsored by Dr. Cook's daughter. Unlike Cook and Barrille, these were experienced, well-equipped mountaineers, and they gave themselves the very best chance of climbing the mountain by flying in, thus avoiding the long trudge up the Ruth Glacier. And yet in fourteen days they reached a high point of only 11,400 feet, during which time they had climbed only six thousand feet and covered only twenty-five miles. Cook claimed to have covered eighty-five miles and climbed nineteen thousand feet in twelve or thirteen days.

His supporters claim that his descriptions of the summit are strikingly similar to those of other climbers who have scaled the mountain, invariably quoting Dr. Hudson Stuck, Archdeacon of the Yukon, who led the first ascent of the higher South Peak of McKinley in 1913. But as Stuck says in his book: "There is no rock of any kind on the South (the higher) Peak above 19,000 feet. The last 1,500 feet of the mountain is all permanent snow and ice."

In 1915 Stuck was to offer a more "decided and deliberate opinion" that Cook's claim was not founded on fact:

> I will venture with all confidence this: that any man who, having read Dr. Cook's book, shall himself climb to the top of the mountain ... will never be convinced by all the special pleading in the world that the man who wrote that book had climbed where he climbed and stood where he stood.

The debate continues to this day, but as Dr. Bradford Washburn points out (and he is the undoubted authority on Mount McKinley by virtue of his climbing record and his map of the McKinley Massif), "those who support Dr. Cook's McKinley claim do not have a single person in their camp who has ever set foot on the mountain, or knows anything whatever about it." He, like all of the other McKinley climbers – and there is not one who believes Cook got nearer to the summit than the head of the Ruth Glacier – have no axe to grind against Cook. "Actually, over quite a long period of years," Washburn says, "I have searched for facts which would make it easier for one to reach reasonable conclusions. It would have been quite exciting to discover new facts which strengthened Dr. Cook's case. Instead, however, as new facts have emerged, every single one of them has been more damaging to him."

One of the main arguments of the Cook supporters on the McKinley issue appears to be that absence of proof is not proof of absence. Another well worn argument is that if he did reach the summit he had a perfect moral right to photograph another peak and use that picture, so-to-speak, to "represent" the summit.

There is also a McKinley-related argument which crops up frequently in the polar controversy: namely, that Cook's success or failure on Mount McKinley in 1906 has no bearing whatsoever on whether he reached the North Pole in 1908, that as long as there is a strong body of supporting evidence for his North Pole claim, it is immaterial whether or not he reached the summit of McKinley.

The supporters of Cook of course concede that if the charge of faking the climb could be proved beyond a reasonable doubt, this would reflect very seriously upon the character of their hero. But what if the character of the man *is* flawed? Would we not then be likely to find similarities between these two seemingly "separate" claims – the fingerprints of deception? The answer to this is a definite yes, providing one knows what to look for.

This was not, however, the quest of those who had sailed from Boston in the sealer *Boethic* on 19th June, 1910. Their skipper was Captain Bob Bartlett and one of the three sportsmen was Whitney. They reached Etah on 25th July and as Paul J. Rainey wrote in an article for *Cosmopolitan Magazine*, although "it was not my original intention to visit the cache at Etah where Cook's records were said to be concealed, or his igloo at Cape Sparbo, I did, as a matter of fact, visit both places, and secured interesting photographs of each." It seems inconceivable that he did not take a close look at that cache since he was close enough to it to take a photograph of Itukusuk standing in the ruins. But that is what he said:

> I refrained from touching or opening it, on account of not wishing to be mixed up in the Peary–Cook controversy. The cache is a stone igloo. The top has fallen in. The contents, whatever they may be, being covered with canvas, it was impossible for me to see anything. It seems peculiar, however, that an explorer, returning from the pole and reaching a point where he could have obtained plenty of help from the Eskimos, should have left valuable records in a place so unprotected.

It appears, however, that Bartlett might have been a little bolder, judging by his remark to a reporter from the *New York World* on his return: "The only articles belonging to Dr. Cook at Etah are some clothing and such like and possibly a sextant. But as for records, you can stake your life that none are there."

The sextant was later found in Itukusuk's possession by the Danish explorer Peter Freuchen and bought from him for an alarm clock "which he immediately took apart and divided among his many friends." But no trace has ever been found or heard of the records.

Cook's hopes of making a comeback and vindicating himself were dealt another blow when he wrote an article for *Hampton's Magazine*. The idea initially had appealed to him, since he would be addressing the same public as Peary had in his long-running serial story, but there had been a catch. What *Hampton's* were wanting from Cook was a confession and he was not prepared to make one. And so, since Cook would not cooperate quite as fully as they had wished, *Hampton's* had taken his story, altered it in parts to read as a plea of insanity, and blazoned the front of the magazine with the words "Dr. Cook's Confession." Cook was hit hard by this and later wrote: "I felt impotent, crushed. In my very effort to explain myself I was being irretrievably hurt. I was being made a catspaw for magazine and newspaper sensation."

There was now only one way that Cook could get his message across to the public: he would write, publish, promote, and distribute his book *My Attainment of the Pole*, and in one of the most extraordinary books that have ever been written by a polar explorer he spewed out his hurt, his hatred of Peary and his truly enormous load of self-pity in the cause, as he says, of truth.

> Only by reading my own story, as fully set down herein, can anyone judge of the relative value of my claim and that of my rival claimant; only by so doing can anyone get at the truth of the plot made to discredit me; only by doing so can one learn the reason for all of my actions, for my failure to meet charges at the time they were made, for my disappearing at a time when such action was unfairly made to confirm the worst charges of my detractors.

It is a ranting, maniacal book which was rejected by several publishers before its author finally decided to finance the publication himself; and its literary style, its hallucinations, and the viciousness of his attacks upon Peary and every institution that had challenged Cook's claims and "attempted to steal" the honours that his achievement had earned, set the work in a class of its own.

Right from the outset he warns the reader that this will be a bloody book: "I shall now, having felt the smarting sting of the world's whip, and in order to justify myself, use the knife." He goes on to accuse Peary of endangering his life "by a dishonest appropriation of food supplies," and in his lectures, he took this issue of his food supplies even further, knowing that it was Peary's policy flatly to refuse to respond:

> As we came back to Greenland we were half starved, almost unable to walk; really at death's door, and we looked around for something to eat. We had left there a camp in which we had packed away food enough for several years. That was our life-saving station; our very existence depended on that camp, but during our absence, during the time that our backs were turned, Mr. Peary came along and took that camp, took all of our food supplies and left us hopelessly stranded to starve.
>
> There Mr. Peary attempted a deliberate murder, for in taking our supplies he knew that he was trying to starve us out, and he was told so by his own men. There Peary did a thing for which he would be hung, and rightly so, in a mining camp.

And yet his book contradicts these assertions:

> So weak that we had to climb on hands and knees, we reached the top of an iceberg, and from there saw Annoatok. Natives, who had thought us long dead, rushed out to greet us . . .
> The world now seemed brighter. The most potent factor in this

change was food – and more food – a bath and another bath – and clean clothes. Mr. Whitney offered me unreservedly the hospitality of my own camp. He instructed Pritchard to prepare meal after meal of every possible dish that our empty stomachs had craved for a year.

There is also documentary evidence from Peary that Cook's accusations are untrue. In his orders to Boatswain John Murphy dated Etah, 17th August, 1908, Peary had stated:

> You will exercise the utmost care and diligence in using and protecting all supplies and equipment left here. Should Dr. Cook return or be brought back in bad condition, you will take every possible care of him, and endeavor to bring him around as speedily as possible. You will take all possible care of his equipment and supplies, and on his return allow him to use them. Any of the supplies from the *Roosevelt* which Dr. Cook needs you will give him.

Cook's book draws his readers into what he describes as the "web of shame" – his conspiracy theory. "I found myself the object of a campaign to discredit me in which, I believe, as an explorer, I stand the most shamefully abused man in the history of exploration." He goes on to blast Peary unmercifully throughout in high-flown insults and colourful footnotes, and devotes four whole chapters at the end of his book to telling how Peary and his supporters by "weaving a leprous blanket of infamy" attempted to cover him. He tells of "the widespread and unprecedented call for 'proofs,' which in some vague way were to consist of unreduced reckonings."

> Mr. Peary had his own – he had buried part of mine. I did not at the time instantly produce these vague and obscure proofs, knowing, as all scientists know, that figures must inevitably be inadequate and that any convincing proof that can exist is to be found only in the narrative account of such a quest.

And yet his own book fails to provide it. What the book does provide, however, are pictures, those fingerprints of deception, and the first to point these out was Donald B. MacMillan who had been with Peary in 1909 and had made (with Itukusuk as one of his companions) an unsuccessful search for "Crocker Land" in 1914. In an article in the *Geographical Review* entitled "Cook's Non-Attainment of the Pole," he had this to say:

> Many of the photographs in Dr. Cook's *My Attainment of the Pole*, New York, 1911, are recognized by both E-took-a-shoo and Ah-pellah. The

photographs facing page 244 marked "Bradley Land Discovered," etc, were taken off the western shore of Axel Heiberg Island, about 550 miles from the Pole.

Facing page 282: Photo "Mending Near the Pole" was taken on West side of Axel Heiberg Island.

Facing page 286: "At the Pole – We were the only pulsating creatures in a dead world of ice." Photos taken in the spring of 1909 near Cape Faraday on east coast of Ellesmere Island about 780 miles from the Pole. The musk-ox boots worn by Ah-pellah were made in the igloo at Cape Sparbo in Jones Sound, following return from the north.

Facing page 298: "First Camp at the Pole, April 21, 1908." Photo taken in spring of 1909 a little south of Cape Faraday on the eastern shores of Ellesmere Island.

Facing page 332: "Back to Land and Life." Taken near Cape Southwest, southern coast of Axel Heiberg Island.

Facing page 332: "Saved from starvation, the result of one of our last cartridges." Taken near Cape Svarten on the north shore of North Devon. The boys had many cartridges at this time. They had four in fact, when they reached Etah.

From conversations with Cook's two boys, MacMillan also reports them as saying that they did not travel beyond the point where their two companions had returned to land and that "after sleeping for two nights, the party returned to the cache on the shores of Axel Heiberg Island, took everything from the cache, and proceeded south, following the western shore." Other explorers were given the same stories by Cook's two boys. Itukusuk had pointed out to Sergeant Stallworthy "the spot where, he said, Dr. Cook took photographs which the latter afterwards claimed to have been taken at the North Pole. This was approximately in latitude 82° North, within sight of land." Itukusuk had also lived in Peter Freuchen's house at Thule for more than two years (being married to one of Freuchen's servants), and both Itukusuk and Awellah had told Freuchen about their trip with the doctor.

There is also the issue of the credibility of the Eskimos' account to consider. The two boys had shown some anxiety about going out of sight of land on the Arctic Ocean, and in *My Attainment of the Pole* Cook comments:

Before leaving us one of the departing Eskimos had pointed out a low-lying cloud to the north of us. "Noona" (land), he said, nodding to the others. The thought occured to me that, on our trip, I could take advantage of the mirages and low clouds on the horizon and encourage a belief in a constant nearness to land, thus maintaining their courage and cheer.

But on my last visit to the Thule District I got this reply from Talilanguaq when I asked him if Cook and his two boys had gone a long way out on to the Arctic Ocean:

> With only two hunters, two sledges, on the way to the North Pole is to commit suicide. When he [Cook] told The People [the Eskimos] that they could see land clouds – they are not fools! You cannot lie to them, because they have been living here a long time, and they know about the hunting places; they know about nature – the whole nature – that's their life!

A partial comment it might be argued, since Talilanguaq is the Eskimo grandson of Admiral Peary, but the fact is, it matters as little to him which white man was first to reach the Pole as it does to any of the other Eskimos in North-West Greenland. He speaks from experience not only as one of the greatest of the present day hunters in the Thule District, but also as the man who was leader of the Eskimos on the successful Monzino expedition to the North Pole in 1971, and one of the supporting Eskimos on the 1978 Japanese North Pole expedition which also reached the Pole. Nor should the folklore of the polar Eskimos be ignored. The stories handed down state that Cook and his two boys did not go more than a few days' travel onto the Arctic Ocean, and to argue that their own story of what they did is invalid because they were uneducated is as insulting as it is absurd, for unlike the white men who came to their country to seek fame and glory, they, the natives, had no need to lie. The story told by Itukusuk and Aapilaq to their fellow tribesmen about their journey with Dr. Cook can be found in Appendix I.

In 1967, with two companions and three teams of dogs, I retraced Dr. Cook's route from Etah to the northern tip of Axel Heiberg Island, and from there on to Devon Island, passing by the great cliffs of Svartevoeg at which Cook and his men had a camp. From the description of his journey to that point we were able to follow his route, although not without some difficulty because of his style of writing. From that point on, however, we have a choice to make between accepting Cook's word, or that of his two companions.

My own acceptance of the Eskimos' version of the story is, however, not simply a gut feeling that their version is the true one. It is a conviction strongly influenced by the fact that two of the pictures in Cook's book I now know for a certainty were used by Cook to deceive.

Like MacMillan, I had been arrested by the picture captioned "Bradley

Cook's map showing his claimed route to the North Pole includes Peary's Crocker Land as well as his own Bradley Land and, north of that, his "Submerged Island" – none of which exist. His map also shows a very narrow channel dividing Ringnes Land through which he claims to have travelled – a channel which in fact is fifteen miles wide at its narrowest.

Land Discovered," facing page 244 in *My Attainment of the Pole*. In recent years the Cook supporters have become convinced that this picture shows an ice island, a very large piece of drifting ice which has broken away from an ice shelf. The drift tracks of several ice islands have been closely monitored over the last thirty years and this has encouraged the Cook supporters to believe that it was an ice island that Cook claims to have seen to the west of his course on 30th March, 1908, at latitude 84°50′N, longitude 95°36′W.

Anyone, however, who has seen the north-west coast of Axel Heiberg Island, and has also seen ice islands from the surrounding sea ice will know that the picture in Cook's book is not an ice island, but a picture of land, and since there is no land where Cook claims to have taken this picture, we may take it that what Cook's two companions told MacMillan was true. It is unlikely that the exact location of the land seen in Cook's picture will ever be determined for, as can readily be seen by comparing some of the pictures in Cook's *To the Top of the Continent* with pictures taken from the same spot by other explorers, Cook took the precaution of waiting until cloud obscured some of the features before taking his photographs, thus making it much harder for later travellers to locate. And he almost certainly took that same precaution with the "Bradley Land" picture.

The search for "Bradley Land" is made even harder since the only picture available is the one in his book, the original plate is missing from the Cook Collection at the Library of Congress, as are also the plates of the two other crucial pictures: those of his "North Pole" camp, and his "summit picture" of Mount McKinley. He also, as we have seen in the case of the "Fake Peak," made sure that pictures, the location of which he did not want anyone to find, were taken off his stated route and in some cases have been printed the wrong way round to confuse the issue further.

The middle picture on his page 244, captioned "Submerged Island of Polar Sea," I discovered was a picture of a glacier and not, as Cook claims, a picture of "old ice" between latitudes 87° and 88°N. The original plate, which I found in the Library of Congress collection of Cook's material, has never been published before. Printed right to the edge of this original plate one can see the land. It will be noticed also that the dog teams are moving towards camera, and yet in the foreground there are the tracks of a third sledge – there were only two sledges on the journey Cook claims to have made.

Cook's supporters argue that his "discovery of an island of glacial land ice within one hundred and twenty miles of the North Pole, and the verification in modern times of the existence of such a phenomenon in the exact area specified by Cook is very strong evidence of his attainment of the North Pole." But on the evidence of this picture it is not, and in any case, old floes such as the ones described by Cook are occasionally to be found much further south on Cook's alleged route.

With the certainty that Cook had studied every description of pack ice that could be found in the literature before committing himself to that journey, he would have known from Peary's description in *Nearest the Pole* that old floes were to be found far out on the Arctic Ocean "which looked as if they did not move even in summer," and Cook may well have got his idea of including a description of these old floes in his story from this source.

Certainly his research, together with his personal observations of the drift of ice off the northern coast of Axel Heiberg Island would have been more than sufficient information for him to come up with a fairly safe guess as to the conditions of ice and the drift of ice further to the north than he actually went. And so, although in theory Cook could, by feeding dog to dog, have made a long journey out onto the polar pack ice, the evidence of his Eskimos, combined with the suspicion aroused by his deliberate deception in some of his picture captions, points to the conclusion that he fell to the same temptation he had on McKinley. He took the easier route to fame – and at the sound of the applause, convinced himself he had earned it.

But there are many who still believe Cook's story, and one of his strongest advocates, and a member of the Frederick A. Cook Society, is Sheldon Cook-Dorough. He tells how Cook's troubles were by no means over during the later years of his life, that he bore a great deal of sorrow:

> Some of that sorrow flowed from the questioning of his claim to the first attainment of the North Pole. Some of that sorrow came from other sources. He entered the oil business in Texas in the 1920's – he was a petroleum geologist. He was accused, tried and convicted of having defrauded stock-holders by falsely stating that the lands of his company were oil potential lands. In the event, after his imprisonment began, these lands indeed came in, many of them, in oil. Probably billions of barrels have been pumped from his lands during the last sixty years.
>
> But nevertheless, he languished in prison until 1930, serving seven years of a fourteen-year sentence, and in 1940 he was felled by a very serious stroke. President Franklin D. Roosevelt in that year conferred full and unconditional pardon upon Frederick Albert Cook, and he was cleared of the stain of the conviction of having defrauded stockholders by falsely indicating that his lands possessed great quantities of oil.
>
> His last years were indeed in many ways sorrowful. But he never wavered in the conviction and in the faith that his claim to the discovery

of the North Pole, and his other achievements in exploration, would receive recognition in full.

A few years before his death on 5th August, 1940, Cook recorded for posterity a final statement. The voice is that of a tired old man. Yet these were his final words:

I have been humiliated and seriously hurt. But that doesn't matter any more. I'm getting old, and what does matter to me is that I want you to believe that I told the truth. I state emphatically that I, Frederick A. Cook, discovered the North Pole.

CHAPTER 21

The Price of Fame

The challenge thrown out by Admiral Schley that Peary should submit his proofs to that same impartial examining body which had so dramatically and effectively rejected the claim of Dr. Cook, had been, for Peary, a sure indication that his own claim was still vulnerable. But the shock wave of that challenge from Schley had also been felt by several of Peary's loyal supporters, with by far the greatest shock, needless-to-say, being felt at the National Geographic Society where the Board of Managers were well aware that Peary's claim would not survive the test that Schley had in mind.

How great then must have been the relief when the problem was very neatly resolved by the publication on Christmas Day of a statement in the *New York Times* by the US Minister to Copenhagen, Dr. Maurice Egan. The University of Copenhagen, the *Times* had quoted Egan as saying, "accepted the word of Commander Peary that he had reached the Pole and the verdict of the National Geographic Society without any desire to examine his proofs." We shall never know whether that statement had been made with the full authority of the faculty or had simply been an unguarded comment. Either way, since it went uncorrected, the explorer was assured of a deluge of medals, for with that acceptance by the Danes, the precedent had been clearly established that Peary's proofs need not be examined since his claim had been seen to be sound.

It was as though Peary had suddenly been picked up by a huge wave of public recognition. Within days the first instalment of his story in *Hampton's Magazine* appeared on the newsstands, with a frontispiece photograph of the portrait bust of Peary by William Partridge and a glowing tribute from Theodore Roosevelt in the form of a letter in his own hand:

On Safari, North of Mt. Kenia, [sic]
Sept. 22nd, 1909

Dear Mr. Bridgman:
    . . . I am inexpressibly rejoiced at his wonderful triumph; and proud beyond measure, as an American, that this, one of the great feats of

the ages, should have been performed by a fellow countryman of ours. It is the great feat of our generation. We are all Captain Peary's debtors – all of us who belong to civilized mankind.

> With heartiest congratulations,
> faithfully yours,
> Theodore Roosevelt

Financially also Peary was now riding high. For that serial in *Hampton's Magazine* which ran to nine ghosted monthly instalments, Peary was paid $40,000. He had also signed a contract with Frederick Stokes for his book with an advance of $15,000, and was soon commanding huge fees from his platform appearances, $7,500 for one of his lectures and never less than $1,000.

But the most heady experience undoubtedly was the evening at the Metropolitan Opera House on 8th February, 1910, at which the municipality of the City of New York, supported by an honorary committee of thirty-one millionaires, gathered to pay tribute to the explorer. It was an event which the *New York Times* described as "one of the most remarkable testimonials ever given to a citizen of the United States." As Charles Evans Hughes, Governor of the State of New York, explained to a delighted audience, it was a tribute which had been delayed by circumstances "not within our control." This being a clear reference to Dr. Cook, the audience had "laughed and cheered [and] Peary had nodded and smiled."

President Taft sent a telegram of congratulations which was read out to the audience by Governor Hughes: "I sincerely hope, as is now proposed, Congress will take some substantial notice of the great achievement which has reflected such great credit on American enterprise, persistence, courage, and endurance."

Here was a sentiment which the *Times* had been pushing ever since the Copenhagen verdict on Cook: "The pity of it is that Peary's triumph should have been clouded, and his just pride tinged with disappointment and vexation ... It can never be wholly made up, but certainly now reparation should be made in every appropriate way. Imposture has met its doom; merit should have its full reward." And a part of that reward came that very evening for he had, besides all the tributes and the cheers, received a cheque for $10,000 from the Civic Forum which immediately and grandly he had announced he would donate to a worthwhile and patriotic cause: to fit out an expedition "for the purpose of exploration and scientific investigation; and to enter the Stars and Stripes in a splendid, manly international race for the South Pole."

He was at that moment almost on the crest of the wave. With the inevitability now of international recognition of his North Pole claim, and with a growing impetus in the campaign for his promotion to the rank of Rear-Admiral, backed by the expressed admiration of two Presidents and the ground-work of Congressional lobbyist, Lucien Alexander, Peary seemed within the stroke of a pen of finally receiving the glory that his years of suffering had earned him. The next day the United States Senate unanimously passed the bill, introduced by Senator Hale of Peary's home state of Maine, to promote and retire him with the rank of Rear-Admiral.

But, then, almost as breathlessly as he had been lifted, his luck fell away. In the House of Representatives a similar bill met with some opposition from an eloquent minority who considered Peary's promotion unjustified on the grounds that he had spent only twelve years on active duty out of a total of twenty-eight years in the Navy, sixteen years having been spent on the "self-imposed task" of trying to reach the North Pole. With questions also raised concerning Peary's claim, the bill had been referred to a Naval Affairs subcommittee for examination of that claim, and by 25th February Peary could see that he was in trouble for the *New York Times* had picked up a rumour as to who his examiners might be:

This board of scientific investigation will be composed of Rear Admiral Melville, U.S.N., retired; Rear Admiral Schley, U.S.N., retired, and Major General A. W. Greely, U.S.A., retired, all of whom have won recognition at the hands of Congress because of their attainments in the Arctic ice fields.

Members of the committee will communicate with Commander Peary to ascertain if the three experts suggested are acceptable to him.

Two of the three most definitely were not. Peary himself, however, was cautious enough to get Representative De Alva Alexander (a good friend of General Hubbard) to write to the Hon. Thomas S. Butler, Chairman of the Committee, and make the point strong and clear:

There are two reasons why Admiral Schley, Admiral Melville, and General Greely should not be asked to pass upon these proofs. First, it would be a reflection upon the National Geographic Society. Secondly, it would be manifestly unfair and unjust, for Admiral Schley is known to be unfriendly, while General Greely is scarcely less undesirable. On the other hand, Admiral Melville has been so pronounced in favor of Peary that any verdict he rendered might not be called impartial.

With these three polar experts removed, Peary had no doubt felt a little safer. He was, however, in for a shock, for although at their first meeting on 4th March there was not one among the seven members of the

Congressional subcommittee who was knowledgeable on the subject of the Arctic, or of navigation, there were three who were, as Dennis Rawlins puts it, "prepared to let loose their curiosity and logic on the explorer."

Peary had clearly been assuming that the Naval Affairs subcommittee would merely go through the motions and endorse the findings of the National Geographic Society's three-man committee, and that he would not even be required to present himself for questioning. This had probably also been the expectation of Hon. Thomas S. Butler, Chairman of that subcommittee, for at the first meeting he invited only Prof. O. H. Tittmann, the Superintendent of the US Coast and Geodetic Survey, and Prof. Henry Gannett, now the President of the National Geographic Society. Admiral Chester, the third member of the National Geographic Society's three-man committee which had passed Peary's claims as sound, was out of the country at that time. During their questioning, however, it became clear not only that Peary's proofs had been examined in a very casual manner, but that there were grounds also for believing that Peary's examiners had been "prejudiced in his favor."

This changed the atmosphere of the hearings, and when further questioning revealed that Peary's observations had been made on "loose slips of paper," that it *was* possible to fake observations, and that Peary's records had not been submitted to any of the ten European Geographical Societies who had awarded him their highest honours – that they had simply taken on trust the judgement of the National Geographic Society – the suspicion of Representative Macon was fully aroused.

He demanded that Peary's original data be submitted for inspection. Peary replied through Representative Alexander that whilst he had no objection to this, he did not want it entered on the record, thus making it public, on the grounds that "it would be breaking faith with his publishers." And so the first round of the Peary Hearings came to an end with Peary badly shaken.

His cause, however, was espoused by many, for Congress were seen to be casting doubt upon the integrity of everyone connected with Peary by challenging the findings of the National Geographic Society. A pamphlet was printed under the title "How Peary Reached the North Pole" which was sent out to members of Congress. Even from the floor of the House there were calls of concern, one of them coming from Representative Joseph H. Moore:

To discredit Robert E. Peary, after all his years of endeavor . . . must necessarily discredit American scientists who have put the stamp of their approval upon his labors . . . Peary's achievements and the report of the National Geographic Society have been received without question by Nansen, The Duke of Abruzzi, Greely, Shackleton, and

Scott. With this strong array it would seem that the only thing for Congress to do would be to accept the verdict of the National Geographic Society without further humiliation of the American explorer.

But the speaker was listing the names of explorers who had sent their congratulations to Peary on the assumption that his proofs had been adequate, and adequately examined. These same explorers were to become significantly silent after it became known that Peary had taken no shots for longitude on his way north to check his drift and direction. At the time, however, the propaganda barrage was fiercely pro-Peary. Even the press joined in the condemnation of those members of the Congressional subcommittee who were demanding more proof from Peary before granting him the thanks he deserved. But all to no avail. The subcommittee had dug themselves in.

Peary, deeply hurt by this, had intensified his quest for promotion at the expense of other demands on his time, one of them being his book. This was his best chance to give a credible and lasting support to that claim which even Peary by now must surely have realised was far too weak to stand on its observations alone, and according to his biographer Hobbs, Peary was hard at work on his book during every spare moment of his frenetic round of engagements. Hobbs quotes Peary as saying that the book had "been planned and written in hotels, on trains and street cars and taxicabs even, on steamers and everywhere and anywhere I might find a few spare hours or minutes during the last year."

Hobbs even adds that "despite the handicaps of the writing of the *North Pole*, its literary quality is of a high order. Peary, like Captain Scott, if he had not chosen the career of an explorer, might have achieved a reputation as a writer." And yet at the time of writing this Hobbs knew that Peary had employed A. E. Thomas as a ghostwriter, having exchanged a great deal of correspondence with Stefansson on this and the subject of "Peary's ignorance of the Eskimo language," two subjects which at that time were regarded as extremely sensitive issues with the Peary family.

This sensitivity was probably a hangover from Peary's own concern that no one should know he had used the services of a ghostwriter. "Thomas' work must be entirely confidential," he had written to his publisher. He was to start work on material ghosted for him by Elsa Barker for the *Hampton's* series, and forward each chapter to Peary for corrections. But using a ghostwriter was a risk, and Peary knew it: "have someone . . . go through the text looking for apparent discrepancies, lack of correlation in sequence of narrative, lack of clearness, etc" he had exhorted his publisher after Thomas had completed the work. In a letter to Andrew Freeman, Thomas admitted: "It is perfectly true that I wrote the bulk of Peary's *North Pole*. I should think 80 per cent would be about right."

But the work as a historical record suffered by this arrangement and its many discrepancies weakened Peary's case. It was almost as though his highest priority was to collect as many honours as possible in order to improve his chances of surviving his forthcoming struggle with Congress. On 26th April he and his family sailed for Europe, the children being taken because never again would they have an opportunity to meet so many distinguished people all gathered to do honour to their father. At the Albert Hall in London, Peary's daughter recalls: "all of Great Britain's famous living Arctic and Antarctic explorers were seated on the platform and when Dad came out, amidst ringing cheers, I nearly burst with pride." Here he was awarded the Royal Geographical Society's special gold medal "For Arctic exploration from 1886 to 1909," its inscription cautiously avoiding the issue which privately was still, by some of the members of the Council, regarded as unresolved. In spite of this caution, however, the President of the Society praised not only Peary before that distinguished gathering (which included the disguised Dr. Cook), but also the Society who had examined his data:

And finally an exceptionally capable committee of his fellow country-men, appointed by the National Geographic Society of Washington, have examined his original records and have emphatically endorsed his claim. This judicial task could not have been more appropriately placed. It is on these grounds that I stand here tonight as the representative of the Royal Geographical Society and, armed with the full authority of its Council, welcome you, Commander Peary, as the first and only human being who has ever led a party of his fellow creatures to a Pole of the Earth.

And so the Royal Geographical Society, the premier authority of exploration, had honoured Peary without seeing his proofs, for although they had requested to see his records before conferring the honour upon him, he had not handed over the copies of his data until after he had received the medal.

During that glorious May and on into the first week of June, Peary toured the capitals of Europe receiving ovations, dining with kings, and collecting every honour that their geographical societies could offer, with the exception of the three Scandinavian countries whose explorers' tracks had crossed those of Peary's. And had he been satisfied with these symbols, perhaps Jo's dream that one day he would find that peace which even he himself so longed for might have come to pass. But Peary needed more, and in seeking promotion to the rank of Rear-Admiral as his country's recognition of his status and his claims, he was to come so very close to losing everything he had gained.

Fortunately he had taken the precaution of having his observations recomputed by Hugh C. Mitchell (who was later to do a similar job for Richard E. Byrd) and Charles R. Duvall, both of the US Coast and Geodetic Survey whose chief was Tittmann, one of the three who had examined Peary's data for the National Geographic Society. The fact that they had been commissioned by Peary at his own expense was not mentioned by Tittmann in his testimony before the Congressional subcommittee on 12th January, 1911. Asked to give his opinion of their professional skill as computers, he had commented: "I think they are unsurpassed anywhere in ability or experience." They were, moreover, Government employees, and there can be little doubt after a close study of the records that Mitchell's testimony, coming at the end of the mauling Peary had received during the three days of the Hearings between 7th–11th January, won the vote in Peary's favour by the narrowest of margins. (See Appendix II.)

The assessment of Mitchell's testimony by Professor of Physics and Astronomy, Dennis Rawlins, is that it was "riddled with misstatements, computational inelegancies, and optimistic assumptions, which were naturally not picked up by the untrained legislators. But the crucial testimony was Mitchell's professional opinion on the genuineness of the data." Mitchell was asked if he considered it possible that anyone could have faked the observations and replied, "No." He was asked to suppose that the figures submitted to him by Peary had been made in Washington, New York, or Boston – how could he have detected it – and replied:

> Well, that is a rather difficult question to answer. I believe it is altogether a matter of experience that any dishonesty in observations or computations will show up in the reduction ... At some point of the work it will come out; yes. That is a belief. That is not a mathematical demonstration.

On 21st January, 1911, the subcommittee's report was sent to the House of Representatives; on 3rd March the bill was finally passed, and on the following day it was signed by President Taft. Peary had won his honours because the wrong questions had been asked.

But at what cost? His wife, in an unpublished note, offers us an answer:

> No one will ever know how the attack on my husband's veracity affected him, who had never had his word doubted in *any* thing at *any* time in his life. He could not believe it. And the personal grilling which he was obliged to undergo at the hands of Congress, while his scientific

observations were examined and worked out, although it resulted in his complete vindication, hurt him more than all the hardships he endured in his sixteen years of research in the Arctic regions and did more toward the breaking down of his iron constitution than anything experienced in his explorations.

On 2nd August, 1916, Representative Henry Helgesen introduced a bill before Congress to repeal the 1911 Act of Congress which had recognised Peary's claim and recommended his promotion. Had there been a second hearing it is very probable that the navigational issues would have been more carefully examined, but on 10th April, 1917, Helgesen died, his bill was dropped, and Peary no doubt breathed a sigh of relief.

The strain, nevertheless, had taken its toll. By the end of that year Peary became ill with pernicious anaemia, and during his last summer on his beloved Eagle Island, knowing he would never be well again, he spent most of the time lying in the sun on a musk-ox rug laid out on the lawn. That island which had given him strength, however, could do no more than comfort him and ease him nearer to the end, and on 20th February, 1920, the spirit finally parted from the body of this exceptional man.

The fame he craved he *had* received. Twenty-two gold medals; three honorary doctorates; the French Cross of Grand Officer of the Legion of Honour; the "Thanks of Congress" for his "Arctic Explorations resulting in reaching the North Pole," and promotion to the rank of Rear-Admiral with retirement at that rank dating from 6th April, 1909, the date he claimed he reached the North Pole. No explorer in the early part of this century received more honours or more symbols of fame.

But what was the price he paid for that fame? The burden of knowing that he had *not* reached the Pole, or his bitterness at being doubted when he was telling the truth? He had only 133 miles to go from the point where Bartlett turned for home. He had the best men, the strongest dogs, and most of all, the need to reach it. How tragic then the irony that north had not been Peary's heading and in spite of all his effort, all his courage and persistence, he failed to reach the Pole.

But surely it is only fair to see the man for what he was, and not for what he failed to be. Those doubts that have for eighty years hung round his controversial claim, distorting every image of the man and his achievements, would surely then be understood, and Peary's striving, wounded spirit finally find peace.

The Eskimo Account of Dr. Cook's Attempt to Reach the North Pole in 1908

The statement made on board the *Roosevelt* by Cook's two Eskimo companions at Etah on 17th August, 1909 concerning the journey they made with Dr. Cook was never accepted by Cook, nor has it ever been regarded as a valid statement by any of his supporters. The two boys, it is argued, were confused by the line of questioning and by the map that was laid out in front of them. It was also suggested that the boys were too afraid of Peary to tell him the truth about where they went. But the main argument put forward by Cook appears as a footnote to page 452 of his book, *My Attainment of the Pole*:

> Among themselves the Eskimos have an intimate way of conveying things, a method of expression and meaning which an outsider never grasps. At most, white men can understand only a selected and more simple language with which the Eskimos convey their thoughts. This partly accounts for the unreliability of any testimony which a white man extracts from them. There is also to be considered an innate desire on the part of these simple people to answer any question in a manner which they think will please. In all Indian races this desire to please is notoriously stronger than a sense of truth. The fact that my Eskimos, when later questioned as to my whereabouts, are reported to have answered that I had not gone far out of sight of land, was due partly to my instructions and partly to this inevitable wish to answer in a pleasing way.
>
> While they spoke among themselves of having reached the "Big Nail," they also said – what they later repeated to Mr. Peary – that they had passed few days beyond the sight of land, a delusion caused by mirages, in which, to prevent any panic, I had with good intentions encouraged an artificial belief in a nearness to land.

Amundsen (who had spent even less time living among the Eskimos than Cook) echoed this in a comment reported in the *New York Times* of 24th January, 1926:

My experience with Eskimos is that they will give you the kind of answer you want. MacMillan said to the Eskimos: "Dr. Cook only away from camp one sleep?" and laid his head on his hands to denote the passing of one night, and the Eskimos nodded "yes." That kind of evidence was used to discredit Dr. Cook.

MacMillan, however, had spent almost five and a half years living and travelling with the Eskimos at the time of writing his article, Dr. Cook's Non-Attainment of the Pole (published in the *Geographical Review*, February 1918), and his travelling companion on his journey in search of "Crocker Land," during which he retraced Cook's outward route as far as the northern tip of Axel Heiberg Island, had been Itukusuk. It is therefore reasonable to assume that MacMillan's command of the Eskimo language by that time had advanced far beyond the need to use sign language to indicate sleep, and that MacMillan had understood correctly what Itukusuk and Aapilaq told him about their journey with Cook and where Cook had taken the pictures which appeared in his book.

Cook's two companions told the same story to Rasmussen and Freuchen in 1910 when the two Danes set up their trading station at Thule. Indeed, Itukusuk, having married one of Freuchen's servants, lived in Freuchen's house for more than two years, so we may be sure that Freuchen in that time had ample opportunity to get at the truth. But still the Cook supporters insist that the Eskimos' statements are worthless on the grounds that they have a different concept of truth.

So what are we to believe? The explorer Vilhjalmur Stefansson in a letter to Peary dated 3rd October, 1910, made this comment:

There are two things I know about Eskimo character – they seldom lie, and they never keep a secret, no matter how solemnly they promise to do so. Keeping a thing secret is in fact the deadliest sin of which the Eskimo knows – this is true of those Eskimos I know, for they generally attribute famine, epidemics, etc., to some member of their tribe having kept something of importance secret.

What Itukusuk and Aapilaq told their own people is therefore the story that needs to be told, and I do not refer to the story given second-hand to Rasmussen which was published in the *New York Times* on 21st October, 1909, but the story handed down by word of mouth among the polar Eskimos themselves. The oral tradition is the voice of their past and the Eskimos respect their past. Stories are always retold exactly as heard, not deviating by a single phrase or word, and one of the great exponents of that art of handing history on was my old friend, Inuutersuaq Ulloriaq.

I knew the hunter Inuutersuaq over a period of twenty years from 1966, when I spent the first of my four winters in the Thule District of North-West Greenland, until his death in 1986 at the age of eighty, and never in all the journeys I made in that happy span of twenty years did I pass through his village of Siorapaluk on my eager way north or my weary return without making a sort of pilgrimage to his tiny, tidy house.

On those visits the old man would get out his map and for hours on end would tell me the stories of journeys he had made "a long time ago," many of them with his wife, Naduk. In 1930 he and Naduk were involved in a search on Ellesmere Island with the Royal Canadian Mounted Police for three missing men from the Kruger expedition, an expedition on which Itukusuk had been the chief hunter of the party. In 1934–5 he and Naduk had been members of the Oxford University Ellesmere Land expedition whose leader was Edward, now Lord Shackleton, the son of the famous explorer, and in 1940 he went there again with the Danish Thule and Ellesmere Land expedition. Through these contacts with the white explorers he developed a certain tolerance for their weaknesses and an interest in their claims, and often our talks would come round to Dr. Cook, since both of us had retraced his route across Ellesmere Island by the Sverdrup Pass, the so-called Musk-Ox Way.

What Inuutersuaq was told by Itukusuk is the truth as Cook's companions saw it. They knew what they did and where they went. What they could never understand was why their white friend wanted to tell a different story. Their own story, as here handed down, is therefore an essential part of the whole.

The testimony of Inuutersuaq Ulloriaq

Dr. Frederick Albert Cook, whom we called Daagitkoorsuaq, was on his own say-say the first white man to reach the North Pole, on 21st April, 1908. But the two young Polar Eskimos who accompanied Cook, Itukusuk (1888–1935) and Aapilaq (1885–1935), knew this was not the case at all.

I will now tell what I have heard about Daagitkoorsuaq from his two companions, their families and the old people in Thule . . .

In Smith Sound between Canada and Greenland there is often open water all year round but in the winter Kane Basin is covered with ice northwards from a line between Cape Sabine and Anoritooq. Cook and his companions took their sledges along the edge of this ice across the sea to Canada where they followed the coast northwards. They made camp in between of course and gradually came to Agpaussat, the large point on the Bache Peninsula (79°N), and from there they followed the big fjord westwards, taking their sledges up a valley so that in this way they could reach the sea ice on the other side overland. I know from my trip with Christian Vibe in 1940 that here one has to make camp two or three times on the way. When they reached the ice in Bay Fjord they travelled across it for some time before they set a course northwards skirting Axel Heiberg Land. As was usual Daagitkoorsuaq went ahead on skis. There can be no question that the travellers lacked anything. In this region there are many polar bears and musk-oxen. While they were following the coast of this very big island, Daagit-koorsuaq was one day very nearly eaten by a hungry polar bear. Pualuna had the following to say about this:

> Before we were to round a small point we made a stop to prepare some hot food. As usual Daagitkoorsuaq set off before the others. They had warned him against travelling alone because the area they were in was covered in polar bear tracks. Daagitkoorsuaq knew he was the leader and so he went on ahead without saying anything. He had hardly disappeared around the point when the sledges which were immediately behind him heard him shouting wildly. Some of the sledge drivers cut dogs loose which made for the polar bear, just in time to prevent him being bitten by the large bear which was standing with its jaws already open. The dogs went for the polar bear and Cook was saved at the last minute.

When they reached the northern tip of Axel Heiberg Land the accompanying sledges turned around to go hunting polar bears and musk-oxen. Among them was Pualuna, Oodaaq's older brother.

Only three people remained, and they spent many days at the northern tip of Axel Heiberg Land with an abundance of provisions and equipment. They were not doing anything in particular but their leader wrote and wrote. The young men were very clear about the fact that the trip was to go to the North Pole, as Cook had shown them a map in Anoritooq and explained to them where it lay.

One day at last the leader said it was time to move on. So they set off for the North Pole. The young men were pleased to be off. Young people do not find it especially entertaining to be stuck in one place. They travelled for a long time towards the north on the two dog sledges with the leader out in front on his skis as usual. The whole time they could make out faintly some of the coast of Grant Land. The young men had still not lost any of their courage for they moved forward the whole time. They were carefree every day. Presently they came to large expanses of drift ice and after having travelled through this for some time ice packs came into sight. The leader stopped then and wanted to go no further. He did nothing but write, as usual. Since the young men had nothing else to do, they passed the time by hitting one another to see which of them was the stronger. Sometimes they built small igloos. There is no doubt that this was the reason for their constant good humour. I do not doubt either that their leader was good to them. Daagitkoorsuaq had a remarkable command of the polar Eskimo language. He had after all been along as doctor and ethnographer during Piulersuaq's winter stay in Cape Cleveland 1881–2.

Eventually they turned around and travelled south through the enormous ice packs between which there were also large holes in the ice with tracts of open water. They continued down alongside Axel Heiberg Land directly towards the sound [Hassel Sound and Penny Strait] before the end of the shady side of

Ellesmere Land. Spring was just around the corner. They were not short of provisions since the place they were in was full of animals to hunt, such as polar bears, musk-oxen, reindeer and seals.

Gradually they came to Hell Gate between Ellesmere Land and Devon Island. I have heard that this sound seldom freezes over, especially when the sea currents are stronger than usual. They could thus go no further. There was already too much open water. Spring had of course arrived. In some places the land was very steep and the ice floor was missing. This is the frozen solid coastal ice which remains long after the sea ice. It can in certain cases be used to drive sledges across.

At Hell Gate they stopped for a long time. Remarkably they had a dinghy with them. I believe it was made of canvas with a wooden frame which could be dismantled. Using the dinghy they ferried all their equipment to the edge of the ice opposite. But they had to leave all the dogs behind and one of the sledges. The young men have since told me that, as the dinghy sailed away from the dogs, they barked so much that they could be heard long afterwards. They never saw the dogs again. This was one of the worst experiences for the two young men.

When they reached the edge of the ice once more they loaded the equipment and the dinghy, which they first dismantled, on the sledge, and then they began to walk, pulling the sledge behind them, across the sea ice in Jones Sound, in the direction of a headland on Devon Island. There they intended to build a house. The ice's surface was covered with many melt water puddles and the travelling was very tiring. Of course they slept when they were tired. The two young men were beginning to lose their good humour. They walked for many days.

Exhausted, they eventually reached the headland at Cape Sparbo in early September 1908. When they had finished organising themselves they inspected the place more closely and found that it was very suitable for wintering. There was a rise on the headland, behind which a plateau rose a long way inland. I saw this place myself from a distance in 1930 with the Canadian Police.

... In the time that followed the leader gave the two men instructions to catch only some of the musk-oxen. He gave as his reason the fact that they would run low on ammunition. But it can be assumed that in reality he did not want them to ruthlessly exploit the musk-oxen; and that he was afraid that if there was too much food it would start to rot. It was mid-summer. The meat had no suet which could be used to make tallow for fuel. When autumn came they could catch a lot and the animals would have grown new coats and would be fatter.

Daagitkoorsuaq was being foolish when he told the two young men that they would run low on ammunition. He should instead have explained to the young men what his real reasons were. When the two energetic young hunters heard that there was a shortage of ammunition they ... caught some musk-oxen with their lances but not very many, because it was a dangerous way to hunt without dogs to attack the animals simultaneously. At this time it was usual to travel with lances as reserve equipment.

They built a house further inland using wood from the dinghy and musk-ox skin with which they covered the house's roof. The house was lovely and warm so they were not worried about freezing.

Autumn came. The musk-oxen were ripe as far as meat and skin were concerned. They could now build up a healthy stock of meat and tallow for fuel. They very likely had blubber oil lamps made of stone with them. Cook could also build up meat supplies for the return trip.

They were glad that they had chosen to build the house further inland. They were in fact never troubled by polar bears, although the headland was visited almost every day by these animals, sometimes a pair or a mother with young. But later in the winter a polar bear appeared who did not want to leave them. It bothered them especially at night. By day it left them. One night, when as usual it returned, the two young men prepared themselves with a lantern and a rifle. They hurried out so that they would surprise the polar bear but they discovered that it was closer than they had imagined. One of the hunters was sure that he could hit the bear because it was very close. So he fired. After the shot they rushed back into the house again without further ado as there was nowhere else to go. The one who had fired the shot said he was sure he had hit it, and that the polar bear cried out when it was hit. All the same they did not dare to go out.

Early next morning, while it was still half dark, they both went out again with a rifle to search for the bear. It was lying dead not far from the house. So now they had got a polar bear. The two young men did not hesitate to tell their leader the good news. This polar bear was moreover the only one that came to visit them. It had in fact been in the habit of feeding from their meat stock.

The three men went without nothing because they had been careful to build up supplies which would last them a long time. Besides going hunting the young men were busy sewing suits of musk-ox skin. They sewed gloves and top-boots for protection against the cold on the return trip. Thus for them the polar night did not seem so long. They were also able to keep themselves amused by wrestling. They probably also cheered Cook up when he was a bit depressed.

When summer eventually arrived they discovered just how much he lied. When he went out walking they saw a map in his papers, on which he had drawn a route all the way to the North Pole. The first time they saw it they had a good laugh because they knew there was no question of anything of the sort.

Although they believed he was lying they did not change their attitude towards him. They thought a lot of him and they knew he thought a lot of them. Only on one occasion did they get angry with him. This was when they had to leave their dogs behind, when there was nothing wrong with them and they were alive and well. They could not forget the howling of the dogs when they realised they were being left behind. It was as if they could hear the dogs howling a long time afterwards.

From the accounts of these young hunters we others could later understand how dogged, patient, obedient and respectful they had been. And this is how it should be when one is with an expedition.

Gradually it began to get light. Before very long the sun returned. Nevertheless they stayed put a long time as it was stormy for many days. But they knew that the storms would stop when March came with its light nights. They also knew that at that time some of their friends from the settlement would set off to hunt bears in Canada. That spring as it happened none went hunting polar bears in Ellesmere Land.

I have heard of no unusual or remarkable occurrences on the return trip. But I have no doubt that they hunted on the way, because this area is inhabited by polar bears and seals. They of course had rifles, harpoons and other weapons with them.

At the end of April 1909 the people of Anoritooq saw a small dot appear on the coast of Canada, when they least expected it. At this point there are only fifty kilometres between Canada and Greenland. It was at night, but this was also the time when the sun begins to shine at night. When they realised that it was three men pushing a sledge, they knew who it was and they drove to meet them on their dog sledges.

People were very happy to learn that the North Pole explorers had reached home unharmed and had survived both the summer and a long winter without the help of a single dog. The young men seemed happy by nature and did not let anything discourage them.

Back home in Anoritooq the two young men were very pleased to see their families and parents fit and healthy. They were interrogated thoroughly as to what the North Pole looked like and whether they had actually reached the North Pole. The polar Eskimos had of course been given to understand by Daagitkoorsuaq that he had reached the North Pole! But when the two young men were asked whether they had really reached the North Pole, they just laughed, perhaps because it made them think of the route which had been drawn to the North Pole but also perhaps because they knew that nothing of the sort had happened. They thought it would be a sin if their leader were to have an inkling of what they had seen. We all knew that the two young men were loyal people.

Although they knew they had looked at the map with their leader's invented route to the North Pole, they never dreamed of going along with the joke. I am saying this because I know that later they were interrogated very thoroughly about the North Pole, by Piulersuaq himself. They of course admitted that he had lied. I am in no doubt either that Daagitkoorsuaq never let the two young men, Aapilaq and Itukusuk, know anything of his lie about them reaching the North Pole. He was able to do this because they did not know where the North

Pole lay, or so he thought then. I have already said that they stopped for a long time in an area where there was enormous drift ice and pack ice which had broken loose from the polar ice. They reached the place in the middle of their most hopeless struggle and camped there. Their leader said nothing to them about having reached the North Pole. When I asked them if there was any land, they said they were not so far from land. They of course meant that they could see some of Cape Columbia on the north coast of Ellesmere Land the whole time. It was moreover the place which Piulersuaq used as a depot and starting point for his trips in 1907 and 1909, when he was on his way to the North Pole.

It was not difficult to guess Daagitkoorsuaq's thoughts:

1 Daagitkoorsuaq was clear in his mind that he could not reach the North Pole. He therefore concentrated persistently on the trip in the large drift ice instead.

2 The two ignorant young men did not know where the North Pole lay.

3 To be able to do what he did, he did not want any adults with him.

After several days in the pack ice they would naturally have turned back because their provisions and equipment would not be sufficient for a trip to the North Pole. I think also that there is a big question mark over whether Daagitkoorsuaq rewarded the two young men with something of use after such a protracted trip. I mention this because I have never heard whether the two young men received anything at all for their efforts, although I have no doubt that they were given rifles, knives and the like, and perhaps even some timber.

I have also heard that Daagitkoorsuaq did not stay long in Anoritooq. He of course knew that in the month of August Peary would return from his North Pole trip. Before spring had fully arrived he had people take him by dog sledge to the district of Upernavik in West Greenland. If this was the case, it cannot have been long before he reached his country, America, and there told of how he had reached the North Pole.

I know that the polar Eskimos have nothing bad to say about Daagitkoorsuaq. Nor about his earlier stay in 1881–2.

Note: Inuutersuaq's report (of which only part is here published) was written in his own language a few years before his death. It was translated from the Inughit language into Danish by Tukumeq Qaavigaq, and the Danish version was adapted for publication by Rolf Gilberg. It was first published by the Greenland Society in 1984 under the title *What Has Been Heard About the First Two North Pole Explorers*. The translation into English is by Translagency Ltd, London. I offer my thanks to the Greenland Society and to Rolf Gilberg for permission to publish this extract.

Appendix II

The Peary Hearings

By the end of 1910 Peary had received recognition as the discoverer of the North Pole by almost every geographical society in the western world. But there was one acknowledgment which he craved more than any other, and in seeking promotion and retirement at the rank of Rear-Admiral as his country's recognition of his status and his claims, he was subjected to a Congressional Hearing during which, as the transcripts of the Hearings show, he came close to losing every honour that he had ever earned.

The so-called Peary Hearings were an ordeal for the explorer which lasted three full days, the 7th, 10th and 11th January, 1911, during which Peary personally defended his claim. The transcripts of those Hearings run to some fifty thousand words, in addition to which there were some thirteen thousand words of supporting documents put on the official record. The strain of that final defence of his claim, and the weaknesses which were clearly exposed yet barely recognised at the time will be seen in the following extracts. The notes in italics will serve as a guide to the crucial issues that were raised in the Hearings, and as comment on what was left unchallenged or hidden between the lines.

SUBCOMMITTEE NO. 8 OF THE COMMITTEE ON NAVAL AFFAIRS
Saturday, January 7, 1911

The subcommittee this day met, Hon. Thomas S. Butler (chairman), presiding.

STATEMENT OF CAPT. ROBERT E. PEARY, UNITED STATES NAVY

MR. BUTLER: Capt. Peary, there are two or three bills awaiting the action of the committee, on which congressional action is necessary. You know what the bills are. Yesterday the subcommittee suggested that you should be invited to come here at 10 o'clock this morning and tell us anything you may see fit bearing upon your trip to the North Pole...

When we adjourned last spring [Monday, 7th March, 1910] some members of the committee desired you to submit some proofs that you had been to the North Pole, had succeeded, before congressional action should be taken on any of the bills, and while I have no disposition whatever to examine you or to cross-examine you, if you have any data or any material to submit to us, which will enable us in our own way to establish the fact, we would be glad to have it . . .

If agreeable to you, begin your narrative where Bartlett left you, and tell us what you can which will help us to understand that you actually did reach the pole . . .

Take your own way and drift along, and, for one member of the committee, I shall be greatly pleased to sit here and listen.

[Peary, as requested, gave a general description of his journey from Bartlett's Farthest North to Camp Jesup; but when asked to explain the magnetic Pole, he ran into his first problem.]

Compass Variation
MR. ENGLEBRIGHT: In using a compass in the northern regions you use it with a calculated variation?
CAPT. PEARY: You use it, checking it by observations wherever you can. Along this coast (indicating on map) there are observations made by the British expedition, from this point (indication) out to about here (indicating). There are other observations made by me out to here (indicating) in the summer of 1906 and up to here (indicating) in the summer of 1900. To give you an idea of what those variations are, here at Roosevelt (indicating) the variation is approximately 95 west. In other words, the north end of the needle points a little south of true west, and as you go west that increases.
MR. ENGLEBRIGHT: Is not that all charted by the Coast Survey and by the maritime nations of the world?
CAPT. PEARY: They have the lines of certain variations, but, of course, the greater the number of observations, the more accurate the data.
MR. ENGLEBRIGHT: Did you have such a chart with you?
CAPT. PEARY: No, sir; I did not have such a chart.
MR. DAWSON: Did you make any observations in the locality which would tend to throw any additional light on the variation of the needle?
CAPT. PEARY: I did not on this last expedition: I did on the previous ones . . .

[Peary at this point side-stepped the issue of why he did not take any observations for magnetic variation by continuing his account of what he did at Camp Jesup, and no one on the committee pressed him to return to that sensitive issue for the obvious reason that they were unaware of its significance. He then told them about his soundings. He even told them that he had lost the line. But again, the committee missed their opportunity to ask him why he had told the US Coast and Geodetic Survey that all of his soundings "were made on the meridian of Cape Columbia" when he had not taken any observations for longitude.]

Appendix II

Faked Observations

MR. BUTLER: We have your word for it, and we have these observations to show that you were at the North Pole. That is the plain way of putting it – your word and your proofs. To me, as a member of this committee, I accept your word; but your proofs, I know nothing at all about.

. . . I will ask you this question: Was it absolutely necessary for you to have been at the North Pole in order to make these observations? Maybe I should not, but I do. I am perfectly satisfied with your statement, but was it necessary to have been absolutely at the pole in order to have made the observations which you did make?

CAPT. PEARY: That is a question on which there has been some discussion. I can answer it by saying that observations have never been made yet that were not made at the place.

MR. BUTLER: You must have been at the place to have made certain observations, and if you were there you were there, but could you have made the figure without having been at the pole, and if you had made the figure without having been there, is there any way to detect your effort?

CAPT. PEARY: That is a thing I can only answer in this way. There is a difference of opinion in regard to that. You will find that some experts will say that observations can be arranged and others will say that they can not.

MR. BUTLER: Observations, in other words, can be written down as having been made by a person who reports to have been at a certain place?

CAPT. PEARY: That has been stated.

MR. ROBERTS: Mr. Gannett and Mr. Tittmann told us that it is possible for a person who has sufficient knowledge to sit down in a department here in Washington and make figures and claim to have been at a point where the so-called observation was made. In other words, that the figures themselves would not carry any proof on their face.

CAPT. PEARY: That is the opinion of an expert.

[*This was Peary's toughest test so far; but Roberts did not press home this line of questioning, and Dawson then changed the subject to the conditions under which the diary was written. In the course of this discussion, Peary gave the committee Bartlett's address, "in case you should care to write him," but they did not follow this up and invite him to offer any statement, nor did the committee call Henson as a witness.*]

The National Geographic Society and the Diary

MR. ROBERTS: . . . If I understand, this identical memorandum book was submitted to the committee of the Geographic Society, was it not? . . . And the members of that committee read all of it carefully?

CAPT. PEARY: No; I will not say they read all of it carefully. It was passed around. I can not say how much they read . . . I do not know whether any one man read right straight through or not.

[*Mr. Macon pressed this issue; but to no avail as the subject was again changed, Peary now being asked to read his diary out loud. And this at one point had embarrassed him.*]

CAPT. PEARY: . . . On the next day, the 6th, I have this entry, after we had built our igloos and entered them: "The pole at last!!! The prize of 3 centuries, my dream and ambition for 23 years." I do not care to read this . . . The only thing about it is it sounds a little bit foolish to be reading it oneself.

[*But Peary was persuaded to continue reading his entry for the record, and when he came to the missing entries, no one asked why he had written nothing at the Pole.*]

CAPT. PEARY: . . . There are no continuous entries after that until Friday, April 9.

MR. MACON: You did not record what you did during the 30 hours you were at the pole?

[*Peary produced memoranda of the events but later admitted the diary contained no entries.*]

CAPT. PEARY: . . . I started back on the afternoon of the 7th. For the 8th I made no entry at all . . .

[*At 12.15 p.m., the subcommittee adjourned. It met again on Tuesday, 10th January, 1911, and amongst other things heard that Peary had submitted to the Navy Department's annual physical tests, and passed. The test taken was on roads in the Chevy Chase area of Washington, D.C. and Peary had walked fifty miles in twenty hours over a period of three consecutive days. He was then asked what his best day's travel was on his return from the Pole, and replied: "Fifty geographical miles, estimated."*]

Soundings

[*A letter from the US Coast and Geodetic Survey to Peary dated 21st October, 1909, was entered on the record in which he had been asked to provide "data for determining their positions." Peary's reply, dated 28th October, 1909, was also put on record, and on the matter of positions he stated "that these soundings were made on the meridian of Cape Columbia, and plotting on that meridian at the latitudes which I think are noted in the table on the profile sheet will give their position." He did not state how he kept such a straight course, nor did any member of the subcommittee ask that crucial question. One good question, however, was asked.*]

MR. ENGLEBRIGHT: . . . On a trip to the North Pole, finding nothing but floating ice, the only possible identification that could be made would be a result of soundings, would it not, that any future explorer could identify the position? In other words, if another explorer should go to the North Pole and within five miles of the pole should drop the lead down and strike bottom in 100 fathoms of water that would show a defect in your report. The fact is there is nothing else a man could do except to take soundings to identify his position or leave a record?

CAPT. PEARY: If a line of soundings were carried to the pole and every one touched bottom that would be an absolute identification and verification right straight through. If a line of soundings were taken and they reported 1,500 feet bottom and somebody else should go there and get only 100 fathoms, that would not look well, but if someone else should go there and should get 2,000 fathoms or 2,500 fathoms, I would say that it would not show anything.

[*It would appear from this comment that Peary does not consider the system of sounding with very fine wire and a weight reliable at the greater depths. It should also be noted that Peary's line of nine soundings was not taken on the meridian of Cape Columbia, as he believed, and to date the only line of soundings that has been made on that meridian was recorded by HMS* Sovereign *in October 1976, and these do not match up with the 1909 data.*

Bartlett's last sounding at latitude 87°15' found no bottom at 1,260 fathoms (7,560 feet). Peary's "five miles from the North Pole," found no bottom at 1,500 fathoms (9,000 feet) and, on reeling in, "the wire parted, as had been feared, and the last lead and nearly all of the wire was lost." Between these soundings, however, they had crossed the submarine Lomonosov Ridge, the highest point of which on the 70th meridian is only 656 fathoms (3,936 feet). So what, if anything, can be deduced from Peary's soundings?

At the North Pole the depth of the ocean bed is now known to be 2,346 fathoms (some 14,000 feet). Peary's 1,500 fathom no bottom would fit this, had he been there, but all the hard evidence indicates that his course had been deflected to the west by the drift of ice. This being the case, both Camp Jesup and his Farthest North could have been over the Lomonosov Ridge, and doubtless it will be argued that this theory is flawed since Peary found no bottom at 1,500 fathoms. But the submarine ridge is not more than twenty-five miles wide in that area and rises steeply from the ocean bed some 1,200 fathoms (7,200 feet) over a distance of only ten miles. He could have been only one or two miles from the escarpment edge and got a 1,500 fathom no bottom, and in any case, his sounding system was unreliable at those depths. Indeed, the last sounding which found bottom on that trip was Marvin's at latitude 85°23', only 137 miles from Cape Columbia, and HMS Sovereign *found the ocean bed to be 260 fathoms deeper in that area. Peary's soundings are therefore of no use as an indicator of either his route or his Farthest North.*]

Witnesses

MR. ROBERTS: . . . I am going to take the liberty of asking you why, when you went to the pole on your final dash, you did not take with you some of the members of your party in order that there might be credible corroborative evidence if the question was ever raised as to attaining the pole? I do not know whether you care to answer that question.

CAPT. PEARY: I have not the slightest objection to answering that question, Mr. Roberts . . . The pole was something to which I had devoted my life; it was a thing on which I had concentrated everything, on which I had expended some of myself, for which I had gone through such hell and suffering as I hope no man in this room may ever experience, and in which I had put money, time, and everything else, and I did not feel that under those circumstances I was called upon to divide with a man who, no matter how able and deserving he might be, was a young man and had only put a few years in that kind of work and who had, frankly as I believed, not the right I had to it. I think that conveys my idea.

[*The committee adjourned shortly after hearing Peary's reason for not presenting himself and his records the previous year, namely, that he was not "ready to have the results of [his] work published."*

The subcommittee met again on Wednesday, 11th January, 1911, when he stated that he had told no one on the ship of his success because: "As is known by the records I was under honorable obligations to furnish the account of my expedition on my return, and I felt that I should protect the account of the journey by reserving it rather than giving it to anyone else previous to reaching home."]

The Diary

MR. ROBERTS: Have you any objection to my reading what is on the outside of it, simply to identify it?

CAPT. PEARY: No, sir.

MR. ROBERTS: (reading) "No. 1, *Roosevelt* to —— and return, February 22 to April 27, R. E. Peary, United States Navy."

[*Surprisingly, Mr. Roberts did not follow this up, and ask why Peary had not completed the title page with the words "North Pole."*]

MR. ROBERTS: Have you any objection to my looking through the book?

CAPT. PEARY: No objection, except that I would like to call your attention to the personal notes.

MR. ROBERTS: . . . Would you leave this book to be examined by the committee?

CAPT. PEARY: I do not care to leave it with the committee or anyone. I do not care to let it out of my possession; it never has been.

MR. ROBERTS: If the members of the committee care to, I would like to have the book examined, particularly with reference to its condition and state. It shows no finger marks or rough usage; a very cleanly kept book.

[*The implication of this remark appears to be that the diary had not been written in the field; but it was taken no further. Nor was any comment made on the consistency of the handwriting throughout the diary, a point remarked upon by a handwriting expert at Scotland Yard's Forensic Science Laboratory in London. My personal belief (having studied the original very closely) is that it was written in the field. The fact that the only direct reference to the North Pole is on a loose-leaf page is, however, significant. The blank pages released Peary from any need to commit himself until he had more time to think through his dilemma.*]

Appendix II

Naval Service
[*This aggressive line of questioning was clearly inspired by the Line Officers in the Navy who objected to a Civil Engineer being given high rank and the "Thanks of Congress" for what in effect was an achievement outside of the naval commitment.*]

MR. MACON: Mr. Chairman, the committee having under consideration a bill for the purpose of promoting Capt. Peary to rear-admiral for the discovery of the North Pole, which, in a sense, would be to place in his hands on the part of the American people a passport into every phase of human society as an American hero, and remembering that this country and every other country has been infested with bogus heroes as well as real ones, I consider that we ought to go into this matter upon the merits of the case and not becloud it by comparing his marches in the polar region with a dog race in Alaska.

MR. BUTLER: Can not that be determined when we meet in executive session?

MR. MACON: I am proceeding now. And not becloud or confuse it with a description of the character of food that he ate while he was on the trip, but that we ought to consider the facts connected with this case and not treat it as a joke. It is too serious a matter, and hence in my examination of the gentleman I propose to deal with the meritorious facts in connection with his case as I see them. Capt. Peary, this being, as I said a little while ago, the consideration of a bill to confer high honors upon you, I want to find out whether or not you are entitled to them, whether your services to the Government have been of such moment as to make you worthy of them. If they have been, I want you to have it. Therefore I will ask you, to start with, how long have you been in the service of the Government in connection with your duties as a naval officer?

CAPT. PEARY: I entered the service on the 26th of October, 1881, I think.

MR. MACON: A little over 29 years?

CAPT. PEARY: The 26th of October, 1881, I think, was the date.

MR. MACON: How much of that time have you devoted to real service in the Navy Department?

CAPT. PEARY: That I cannot answer off hand. I think this is stated in a letter from the Secretary of the Navy to this committee; it was written last winter.

MR. MACON: You can approximate it in years; we do not ask for months or days.

CAPT. PEARY: That information, I think, will be found in detail on page 23 of Mr. Moore's speech.

MR. MACON: Mr. Moore's speech? You can not approximate it, then?

CAPT. PEARY: Not unless it is given there.

MR. MACON: Then I will ask you if you can approximate how many years you have devoted to polar or arctic explorations? I will not say polar explorations, because I do not believe you have been in search of the pole all the time you have been out.

CAPT. PEARY: My first expedition was in 1886. The answer to that question is also given in detail on page 6 of Mr. Moore's speech.

MR. DAWSON: I suggest that both statements go into the record.

MR. MACON: I am trying to find out from him. He is supposed to know as much about it as Mr. Moore.

CAPT. PEARY: These are official documents.

MR. MACON: He is supposed to know about the official records. I know as much about the time I have given to my duties as Congressman since I have been a Member of Congress as my official record could disclose.

MR. DAWSON: Of course, if the gentleman from Arkansas does not want the facts to go into the record ----

MR. MACON: That is what I am after. I am after the facts. That is exactly what I am after. I am not after second-handed facts; I want them first-handed ... yesterday the captain stated to the committee that this matter had been his lifework; that his soul, practically, was wrapped in it to the extent that he was not willing to share any part of the glory of it with anybody on the face of the earth. Now, if he has made a lifework of it, if he has been so wrapped in what he was doing, then he ought to have felt enough interest to be able to give us the information of his own knowledge.

CAPT. PEARY: I am unable to answer that question in detail without information or the written record.

MR. MACON: Will you put it in the record?

CAPT. PEARY: I will ask the committee to accept the statement of the Navy Department for the time I was on leave, and that the time I was on leave subtracted from the total time since I entered the service in October 1886, will give you the amount of time I have been on duty.

MR. ROBERTS: There (handing paper to Capt. Peary) is the whole record from the Navy Department if you care to look it over in order to answer the question.

CAPT. PEARY: (after examining letter) I will say that the letter here states that I performed active duty for 12 years and 9 days. That would be up to the date of this letter, February 11, 1910. I have been unemployed for 16 years, 1 month, and 16 days. Of this unemployed duty approximately 13 years and 5 months have been spent on leave while unattached, and the balance on waiting orders or leave on duty. (With the exception of two days of duty, October 25 and October 26), according to this report, I was on "leave without pay."

MR. MACON: For 6 months during 16 years you did not receive pay?

CAPT. PEARY: That is the statement. That would be essentially in accordance with my recollection.

[*After another diversion into the subject of soundings, Macon asked Peary how many observations were taken on his journey, and noted from Peary's reply that only three latitude shots were taken and no observations for longitude as far as Bartlett's Farthest North. And at that point the subcommitee had taken a break for two hours.*]

Appendix II

Observations

MR. MACON: I believe we left off with the observations. We had just taken up the subject of observations. I believe I asked you to tell the committee what observations were taken on this trip, the number and character of them, and you explained certain ones. You said, I believe, that you took no longitude observations at all?

CAPT. PEARY: I took no observations for longitude at any time on the trip.

MR. MACON: I am advised by astronomers and geographers and explorers and scientists that it is impossible for any one in a broad field, as you were going over on your explorations of the North Pole, to tell exactly the direction they were traveling unless they took longitude observations. What do you say about that?

CAPT. PEARY: I should say that would be an opinion to be left to experts.

MR. MACON: Then, if the experts differed about the matter, there would be some confusion?

CAPT. PEARY: Yes, sir.

MR. MACON: What is your opinion about it?

CAPT. PEARY: My opinion is that we were able to keep our course. My opinion also is that at the time of the year, and under the conditions existing there, any attempt at taking longitude observations would have been a waste of time.

MR. MACON: Why so?

CAPT. PEARY: In the middle part of the journey the altitude of the sun was so low that presumably any longitude observations would have been unnecessary, and in the neighborhood of the pole it is generally recognized that longitude observations are not practicable with any degree of accuracy.

MR. MACON: Then, you do not hold to the teachings of other scientists, which is to the effect that unless you take the longitude observations you cannot know exactly the direction in which you are traveling?

CAPT. PEARY: I do not think that I care to go into a discussion of general principles. I will state the facts, and also my determination of those facts, to the committee or to any experts.

MR. MACON: You are an explorer, so reputed, and we want to find out whether or not you knew what you were doing. When you send a man into the field to plough he must know something about the work or he will not do much intelligent work.

CAPT. PEARY: I do not care to go into a discussion of general principles. I am willing to give the facts in regard to the work.

MR. MACON: You have no scientific opinion to offer?

CAPT. PEARY: No more than was contained in my earlier replies – that I thought any attempt to take longitude observations would have been a waste of time.

[*This is an astonishing reply, and one which several "revisionists" who support Peary's claim persist in believing. Larry Schweikart, Assistant Professor of History at the University*

of Draton, in his article in the May 1986 number of The Historian, *is a case in point.*
He takes as proof of Peary's ability to navigate by dead-reckoning a comment made in
the English edition of my own book Across the Top of the World, *in which I said:*
"Our final approach to the Pole was made on dead-reckoning using a very hazy sun for a
general direction." He goes on to say that "Uemura and Herbert duplicated Peary's
'incredible navigational folly,' [not taking observations for longitude] indicating that Peary's
methods were, and are, sound."

This reading is utterly absurd. We checked our dead-reckoning against our position fixes
– a latitude shot at local noon and a full position fix at the end of each day when the sun
was visible (or the stars and planets during the first month of the journey). Rarely did we
travel for more than four days without being able to get a position fix, and those fixes are
vital. Without a knowledge of one's position and a regularly up-dated check on the variation
of the compass, it is impossible to reach the North Pole.

Again, on the issue of Peary's speeds, Schweikart compares them with a dog-sledge race
and claims that the racers' speeds of five miles per hour "clearly demonstrate the plausibility
of Peary's return rate of 2.16 miles per hour." He quotes me again as saying that near
the Pole "conditions got better all the time. The surface was so good that once or twice the
dogs actually broke into a gallop." But he does not mention our average distances for the
obvious reason that to compare them with Peary's would totally destroy his argument. The
plain fact is that Peary's claimed speeds are extremely dubious and no amount of theory
will make them any less so.]

MR. MACON: How many observations were taken by you after you left Mr. Bartlett,
at 87° 47', between that and the North Pole, a distance of 133 miles – observations
of any kind?

CAPT. PEARY: I would like to say that I took in all 13 single or 6.5 double
observations of the sun at two different stations in three different directions at
four different times.

MR. MACON: Where were they taken?

CAPT. PEARY: Three sets of those observations were taken at Camp Jesup, and
one set was taken at a point an estimated distance of 10 miles beyond that camp.

MR. MACON: Camp Jesup was right at the pole?

CAPT. PEARY: It was the pole camp.

MR. MACON: Then you took no observations, longitude or otherwise for a distance
of 133 miles after you left Bartlett at 87° 47'?

CAPT. PEARY: No, sir.

MR. MACON: And without that you managed to make a straight course to the pole
without anything except conjecture or estimate to guide you. Is that it?

CAPT. PEARY: I leave the observations to answer that question. I am satisfied that
I made that distance, was in fairly close limits as I have done on other journeys
on previous expeditions.

MR. MACON: . . . How did you come to the conclusion that you were 4 or 5 miles from the pole toward the Bering Sea when you had not taken any longitude observations?

CAPT. PEARY: I did not know that until I had taken my observations.

MR. MACON: But you took no longitude observations?

CAPT. PEARY: I took no observations for longitude.

MR. MACON: What character of observations led you to conclude that you were west of the pole 4 or 5 miles?

CAPT. PEARY: The observations taken by me at those two places of which I speak. After I had taken the series of observations which I had noted, I felt I knew approximately my position as indicated in the book.

[Peary was clearly under tremendous pressure at this point, but neither Macon nor any of the other members of the subcommittee had the navigational knowledge to pin him down and he was saved by the bell at the count of nine. From this point on, however, Macon became utterly absurd, and lost not only his way, but also his argument, and his cool.]

MR. MACON: Explorers and a certain class of scientists tell us that conditions are such in the Arctic Zone that . . . an ordinary hare would be the size of a good-sized animal, and that an object that might appear small here would be about the size of a mountain . . . if that condition does exist, that an animal is so magnified or an object is so magnified, how do you explain to the committee that you took a correct observation?

MR. DAWSON: It would not affect the instrument?

CAPT. PEARY: It would not affect the instrument.

MR. ENGLEBRIGHT: And it would not affect the eye?

CAPT. PEARY: I do not see how the eye would be affected in that way.

MR. MACON: The same eye that looked through the instrument would look at the animal.

MR. MACON: . . . Would recomputing the records of your observations be satisfactory evidence of where you were when they were taken – recomputed here in Washington?

CAPT. PEARY: I do not know that I understand that question.

MR. MACON: I ask you if a recomputing of your records, the records of your observations, would be a satisfactory evidence?

CAPT. PEARY: I should say that it would be generally so considered.

MR. MACON: Then, when they could not rely upon them, you appear to differ from them – Messrs Gannett and Tittmann – who passed upon your record. Your narrative could have been written here in Washington or at Bartlett's Camp. That could not be considered competent or satisfactory evidence by geographers or scientists, could it?

MR. BATES: This witness is not here to be lectured.

MR. MACON: I am asking questions.

MR. BATES: I submit, Mr. Chairman, that this witness is not here to be lectured.

MR. MACON: I am not lecturing him.

MR. BATES: You are giving an opinion, Mr. Macon.

MR. MACON: If I am offensive to the gentleman from Pennsylvania ----

MR. BATES: No, you are not, but you are taking up valuable time.

MR. MACON: My time is as valuable to me as it is to you, and I insist I am taking up time trying to ascertain the truth – not what pemmican is made of. You did not complain when they were asking about immaterial things this morning.

MR. BATES: I objected because the gentleman's remarks were, in a sense, a severe stricture on the witness, who came before us at our request.

MR. MACON: I am asking him questions. He can decline to answer any one of them if he wants to.

MR. BUTLER: Ask a question, Mr. Macon. We invited Capt. Peary to come, and I am sure he will answer anything he feels he can answer.

MR. MACON: Captain, did you find any evidence of increase or diminution of weight at the pole?

CAPT. PEARY: I did not, except the weight of the members of the party and the dogs.

MR. MACON: I mean change in weight except for lack of foodstuff?

CAPT. PEARY: I beg your pardon?

MR. MACON: Did they change except perhaps for lack of foodstuff?

CAPT. PEARY: Not that I noticed; no.

MR. MACON: Did you find any decided atmospheric changes?

CAPT. PEARY: I did not.

MR. MACON: Did the needle answer to the primary or the secondary magnetic pole?

CAPT. PEARY: The direction of the compass was fairly constant there.

MR. BUTLER: Will you tell me, please, what that means?

MR. MACON: I asked him whether the needle answered to the primary or secondary magnetic pole.

MR. BUTLER: What are they?

MR. MACON: Oh, they are known in science.

MR. BATES: Where did you find that question?

MR. MACON: They are known in science.

MR. BATES: But I am not a scientific person.

MR. DAWSON: I would be glad if the gentleman from Arkansas would explain.

MR. MACON: The gentleman from Arkansas is going to ask questions, and he is not going to ask any foolish ones either.

MR. ENGLEBRIGHT: Is he trying to test the Captain's knowledge on science by asking such questions – ridiculous questions?

MR. MACON: I have asked no ridiculous questions.

MR. ENGLEBRIGHT: Did you ever hear of a primary or secondary magnetic pole?

MR. MACON: Yes, I have.

MR. ENGLEBRIGHT: Where – in Arkansas?

MR. MACON: Where I have heard of everything else – no; in Washington. And I want to say to the gentleman from California if he intends it as a slur in regard to Arkansas, that it is unworthy of him.

[*Macon regained some of his composure but very little of his earlier sting, even on the subject of Peary's speeds and distances, and from the transcripts his aggression appears to have eventually irritated Peary who, up to this point, had suffered his interrogator with great dignity. "No," Peary corrected Macon on the distances he was extracting; but Macon ploughed on. "Excuse me ----" Peary exclaimed three times before he could get his correction recorded.*

But he did get in one good shot and no one even noticed.]

MR. MACON: Did you take into account any detours, by reason of having to go around any object, any obstruction, or going over obstructions, did you make any estimate about them?

CAPT. PEARY: My estimate of the distance, as I have stated, was that it was 10 miles to my farthest point [from Camp Jesup] and 8 miles to the point to the right – I was about to say east, but there is no east or west there.

[*Peary simply avoided the question. Macon had then asked him how many days behind Bartlett he was in reaching the ship, and on getting Peary's astonishing reply of only four days, no one took it up.*]

Proofs

MR. MACON: There having been quite a rivalry between your friends and the friends of Dr. Cook over the discovery of the pole and his having submitted his proofs, as they are called, to the Copenhagen University, I want to ask you if you would be willing on account of that rivalry to have your proofs submitted to the same tribunal, to be passed upon by it?

CAPT. PEARY: I should prefer not to go into that question at all. I think the question is one that could be answered for himself by any and every member of the committee.

MR. MACON: Now, the gentlemen who were before us last spring said that they were of a subcommittee that examined your proofs, and they admitted that they had made up their minds about your having discovered the pole before they saw any of them at all. Therefore they could not have been an impartial jury to sit upon your case. That is the reason why I ask whether or not you would be willing to allow your proofs now to be submitted to the same impartial tribunals that passed upon the credibility of Dr. Cook's proofs. If you are not willing to submit proofs to them, all you have to do is to say so; nobody has any power to make you do so.

MR. BUTLER: My recollection is that the Danes concluded that Cook reached the North Pole ----

MR. MACON: No, that was all done before they examined the proofs-----

MR. BUTLER: They did that before they examined the proofs?

MR. MACON: Yes.

MR. DAWSON: Cook exploded in the meantime, did he not?

MR. MACON: No, he did not explode at all.

MR. BUTLER: What was the question?

CAPT. PEARY: I think I answered the last question.

MR. MACON: The question I asked was whether he would be willing to submit his proofs, that he said he did not want to go into that subject. In other words, he declines to say whether he will or will not. Of course that will carry the idea that he refuses to do so.

MR. BATES: Nothing of the sort.

MR. MACON: It does. Captain, have your proofs been submitted to any geographical or scientific society to be passed upon except this National Geographic Society?

CAPT. PEARY: This is a copy of the letter received by me from Maj. Leonard Darwin, president of the Royal Geographical Society of London (indicating). This is a copy of a letter received by me from Mr. Douglas W. Freshfield, member of the council of the Royal Geographical Society.

(Capt. Peary read the two letters referred to, as follows:)

Royal Geographical Society,
1 Savile Row, Burlington Gardens,
London W. December 5, 1910

Commander R. E. Peary,
Eagle Island, South Harpswell, Me., United States.

Dear Commander Peary,
Please accept our sincere thanks for the documents you have sent us, including copies of the observations taken by you at the pole. They have been thoroughly examined by us. In the opinion of my council there is nothing in this or any other new matter which has come to their notice that in any way affects the position indicated by me when I, on behalf of the society, presented you with a special gold medal at the Albert Hall for your explorations, during which you were the first to reach a pole of the earth.

With best wishes, believe me, yours sincerely,
LEONARD DARWIN, President R.G.S.

[*These letters, and the testimony of Tittmann and Mitchell on Peary's observations saved him, for it was assumed that the Royal Geographical Society and the two US Coast and Geodetic Society computers would have taken into account all of the navigational issues.*

But this they had not done. The RGS was presented by Peary with seven pages of copies of his observations, and five typed pages of extracts from his diary. They were already committed to presenting him with the special gold medal and had no choice, if they were to avoid an extremely embarrassing situation, but to assume that his data had been observed at the Pole, and to go through the motions of checking it.]

MR. ROBERTS: Just one question . . . I forgot. You spoke of submitting copies of your records to the Royal Geographical Society of London. Did they request you to do so?
CAPT. PEARY: I was asked if I would bring my records with me.
MR. ROBERTS: On what occasion?
CAPT. PEARY: When I went over there; I stated that I would bring them and submit them to the Society.
MR. ROBERTS: Did you take the originals?
CAPT. PEARY: I did.
MR. ROBERTS: But you submitted copies?
CAPT. PEARY: I submitted copies.
MR. ROBERTS: That was *after* the award of the medal?
CAPT. PEARY: Yes.

[*Thus the prize was won.*]

References

Note: P refers to Peary. Book publication details are supplied in full in the bibliography.

PROLOGUE   *page 11*

11 P to Congressional subcommittee: Committee on Naval Affairs, Subcommittee on Private Bills, the so-called Peary Hearings, 11th Jan, 1911, p 84.

18 'The Pole at last': Robert E. Peary, *The North Pole* (1910), p 257.

CHAPTER 1   Guests of Honour   *pages 21–33*

Note: Quotations from speeches made at the banquet held at the Willard Hotel in Washington, D.C. on 15th Dec, 1906, can be found in the *National Geographic Magazine*, January, 1907.

25 'I would rather die': Frederick A. Cook, autobiographical sketch (unpublished), Stefansson Collection. See also Hugh Eames, *Winner Lose All*, (1973) pp 24–5.

25 'You are through': Ibid., pp 24–5.

26 'fascination which makes men risk': Frederick A. Cook, *My Attainment of the Pole* (1911), p 28.

29–30 Belmore Browne: *The Conquest of Mt. McKinley* (1913), pp 70–1.

33 'I had no money': Cook, *My Attainment of the Pole*, op. cit., p 29.

CHAPTER 2   The Sheltered Years   *pages 34–43*

34 'the purest accident': Fitzhugh Green, *Peary: the Man Who Refused to Fail* (1926), p 52.

34 John E. Weems: *Peary: The Explorer and the Man* (1967), pp 68–9.

35 'It is impossible to point': Peary, *The North Pole*, op. cit., p 25.

35–6 'One of the tonic themes': Green, op. cit., pp 18–20, 20–1.

37 Marie Peary Stafford: *Discoverer of the North Pole* (1959), pp 12–15.

37 'living alone with his mother': Green, op. cit., p 21.

38 P to his mother: letters dated 18th June, 1865 and 28th Feb, 1868.

39 'In the early years': Cook, *My Attainment of the Pole*, op. cit., p 26.

40 'The study of nature': essay, 3rd Feb, 1872.

40 'About nine o'clock': P diary, 12th Jan, 1873.

41 'lonesome, oh so lonesome': P diary, 17th Oct, 1873.

41 'Mother is so weak.': P diary, 8th Jan, 1874.

42 'I have asked myself': P to Mary Kilby, 16th May, 1875.

42 'How many have wished': P to Mary Kilby, 6th May, 1877.

43 'I am trying an experiment': P to Mary Kilby, 10th Oct, 1877.

CHAPTER 3 The Uncertain Direction of Fame *pages 44–51*

45–7 P to his mother: 16th Aug, probably 1880.

47 'stay where he was': Marie Peary Stafford, *Discoverer of the North Pole*, op. cit., p 35.

47 'my fortune or misfortune?': P to his mother, 10th October, 1880.

48 'these glorious influences': P, draft MS, 1881.

50 'satisfied from his showing': Green, *Peary: the Man Who Refused to Fail*, op. cit., p 34.

50 P to his mother: 14th Dec, 1881.

50 Buying Eagle Island: Marie Peary Stafford, op. cit., p 49. According to her son, Commander E. Stafford, U.S.N. (Rtd.), Peary bought Eagle Island "with the first $500 he was able to set aside" two years after graduating from Bowdoin College (i.e. in 1879).

51 P to his mother: 28th Dec, 1884.

51 The three months in Nicaragua: P diary, 4th and 6th Feb, 1885.

51 'I came upon a fugitive paper': Peary, *Northward Over the Great Ice* (1898), Vol 1, p xxxiv.

CHAPTER 4 The Persistent Devil, *pages 52–63*

52 Secretary of the Navy to P: letter dated 14th April, 1886.

55 William Scoresby: 'The Polar Ice' (Caedmon of Whitby, 1980, reprint of 1815 paper), pp 329–33.

58 I. I. Hayes: *The Open Polar Sea* (1867) pp 1–2.

60 Capt. Sir G. S. Nares, R.N.: *A Voyage to the Polar Sea* (1878), Vol 1, pp 394–5.

61 Adolphus W. Greely: *Three Years of Arctic Service* (1886), Vol 1, Preface p vi.

61–2 'There should be one head': P diary, 1885. National Archives. See also: Weems, *Peary: the Explorer and the Man*, op. cit., pp 71–3.

CHAPTER 5 Fame – One Way or Another, *pages 64–74*

64 Greenland Ice Cap 'attainment': Peary, *Northward Over the Great Ice*, op. cit., Vol 1, p 39.

64 'an invaluable fund': Ibid., p 39.

65 Fridtjof Nansen: *The First Crossing of Greenland* (1896), Vol 1, pp 505–6. See also J. Gordon Hayes, *Robert Edwin Peary*, p 16.

65 Fitzhugh Green: *Peary: The Man Who Refused to Fail*, op. cit., p 52.

66 'I am too impatient': P diary, 27th May, 1886.

66 'I can't get along without': Bradley Robinson, *Dark Companion* (1947), p viii, Foreword by Donald B. MacMillan.

66   Henson's mixed race: Ibid., p 5.

67   Childs to Henson: Ibid., pp 26–7.

67   'a strangely grotesque pair': Ibid., p 21.

67   Childs to Henson: Ibid., p 28.

68   First meeting of Henson and P: Ibid., p 52.

68   P's mother to P: 10th March, 1887.

69   Robert E. Peary, 'Recent Nicaragua Ship Canal Surveys': (*Proc. Amer. Assoc. Adv. Sci.* 37th Meeting held in Cleveland, Aug 1888, and Salem, May 1889), pp 386–91.

70   'I shall be indispensable': P to his mother, 6th May, 1888.

71   'This forestalling of my work': Peary, *Northward Over the Great Ice*, op. cit., Vol I, p xxxvii (Introduction).

71   'Nansen's Greenland plan': Nansen' *The First Crossing of Greenland*, op. cit., Vol 1, pp 3–4.

CHAPTER 6 The Vision *pages 75–89*

75   'Scores of whistles': Peary, *Northward Over the Great Ice*, op. cit., Vol 1, p 43.

75   'Now I feel': P to his mother, 11th June, 1891.

76   'Thanks to the professional skill': Peary, *Northward Over the Great Ice*, op. cit., Vol 1, p 65.

76   'They were all young': Ibid., p 45.

77   'His intelligence and faithfulness': Ibid., pp 45–7.

77   'Possessed of health': Ibid., p 47.

77–8 'She has been': Josephine Diebitsch-Peary, *My Arctic Journal* (1893), pp 3–5.

80   'I wished to become well acquainted': Peary, *Northward Over the Great Ice*, op. cit., Vol 1, p 74.

80–1 Cook's report: Ibid., pp 114–21.

82–3 JP on the Eskimos: Josephine Peary, op. cit., pp 41, 89–90, 125–8.

83   'a systematic series of interviews': Peary, *Northward Over the Great Ice*, op. cit., Vol 1, pp 153–4.

83   'On one side of the stove': Ibid., p 175.

84–6 The collapse of the igloo: Ibid., pp 199–210.

86   'I was more or less in the dark': Ibid., pp 277–8.

87   'A few steps more': Ibid., pp 345–6.

88   Congressional Record: speech by Hon. Henry T. Helgesen in the House of Representatives, 13th Jan, 1916.

88   P on Verhoeff's death: Peary, *Northward Over the Great Ice*, op. cit., Vol 1, pp 415–16.

89   Nansen to P: 29th Sept, 1891.

CHAPTER 7 The Deepening Obsession *pages 90–109*

90   P's objectives: Peary, *Northward Over the Great Ice*, op. cit., Vol 2, p 550.

90   Wistar's support: Ibid., Intro. p 43.

91   'I had six months': Ibid., Intro. p 43.

91   Pond on P's lecture tour: Green, *Peary: the Man Who Refused to Fail*, op. cit., p 104.

92   'To Dr. Cook's care': Peary, *Northward Over the Great Ice*, op. cit., Vol 1, pp 423–4.

92   'The report would be incomplete': *New York Herald*, 28th Sept, 1909.

93   'Here was the only break': Cook, Autobiographical Sketch, op. cit.

94   P on birth of daughter: Peary, *Northward Over the Great Ice*, op. cit., Vol 2, pp 68–70.

94–5 'a big wave': Ibid., pp 70–6.

95   'I'll conquer yet': Weems, *Peary: the Explorer and the Man*, op. cit., p 138.

95   'For thirty-four hours': Peary, *Northward Over the Great Ice*, op. cit., Vol 2, pp 97–100.

95   P turns back: Ibid., pp 112–13.

96   'The causes of failure': Ibid., p 120.

96–7 P's footnote: Ibid., p 159.

97   Cook on Astrup's death: Cook, *My Attainment of the Pole*, op. cit., pp 38–9 (footnote).

97–8 Cook on Verhoeff's death: Ibid., p 63.

98   'the first white persons': Peary, *Northward Over the Great Ice*, op. cit., Vol 2, p 123.

98   Search for the meteorites: Ibid., pp 127–55.

98–9 Lee to his mother: Weems, op. cit., p 148.

99   'Davidson and Carr': Peary, *Northward Over the Great Ice*, op. cit., Vol 2, p 115.

99   Samuel J. Entrikin: *Tourist Magazine*, Dec 1910, pp 453–6.

99   'Peary's failure': Ibid.

100 Baldwin on P: Ibid., pp 467–8.

102 'After the first three days': Peary, *Northward Over the Great Ice*, op. cit., Vol 2, pp 293–4.

102 'the idea of abandoning': Ibid., p 299.

105 'The traveling is good': Peary, *Northward Over the Great Ice*, op. cit., Vol 2, p 447.

105 'Never shall I forget': Ibid., pp 467–8.

106 P's mother to P: 10th March, 1895, delivered by *Kite*, Aug 1895.

106 'the region of one hundred tons': Peary, *Northward Over the Great Ice*, op. cit., Vol 2, p 599. Note: the actual weight of the largest meteorite is 34 tons, not as Peary states 90–100 tons.

106 P on the meteorites: Ibid., pp 553–4, 572–4, 618.

107 'five big barrels': Kenn Harper, *Give Me My Father's Body* (Blacklead Books, Frobisher Bay, NWT, 1986), p 34. Also: *World*, 6th Jan, 1907.

107 'The ship's men': P diary, 22nd Aug, 1896.

107 'Peary did not donate': Harper, op. cit., p 77.

References

108 'As I sit here writing': Peary, *Northward Over the Great Ice*, op. cit., Vol 1, p 508.

108 'acting on the Eskimos' own suggestion': Harper, op. cit., p 33.

CHAPTER 8 The Years of Doubt and Suffering – Part 1   *pages 110–130*

110 'Shoot forward to the Pole': P memo in 1885 diary.

110–11 'The lateness of the season': Robert E. Peary, *Nearest the Pole* (1907), p 296.

111 Otto Sverdrup: *New Land* (Longmans, London, 1904), Vol, 1 p 1.

111 Dennis Rawlins: *Peary at the North Pole, Fact or Fiction* (1973), p 40.

112 'meeting with Sverdrup': P to his wife, 27th Aug, 1899. See also: Sverdrup, op. cit., Vol 1, pp 58–61.

112 Bradley Robinson: *Dark Companion*, op. cit., p 132.

114 'in readiness to start': Peary, *Nearest the Pole*, op.cit., p 305.

114 'A little remaining oil': Ibid, p 308.

114–15 'My God, Lieutenant': Robinson, op. cit., p 135.

115 Quotation from Seneca: Weems, *Peary: the Explorer and the Man*, op. cit., p 337, note 5 which reads: 'Hobbs mentioned this quotation without documentation in his biography of Peary (p. 213). Since then it has appeared in numerous other books and articles. Neither Peary nor Dedrick, the only two men at Fort Conger capable of keeping literate diaries, mentioned the quotation, but one would not expect Peary to. Inside the cover of Peary's diary beginning April 4, 1901, is an inscription, with no elaboration, obviously printed by him: '*Inveniet viam, aut faciet,*' which is in the third person singular of the verb, not first person: "He will find a way or make one." '

115 Removing P's toes: Weems, op. cit., p 337, note 4 which reads: "Peary diary, January 18th, 1899, in Dedrick's handwriting. Eventually Peary lost eight toes, in two subsequent operations."

115 'the character of the road': Peary, *Nearest the Pole*, op. cit., p 309.

116 'I bent down': Lin Bonner, article in *Liberty*, 17th July, 1926, p 19.

116 Henson was not present: Robinson, op. cit., p 141.

116 Henson was present: Robert H. Fowler, 'The Negro Who went to the Pole with Peary', *American History Illustrated*, April 1966, p 10. See also *Liberty*, op. cit., p 19.

116 'to push northward': Sverdrup, op. cit., Vol 1, p 116.

117 'You must take your chances': Ibid., p 117.

117 'clear across to the Greenland shore': Peary, *Nearest the Pole*, op. cit., pp 310–11.

118 'I completed the work': Ibid., pp. 311–12.

118 Adolphus W. Greely: *Three Years of Arctic Service*, op. cit., Vol 2, p 68.

119 'monotony of Arctic life': Ibid., Vol 2, p 70.

119 'The saddest part': Robert E. Peary, 'The Discovery of the North Pole', *Hampton's Magazine*, Vol. xxiv, No. 3, March 1910, p 336.

359

119   P to Bridgman: Explorers' Club Archives, 1902. See also, Rawlins, op. cit.,
      p 55.

119   'the scientific records': Peary, *Nearest the Pole*, op. cit., p 321.

123   wintering at Etah: Peary, *Nearest the Pole*, op. cit., p 316.

123   'On leaving Etah': Ibid., p 321.

124   The thin ice: Ibid., pp 322–3.

124   'the Arctic *Ultima Thule*': Ibid., p 326.

124   'the edge of the disintegrated pack': Ibid., p 327.

125   'looked like a vast field of snow': Robinson, op. cit., p 162.

129   'April 15th I left Conger': Peary, *Nearest the Pole*, op. cit., p 334.

130   'April 30th, at Hayes Point': Ibid., p 334.

CHAPTER 9 The Years of Doubt and Suffering – Part 2   *pages 131–143*

131   'not even able to buck': Harold Horwood, *Bartlett* (1977), p 55.

132–5   Marie Ahnighito Peary: *Snow Baby* (1935), pp 70–1, 72–3, 74–5,
      86–7, 88–9, 128–9.

138   Weems: *Peary: the Explorer and the Man*, op. cit., p 190.

139   'After a few days' rest': Peary, *Nearest the Pole*, op. cit., p 335.

139–40   Cook's first impression: Cook, unpublished autobiographical sketch,
      op. cit.

140   'I would rather die': Hugh Eames, *Winner Lose All*, op. cit., pp 24–5.

140   'through as a traveler': Ibid., pp 24–5.

141   Cook on Dedrick: Cook, *My Attainment of the Pole*, op. cit. (footnote),
      pp 434–5.

142   Tornarssuk: Kaj Birket-Smith *Eskimos* (Crown, NY, 1971), p 188. See also:
      Knud Rasmussen, *Greenland by the Polar Sea* (Heinemann, London, 1921),
      p 30, and Erik Holtved, 'Tornarssuk, an Eskimo Deity', *Folk Magazine*,
      May 1963, pp 157–72.

142   'highest honored son': Robinson, *Dark Companion*, op. cit., p 167.

142   '400 miles of the most arduous traveling': Peary, *Nearest the Pole*, op. cit.,
      p 341.

142   'The game is off': Ibid., p 344.

143   'I close the book': P diary, 6th May, 1902.

143   'My feelings are not of the brightest': P diary, 24th May, 1902.

143   'As I look about': P diary, 6th June, 1902.

CHAPTER 10   The Weather-Beaten Fanatic *pages 144–160*

144   'an extended scheme of exploration': Peary, *Nearest the Pole*, op. cit., p 295.

145   'The personal effects': Ibid., pp 286–7.

146   Dedrick to P: *New York Herald*, 10th Nov 1902. Also Andrew A. Freeman,
      The Case for Doctor Cook (1961), p 71.

146   Bridgman to Cook: Freeman, op. cit.

146   Dedrick's bonus: Ibid.

146–7 'with a new rifle': Ibid., p 72.

147 'grit and loyalty': Peary, *Northward Over the Great Ice*, op. cit., Vol 2, pp 293–4.

147 'speed away to the Pole': P diary, 1885.

147 'Peary Channel': Peary, *Northward Over the Great Ice*, op. cit., Vol 1, p 346.

148 Green: *Peary: the Man Who Refused to Fail*, op. cit., p 156.

148 'an uneventful voyage': Peary, *Nearest the Pole*, op. cit., p 349.

149 'might detract from the interest': *New York Tribune*, 19th Sept, 1902. Also Freeman, op. cit., p 74.

149 Bridgman to press: *New York Times*, 22nd Sept, 1902.

149 'practically insane': *New York Times*, 22nd Sept, 1901.

149–50 Dedrick to *New York Herald*: 10th Nov, 1902.

150 'The members having lost hope': Green, op. cit., pp 192–3.

150 William Herbert Hobbs: *Peary* (1936), p 255.

154 P to Bryant: 17th Jan, 1903.

156 Bryant's reply: Green, op. cit., p 241.

157 Admiral Beaumont: *Geographical Journal*, Vol. 22, 1903, pp 669–70.

157 Incorporation of Peary Arctic Club: Peary, *Nearest the Pole*, op. cit., pp 288–9.

158 Commander Edward Stafford: 'Peary and his Promised Land', unpublished article.

158 The meeting with Jesup: Weems, *Peary: the Explorer and the Man*, op. cit., p 204. The amounts of money differ from those mentioned by Peary in *Nearest the Pole*, op. cit., pp 355–9.

158–9 Marie A. Peary: *Snow Baby*, op. cit., p 226.

159 Jo to P: 17th June, 1904. National Archives.

159 *New York Sun*: 14th Sept, 1904.

159 'Next summer I shall start north': *New York Sun*, 15th Sept, 1904.

160 *New York Tribune*: 9th July, 1905.

160 'bowing to the plaudits': *New York Times*, 17th July, 1905.

160 'I am going in God's name': Freeman, op. cit., p 82.

CHAPTER 11 Farthest North, 1906? Part I *pages 161–176*

161 P on his crew: Peary, *Nearest the Pole*, op. cit., pp 4–6.

162 'without dropping anchor': Ibid., pp 21–2.

162 Departure from Etah: Ibid., p 33.

163 'three musk-oxen': Ibid., p 35.

163 'Up to this time': Ibid., p 35.

163 Nares: *A Voyage to the Polar Sea*, op. cit., Vol 1, pp 101, 103

163 'I determined to test my belief': Peary, *Nearest the Pole*, op. cit., p 36.

164 P sets out for Lake Hazen: Ibid., p 333.

164 'In all my experiences': Robert E. Peary, 'Ice Navigation', *Century Magazine*, Sept 1917, p 761.

164–5   *Roosevelt* grinding through the floes: Peary, *Nearest the Pole*, op. cit., pp 44–5

165   'A wild morning': Ibid., p 47.

165–6   'Since leaving Etah': Ibid., pp 50–1.

166   'Its slow resistless motion': Ibid., pp 58–9.

166–7   'This meat': Ibid., pp 64–5.

167–8   'a period of constant anxiety': Ibid., p 93.

168   Henson's version: Robinson, *Dark Companion*, op. cit., p 191.

170   'Professor Marvin, Bartlett, Dr. Wolf': Ibid., pp 191–2.

170   'the floe on which my igloos were built': Peary, *Nearest the Pole*, op. cit., p 105.

171   'A few moments' conversation': Ibid., p 106.

171   'Though I fight': Ibid., pp 111–12.

171   'a broad lead': Ibid., p 115.

172   'somewhat farther west': Ibid., p 117.

172   'On the 15th': Ibid., p 114.

172   'the work went on': Ibid., pp 109–10.

173   'my little brown children': Ibid., p 124.

173   'more or less worried': Ibid., p 125.

175   Thomas F. Hall: *Has the North Pole Been Discovered?* (1917), p 292.

175   'On the old floes': Peary, *Nearest the Pole*, op. cit., p 129.

175   Rough ice catching blown snow: Ibid., p 124.

175   'It was evident': Ibid., p 130.

CHAPTER 12 Farthest North, 1906? Part 2   *pages 177–190*

177   'stopped by open water': Peary, *Nearest the Pole*, op. cit., p 130.

177   'bent every energy': Ibid., p 130.

177–8   'The first march': Ibid., p 131.

178   'covered thirty miles': Ibid., pp 131–2.

178–9   'Our stay in camp': Ibid., p 132.

181   'a region of open leads': Peary, *Nearest the Pole*, op. cit., pp 133–5.

184   'already made a good day's march': Ibid., p 139.

185   'some difficulty in picking up trail': Ibid., p 139.

186   'remove every scrap': J. Gordon Hayes, *Robert Edwin Peary*, op. cit., p 68.

186   March into Storm Camp: Peary, *Nearest the Pole*, op. cit., p 141.

186   'I alone of the party': Ibid., p 142.

187   'in this dismal camp': Ibid., pp 144–6.

187   Return of scouts: Ibid., pp 144–6.

187–8   'Once started': Ibid., pp 145–6.

188   'conglomeration of fragments': Ibid., pp 146–7.

188   'I headed directly': Ibid., p 148.

188–9   Inuutersuaq Ulloriaq: 'What has been heard about the first two North

References

Pole explorers' (*Gronland*, the magazine of the Greenland Society, No. 3, 1984), pp 61–87.

189   Hall: *Has the North Pole Been Discovered?*, op. cit., p 286.

190   'What a delicious thing rest is': Peary, *Nearest the Pole*, op. cit., p 168.

CHAPTER 13 Farthest North, 1906? Part 3   *pages 191–201*

191   J. Gordon Hayes, *Robert Edwin Peary*, (Grant Richard & Humphrey Toulmin, London, 1929, page 54.

192   Peary – letter to Peary Arctic Club, dated 11th January, 1903. National Archives. Also: Peary, *Secrets of Polar Travel*, (The Century Co, New York, 1917), pp 185–189.

192   'an ample supply of cutlery': Peary, *Secrets of Polar Travel*, op. cit., p 186.

193   'I have used the Eskimos': Ibid., p 179.

193   'The language of the Eskimos': Ibid., p 183.

193   Bartlett on P: Robert A. Bartlett *The Log of Bob Bartlett* (1928), pp 149–51.

194   P to Jo: 27th Aug, 1899.

194   'One must make a psychological study': Peary, *Secrets of Polar Travel*, op. cit., pp 183–5

194   'Today has seen the accomplishment': Peary, *Nearest the Pole*, op. cit., p 182.

195   P's cairn note: Dr. G. Hattersley-Smith, 'Peary's North Pole Journey' (*The Beaver*, Summer, 1961).

195   The homeward trek: Peary, *Nearest the Pole*, op. cit., p 147.

196   'A day's march?': Ibid., p 190.

196   'In today's march': Ibid., p 192.

196   'North stretched . . . the polar pack': Ibid., p 202.

196–7   'The clear day': Ibid., p. 207.

197   'With the completion of my work': Ibid., p 208.

197   'no reason to complain': Ibid., p 209.

197   'a striking picture': Ibid., p 211–12.

198   'the devil-inspired labyrinth': Ibid., p 225.

198   'with open water': Ibid., p 234.

198   *Roosevelt* damaged: Ibid., pp 235–6.

198   'My kamiks were cut through': Ibid., p 240.

198   'I should have thought': Bartlett, op. cit., p 166.

199   'I used to go on deck': Ibid., pp 168–9.

199–200   'Peary had promised': Robert A. Bartlett, 'Bringing the Crippled *Roosevelt* Home' (in *Told at the Explorers' Club* (1931), pp 31–3.

200   'it wasn't a nice feeling': Bartlett, *Log of Bob Bartlett*, op. cit., pp 172–5.

201   *Boston Herald*: 24th Nov, 1906.

201   Jo to Peary, 17th June, 1904.

CHAPTER 14 The Threat of Dr. Cook   pages 202–215

202 Robert A. Bartlett: *Log of Bob Bartlett*, op. cit., pp 177–8.

202 'I have never spent': Peary, *Nearest the Pole*, op. cit., pp 276–9. Also P diary, 20th Dec, 1900.

204 P to Roosevelt: see Hobbs, *Peary*, op. cit., p 319.

206 'an absolutely paralysing defeat': Peary, *North Pole*. (Hodder ed.,), p 28.

207 Jo Peary to Osborn: 15th March, 1908.

207 P on Cook: Peary, *Northward Over the Great Ice*, op. cit., Vol 1, pp 423–4.

207 Prof. G. Frederick Wright to E. C. Rost: 28th Dec, 1914. Congressional Record, 8th Feb. 1915, 'Extension of Remarks of Hon. William J. Field – The North Pole Controversy'.

207 Bridgman on Cook: *Brooklyn Standard Union*, 2nd Dec, 1893.

208 'skill, energy, and persistence': Roald Amundsen, *New York American*, 19th Sept, 1909.

208 'a genius': Roald Amundsen, Associated Press to *New York Times*, 24th Jan, 1926. Also Freeman, *The Case for Dr. Cook*, op. cit., p 303.

209 'An Arctic expedition': Cook, *My Attainment of the Pole*, op. cit., pp 24, 29–30.

209 'We'll fit this expedition': Freeman *The Case for Doctor Cook*, op. cit., p 95.

210 'Ordinarily, Annoatok': Cook, *My Attainment of the Pole* op. cit., p 68.

211 Jo to P: 17th Nov, 1907.

211 'He did not care to serve': Freeman, op. cit., p 99.

212 'During those dizzy hours': Cook, *My Attainment of the Pole*, op. cit., p 43.

213–14 Cook on sledging: Ibid., pp 130–2.

214 Cook on a collapsible boat: Ibid., p 134.

215 'My heart was high': Ibid., pp 155–6.

CHAPTER 15 The Final Arrow   pages 216–235

216 'heart stirring farewells': Peary, *The North Pole*, op. cit., p 38.

216 'Men in the streets': Robinson, *Dark Companion*, op. cit., pp 210–11.

216 Bartlett on President's inspection: *Log of Bob Bartlett*, op. cit., p 183.

216 'Mr. President': Peary, *The North Pole*, op. cit., p 39.

217 'Another farewell': Ibid., pp 40–1.

217 Henson on Marvin: Henson, *A Negro Explorer at the North Pole* (Stokes, NY, 1912), pp 18–19.

217 Henson on Borup: Ibid., p 17.

217–18 Marvin to Bement: Marvin's letters to L. C. Bement quoted in this chapter are believed to be among the last he wrote. They are all quoted from Freeman, *The Case for Doctor Cook*, op. cit. (note), p 281.

218 'The man could hardly walk': Excerpts from a letter of Henry Johnson's in *Tourist Magazine*, Oct 1910.

218–19 Cook to Franke: Freeman, op. cit., p 109.

218 'obtained all the Eskimos': Peary, *The North Pole* (Stokes ed.), p 77.

References

219 'Commander Peary gave me': Henson, op. cit., pp 29–30.

220 Siorapaluk to Malaurie: Jean Malaurie, *The Last Kings of Thule* (1982), p 234.

220 'He showed me a letter': Peary, *The North Pole* (Stokes ed), p 79.

220–1 'Pushing his way': Robinson, op. cit., pp 213–14.

221 'just as the enemy': Freeman, op. cit., pp 114–15.

221 'one narwhal tusk': Eames, *Winner Lose All*, op. cit., p 82.

221 'This house belongs': Frederick A. Cook, *Return from the Pole* (1953), pp 218–19.

222 Marvin to Bement: 15 Aug, 1908.

224 'Ahead of me': *Hampton's Magazine*, Jan 1910, p 24.

224 'I had planned': Peary, *The North Pole* (Hodder ed.), p 136.

225 'That last day': Ibid., p 177.

225 'From Cape Columbia': Peary, *The North Pole* (Stokes ed.), p 193.

226 'a physical impossibility': Ibid., pp 204–6.

226 'Twenty-four hours': Ibid., p 207.

226 'a little south of true west.' Peary, *Nearest the Pole*, op. cit., pp 126–7.

227 'The wind was from the east': Peary, *The North Pole* (Stokes ed.), pp 215–16

227 'the lateral movement': Ibid., p 222.

228 'more mental wear and tear': Ibid., p 228.

228 'I would see them talking': Ibid., p 230.

228 John W. Goodsell: *On Polar Trails* (1983), p 122.

229 'Two of them were rendered unconscious': Peary, *The North Pole* (Stokes ed.), p 230.

229 'MacMillan was invaluable': Ibid., p 231.

230 'Marvin came': Ibid., p 235.

230 'That night was one of the noisiest': Ibid., p 240.

230 'I knew from experience': Ibid., pp 240–1.

231 'with good weather': Ibid., p 242.

231 'kept the parties closer together': Ibid., p 245.

231 'Included in these marches': Ibid., p 249.

231–2 'on reaching my highest record': Ibid., pp 253–8.

232 'on the opposite side': Ibid., pp 260–1.

233 'The entire region': Ibid., p 265.

233 'This northerly wind': Ibid., p 265.

233 'we should undoubtedly have covered': Ibid., p 266.

233 'Our latitude was': Ibid., p 268.

234 P chooses Henson for Pole: Ibid., pp 272–3.

234 'I can't get along without him': Robinson, op. cit., p viii, Foreword by Donald B. MacMillan.

234 'I felt a keen regret': Peary, *The North Pole* (Stokes ed.), p 268.

234–5 'Every nerve must be strained': Ibid., pp 269–71.

235 'Up to this time': Ibid., p 274.

CHAPTER 16 The North Pole – or Not *pages 236–258*

236 'It was a fine marching morning': Peary, *The North Pole* (Stokes ed.), p 275.

236 'well over the 88th parallel': Ibid., pp 276–7.

237 'The moon had been our friend': Ibid., pp 278–9.

237 'All day long': Ibid., p 279.

237 'The surface of the ice': Ibid., p 280.

237 'a man who should wait': Ibid., p 281.

238 'Toward the end of the march': Ibid., p 282.

238 'I knew of course': Ibid., p 283.

239 'Sometimes I would climb': Ibid., p 283.

241 Isaiah Bowman Papers: Johns Hopkins University, Eisenhower Library.

242 Peary Hearings, Committee on Naval Affairs, Subcommittee on Private Bills (Subcommittee No. 8), afternoon session, 11th Jan, 1911, 'Statement of Capt. Robert E. Peary, US Navy, continues', pp 99–100.

242 'a colorless pall': Peary, *The North Pole* (Stokes ed.), p 284.

242 'some strange shift of feeling': Ibid., p 285.

242 'I, who had walked': *Boston American*, Henson's story, 17th July, 1910.

242 and 244 'The last northward march': Peary, *The North Pole* (Stokes ed.), p 287.

244 P 'the first to leave camp': 'A Negro at the North Pole', by Matthew Henson, *World's Work*, Vol 19, No. 6, April 1910, p 12834.

244 'Peary, he stayed back': Fowler: 'The Negro Who Went to the Pole with Peary', *American History Illustrated*, Vol I, No. 1, April 1966, pp 47–8.

245 Thomas to Freeman: Freeman, *The Case for Doctor Cook*, op. cit., p 208. Also: Weems, *Peary the Explorer and the Man*, op. cit., note no. 35, p 345.

245 'After the usual arrangements': Peary, *The North Pole* (Stokes ed.), p 287.

245 'I believe that the full distance': *Boston American*, op. cit.

245 'Don't you want me to be with you?': *American History Illustrated*, op. cit.

246 P vets Henson's book: P had insisted that Henson cut out of the book his account of P's dismissal of the two Eskimos at the Big Lead. See Fowler, op. cit.

246 'prospects for getting a sight': Henson, *A Negro Explorer at the North Pole*, op. cit., pp 132–3.

246–7 Peary Hearings: op. cit., p 100.

247 'repairing a sledge': *Boston American*, op. cit.

248 'gone about one and a half hours': *American History Illustrated*, op. cit.

249 'I was sure that he was satisfied': Henson, *A Negro Explorer at the North Pole*, op. cit., p 135.

250 'It was my boy Ootah': *Boston American*, op. cit.

251 'All the plans': Peary, *The North Pole* (Stokes ed.), p 302.

254 'Though intensely conscious': Ibid., p 301.

254 'From the time': *Boston American*, op. cit.

255 'The thing which it was intended': Peary, *The North Pole* (Stokes ed.), p 316.

255 'My heart thrilled': Ibid., p 317.

255   'Have you heard about poor Marvin': Ibid., pp 317–18.

255–6   Robert A. Bartlett: *Log of Bob Bartlett*, op. cit., pp 197–8.

256   'From the time of my arrival': Henson, *A Negro Explorer at the North Pole*, op. cit., p 153.

256   Goodsell: *On Polar Trails*, op. cit., p 183.

256   'Arrived on board yesterday': George Borup, *A Tenderfoot With Peary* (1911), p 231.

256   'arrange the results': Peary, *The North Pole* (Stokes ed.), p 327.

CHAPTER 17 The Onus of Proof   *pages 259–272*

260   P's plan: Peary, *The North Pole* (Stokes ed.), p 4.

261   Peary Hearings: op. cit., p 69.

262   Will Steger news release: (Westmorland Larson & Hill, Duluth, Mn), 8th May, 1985.

262   Steger on P's mileage: Will Steger with Paul Schurke, *North to the Pole* (1987), p 303.

263   'From here to the Pole': Peary, *The North Pole* (Stokes ed.), p 306.

263–4   'traveling nearly before the wind': Ibid., pp 305–306.

264   Nansen's law of drift: P. Gordienko, 'Arctic Ice Drift', Publication No. 598; *Arctic Sea Ice* NAS/NRC, Washington, D.C., Dec, 1958, p 21.

267   Magnetic variation: Peary Hearings, op. cit., p 26.

271   Steger on sastrugi: Steger, op. cit., p 302.

CHAPTER 18 The Gold Brick   *pages 273–290*

273   'The true explorer': Peary, *Nearest the Pole*, op. cit., p ix.

274   'Every time I met Dr. Cook': Bartlett, *Log of Bob Bartlett*, op. cit., p 202.

274   'Mr. Peary's attitude': Cook, *My Attainment of the Pole*, op. cit., pp 69–70 (footnote).

274   'in the event of Dr. Cook': Freeman, *The Case for Doctor Cook*, op. cit., p 99.

275   'We stopped at Cape Saumarez': Peary, *The North Pole* (Hodder ed.), p 295.

275   'Peary was not especially concerned': Bartlett, op. cit., p 204.

275–6   'To us, up there at Etah': Henson, *Negro Explorer at the North Pole*, op. cit., pp 177–8. See also: Robinson, *Dark Companion*, op. cit., p 236.

276   'unshaken by cross-examination': Cook, *My Attainment of the Pole*, op. cit., p 201 (footnote).

279   Barton W. Currie: *New York World*, 29th Sept, 1909.

280   Minik on P: Harper, *Give Me My Father's Body*, op. cit., p 135.

281   'You're a race of scientific criminals': *Evening Mail*, 9th July, 1909.

282   Marie Peary: *Snow Baby*, op. cit., pp 242–3.

283   'crowned with roses': W. T. Stead, 'Dr. Cook: the Man and the Deed', *American Review of Reviews*, Oct 1909'. p 438.

283 'I am proud': Freeman, op. cit., p 152.

283 'a naive, inexperienced child': Stead, op. cit., p 43.

284 'Compared with our best men': Ibid., p 445.

284 'too honest and too limited': Ibid., p 448.

286 P's 'brief summary': Robert E. Peary, 'Discovery of the Pole', *World's Work*, Oct 1909, p 12103.

286 'Her happiness was clearly evident': *New York Times*, 11th Sept, 1909.

286 Barton Currie: *New York World*, 20th Sept, 1909.

289 Cook's arrival at New York: *New York Herald*, 22nd Sept, 1909.

289–90 Marie Peary: op. cit., pp 245–6.

290 'What I have to say': *New York World*, 22nd Sept, 1909.

290 'Acting on the advice': Freeman, op. cit., p 167.

CHAPTER 19 The Tarnished Prize *pages 291–306*

291 Printz on Cook: *New York Sun*: 6th Sept, 1909.

292 'as loyal and responsive': *New York Times*, 11th Sept, 1909.

292 Green: *Peary*, op. cit., p 198.

293 Whitney's telegram: Eames, *Winner Lose All*, op. cit., p 146.

293 'disturbed by the growing uncertainty': Cook, *My Attainment of the Pole*, op. cit., p 504.

293 'The scientists are the ones to say': *New York Times*, 27th Sept, 1909.

293 Currie on Whitney: *New York World*, 4th Oct, 1909.

293 'I cannot conceive': *New York Times*, 27th Sept, 1909.

294 'Peary had suffered a mental breakdown': William R. Hunt, *Stef*, (1986) p 229.

294 Tarr to Bridgman: *New York Times*, 30th Sept, 1909.

295 Explorers' Club to investigate Cook: Proceedings of the Explorers' Club, New York, 24th Dec, 1909.

295 'perused a batch of letters': *New York Times*, 15th Oct, 1909. See also Freeman, *The Case for Doctor Cook*, op. cit., p 178.

295 'Barrille's affidavit': *New York Globe*, 14th Oct, 1909.

295 Herschel Parker: *New York Times*, 29th Oct, 1909. See also *New York Times*, 9th Sept, 1909.

296 Press against Cook: *New York Globe*, 18th Oct, 1909. Also *New York Times*, 18th Oct, 1909.

296 'hardships in the long polar night': Terris Moore, *Mt. McKinley: the Pioneer Climbs* (1967), p 66.

296 'On every side I sensed hostility': Cook, *My Attainment of the Pole*, op. cit., pp 505–6.

296 'thirty pieces of silver': *New York Herald*, 29th Oct, 1909.

297 'I've got the Opera House tonight': *New York Times*, 29th Oct, 1909.

297 'I have stated': *Anaconda Standard*, 30th Oct, 1909.

298 and 299 National Geographic Society summary of Board of Managers'

action: from 1st Oct, 1909 to 1st Feb, 1910. NGS Archives. See also: Committee on Naval Affairs Subcommittee on Private Bills, March 4, 1910, pp 9–11.

298 'Peary willing': *New York Times*, 2nd Oct, 1909.

300 Peary Hearings, p 12.

300 Gannett on P: Ibid., pp 12, 15

300 Marie Peary: *Snow Baby*, op. cit., p 255.

301 P examined by NGS: Peary Hearings, pp 7–8, 10, 13–15.

302 'little less than an insult': *New York Times*, 12th Dec, 1909.

303 'plots to steal his records': *New York Times*, 27th Dec, 1909.

303 Lonsdale on Cook's disappearance: *Travel Magazine*, June 1910.

303 Cook to his wife: letter in *New York Times*, 27th Dec, 1909.

304 Lonsdale to *New York American*: 10th Dec, 1909.

306 Rasmussen on Cook: *New York Times*, 22nd Dec, 1909

306 'The greatest of the earth's trophies': *Brooklyn Standard Union*, 21st Dec, 1909.

306 W. S. Schley: *New York American*, 22nd Dec, 1909.

306 'Cook was too hastily acclaimed': *New York Sun*, 22nd Dec, 1909.

CHAPTER 20 The Burden of Truth *pages 307–321*

307 Fiala on Cook: *New York World*, 3rd Oct, 1910.

307 'Few men in all history': Cook, *My Attainment of the Pole*, op. cit., p 4.

309 'allow the atmosphere to clear': Cook, *My Attainment of the Pole*, op. cit., p 5.

309 'the rough material': *Philadelphia Evening Bulletin*, 15th Sept, 1909.

309 'she had no address': Freeman, *The Case for Doctor Cook*, op. cit., p 212.

310 'still under an assumed name': Ibid., p 213.

310 Terris Moore: *Mt. McKinley: the Pioneer Climbs* (1967), p 83.

311 Rusk on Cook: Ibid., p 85.

311–12 Hudson Stuck: "The Ascent of Denali" (New York, 1914).

312 Stuck on Cook's book: *New York Evening Post*, 30th March, 1915.

312 Dr. Bradford Washburn: letter to author, 11th Dec, 1986. See also *American Alpine Journal*, 1958, p 3.

312 'I have searched': Washburn to Editor of *Arctic*, June 1984.

313 Rainey: *Cosmopolitan Magazine*, Dec 1910.

313 Bartlett: *New York World*, 18th Sept, 1910.

313 Peter Freuchen: *Arctic Adventure*, op. cit., p 31.

313 'I felt impotent': Cook, *My Attainment of the Pole*, op. cit., p 555.

314 'Only by reading: Ibid., p 6.

314 'As we came back': Cook lecturing at Benton Harbor, Michigan, 18th Nov, 1913.

314 'So weak that we had to climb': Cook, *My Attainment of the Pole*, op. cit., pp 436–7.

315 'a campaign to discredit me': Cook, *My Attainment of the Pole*, op. cit., p 8.

315 'weaving a leprous blanket': Ibid., pp 509–10.

315 'Mr. Peary had his own': Ibid., p 9.

315–16 MacMillan on Cook's photographs: Donald B. MacMillan, notes in *Geographical Review*, 1918. See also Terris Moore, *Mt. McKinley: the Pioneer Climbs*, op. cit., pp 189–94.

316 'after sleeping for two nights': Ibid.

316 Itukusuk's evidence: Edward Shackleton, *Arctic Journeys* (ed. Hodder, 1936), p 34. See also William R. Hunt, *To Stand at the Pole* (Stein & Day, NY, 1981), pp 259–66.

316–7 'Before leaving us': Cook, *My Attainment of the Pole*, op. cit., p 206.

317 Talilanguaq Peary: interviewed in film *The Noose of Laurels*. Central Television, first screening in UK 12th April, 1988.

319 'an island of glacial land ice': Sheldon Cook-Dorough to the author, 30th Dec, 1986.

320–21 Cook's later years: Sheldon Cook-Dorough, interview in film *The Noose of Laurels* op. cit., 12th April, 1988.

CHAPTER 21 The Price of Fame *pages 322–329*

322 'accepted the word of Commander Peary': *New York Times*, 25th Dec, 1909.

322–3 Roosevelt to Bridgman: *Hampton's Magazine*, Jan 1910.

323 Metropolitan Opera House evening: *New York Times*, 9th Feb, 1910.

323 'for the purpose of exploration': Hobbs, *Peary*, op. cit., p 399.

324 House of Representatives opposition: Memorandum for the Secretary of the Navy from R. F. Nicholson, Chief of Bureau, 10th Feb, 1910. See Peary Hearings op. cit., pp 94–7. National Geographic Archives.

324 'This board of scientific investigation': *New York Times*, 26th Feb, 1910.

324 Representative De Alva Alexander to Representative Thomas S. Butler: 26th Feb, 1910.

325 Dennis Rawlins: *Peary at the North Pole: Fact or Fiction?* op. cit., p 214.

325 'breaking faith with his publishers': Peary Hearings, op. cit., p 23.

325–6 Representative Joseph H. Moore in the House of Representatives: 15th March, 1910.

326 P on writing his book: Hobbs, *Peary* op. cit., pp 406–7.

326 Stefansson: Hunt, *Stef*, op. cit., p 231.

326 P on his ghostwriter: to Frederick Stokes (his publisher), 12th July, 1910. See also Hunt, *Stef*, op. cit., p 138.

326–7 Thomas to Freeman: Freeman, *The Case for Doctor Cook*, op. cit., p 208.

327 Marie Peary: *Snow Baby*, op.cit., p 258.

327 'an exceptionally capable committee': Freeman, op. cit., p 211.

328 Rawlins on Mitchell: Rawlins, op. cit., p 237.

328 Mitchell's evidence: Peary Hearings, op. cit., p 142.

Bibliography

Books: primary sources

Astrup, Eivind. *With Peary Near the Pole*. London: Pearson, 1898.

—— *At the Pole with Peary and Cook*. Portland, Maine: Nelson, 1909.

Bartlett, Robert A. *The Log of Bob Bartlett*. NY: Putnam, 1928.

Borup, George. *A Tenderfoot With Peary*. NY: Stokes, 1911.

Cook, Frederick A. *My Attainment of the Pole*. NY: Polar Publishing Co., 1911.

—— *Return from the Pole*. (Edited by Frederick J. Pohl.) NY: Pellegrini & Cudahy, 1951; London: Burke, 1953.

—— *Through the First Antarctic Night*. NY: Doubleday & McClure, 1900; London: Heinemann, 1900.

—— *To the Top of the Continent*. NY: Doubleday, 1908; London: Hodder & Stoughton, 1908.

Eames, Hugh. *Winner Lose All: Dr. Cook and the Theft of the North Pole*. Boston: Little, Brown, 1973.

Freeman, Andrew A. *The Case for Doctor Cook*. NY: Coward, McCann, 1961.

Gibbons, Russell W. *The Historical Evaluation of the Cook–Peary Controversy*. Ohio Northern University: Department of History, 1956 (revised).

Green, Fitzhugh. *Peary: the Man Who Refused to Fail*. NY: Putnam, 1926.

Hall, Thomas F. *Has the North Pole Been Discovered?* Boston: Badger, 1917.

—— *Has the North Pole Been Discovered?* vol. 2, supplement. Omaha: privately printed, 1920.

Hayes, J. Gordon. *The Conquest of the North Pole*. NY: Macmillan, 1934; London: Thornton Butterworth, 1934.

—— *Robert Edwin Peary*. London: G. Richards & H. Toulmin, 1929.

Henson, Matthew A. *A Negro Explorer at the North Pole*. NY: Stokes, 1912.

Hobbs, William Herbert, *Peary*. NY: Macmillan, 1936.

Hunt, William. *To Stand at the Pole*. NY: Stein & Day, 1981.

Lewin, W. Henry. *The Great North Pole Fraud*. London: C. W. Daniel, 1935.

MacMillan, Donald B. *How Peary Reached the Pole*. Boston: Houghton Mifflin, 1934.

Peary, Josephine Diebitsch. *My Arctic Journal*. NY: Contemporary Publishing, 1893; London: Longmans, Green, 1893.

Peary, Marie Ahnighito. *Snow Baby*. London: Routledge, 1935.

Peary, Robert E. *Nearest the Pole*. NY: Doubleday, 1907; London: Hutchinson, 1907.

—— *The North Pole*. NY: Stokes, 1910; London: Hodder & Stoughton, 1910.

—— *Northward Over the 'Great Ice'*. 2 vols. NY: Stokes, 1898; London: Methuen, 1898.

—— *Secrets of Polar Travel*. NY: Century, 1917.

Rawlins, Dennis. *Peary at the North Pole, Fact or Fiction?* NY: Luce, 1973.

Robinson, Bradley. *Dark Companion*. NY: McBride, 1947; London: Hodder & Stoughton, 1948.

Rost, Ernest C. *Mount McKinley: Its Bearing on the Polar Controversy*. Washington, DC: Milan & Sons, 1914.

Stafford, Mary Peary. *Discoverer of the North Pole*. NY: Morrow, 1959.

Weems, John Edward. *Peary, The Explorer and the Man*, Boston, 1967; London: Eyre & Spottiswoode, 1967.

—— *Race for the Pole*. NY, 1960.

Whitney, Harry Payne. *Hunting with the Eskimos*. NY: Century, 1911.

Wright, Theon. *The Big Nail*. NY, 1970.

Books: secondary sources

Abramson, Howard. *National Geographic: Behind America's Lens on the World*. NY: Crown Publishers, 1987.

Abruzzi, Duke of the. *On the 'Polar Star'*. 2 vols, London: Hutchinson, 1903.

Allen, Everett. *Life of Donald MacMillan*. NY: Dodd, 1962.

Amundsen, Roald. *My Life as an Explorer*. NY: Doubleday Doran, 1927; London: Heinemann, 1927.

—— *The South Pole*. NY: Lee Keedrick, 1913; London: Murray, 1912.

Amundsen, Roald *et al*. *First Crossing*. NY: Doran, 1927.

Amundsen *et al*. *Polar Flight*. NY: Dodd, 1925; London: Hutchinson, 1925.

Anderson, J. R. L. *The Ulysses Factor*. London: Hodder & Stoughton, 1970; NY, 1970.

Angell, Pauline. *To the Top of the World*. Chicago: Rand McNally, 1964.

Balch, Edwin Swift. *Mount McKinley and Mountain Climbers' Proofs*. Philadelphia: Campion, 1914.

—— *Mount McKinley and Mountain Climbers' Proofs*. Philadelphia, 1914.

—— *North Pole and Bradley Land*. Philadelphia, 1913.

Balchen, Bernt. *Come North with Me*. NY: Dutton, 1958.

Barclay, George Lippart. *The Greely Arctic Expedition*. Philadelphia: Barclay, 1884.

Barclay, W. S. *The Land of Magellan*. London: Methuen, 1920.

Bartlett, Bob. *Sails Over Ice*. NY: Scribner, 1934.

Birket-Smith, Kaj. *Eskimos*. NY: Crown, 1971.

Blake, E. Vale, ed. *Arctic Experiences, Containing Capt. George E. Tyson's Wonderful Drift on the Ice-Floe*. London: Sampson.

Brady, William A. *Showman*. NY: Dutton, 1937.

Bridges, E. Lucas. *Uttermost Part of the Earth*. London: Hodder & Stoughton, 1948.

Brown, William Adams. *Morris Ketcham Jesup*. NY: Scribner, 1910.

Browne, Belmore. *The Conquest of Mt. McKinley*. NY: Putnam, 1913.

Bryce, George. *The Siege and Conquest of the North Pole*. London: Gibbings, 1910.

Burrage, Henry S. *Thomas Hamlin Hubbard*. Portland, Me.: 1923.

Byrd, Richard. *Skyward*. NY: Putnam, 1928.

Cook-Dorough, Sheldon. *Frederick Albert Cook – The Major Expeditions, A brief summary*. NY: Sullivan County Historical Society, Hurleyville, 1988.

Corner, George. *Dr. Kane of the Arctic Seas*. USA: Temple University, 1972.

Cross, Wilbur. *Ghost Ship of the Pole*. NY: Sloane, 1960.

Davis, Burke. *The Billy Mitchell Affair*. NY: Random House, 1967.

Davis, Rear-Admiral C. H., USN. *Narrative of the North Polar Expedition U.S. Ship Polaris*. Washington DC: Government Printing Office, 1876.

De la Croix, Robert. *Mysteries of the North Pole*. (Translated by Edward Fitzgerald.) NY: John Day, 1956.

DeLong, George W. *Voyage of the Jeannette*. Boston: Houghton Mifflin, 1884.

Dolan, Edward. *Matthew Henson, Black Explorer*. NY: Dodd, Mead, 1979.

Dunn, Robert. *The Shameless Diary of an Explorer*. NY, 1907.

Elder, William. *Biography of Elisha Kent Kane*. Philadelphia: Childs & Peterson, 1858.

Everett, Marshall. *The True Story of the Cook and Peary Discovery of the North Pole*. Chicago: Educational Company, 1909.

Fairley, T. C. *Sverdrup's Arctic Adventure*. Toronto: Longman, 1959.

Fiala, Anthony. *Fighting the Polar Ice*. NY: Doubleday, Page, 1906.

Fisher, Margery and James. *Shackleton*. London: Barrie, 1957; Boston: Houghton Mifflin, 1958.

Fox, Margaret. *Love-Life of Dr. Kane*. NY: Carleton, 1866.

Freuchen, Peter, and Finn Salomonsen. *The Arctic Year*. NY: Putnam, 1958.

—— *Vagrant Viking*. NY: Messner, 1953.

—— *Arctic Adventure*. NY: Farrar and Rinehart, 1935; London: Heinemann, 1936.

—— with David Loth. *Peter Freuchen's Book of the Seven Seas*. NY: Messner, 1957.

Gibbs, Philip. *Adventures in Journalism*. London: Heinemann, 1923; NY: Harper, 1923.

Goodsell, John W. *On Polar Trails*. Austin, Texas: Eakin Press, 1983.

Greely, Adolphus W. *Report of the US Expedition to Lady Franklin Bay, Grinnell Land*. Washington, DC: House Miscellaneous Documents, 1st Session 49th Congress, 1885–6, vol. 22 (in two parts), Government Printing Office, 1889.

—— *Handbook of Polar Discoveries*. Boston: Little, Brown, 1910; London: Fisher Unwin, 1910.

—— *The Polar Regions in the Twentieth Century*. NY: Little, Brown, 1928; London: Harrap, 1929.

—— *Reminiscences of Adventure and Service*. NY: Scribner, 1927.

—— *Three Years of Arctic Service*. NY: Scribner, 1886; London: Bentley, 1886.

—— *True Tales of Arctic Heroism in the New World*. NY: Scribner, 1912.

Green, Lawrence. *America Goes to Press*. NY: Bobbs-Merrill, 1936.

Haig-Thomas, David. *Tracks in the Snow*. NY: Oxford, 1939.

Harper, Kenn. *Give Me My Father's Body*. Frobisher Bay: Blacklead Books, 1986.

Harrison, Alfred H. *In Search of a Polar Continent*. Toronto: Musson, 1908.

Hayes, Isaac Israel. *Arctic Journey*. Boston: Brown, 1860.

—— *The Open Polar Sea*. NY: Hurd, 1867; London: Sampson Low, 1886.

Hendrik, Hans. *Memoirs of Hans Hendrik, the Artic Traveller*. (ed. Dr. Henry Rink.) London: Trubner, 1878.

Herbert, Marie. *The Snow People*. London: Barrie & Jenkins, 1973.

Herbert, Wally. *The North Pole*. London: Sackett & Marshall, 1979.

—— *Across the Top of the World*. London: Longman, 1969; NY: Putnam, 1971.

—— *Polar Deserts*. London: Collins, 1971.

—— *Eskimos*. London: Collins, 1976.

—— *Hunters of the Polar North*. London: Time-Life, 1981.

High, Fred. *The Case of Dr. Cook*. Chicago: Fred High, 1914.

Hoehling, A. A. *Jeannette' Expedition*. London: Abelard, 1967.

Horwood, Harold. *Bartlett, The Great Canadian Explorer*. NY and Toronto: Doubleday, 1977.

Houben, H. H. *Call of the North*. London: Mathews & Marrot, 1932.

Hoyt, Edwin P. *The Last Explorer*. NY: Day, 1968.

Hunt, William R. *Stef*. Vancouver: University of British Columbia Press, 1986.

Huntford, Roland. *Scott & Amundsen*. London: Hodder & Stoughton, 1979; NY: Putnam, 1980.

Ingersoll, Ernest. *The Conquest of the North*. NY: Hammond, 1909.

Ingleford, Cdr. E. A. *A Summer Search for Sir John Franklin*. London: Harrison, 1853.

Johnson, W. N. *Did Commander Peary 'Achieve' the North Pole?* Chicago: Dvorak & Weiser, 1915.

Kane, Elisha Kent. *Arctic Explorations in the Years 1853, '54, '55*. 2 vols. Philadelphia: Childs & Peterson, 1856.

—— *The U.S. Grinnell Expedition*. NY: Harper, 1854.

Keely, Robert N., and G. G. Davis. *In Arctic Seas: The Voyage of the 'Kite'*. Philadelphia: Thompson, 1893.

Kersting, Rudolph. *The White World*. NY: L. Scribner, 1902.

Kirwan, L. P. *The White Road: A History of Polar Exploration*. London: Hollis & Carter, 1959.

Kugelmass, J. Alvin. *Roald Amundsen*. Kingston, Chicago, 1955.

Kuralt, Charles. *To the Top of the World*. NY: Holt, 1968.

Loomis, Chauncey. *Weird and Tragic Shores*. NY: Knopf, 1971.

MacMillan, Donald B. *Etah and Beyond*. NY: Houghton Mifflin, 1927.

—— *How Peary Reached the North Pole*. Boston: Hale, Cushman & Flint, 1933.

Malaurie, Jean. *The Last Kings of Thule*. NY: E. P. Dutton, 1982.

Markham, Capt. Albert H. *The Great Frozen Sea*. London: Daldy Isbister, 1878.

Markham, Sir Clements R. *The Lands of Silence*. Cambridge: University Press, 1921.

Melville, George. *In the Lena Delta*. Boston: Houghton Mifflin, 1884.

Mikklesen, Ejnar. *Lost in the Arctic*. London: Heinemann, 1913.

Miller, Floyd. *Ahdoolo!* NY, 1963.

Miller, J. Martin (ed.). *Discovery of the North Pole*. Philadelphia: Parker, 1909.

Mirsky, Jeannette. *To the North*. NY: Viking, 1934.

Mitchell, H., and Duvall, C. (and Hubbard, T.). *Acts*. IGC 10:682.

Mitchell, William. *General Greely*. NY: Putnam, 1936.

Montague, Richard. *Oceans, Poles, and Airmen*. NY: Random House, 1971.

Moore, Terris. *Mt. McKinley*. University of Alaska Press, 1967.

Morris, Charles (ed.). *Finding the North Pole*. (n.p.) W. E. Scull, 1909.

Mowat, Farley. *The Polar Passion*. Toronto: McClelland & Stewart, 1967.

Nansen, Fridtjof. *Farthest North*. 2 vols. NY: Harper, 1897; London: Newnes, 1898; Chatto, 1955.

—— *The First Crossing of Greenland*. London: Longman, 1896.

—— *In Northern Mists: Arctic Exploration in Early Times*. London: Heinemann, 1911.

Nares, George. *Voyage to the Polar Sea*. London: Sampson Low, 1878.

National Geographic Society. *Great Adventures with the National Geographic*. Washington, D.C., 1963.

Neatby, L. H. *Conquest of the Last Frontier*. Athens: Ohio University, 1966.

Nobile, Umberto. *My Polar Flights*. NY: Putnam, 1961.

Noyce, Wilfrid. *Springs of Adventure*. London: Murray, 1958.

Papanin, Ivan. *Life on an Ice Floe*. NY: Messner, 1939.

Parry, William Edward. *Journal of a Voyage for the Discovery of the North-West Passage from the Atlantic to the Pacific*. London: Murray, 1821.

Payer, Julius. *New Lands, Arctic Circle*. NY: Appleton, 1877.

Phipps, C. J. *A Voyage Towards the North Pole*. (1773), facsimile reprint: Caedmon of Whitby Press, 1978.

Putnam, George Palmer. *Mariner of the North: The Life of Captain Bob Bartlett*. NY: Duell, Sloan and Pearce, 1947.

Quigley, Carroll. *Tragedy & Hope*. NY: Macmillan, 1966.

Rasky, Frank. *North Pole or Bust*. Toronto: McGraw-Hill, Ryerson, 1977.

—— *The Polar Voyages*. Toronto: McGraw-Hill, Ryerson, 1976.

Rasmussen, Knud. *Greenland by the Polar Sea*. London: Heinemann, 1921.

——*People of the Polar North*.

Reed, William. *The Phantom of the Poles*. NY: Rockey, 1906.

Reeves, Edward Ayearst. *The Recollections of a Geographer*. London: Seeley, Service, 1935.

Ross, John. *Narrative of a Second Voyage in Search of a North-West Passage*. London: PUBLISHER?, 1835.

Schley, Winfield S. *The Rescue of Greely*. NY: Scribner, 1885.

Scoresby, William, Jnr. *The Polar Ice*. (1815) and *The North Pole*. (1828). Caedmon of Whitby Press, 1980.

—— *The 1806 Log Book Kept by William Scoresby*. Caedmon of Whitby Press, 1981.

Shackleton, Edward. *Arctic Journeys: the Story of the Oxford University Ellesmere Land Expedition, 1934–5*. London: Hodder & Stoughton.

Silverberg, Robert. *Scientists & Scoundrels*. NY: 1965.

Stamp, Tom and Cordelia. *William Scoresby – Arctic Scientist*. Caedmon of Whitby Press, 1976.

Stefansson, Vilhjalmur. *Arctic Manual*. NY: Macmillan, 1957.

—— *The Friendly Arctic*. NY: Macmillan, 1921.

—— *The Problem of Meighen Island*. NY: privately printed, 1939.

——*Unsolved Mysteries of the Arctic*. NY, 1939.

—— *Discovery*. NY: McGraw-Hill, 1964.

——*Great Adventurers and Explorations*. NY: Dial, 1952.

—— *Greenland*. NY: Doubleday, 1943.

Steger, Will. *North to the Pole*. NY: Times Books, 1987.

Stuck, Hudson. *The Ascent of Denali: a Narrative of the First Complete Ascent of the Highest Peak in North America*. NY: Scribner, 1914.

Bibliography

Sverdrup, Otto. *New Land.* London: Longman, 1904.

Todd, A. L. *Abandoned: The Story of the Greely Arctic Expedition 1881–1884.* NY: McGraw-Hill, 1961.

Victor, Paul-Emile. *Man and the Conquest of the Poles.* NY: Simon & Schuster, 1963.

Villarejo, Oscar M. *Dr. Kane's Voyage to the Polar Lands.* Philadelphia: University of Pennsylvania, 1965.

Washburn, Bradford. *Mount McKinley and the Alaska Range.* Boston: Museum of Science, 1951.

Washburn, Bradford. unpubl. ms on Cook-McKinley, AAC.

West, Richard S., Jr. *Admirals of American Empire.* Indianapolis: Bobbs-Merrill, 1948.

Magazine Articles

Adams, Cyrus. 'The North Pole at Last.' *American Review of Reviews*, October, 1909.

American Alpine Journal, 1946.

'Arctic Cache.' *Time*, May 26, 1952.

'Arctic Sea Ice.' Proceedings of Conference, February 1958, NAS/NRC Publication No. 598, December, 1958.

Balch, Edwin Swift. 'Dr. Cook and Crocker Land.' *Scientific American*, October 23, 1915.

—— 'Letter to the Editor.' *Independent*, February 27, 1926.

—— 'Present Status of the North Pole Question.' *Scientific American*, March 18, 1916.

Bonner, Lin. 'Matt Henson: First to Reach the Pole.' *Liberty*, July 17, 1926.

Bradley, John R. 'My Knowledge of Dr. Cook's Polar Expedition.' *Independent*, September 16, 1909.

'Camera Eye vs. Dr. Cook.' *Life*, August 20, 1956. (Comparative photographs that seek to refute Cook's claim to climbing Mount McKinley.)

'Collapse of a Colossal Falsehood.' *Outlook*, January 1, 1910.

Cook, Frederick A. 'Letter to the Editor.' *Time*, March 30, 1936.

—— 'North Pole at Last.' *World's Work*, October, 1909.

[Cook, Frederick A., obituary] *Time*, August 12, 1940.

'Cook's Case.' *Newsweek*, September 24, 1951.

'Cook's Confession.' *Current Literature*, January, 1911.

'Cook's Discovery of the North Pole.' *Scientific American*, September 11, 1909.

Curtis, Heber D. 'Navigation Near the Pole.' US Naval Institute *Proceedings*, January, 1939.

Day, G. C. 'Locating the Pole.' *Harper's Weekly*, October 16, 1909.

Decker, Karl. 'Dr. Frederick A. Cook – Faker.' *The Metropolitan Magazine*, January, 1910.

'Discovery of the North Pole.' *Journal of American History*, no. 3, 1909.

'Discovery of the Pole.' *Life*, May 14, 1951.

'Doctor Cook's Own Story.' *Hempton's*, January–February, YEAR?

'Dr. Cook's Confession Exposed.' *The Platform*, June, 1915.

'Dr. Cook as an Object Lesson.' *Scientific American*, October 2, 1915.

'Dr. Frederick Cook's Record Audiences.' *The Lyceum Magazine*, October, 1913.

Egan, Maurice F. 'Dr. Cook in Copenhagen.' *Century*, September, 1910.

Entrikin, Samuel J. *Tourist Magazine*, NY, December, 1910.

'Errors of Observation at the North Pole.' *Current Literature*, October, 1909.

Bibliography

Euller, John. 'The Great North Pole Lie.' *Bluebook*, September, 1953.

'Explorer.' *Newsweek*, November 10, 1934.

Fields, William J. 'Extension of Remarks . . . in the House of Representatives, Monday, February 8, 1915.' *Congressional Record*, February 10, 1915.

Fowler, Robert H. 'The Negro Who Went to the Pole with Peary.' *American History Illustrated*, April, 1966.

'General Greely – Reluctant Peary Doubter.' *Independent*, October 17, 1925.

Gibbons, Russell W. 'According to the Author . . .' *Yankee*, December, 1969.

'Go to the Best Jail, Urges Dr. Cook.' *Literary Digest*, February 1, 1930.

'Gold Brick?' *Time*, December 4, 1939.

Grosvenor, Gilbert H. 'National Geographic Society and its Magazine.' *National Geographic Magazine*, 1957.

Grosvenor, Gilbert, and Thomas W. McKnew. 'We Followed Peary to the Pole.' *National Geographic Magazine*, October, 1953.

Hattersley-Smith, G. 'Peary's North Pole Journey.' *Beaver*, 1961.

Helgesen, Henry T. 'Extension of the Remarks . . . in the House of Representatives, Tuesday, January 25, 1916.' *Congressional Record*, 1916.

Henson, M. 'Negro . . . NP,' 4/'10, *World's Work*, 19:12825.

——'Real Story . . .' Boston. *American* 7/17/10.

Herbert, Wally. 'Commander Robert E. Peary – Did He Reach The Pole.' *National Geographic Magazine*, September, 1988.

'Historic Swindle.' *Nation*, December 23, 1909.

Hobbs, William Herbert. 'Admiral Peary, the Discoverer of the North Pole.' *Scientific Monthly*, May, 1935.

Holtved, Erik. 'Contributions to Polar Eskimo Ethnography.' *Meddelelser om Grønland*, vol. 182, no. 2, Copenhagen: C. A. Reitzels Forlag, 1967.

——'Tornarssuk, An Eskimo Deity.' *Folk Magazine*, May, 1963.

'Honors to Peary.' *Nation*, November 11, 1909.

'Hot Shot for Mr. Peary.' *The Platform*, October, 1913.

Hrdlicka, Ales. 'An Eskimo Brain.' *American Anthropologist*, vol. 3 (1901): 454–500.

——'Contribution to the Anthropology of Central and Smith Sound Eskimo.' *Anthropological Papers of the American Museum of Natural History*, vol. 5 (1910): 175–280.

Hubbard, Thomas H. and others. 'To Students of Arctic Exploration: the Geographic Position of Camp Jesup and the Reduction of the Observations of R. E. Peary in the Vicinity of the North Pole.' Reprinted from *Acts of the 10th International Congress of Geography*, Rome, 1913.

Hussey, E. F. 'Dr. Cook's Pemmican.' *Independent*, November 11, 1909.

'Is It a Lie?' *Independent*, October 21, 1909.

Isachsen, Gunnar. 'Peary's Marches on His North Pole Expedition, 1909.' *Geographical Review*, January, 1929.

Kelly, Tom. 'The Great North Pole Cover Up.' *Washingtonian Magazine*, January, 1974.

Kennan, George. 'Arctic Work and Arctic Food.' *Outlook*, October 16, 1909.

—— 'Commander Peary's Return.' *Outlook*, October 2, 1909.

—— 'Waiting for Peary.' *Outlook*, September 25, 1909.

Koenig, L. S. and others. 'Arctic Ice Islands.' *Arctic*, July, 1952.

Lonsdale, Walter. 'The real story of Dr. Cook.' *Travel Magazine*, June, 1910.

MacMillan, Donald B. 'Peary as a Leader.' *National Geographic*, April, 1920.

'Map of Routes of Cook and Peary.' *World's Work*, November, 1909.

'Negro at the North Pole.' *Literary Digest*, March 16, 1912.

'New Charges Against Dr. Cook.' *Outlook*, December 18, 1909.

Nordmann, Charles. 'How to Recognize the North Pole.' *Living Age*, October 10, 1925.

'North Pole.' *Outlook*, September 18, 1909.

'Old Hoax Revived.' *Outlook*, February 10, 1926.

Osbon, Bradley. 'Cook and Peary'. 9–11/10, *Tourist*, vol. 6.

Paradyne, Henry. 'Dr. Cook's Achievements.' *Harper's Weekly*, September 25, 1909.

Peary, Josephine Diebitsch. 'A Lady Among the Eskimos.' *Spectator*, September 29, 1894.

[Peary, Josephine Diebitsch, obituary] *Time*, January 2, 1956.

Peary. 'Nearest the North Pole.' 2-3/1907, *Harper's*, vol. 114.

Peary, Robert E. 'Discovery of the Pole: Peary's First Account.' *World's Work*, October, 1909.

——'Discovery of the North Pole.' 1–9/10, *Hampton's*, vol. 24 and 25.

—— 'Ice Navigation.' *Century*, September, 1917.

—— 'My Plans for Reaching the Pole.' *Harper's Weekly*, July 9, 1904.

—— 'Sledge-traveling.' *Century*, November, 1917.

—— 'What I Expect to Find at the North Pole.' *Ladies' Home Journal*, March, 1905.

—— 'The Discovery of the North Pole.' *Hampton's Magazine*, July, 1910.

'Peary and Congress.' *Nation*, March 17, 1910.

'Peary as His Friends Portray Him.' *Current Literature*, May, 1910.

'Peary's Cairn Is Found.' *Life*, October 11, 1948.

'Peary's Discovery of the North Pole.' *Scientific American*, September 18, 1909.

—— 'Peary Arctic Club Expedition to the North Pole, 1908–9.' *The Geographical Journal*, August, 1910.

Pillion, John R. 'Extension of Remarks . . . in the house of Representatives, Monday, April 21, 1958, and Tuesday, April 22, 1958.' *Congressional Record*, 1958.

'Pole at Last.' *Independent*, September 9, 1909.

'Psychology of the Cook Fake.' *Independent*, December 30, 1909.

Rand, Sturgis. 'Robert E. Peary and His Campaign for the Pole.' *McClure's*, February, 1902.

'Rewards and Penalties of Polar Exploration.' *Scientific American*, April 22, 1911.

Roosevelt, Theodore. 'Is Polar Exploration Worth While?' *Outlook*, March 1, 1913.

Rosa, Nicholas. 'First to the North Pole.' *Oceans*, May, 1981.

'Scientific Press on the Polar Expedition of Doctor Cook.' *Current Literature*, December, 1909.

Schweikart, Larry. 'Polar Revisionism and the Peary Claim.' *The Historian*, May, 1986.

Scoresby, William. 'The Polar Ice.' Caedmon of Whitby, 1980 reprint of 1815 paper.

Shea, William E. 'Did Peary Touch the Pole?' *Independent*, June 12, 1926.

—— 'Is the North Pole Still Undiscovered?' *Independent*, August 22, 1925.

Stafford, Edward Peary. 'Peary and the North Pole.' 12/71, NIP:44

[Stafford] Marie Ahnighito Peary. 'My Arctic Pets.' *Good Housekeeping*, March and May, 1931.

——'The Snow Baby Returns.' *Good Housekeeping*, April, 1933.

Stafford, Marie Peary. 'The Peary Flag Comes to Rest.' *National Geographic*, October, 1954.

Stanton, Theodore. 'Dr. Cook at Copenhagen.' *Independent*, October 7, 1909.

Stead, W. T. 'Dr. Cook: The Man and the Deed.' *American Review of Reviews*, October, 1909.

Stefansson, Vilhjalmur. 'Claims to Polar Discovery.' *Saturday Review*, December 8, 1951.

'To Meet Mr. Peary.' *Current Literature*, September, 1902.

'Trouble for Peary.' *Current Literature*, April, 1910.

Ward, Henshaw. 'Peary Did Not Reach the Pole.' *American Mercury*, September, 1934.

Washburn, Bradford, and Adams and Ann Carter. 'Doctor Cook and Mount McKinley.' *American Alpine Journal*, 1958.

'When Cook Came to Copenhagen.' *Collier's*, September 25, 1909.

Wirth, Eve R. 'First to the North Pole – Last to Win Victory.' *Compass*, 1981.

'Wonderful Adventures of Dr. Cook.' *Living Age*, July 6, 1912.

Zavatti, Silvio. 'Who Reached the North Pole First?' Translated from *L'Universo*, bi-monthly review of the Military Geographic Institute, November–December, 1957.

Miscellaneous Publications

Borup, George. 'Notes . . .' (1908–09 diary), AGS archives.

Byrd letter to Alfred Collins, 11/6/26 (copy Natl. Arch.)

Byrd. 'Navigation . . .', 11/24/26 (carbon copy Natl. Arch.)

Christie, R. L. 'Fort Conger: Crossroads of the High Arctic.' Musk-Ox, No. 34, 1986.

Curtis, Heber D., and others. 'Peary's North-Pole Observations: A Collection of Reductions and Discussions.' [n.p., n.d.] (Typewritten manuscript in the Library of Congress. The findings are favourable to Peary.)

Helgesen, Henry T. 'Speech of Hon. Henry T. Helgesen, of North Dakota, in the House of Representatives, January 13–16.' Washington: Government Printing Office, 1916.

Leitzel, Ted. 'The Untold Story of the Cook–Peary Polar Controversy.' (A collection of magazine articles by Leitzel from *Real America*, October, 1935–January, 1936, reprinted by Russell W. Gibbons in April, 1965, for the Dr. Frederick A. Cook Society.)

Marvin, Ross. Diaries. Chemung County Hist. Soc., Elmira.

Moore, J. Hampton. 'Peary's Discovery of the North Pole; A Speech by Hon. J. Hampton Moore of Pennsylvania in the House of Representatives, March 22, 1910.' Washington: Government Printing Office, 1910.

Phillips Parmenter, Caroline. 'High Arctic Historical Archaeology, 1979 Season.' Research Bulletin, Ministry of the Environment, Ottawa, 1980. No. 139, August 1980.

——'Historical Archaeology in the Eastern High Arctic.' Op. cit., no. 137, August 1980.

'Pole Nord 1983.' (History of its Conquest . . .), ed: Jean Malaurie, Editions du Centre National de la Recherche Scientifique, Paris 1987.

Rawlins, Dennis. 'Evaluating Claims of North Polar Priority.' *Norse Geogr. Tidsik*, 26:135–40.

—— 'A Retrospective Critique of Peary's North Pole Claim.' *Polar Notes*, October, 1970.

Films

'The Arctic Adventure.' (Running time, 1hr 53mins). Written and directed by Philip Hudsmith, produced by Lyle Bebensee, Lyle Bebensee Productions, 1978.

'Race for the Pole.' Documentary Drama, CBS/ITT Production, first screened 1984.

'The Noose of Laurels.' (Running time, 56mins). Written and presented by Wally Herbert, directed by Edwin Mickleburgh, producer Roger James, Central Television production, first screened 12th April, 1988 in England.

Picture Credits

between pages 128–9
Wally Herbert: portrait drawing of Peary; Fort Conger; the coastal ice-foot.
Library of Congress: Josephine Diebtisch Peary; Jo, Marie and Sam Bartlett; Aleqasina; Peary and
  Jo; Henson and friends; Farthest North, 1906; the deck load of dogs; approaching the Big Lead;
  Henson portrait photograph; the homeward trail; signpost at Cape Aldrich.
National Archives: Peary in Nicaragua; Jo goes ashore; Peary's log; Peary's memo.
National Geographic Society: Eskimo girl washing; Peary hands out gifts; *Roosevelt* wintering at
  Cape Sheridan; hard going across pack ice; Camp Jesup; Peary reads his sextant; Peary portrait
  photograph; Peary's claimed North Pole photograph; the flag party returning to camp.
Nearest the Pole by Robert E. Peary (Doubleday/Hutchinson): Peary's cabin on *Roosevelt*.

between pages 288–9
Frederick A. Cook Society: Cook's Mount McKinley picture; Cook's claimed North Pole picture;
  Cook's cropped submerged island picture; Cook's 'Bradley Land'.
Wally Herbert: portrait drawing of Cook; Eagle Island; Peter Peary and background photograph.
Library of Congress: Cook in 1906; Cook's submerged island uncropped; Cook's winter den; hunting
  musk-oxen; Peary addressing a crowd; Jo greeting Peary; Peary hatted; Peary at desk; Peary
  seated with Jo and Robert Jnr.
National Geographic Society: Peary presenting his proofs.
Politikens Press Foto: Copenhagen banquet.
Royal Geographical Society: Peary's RGS medal.
Edward P. Stafford: Peary with Jo on Eagle Island; Peary with wife and children; Rear-Admiral
  Robert E. Peary.
Dr. Bradford Washburn: Mount McKinley massif.

Index

Index

About the Author

British explorer Wally Herbert's polar career spans thirty-one years, thirteen of which he spent in the Antarctic and the Arctic. He led the first crossing of the Arctic Ocean via the Pole in 1968–69, traveled extensively over Peary's and Cook's routes in Greenland and Ellesmere Island, and revisited the North Pole for this book. The Polar Medal and Bar as well as the Founder's Medal of the Royal Geographic Society are among his honors. A mountain range and plateau in the Antarctic are named for him, and the northernmost mountain in the Svalbard Archipelago in the Arctic also bears his name. He is married and has two daughters.